MAP OF MEMBER
COUNTRIES OF ASEAN

GW00702446

SOUTHEAST ASIAN AFFAIRS 2010

The **Institute of Southeast Asian Studies (ISEAS)** was established as an autonomous organization in 1968. It is a regional centre dedicated to the study of socio-political, security and economic trends and developments in Southeast Asia and its wider geostrategic and economic environment. The Institute's research programmes are the Regional Economic Studies (RES, including ASEAN and APEC), Regional Strategic and Political Studies (RSPS), and Regional Social and Cultural Studies (RSCS).

ISEAS Publishing, an established academic press, has issued more than 2,000 books and journals. It is the largest scholarly publisher of research about Southeast Asia from within the region. ISEAS Publishing works with many other academic and trade publishers and distributors to disseminate important research and analyses from and about Southeast Asia to the rest of the world.

SOUTHEAST ASIAN AFFAIRS 2010

Edited by
Daljit Singh

INSTITUTE OF SOUTHEAST ASIAN STUDIES
Singapore

First published in Singapore in 2010 by
ISEAS Publishing
Institute of Southeast Asian Studies
30 Heng Mui Keng Terrace
Pasir Panjang
Singapore 119614
E-mail: publish@iseas.edu.sg
Website: http://bookshop.iseas.edu.sg

The responsibility for facts and opinions in this publication rests exclusively with the authors and their interpretations do not necessarily reflect the views or the policy of the publisher or its supporters.

ISEAS Library Cataloguing-in-Publication Data

Southeast Asian affairs.
1974–
Annual
1. Southeast Asia — Periodicals.
I. Institute of Southeast Asian Studies.
DS501 S72A

ISSN 0377-5437
ISBN 978-981-4279-81-9 (soft cover)
ISBN 978-981-4279-82-6 (hard cover)
ISBN 978-981-4279-83-3 (PDF)

Typeset by International Typesetters Pte Ltd
Printed in Singapore by Utopia Press Pte Ltd

Contents

Foreword

The good news in 2009 was that the global economic crisis affected Southeast Asia less than had earlier been feared, and towards the end of the year most regional countries were poised for a sharp recovery. Yet, uncertainties and challenges for the future remained in view of the sluggish growth and indebtedness in the developed world.

In the realm of politics, the re-election of President Susilo Bambang Yudhoyono in Indonesia with a landslide majority in a peaceful election was a clear plus for both Indonesia and the region, notwithstanding the unfortunate attempts towards the later part of the year by certain forces to weaken the anti-corruption efforts of the government and to undermine two widely respected members of the President's government, namely Vice-President Boediono and Finance Minister Sri Mulyani, over the issue of the bailout of Bank Century.

Politics in Malaysia was unsettled while in Thailand it remained tumultuous. In Malaysia, Prime Minister Najib Tun Razak's well-conceived 1Malaysia concept seemed to lose its momentum amidst racial and religious tensions caused partly by attacks by extremists on religious establishments. Political uncertainty was also accentuated by the impending trial of opposition leader Anwar Ibrahim on sodomy charges. In Thailand, the destabilizing and disruptive street politics used by the anti-Thaksin yellow shirted mobs in 2008 to oust perceived pro-Thaksin governments were emulated in 2009 by the pro-Thaksin red shirts against Prime Minister Abhisit.

Politics in the rest of Southeast Asia was comparatively more quiescent and "normal". In Myanmar, always an exception to the Southeast Asian norm, the generals were preparing for elections in 2010 for a new constitutional order that would be dominated by the military.

Meanwhile, the Association of Southeast Asian Nations (ASEAN) continued its evolution towards a more rules-based organization with the efforts directed at strengthening procedures for dispute settlement and implementation of agreements. During the year a comprehensive free trade agreement (FTA) was concluded with Australia and New Zealand and another involving trade in goods was signed with India. Meanwhile the FTA with China on trade in goods was due to be implemented on 1 January 2010, even though tariff reductions with China had been proceeding for some years.

ASEAN's centrality in East Asian regionalism was challenged by two proposals for a new "architecture": one by Australian Prime Minister Kevin Rudd for an Asia-Pacific Community and another by Japanese Prime Minister Yukio Hatoyama for an East Asian Community. However it was clear by the end of the year that it would be very difficult to establish a new overarching "architecture". Cooperative mechanisms are more likely to grow organically, often even haphazardly, as pragmatic responses to needs and then evolve as they adjust to new exigencies, which was the way ASEAN evolved. More importantly, as Ezra Vogel has recently pointed out, regionalism in East Asia has been largely fruitful over the past decades and "existing forums offer the best opportunity for leaders in the Asia-Pacific to work together in solving regional and global problems".

Southeast Asian Affairs 2010, like the previous thirty-six editions of this flagship publication of ISEAS, provides an informed and readable analysis of developments in the region. I am confident that it will continue to be of interest to scholars, policymakers, diplomats, students, and the media. I wish to thank the editor and the contributors for the work they have put in to bring out this volume.

K. Kesavapany
Director
Institute of Southeast Asian Studies
March 2010

Introduction

With a gross domestic product (GDP) about the size of India's and growing in recent years at over 6 per cent a year, relatively open economies, a population approaching 600 million, location on the strategic sea routes between the Pacific and Indian Ocean, and the leverage in international relations provided by the Association of Southeast Asian Nations (ASEAN), the vibrant and very diverse region of Southeast Asia seems destined to play an increasingly important role in Asian affairs.

However, in viewing the condition of Southeast Asia in any particular year one is faced with both the positive and negative, a situation akin to a glass being half full or half empty, depending on the perspective of the viewer. Official elites, especially in Southeast Asia, often tend to highlight the full, while less sympathetic critics tend to emphasize the empty parts. The year 2009 continued to present this mixed picture, with both encouraging and troubling trends and developments. Economic indicators have been encouraging, and the economies will also benefit from the rise of China and India. However, GDP, even GDP per capita, while undeniably vital, are not deities exclusively determining the progress of countries and societies. Even as significant poverty remains in the region, serious shortcomings in governance abound in many countries.

In this Introduction it is of course impossible to draw out all the rich insights about the region and its component countries presented by the contributors to this volume. I can only, very selectively, highlight some trends and developments, focusing first on regional issues and then some individual countries.

Resilience in Coping with the Economic Crisis

Although Southeast Asia was significantly affected by the global economic crisis, thereby disproving the decoupling theorists, the adverse effects were not as dire as many had feared. Indeed, as Manu Bhaskaran shows in his economic review of Southeast Asia in this volume, regional economies manifested a surprising resilience in the face of the crisis. Bhaskaran attributes this to stronger financial sectors than during the time of the 1997–98 Asian crisis, better policy responses and macro-economic management, and, generally, the existence of more and better shock absorbers and fewer shock amplifiers. At the end of 2009 regional economies seemed poised for a good rebound, though the challenges of building longer-term resilience to cope with the uncertainties of a changing post-crisis global economy would continue to test state authorities.

Still in a Happy Spot in Major Power Relations, but Some Underlying Unease

Southeast Asia continued to be generally at peace, notwithstanding mistrust and problems in several interstate relationships and domestic political tensions, with pockets of violence, within some countries. The region also remained encased in a fairly comfortable zone of reasonably good relations between the major powers in the Asia-Pacific. As Robert Sutter points out in his chapter, despite Sino-American competition, these two great powers had overriding imperatives to remain committed to constructive engagement. Southeast Asia also saw enhanced U.S.-engagement during this first year of the new Obama administration, including the signing by the United States of ASEAN's Treaty of Amity and Cooperation and overtures to Myanmar (see below). However, a meaningful trade agenda was conspicuously lacking.

Sutter, in his chapter, explains the strength of the U.S. position in Asia relative to other major powers. While this reality was appreciated by many Asian states, some underlying unease in the region about the longer-term balance and relations between the major powers still existed — generated in part by major power competition for influence, military modernizations among the rising Asian powers, Japan's domestic political changes and search for a new identity, China's posture in relation to the South China Sea, and, more recently, possible adverse effects of the financial and economic crisis on the longer-term strategic posture of the United States. On the last point, the concern was that if American politicians could not come together to make the politically painful choices to deal with the country's enormous deficits and public debt in the coming years, at some point defence expenditure, together with U.S. overseas commitments, could face curtailments.

ASEAN Regionalism: Doing the Difficult Part

ASEAN regionalism continued to advance, though slowly and cautiously. The ASEAN Charter for the first time commits ASEAN states to norms about internal behaviour and also seeks to improve implementation procedures for

ASEAN agreements. In 2009 the ASEAN countries' Committee of Permanent Representatives started to function in Jakarta to facilitate implementation. The terms of reference of the ASEAN Inter-governmental Commission on Human Rights (AICHR) were adopted and members of the commission appointed. Though the very formation of the AICHR is a step forward, in view of the traditional sensitivity among many ASEAN countries about domestic discussion of such issues, it lacks an enforcement mechanism. As Joseph Liow says in his opening chapter, this, together with the continued primacy of the principle of non-interference in internal affairs, means that "progress towards a regional norm that defines, honours, and defends human rights in an active and substantive fashion will likely be incremental". Or as Rodolfo Severino puts it cautiously in his chapter on ASEAN, implementation would depend on "the collective will of the member states and on their perceptions of how implementing those provisions will serve the interests of the nation, the regime, or even, politically or personally, the leaders themselves" as in "other regional associations of sovereign states, except … the European Union."

ASEAN: Free Trade Agreements (FTAs) with Outside Countries

ASEAN signed its free-trade-in-goods agreement with India in August 2009 which provides for the start of tariff reductions on 1 January 2010 with a view to their elimination by different dates for different ASEAN countries. ASEAN's FTA with Australia and New Zealand, concluded in February 2009, barely received media attention. Yet, as Rod Severino points out, it is the most comprehensive of ASEAN's FTAs, covering not only tariff reductions and elimination, rules of origin and customs procedures, but also sanitary and phytosanitary measures, product standards and technical regulations, trade in services, movement of people, electronic commerce, investments, intellectual property, competition, and dispute settlement. Receiving much more media attention was the scheduled elimination of tariffs on goods between China and the ASEAN Six by 1 January 2010, even though it was relatively a non-event because tariff reduction had been going on since 2005 and by 1 January 2010 up to 150 tariff lines could still remain protected up to 2012.

Challenges to ASEAN-centred Regional Security Order

ASEAN also faced new uncertainties about the future of the regional security architecture in which at present ASEAN-anchored forums like the ASEAN

Regional Forum (ARF), the ASEAN Plus Three (APT), and the East Asia Summit (EAS) play a vital role. Two new schemes, Australian Prime Minister Kevin Rudds's proposal for the establishment of an Asia-Pacific Community (APC) and the Japanese Prime Minister Yukio Hatoyama's idea of an East Asian Community (EAC) modelled on the EU drew considerable attention in the media and in government and academic circles, and both are well covered in Joseph Liow's chapter. Although neither proposal gained much traction by the end of the year, they drove home the message that ASEAN could not take its centrality in the regional order for granted and in the end what the major players want would have an important bearing on the future of the regional security architecture.

The APC, first proposed in 2008, was seen as a more serious challenge than the EAC, in part because of divisions within ASEAN over it. In 2009 the Australian proponents of the APC, realizing that a new overarching architecture would be difficult to set up, suggested that the APC could be built around one of the existing forums, like the East Asia Summit. Attempts were made to assure ASEAN of its continuing importance and centrality, but sceptics in ASEAN wondered how Canberra would propose to square the circle of having, on the one hand, a smaller, more compact forum, and on the other hand keeping the existing inclusiveness (with sixteen members, and eighteen if the United States and Russia are admitted) and the "driving" role of ASEAN. To the sceptics the proposal still smacked of an attempt to build a concert of some big and a few middle powers in which ASEAN would be sidelined.

Hopefully, such challenges may yet propel ASEAN to get its act together. As Joseph Liow puts it: "Time and again, it has been forces beyond the control of Southeast Asian states that have forced their hand on matters of regional integration. This appears to be happening once more. As ASEAN faces up to the challenge, not only of rising Indian and Chinese power, but also the emergence of alternative visions of regional order that threatens the 'ASEAN Way' with irrelevance, the members of the forty-two-year-old regional organization must yet again set aside their differences and apprehensions towards one another — and these are deep-seated apprehensions indeed — in order for the organization to remain relevant."

Indonesia: Looking Up, Yet Held Back by Domestic Constraints

The third successful elections since 1998 marked a milestone in the country's democratic consolidation. President Susilo Bambang Yudhoyono became the first Indonesian president to be democratically re-elected. The economic performance was positive as the country was spared the worst effects of the global crisis, thanks in part to a big stimulus package (the growth rate declined but remained well above negative territory while unemployment actually fell). The terrorism threat continued on its downward trend, notwithstanding the bombings in Jakarta in July 2009. Aceh demonstrated further stabilization when Partai Aceh, the party of former GAM (Free Aceh Movement) members, won a landslide (with a near majority) in the provincial parliament and became the largest party in sixteen of the twenty-three district parliaments. Significantly, in the presidential election, President Yudhoyono won 93 per cent of the vote in Aceh, by far the best anywhere in Indonesia.

Yet, as Edward Aspinall notes in his chapter, Indonesia has seen average economic growth rates over the period of the first Yudhoyono administration at 5.7 per cent per annum, well below the government's 7 per cent target, and serious problems remain in spurring infrastructure development, manufacturing growth, and achieving poverty reduction goals. Perhaps more troubling, the later part of 2009 glaringly exposed a pervasive culture of corruption in key state institutions, including law enforcement agencies, and attempts by them to undermine the anti-corruption agency. The President himself came under unfavourable public light for his apparent complacency and indecisiveness in the face of these developments. As Aspinall puts it cautiously in the conclusion of his chapter: "It is … far too early to talk about a crisis of Indonesian democracy…. But it would be equally wrong to ignore the problems and adopt a merely celebratory tone…. Viewed favourably, as most Indonesian voters apparently do, the first Yudhoyono term was a period of consolidation, and of modest progress. Viewed in another light, it was a period of stasis, perhaps even stagnation. Yudhoyono's next term in office promises to be — quite literally — more of the same…. in 2009 there were signs that the long-term effects of [his highly cautious] approach might fall short of what many Indonesians desire out of their democracy, even if they expect little more from it."

…But with New Foreign Policy Directions

The changes on Indonesia's domestic political scene since the fall of former President Suharto have been followed by changes in foreign policy. To be sure the country's national interests dictate important areas of continuity, but there have also been significant changes. Dewi Fortuna Anwar sets them out in her chapter on "The Impact of Domestic and Asian Regional Changes on Indonesia's

Foreign Policy". After more than thirty years of Suharto's style of making and conducting foreign policy, countries of this region have to get used to the new realities in which democracy and multiple centres of power — in particular a powerful Parliament that is eager to flex its muscles — shape the formulation and execution of foreign policy. While ASEAN remains a cornerstone of Indonesia's foreign policy, says Anwar, the emphasis on democracy and human rights has introduced "new priorities and attitudes" which affect Indonesia's relations with its ASEAN neighbours. She also explains how Indonesia is engaging the major powers, including rising Asian powers, with its "free and active" foreign policy On the whole, after several years of preoccupation with internal problems, the country is stepping out, with more confidence, as an actor on the international scene. Its international profile is also highlighted by its membership of the G-20 forum.

Myanmar: Taking a Step Forward

Barring the political ripples caused by the escapades of American John William Yettaw, nothing that was extraordinarily dramatic or unexpected happened in Myanmar in 2009. There were signs of hope as the country prepared to establish a new constitutional order, with elections expected in 2010. Whatever the limitations, if successfully implemented, it would be a break from the political stagnation of two decades and thus a step forward. There was increased uncertainty and even fears of volatility among some opposition and ethnic groups as they contemplated the future and prepared to deal with the new political landscape. Martin Smith's analysis in this volume of the ethnic issues serves as a timely reminder that their management in this country, one of the most ethnically diverse, has always been a major challenge for any central government, democratic or non-democratic, and will continue to be so in the lead-up to and after the establishment of the new constitutional order. The regime seemed confident that it would successfully implement the new order, making 2010 a landmark transitional year as 1988 and 1974 were in earlier periods.

The change in America's Myanmar policy under President Barack Obama suggested that strategic considerations now feature in Washington's policy, not just democracy and human rights. The tone of the bilateral relationship has certainly improved. However, as Robert Taylor points out in his review, the sanctions mandated by Congress remain in place and demands continued to be made by the U.S. government on the Myanmar junta's policies in relation to the coming elections. Any significant breakthrough in U.S.-Myanmar relations is unlikely at this sensitive time when the regime is preoccupied with ensuring the successful implementation of the new constitution. If the U.S. approach to Myanmar now seemed somewhat more nuanced and sophisticated, observes Taylor, the EU sent conflicting signals during the year, while China and India continued to develop their relationship with Myanmar.

Malaysia: Can Prime Minister Najib Razak Pull it Off?

Many analysts were of the view that Malaysia needed reforms in its governance and its political economy if the UMNO (United Malays National Organisation)-led ruling coalition, the Barisan National (BN), was to recover its electoral fortunes. During 2009 BN lost four of the five by-elections it contested in the peninsula. The two main partners of UMNO in the BN coalition — the Chinese-based Malayan Chinese Association and the Indian-based Malayan Indian Congress — were in disarray because of internal power struggles and scandals. Since powerful entrenched vested interests in UMNO seemed dead against change, it might be difficult for Prime Minister Najib Razak to have the broad spectrum of support from within UMNO and its supporters to promote his 1Malaysia concept, however well-intentioned. Some have even suggested that the extremists might seek to rally Malay support for UMNO by frightening the community into thinking that their special position, even their religion, was under threat. The incidents of violence against churches in 2009 underscored the dangers.

However, James Chin, in his review of Malaysia, draws attention to the advantages that the BN still possessed and the Prime Minister's political skills to exploit them. Najib could increase support for the ruling coalition, especially among the non-Malays, by highlighting the positive aspects of policy and by taking steps to improve the economy, without necessarily having to make major changes to the existing pro-Malay policies. Chin in fact sees Najib's political stature as having risen as the year 2009 progressed and opines that if general elections had been held at the end of 2009 or early 2010 the BN would have recovered its two-thirds majority in Parliament.

The opposition alliance (PR or Pakatan Rakyat), despite winning a number of by-elections, and despite the corruption and other scandals affecting the BN, was hobbled by the charges of sodomy against its leader, Anwar Ibrahim, who could be put away for an extended period of time if convicted; the pro-BN orientation of the civil service and police in states controlled by PR; and by defections from the ranks of opposition parliamentarians and assemblymen. Chin alludes to attempts to destabilize PR-led state governments by investigations of its members for corruption and other offences.

Thailand: The Curse of Street Politics

There was no end in sight to the political disorder in Thailand, driven as it was by deep underlying fissures in the country's body politic. The age and the frail health of the King injected a particularly worrisome element in the situation. As Chairat Charoensin-o-larn says in his review of Thailand, the hopes of a return to normalcy, the same hopes that the coup of 19 September 2006 had stirred, still remained unfulfilled, with Thailand having a barely functioning government. Predictably, in 2009 the pro-Thaksin red shirts were emulating the disruptive tactics used by the anti-Thaksin yellow shirts in 2008 to bring pressure on the Abhisit Vejjajiva government to resign and hold elections. The traditional Songkarn days celebrations were marked by a bloody riot; ASEAN leaders had to be hurriedly evacuated from the ASEAN summit disrupted by the red shirts in Pattaya; and Premier Abhisit was harassed by the red shirts wherever he went. The only difference, and a critical one, was that the same military that had connived at the disruptive acts of the yellow shirts in 2008, including the occupation of the country's international airport, protected the Abhisit government in 2009. Indeed, as Chairat points out in his chapter, the military has been the biggest beneficiary of the political turmoil of recent years: its budget has almost doubled and it has become a decisive factor and referee in the political game, with any sitting government dependent on it for its support. Chairat also observes that the three years of turmoil has damaged the credibility and legitimacy of Thailand's political and social institutions.

Meanwhile, the insurgency in the south of the country raged on, with no end in sight. The idea of some devolution of power to the southern Muslim provinces in some kind of limited autonomy arrangement remained anathema to the Thai elite.

Vietnam: The China Factor

Vietnam, the biggest country on mainland Southeast Asia in terms of population size, and of considerable strategic importance, saw an economic growth rate of 5.3 per cent in 2009, standing out, alongside Indonesia and Laos, as one of a few countries in the ASEAN grouping that grew more than 2 per cent. Alexander Vuving, in his review of Vietnam, notes that the country was not without significant economic vulnerabilities. He also observes that in recent years there has been a considerable widening of space for public discussion and 2009 saw a dramatic development of civil society.

Developments in Vietnam's relations with China are covered in both Vuving's and Carl Thayer's chapters. China's assertiveness in the South China Sea, felt particularly sharply by Vietnam over the course of 2009, seemed to show to Hanoi that its policy of deference to China over the years was not entirely effective and needed to be complemented by more vigorous national efforts to protect its vital interests. China's diplomatic and economic inroads into Laos and Cambodia in recent years were also viewed with concern. As Vuving puts it: "Chinese activities ... have left the Vietnamese little doubt that China's intentions include control of the South China Sea, which Vietnam sees as its front door, and influence in mainland Indochina, which Vietnam regards as its backyard." Vietnam took steps in 2009 to modernize its military forces and increase cooperation with Laos and Cambodia, even as it continued its web of dense relations and exchanges with China at the party-to-party, state-to-state, and military-to-military levels — demonstrating, as Carl Thayer puts it, that, as the weaker party, it would continue to use the levers of both cooperation and struggle in managing its relations with China.

The year 2009 also saw the emergence of anti-China nationalism as a powerful force in domestic Vietnamese politics. The network of groups opposed to the big bauxite-mining project to be undertaken by China in the central part of South Vietnam grew into a national coalition of mainstream elite motivated by nationalist and human security concerns, forcing the authorities to resort to a crackdown and start a campaign against "the strategy of peaceful evolution". Vuving assesses that the clampdown "did not seem to create the necessary fear".

The Rest of Southeast Asia: Relatively Quiescent, with Business as Usual

In the Philippines, the second most populous country in Southeast Asia, after Indonesia, the political elite was preoccupied with the elections due in 2010. The country weathered the global economic crisis without falling into recession, thanks to beneficial policy reforms carried out earlier and a generous stimulus package. However, the challenges of governance were highlighted again by events towards the end of 2009. The destruction caused by tropical storm Ketsana and Super Typhoon Parma showed a failure to provide adequately, on a long term basis, the infrastructure needed to cope with such natural disasters which are all too common in the Philippines.

The massacre of fifty-seven people associated with Mayor Andal Ampatuan Jr. in Maguindanao in the south was a reminder not just of election-related violence in the country and the existence of private armies but also of the continuing hold of wealthy and powerful clans on the political system. Herman Kraft in his chapter observes that elections in the Philippines "have always energized people with the prospect of change.... It is, however, very difficult to understand why this should be so, considering the kind of leadership that electoral exercises have given the country." A bright spot, though, was the resumption of peace talks between the government and the Moro Islamic Liberation Front in Kuala Lumpur with the Malaysian government acting as facilitator and an International Contact Group set up in the Malaysian capital to provide support. However, a bumpy road lay ahead in the negotiations. The conflicts with the communist New People's Army and with the Abu Sayyaf Group continued.

In Singapore, as Azhar Ghani says in his review, "despite the unusual challenges in 2009, in some fundamental ways, it was reassuringly business-as-usual". As the most internationalized and export-dependent economy in Southeast Asia, there was much preoccupation with economic issues as the country experienced its first recession since 2002. There was some questioning of Singapore's longer-term growth model by critics who argued that the striving for maximum growth with increasing dependence on foreign workers, who already constituted about one-third of the workforce and took up seven of the ten new jobs created in 2008, produced unintended negative effects and delivered too little of the benefits of growth to Singaporeans relative to foreigners and foreign firms. The subject of foreign workers remained a touchy one and the government was paying more attention to its various dimensions. An Economic Strategies Committee (ESC) was also set up to come out with recommendations on how to keep the economy growing in the next decade and to spread more gains to Singaporeans. The government announced some tweaking of the system to allow for a greater diversity of views in Parliament and some relaxation of rules on films and online material with political content.

In Cambodia the economy suffered an estimated contraction of 2.5 per cent after five years of high growth, but this did not bring about social or political unrest. Indeed Prime Minister Hun Sen continued to ride high in popularity and, as Carolyn Hughes affirms in her review, there was further entrenchment of the hold of his Cambodian People's Party on local politics, facilitated by the patronage system. The Khmer Rouge tribunal continued its work. Hughes observes that while it has increased the level of interest in its work in Cambodia, the handful of punishments which it is likely to deliver will neither adversely affect stability nor satisfy those who think that it could reform Cambodia towards becoming a country governed by the rule of law. The diplomatic row with Thailand did not seem to affect day-to-day business relations between the two countries, with Thailand remaining an important investor.

Among the remaining two members of ASEAN, there was more continuity than any significant change in basic trends. In her review of Brunei Pushpa Thambipillai discusses developments in a generally stable and well-managed sultanate with a pro-active and shrewd ruler who is focusing on modernization with stability, friendly ties and cooperation with other countries, and longer-term plans for socio-economic development of his country. On Laos, Holly High dwells mainly on the process of "resourcification" and resource contestation and their political and other dimensions, while Omkar Lal Shrestha deals with the country's economic performance and prospects.

Finally, the only non-ASEAN country of the region, Timor Leste, which has been shaken by traumatic events in its recent past. Selver Sahin argues in her chapter that while 2009 was marked by relative stability and security in the sense of absence of rioting and gang violence, little progress had been made towards addressing the structural problems that had triggered the 2006 crisis. Her chapter examines the formidable challenges facing the country like security sector reform, weaknesses in the rule of law, and socio-economic development.

Apart from the eleven country reviews and the four regional chapters, this volume of *Southeast Asian Affairs* has seven country-specific thematic chapters. Those so far not mentioned in this Introduction include Lee Hock Guan's chapter on the limits of Malay educational and language hegemony, Michael Koh's on the development of arts and culture in Singapore, and Pavin Chachavalpongpun's on "unity" as a discourse in Thailand's polarized politics. Each makes its unique contribution to understanding important or interesting facets of the countries discussed.

Southeast Asian Affairs seeks to accommodate a variety of views and opinions, both Southeast Asian and others, for which the contributors alone are responsible. I would like to thank all the contributors for making this volume possible. Special thanks go to Holly High and Omkar Lal Shrestha for contributing the two chapters on Laos at short notice because the original writer on Laos had to withdraw for unforeseen reasons.

I also thank Stephen Logan of ISEAS Publishing for his meticulous copy-editing and his composure and helpfulness under pressure in accommodating the many amendments, and Ms Betty Tan who, in addition to many other duties, served as a very efficient secretary to the *Southeast Asian Affairs 2010* project. Finally, I thank Mrs Triena Ong, Managing Editor and Head ISEAS Publishing; Dr Chin Kin Wah, ISEAS Deputy Director; and ISEAS Director Ambassador K. Kesavapany. All three had useful advice to offer or lent a sympathetic ear when I went to see them about some problem or other.

Daljit Singh
Editor
Southeast Asian Affairs 2010

The Region

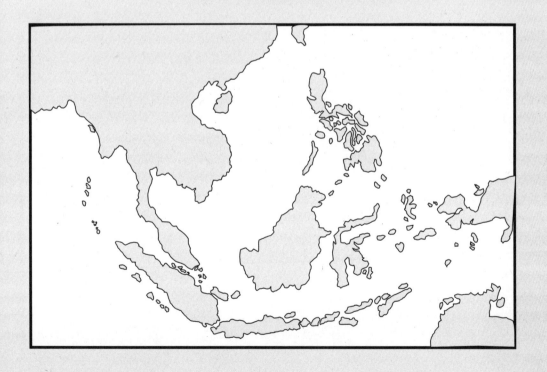

SOUTHEAST ASIA IN 2009
A Year Fraught with Challenges

Joseph Chinyong Liow

Introduction

For Southeast Asia, the past twelve months have proven eventful on several counts. At the positive end of the spectrum, the region managed to weather the economic storm caused by the global credit crunch by minimizing its corrosive effects on local economies and populations, in no small part due to lessons learnt from the economic crisis of a decade ago. Meanwhile, advances were made in regional integration, culminating in the formation of the ASEAN Intergovernmental Commission on Human Rights, while anxieties over American commitment to Southeast Asia — an issue which seized regional leaders for the most part of the administration of George W. Bush — were soothed somewhat with Washington's signing of the Treaty of Amity and Cooperation. On the other hand, the past year also witnessed severe strains on several bilateral relationships among Southeast Asian states, the postponement of an ASEAN Summit under dramatic circumstances, and the emergence of new conceptions of regionalism that threaten to displace ASEAN, along with its norms and values, as the core of multilateral initiatives in the Asia-Pacific region. These developments are likely to evolve further in the coming years, with both positive and negative implications for the region.

ASEAN

The monumental signing and ratification of the ASEAN Charter by ASEAN members in 2008 committed the regional organization to two summit meetings a calendar year instead of the previous practice of one summit over a twelve month period (from mid-year to mid-year). However, in order to facilitate the

JOSEPH CHINYONG LIOW is Associate Professor at the S. Rajaratnam School of International Studies, Nanyang Technological University, Singapore.

transition to the new schedule with minimal disruption, the appointed ASEAN Chair for the year of 2008 was to hold that position for eighteen months instead of twelve, during which time it would host a total of three summit meetings along with the accompanying ASEAN Plus Three and East Asian Summit gatherings.[1] By way of alphabetical rotation, Thailand succeeded Singapore as the ASEAN Chair in 2008. On the surface, it seemed like a routine transition from one core founder member to another. What transpired during Thailand's tenure, however, was anything but routine.

The September 2006 military coup in Thailand had plunged the kingdom into a deep political crisis from which it has yet to recover. The coup precipitated widespread political protests as supporters and opponents of deposed Prime Minister Thaksin Shinawatra tussled for primacy in Thai politics as street demonstrations became all too frequent. By September 2008, the animosity between both factions turned decidedly hostile with the outbreak of violence, forcing the Thai government to declare a controversial state of emergency. The Fourteenth ASEAN Summit scheduled for December was subsequently postponed because of attendant security concerns. ASEAN leaders eventually reconvened in the central resort towns of Hua Hin and Cha-am between 27 February and 2 March 2009. During these meetings, further advancements were made toward regional integration. ASEAN leaders signed the Cha-am Hua Hin Declaration on the Roadmap for an ASEAN Community, and also adopted a series of other documents, including the ASEAN Political-Security Community Blueprint, and the ASEAN Socio-Cultural Community Blueprint. In addition to that, the ASEAN-Australia–New Zealand Free Trade Agreement was signed, creating one of Asia's largest free trade zones. Even though the meetings between ASEAN leaders proceeded without distraction, Thai authorities took the decision to postpone the association's meetings with dialogue partners yet again, rescheduling them for the resort of Pattaya on 10–12 April 2009. In hindsight, this proved to be an ill-fated decision.

As ASEAN and regional leaders gathered in Pattaya, the deepening of Thailand's political malaise saw pro-Thaksin "red-shirt" supporters storm the site of the summit meeting on 10 April, forcing the besieged government of Prime Minister Abhisit Vejjajiva to suffer the ignominy of having to cancel the summit at the eleventh hour and evacuate visiting leaders from ASEAN and its dialogue partners by helicopter to a nearby military airbase. For the Thai government, the entire episode was all the more embarrassing for the fact that Pattaya was initially chosen because it was assumed to be far enough from Bangkok, where demonstrations were most intense, and hence safe from the threat of disruption.

Given the dramatic circumstances surrounding the Fourteenth ASEAN Summit, the gathering of the ten ASEAN states and their six dialogue partners back in Hua Hin and Cha-am for the Fifteenth iteration of the meeting on 23–25 October was considerably less eventful. At the meeting, ASEAN leaders and their dialogue partners reaffirmed their commitment to enhancing regional trade and economic integration and declared their intention to explore regional approaches to tackling the challenges posed by climate change. However, it was the inauguration of the ASEAN Intergovernmental Commission on Human Rights (AICHR) that captured the headlines. The birth of the AICHR was the culmination of sixteen years of intermittent discussions within ASEAN regarding the establishment of a regional consensus on the prickly issue of human rights. While ASEAN can be lauded for establishing an institutional mechanism and taking the bold step towards respect for innate and law-based rights within a Southeast Asian context in which domestic discussion of such issues have long been silenced by authoritarian regimes, many deficiencies remain. Most glaring of all is the AICHR's lack of enforcement power and the continued primacy of the principle of non-interference in members' affairs, which effectively holds the AICHR hostage. This means that progress towards a regional norm that defines, honours, and defends human rights in an active and substantive fashion will likely be incremental.

Notwithstanding the success of the Fifteenth summit, it barely papered over the cracks in the ASEAN principles and process that were revealed by the earlier crises surrounding Thailand's difficulties in discharging its responsibilities as ASEAN Chair. When ASEAN demonstrated characteristic reluctance to intervene in the domestic affairs of a member state at the height of the Thailand political quagmire, what resulted was the cancellation not only of the ASEAN Summit, but the ASEAN Plus Three Summit and East Asian Summit as well. In other words, regional interests were held captive to ASEAN's prioritization of sovereignty. Moreover, ASEAN's inability to press the regional agenda in the wake of domestic political obstacles was coming at a time when ASEAN faced pressure from alternative models of regionalism. As this chapter will discuss in greater detail later, ASEAN's approach to regionalism is already being challenged by alternative ideas of regional security architecture being propounded by powers external to Southeast Asia. In addition to that, there had over the past year also been progress in parallel sub-ASEAN CMLV (Cambodia, Myanmar, Laos, and Vietnam) summits as well as emergent configurations of sub-regional (and sub-national) economic networks driven by trade between China's southern provinces (such as Yunnan and Guangxi) and the northern provinces of mainland Southeast Asian states such as the Greater Mekong Subregion and the Pan-Beibu Gulf

Region. While the latter initiatives can be viewed as part of wider China-ASEAN engagement, they also raise the question of how the potential these initiatives possess can be husbanded to advance economic relationships among ASEAN states, and between ASEAN and China, without jeopardizing the stuttering process of regional economic integration and inadvertently reinforcing fears of the creation of a multi-tiered ASEAN.[2]

Intra-ASEAN Disputes

Prospects for deeper ASEAN integration were also hampered by strains in several bilateral relationships among Southeast Asian states caused by a combination of competing interests, political brinkmanship, and nationalism. Among these, it was the friction between Thailand and Cambodia that proved most alarming.

Differences between Thailand and Cambodia over the land around Preah Vihear Temple, located at the Thai-Cambodian border, have existed for decades. Although the International Court of Justice had ruled in 1962 that the temple belonged to Cambodia, the most accessible entrance to the ancient Khmer temple is situated in northeastern Thailand. The border between the two countries had never been completely demarcated, at least in part because it is still littered with landmines left over from the war in Cambodia.[3] Tensions came to a head after the temple was granted UNESCO World Heritage status, and spilt over into open hostilities in July 2008 as both Cambodia and Thailand mobilized military forces in the region. A skirmish near the temple took place in April 2009, resulting in three deaths. On 25 June, both sides reinforced their respective military presence at the disputed border after the Thai government renewed its campaign against the listing of the temple as a World Heritage site and announced it planned to ask UNESCO to review the World Heritage status given to the temple. Cambodian Prime Minister Hun Sen retaliated by issuing orders for troops to shoot any Thai trespasser — civilian or military — after Thai protestors linked to the People's Alliance for Democracy rallied at the disputed border.[4] Cambodian Foreign Minister Hor Namhong's letter to Thai Foreign Minister Kasit Piromya (dated 12 October 2009) requested that the border dispute between the two countries be included on the ASEAN agenda for the summit scheduled at the end of October, just as Kasit mentioned a week earlier that he would seek a "neutral organization" to "provide an avenue for Thailand and Cambodia to settle the dispute."[5] In an apparent U-turn, Thailand responded that the border dispute with Cambodia should not be internationalized nor brought up within the ASEAN framework. Rather, it was suggested that the vehicle of the Thai-Cambodian

Joint Boundary Commission be used as a foundation for a policy edifice towards peaceful resolution.

Notwithstanding this rhetoric, diplomatic tensions between Thailand and Cambodia escalated when Hun Sen declared during an interview at the Fifteenth ASEAN Summit that if Thaksin Shinawatra were to enter Cambodia, it was Cambodia's sovereign right to decline any request for extradition. Further fanning the flames, he later moved to appoint Thaksin as his economic advisor. Hun Sen's statement was met with anger in Thailand, with Kasit warning that "if Cambodia loves Thaksin that much, the ties with Thailand will certainly have problems."[6] Thai Prime Minister Abhisit Vejjajiva followed up his Foreign Minister's remarks by responding that his Cambodian counterpart would have to make a choice between his personal relationship with Thaksin and good relations with Thailand.[7] In a further escalation, Phnom Penh and Bangkok moved to recall their respective ambassadors. Matters took a turn for the worse in November when Cambodia rejected a request from Thailand for Thaksin's extradition, and instead imprisoned a Thai employee of the Cambodia Air Traffic Service who was accused of stealing Thaksin's flight schedule and passing it on to diplomats at the Thai embassy in Phnom Penh. Bangkok retaliated by warning that it had no intention of withdrawing its troops stationed at the disputed Preah Vihear Temple area. Meanwhile, domestic constituencies in the country called for the government to cancel all agreements with Cambodia. Relations with Thailand were not the only bilateral ties strained by Hun Sen's support for Thaksin; the Myanmar junta also expressed displeasure when Hun Sen compared Thaksin's "persecution" with that of Aung San Suu Kyi.[8]

Mirroring developments in mainland Southeast Asia, relations between Indonesia and Malaysia plummeted during August and September 2009 when a number of Indonesian political parties, non-governmental organizations, lobby groups, and self-proclaimed "patriotic militias" called on the Indonesian Government to take stern action against Malaysia on the grounds that the latter had offended Indonesian national pride and sensitivities. The catalyst that sparked the latest round of sabre-rattling between the two countries was the airing of a Malaysian tourism promotional advertisement on the Discovery Channel that featured a segment on the Pendet dance of Bali. This was seen and cast by the Indonesian media as another instance of Malaysia "stealing" elements of Indonesian culture and claiming it as Malaysian. Despite the facts behind the case — the ad was produced by a non-Malaysian company that later apologized for the error and admitted that it was they, and not the Malaysian Government, that were responsible for the mistake — the prevailing mood in Indonesia was anti-Malaysian, providing the pretext and justification for anti-Malaysia demonstrations in the country. Demonstrations were held in Jakarta and several other cities in Java, leading to at least one reported incident of a protest in Jakarta in front of the Malaysian embassy where the Malaysian flag was burned. Local media reports also noted that harassment of Malaysian students took place in Jakarta and Jogjakarta, where homes rented by Malaysian students were pelted with eggs and the walls defaced.

On the occasion of Malaysia's independence day (31 August), more than one hundred official Malaysian governmental websites were hacked by Indonesian hackers who defaced the sites and replaced them with pro-Indonesian slogans. By early September the anti-Malaysian mood took to the streets with vigilante groups unilaterally patrolling Jakarta in search of Malaysian citizens, purportedly to drive them from the country.[9] The same vigilante groups also threatened to take their violence to the more cosmopolitan parts of Jakarta and to target the area around the Malaysian embassy specifically. These developments were duly reported in Malaysia by both the pro-government and alternative media, and led to calls for the Malaysian Government to ensure the safety of Malaysian tourists and students in the neighbouring country.

Thus far, the Malaysian Government's reaction to the dispute with Indonesia has been a mixture of bewilderment and inaction. Malaysian politicians, including Prime Minister Najib Razak, have exercised restraint and only issued mild statements of caution meant for Malaysian tourists and students currently living and travelling to Indonesia. On 17 September, foreign ministers of both countries met in Jakarta in an attempt to calm tempers on both sides. There have been no acts of reprisal against Indonesians in Malaysia, no burning of the Indonesian flag, and no groups that have systematically retaliated against Indonesian nationals in the country.

However, it should also be noted that the relatively passive reaction on the part of the Malaysian authorities has in fact paradoxically contributed to the deepening of the crisis, for it reinforces the impression that the Malaysians are heedless of the worries and concerns of Indonesians. The most glaring instance of this passive indifference involves the case of the Indonesian model, Manohara Pinot, who was married to a member of the Kelantan royal family. Following the breakdown of their relationship, Manohara alleged that she was physically and psychologically abused by her Malaysian spouse, and had tried to end the marriage and return to Indonesia. Manohara was, however, prevented from doing so, leading her family to allege that she had been kidnapped by members of the royal family. In the end, Manohara managed to return to Indonesia via Singapore, and upon her return was welcomed by anti-Malaysian nationalists. In the wake of the Manohara issue, her story was played up by the tabloid media and later serialized into a soap opera entitled *Tangisan Isabella* (The tears of Isabella), which features an Indonesian model who is kidnapped and abused by a foreign royal family who speak with a clearly Malaysian accent.

The Malaysian government's reluctance to intervene in the case of Manohara when she was resident in Malaysia added to the impression that the Malaysian government was heedless of the safety and welfare of Indonesians. Manohara's mother has also claimed that she was denied access to her daughter and not allowed into the country; a claim that was taken up by the anti-Malaysian nationalist lobby there. The Malaysian government, on the other hand, explained its own reluctance to intervene on the grounds that the federal government did not have the right to interfere in the private domain of citizens and their married lives. This explanation did not go down well in Indonesia.

Relations with the Major Powers

In many respects, developments in Southeast Asia's relations with the United States were by far the most significant among the major powers over the past year. Under the administration of former President George W. Bush, Washington's preoccupation with its global war on terror, its enunciation of a Bush Doctrine premised on the notion of pre-emptive war, and its subsequent invasion of Iraq strained relations with Indonesia and Malaysia — both core members of ASEAN — and raised some apprehensions about American credibility and leadership in the Asia-Pacific region.[10] In stark contrast, Barack Obama's presidential campaign promise of a more finessed foreign policy posture that would stress the need to strengthen relations with allies and friends in Southeast Asia was met with both relief and anticipation in a region for which the matter of deficit in American policy attention, whether real or perceived, has always been a matter of some consternation. The fact that the new American President had his own personal experience with Southeast Asia during his formative years — he grew up in Jakarta and spent four years in an Indonesian public school — fueled romantic expectations in certain quarters that Southeast Asia might command a special place in Obama's foreign policy, thereby heralding a new era in U.S.-ASEAN relations.

To these ends, initial developments have on balance been promising. Since Obama's inauguration in early 2009, Secretary of State Hilary Clinton has already been dispatched to Southeast Asia twice — she visited Indonesia in February as part of her Asian tour after assuming her post, and was in Thailand later in July to participate in the ASEAN Regional Forum. It was during the latter visit that the Treaty of Amity and Cooperation, which committed Washington to the norms and code of conduct that has governed Southeast Asian regional affairs for more than three decades, was signed. During her visits, Clinton made clear that it was Washington's intention to counter China's growing influence and soft power in the region with its own "smart power" offensive.

This seeming shift in thinking in Washington circles on Southeast Asia — and, more broadly, the Asia-Pacific — was further reinforced by Secretary of Defence Robert Gates during his participation at the Shangri-La Dialogue in Singapore in June. During the meeting, Gates noted that "while continuing to fulfill our commitments to the permanent presence of, and direct action by, U.S. forces in the region — places ever greater emphasis on building the capacity of partners to better defend themselves."[11] The United States has actively participated in the global response to the economic crisis, the pandemic flu threat, and anti-piracy initiatives, among other security challenges faced by the region. Placing especial emphasis on maritime security, as well as on anti-piracy and non-proliferation efforts, the United States Pacific Command has worked closely with several regional navies to secure waterways used by drug smugglers, weapons smugglers, and terrorist groups. In terms of the American leadership that can be expected, Gates pointed out that the United States, in negotiating accession to the Treaty of Amity and Cooperation, has shown its willingness to consider regional norms when taking into account its relationships around the world.

Notwithstanding the discernibly more conciliatory tone of Washington's diplomatic rhetoric towards Southeast Asia, ASEAN should also be cognizant of two underlying messages that have also been conveyed. First, as part of its re-engagement with Southeast Asia, Washington has made clear that its attention in the coming years will likely focus on Myanmar. This was illustrated in Secretary Clinton's call for ASEAN member states to press for democratic change in Myanmar, as well as her warning that American interests in the region have also been piqued by suspicions that North Korea had been transferring nuclear technology to Myanmar, and was then made abundantly clear when President Obama made a personal request during the ASEAN-U.S. Summit for the house arrest of opposition leader Aung San Suu Kyi to be lifted.[12] Given how Myanmar continues to be a source of frustration for ASEAN and a threat to its credibility, the onus may well be on the organization to demonstrate that it can "keep its house in order" through its preferred approach of constructive engagement towards Myanmar articulated more than a decade ago. Second, it is also clear that along with its re-engagement, Washington expects Southeast

Asian partners to make a more concerted contribution to their own security, as opposed to over-reliance on the United States

Unlike the closely watched improvements in ASEAN-U.S. ties, advancements in relations with China over the past year have been comparatively low key, though no less significant. In a situation reminiscent of the regional financial crisis of the late 1990s, the global credit crisis afforded China an opportunity to enhance its credentials as a regional leader and player of consequence in economic affairs, not to mention a constructive regional leader. With the ASEAN-China Summit scheduled for April in Pattaya postponed due to anti-government protests elaborated earlier, China moved swiftly to invite regional leaders and captains of industry to the island of Hainan for the annual Boao Forum, which provided a platform for emerging economies to discuss the challenges and responses to the economic downturn. China further cemented its leadership role in the region through the provision of a US$10 billion investment cooperation fund to finance infrastructure development linking China and its regional neighbours, and an offer of a further US$15 billion in credit (in the form of rescue packages) to Southeast Asian countries in need of assistance to weather the crisis. In addition, Premier Wen Jiabao further pledged in Hainan that China would take a proactive role in pursuing closer trade and economic cooperation with the region. As a demonstration of Chinese sincerity, he announced that Beijing would encourage trade settlement in Chinese currency so as to help ease potential foreign exchange shortfalls, thereby facilitating more bilateral trade and investment.[13]

Beneath these demonstrations of altruism, however, lay a pragmatic logic for greater engagement with Southeast Asia. Notwithstanding its offer of aid to Southeast Asia, China was itself not unscathed by the global credit crisis. The downturn in the U.S. economy had a significant impact on Chinese manufacturing, and Southeast Asian markets proved crucial as they could help absorb some of China's excess manufacturing output. In addition to that, the investment in infrastructure development in regional countries also served to meet the employment needs of Chinese labour.

In strategic affairs, however, an abiding concern for Southeast Asia remains the stability of China's relations with the United States, upon which regional security is hinged. By this token, while the bilateral relationship between the two major powers remained for the most part stable over the year, the incident involving the harassment of U.S. Navy spy ship, *Impeccable*, by Chinese navy and civilian patrol vessels south of Hainan Island in March 2009 caused concern in some Southeast Asian capitals. While Beijing claimed that the *Impeccable* was involved in "illegal activities" in its exclusive economic zone, some in the region preferred to view the incident through the lens of Chinese assertiveness in the South China Sea.

While continuity defined much about China–Southeast Asia relations, the region's relations with Japan appear primed for change. The election of Yukio Hatoyama, the Democratic Party of Japan candidate for the September 2009 elections, broke the erstwhile stranglehold of the Liberal Democratic Party on Japanese politics in national polls. Setting a fresh tone for Japanese foreign policy, Hatoyama came into office proclaiming resolve to improve relations with China while also reducing Japan's traditional dependence on America's security assurances. As a demonstration of this intent, Hatoyama pledged not to visit the controversial Yasukuni Shrine, and proclaimed "Japan now needs to make a clear shift from diplomacy that follows a U.S. lead."[14] While it remains unclear whether the new Japanese momentum towards a foreign policy oriented more towards China and East Asia, and away from the United States, can be sustained, the new Prime Minister's immediate attempt to make a personal imprint on regional affairs through the articulation of his vision for an East Asia Community — an issue to be taken up later in this chapter — indicates that Southeast Asia may at least for the time being be dealing with a Japan that appears to be moving away from the familiar passivism and American orientation of the Liberal Democratic Party administration towards a more activist, independent foreign policy.

As for India, Prime Minister Manmohan Singh reiterated India's commitment to deepening economic and political engagement with Southeast Asia on the basis of its "Look East" policy during his meetings with ASEAN counterparts at the East Asian Summit. As the Southeast Asian region gradually recovers from the global credit crunch and the Indian economy continues to grow, the potential weight that India will command has become all the more visible as New Delhi gradually eases into deeper integration with the region. Giving substance to this, after eight years of negotiations India finally signed the much-awaited India-ASEAN Free Trade Agreement (FTA) at the sidelines of the meeting of ASEAN Trade Ministers in August. The FTA will eliminate tariffs on eighty per cent of goods traded between the two parties. Forecasting the anticipated acceleration of ties on the back of the FTA, a scholar of India-ASEAN relations has speculated that "India-ASEAN trade has risen from around US$7 billion in 2000–01 to US$39 billion in 2007–08. With tariffs rationalized, it is expected to rise even further to its target of US$50 billion by 2010."[15] The deepening of economic cooperation with Southeast Asia accompanies India's commitment to playing a more active role in security issues in the region, including its participation in the ASEAN Regional Forum (ARF), joint military exercises with several Southeast Asian counterparts, and active contribution to maritime security in the Strait of Malacca. Indeed, in a demonstration of Southeast Asia's receptivity to a more active and prominent role for India in regional affairs, Indonesia, for a long time a littoral state that harboured reservations towards external parties' involvement in maritime patrols in the Strait of Malacca, issued an invitation to the Indian Navy in March 2009 to help maintain security in the strait.[16] Notwithstanding these advancements, there remains a sense in some ASEAN quarters that having integrated into East Asia, India appears content to just "be at the table".

South China Sea

Long seen as a potential security flashpoint in Southeast Asia, territorial claims over the South China Sea islands continue to be a diplomatic irritant and a test of conflict resolution resolve of regional states. For the most part, diplomatic initiatives, both at the bilateral and multilateral level, over the past several years have at a minimum fostered a climate of dialogue and restraint. Be that as it may, away from the media spotlight claimant states remain unstinting in their assertion of sovereignty over their respective claims in the South China Sea.

The South China Sea territorial disputes have recently escalated again due to new claims submitted by the Philippines, Malaysia, and Vietnam to the United Nations Commission on the Limits of the Continental Shelf (UNCLCS) in response to directives that states that joined the United Nations Convention on the Law of the Sea (UNCLOS) before 1999 had to submit their supplementary claims to economic rights when their continental shelf extends more than 200 nautical miles beyond a baseline by 13 May 2009. Predictably, China reacted negatively to the submissions by these claimant states, and branded these actions a violation of its jurisdiction and sovereign rights over the South China Sea.[17] As a further response, Beijing also established a new Department of Boundary and Ocean Affairs and enhanced its patrolling capabilities in an attempt to further assert its presence in the South China Sea. In addition to this, in a move that could potentially unravel all diplomatic progress hitherto, Beijing has also begun to call into question the need for ASEAN to take a unified position on the South China Sea, particularly since the majority of ASEAN members have no claims in the area.

Differences over the South China Sea are not confined to relations between Southeast Asian claimants and China alone. To be sure, points of divergence and contention also exist between the Southeast Asian claimant states of Malaysia, Vietnam, the Philippines, and Brunei. As but one example, Malaysia has continued to oppose the internationalization of the issue even as Vietnam and the Philippines attempt to build on the momentum created by the South China Sea Declaration of 2002 and push for the creation of a code of conduct which continues to hang in the balance. These unresolved differences, and the absence of any institutional mechanisms to manage any manner of conflict in the area, mean that the South China Sea will remain at the back of the minds of regional security planners for the foreseeable future, even as regional integration deepens.

Regional Security Architecture and Community Building

In response to major global economic and geostrategic upheavals, countries in the Asian region are looking towards community building as a solution. To that end, one of the notable developments over the past twelve months was the articulation of new and alternative frameworks for regionalism. Two in particular gained much attention and warrant closer scrutiny — the proposal espoused by Australian Prime Minister Kevin Rudd for the creation of an Asia-Pacific Community, and the East Asian Community aggressively advocated by Japan's new Prime Minister Yukio Hatoyama. While very much still exploratory in nature, these initiatives are likely to spark debates and discussions in the years to come, with potential implications for how regional affairs are organized as well as the centrality of Southeast Asia in these frameworks.

Asia-Pacific Community

When the Asia-Pacific Community (APC) proposal was first articulated, Kevin Rudd suggested that it would serve to manage the transformation of Asia's international system to accommodate the growing power of China and India, while at the same time rectifying what he observed to be the problem of incapacity on the part of extant institutions.[18] In his keynote address to the Shangri-La Dialogue held in Singapore in June, Rudd asserted that "managing major power relations, particularly in the context of the rise of China and India, will be crucial to our collective future. This will place a premium on wise statecraft, particularly the effective management of relations between the US, Japan, China and India."[19] Underlying this logic was a perception that there were far too many regional institutions doing far too little in the Asia-Pacific region. This point was stressed further by Richard Woolcott, Rudd's special envoy dispatched to ascertain the views of regional countries to the Prime Minister's new regional initiative, who noted in his whirlwind tour of Southeast Asia that none of the existing regional multilateral arrangements had the mandate, the membership, or the ability to deal comprehensively with the economic, security, and political issues identified in the Rudd proposal. Summarizing the incapacity of extant organizations, Woolcott pointed out that "APEC [Asia-Pacific Economic Cooperation] does not include India and its mandate is primarily economic. The EAS [East Asia Summit] does not include the United States and Russia. While the ARF does include all the principal countries, it is widely seen as being too large, with 27 countries; it does not meet at HOG [heads-of-government] level; and when a serious regional issue arose, such as North Korea's nuclear capability, it was handled by a new arrangement, the Six Party Talks, although all six countries were members of ARF."[20] To surmount these obstacles, Rudd proposed the establishment by 2020 of the APC that would include the large and middle powers in the Asia-Pacific region — primarily the United States, China, Japan, India, Australia, South Korea, and Indonesia — who would deal with the entire spectrum of security, economic, and political challenges confronting the region.

While the Australian proposal for an APC remains very much in the embryonic stages, it is perhaps apropos to consider its potential and implications should it gain traction in the coming years. To that end, a raft of issues can be flagged, chief of which would be the matter of membership. The question of "who's in; who's not" has always remained a sensitive issue in the region when it comes to establishment of regional institutions. Since the end of the Cold War and the proliferation of such multilateral initiatives, the geopolitical footprint of the "Asia-Pacific", and which countries fall within it, has always been subject to intense debate and diplomatic bargaining. At first glance, this problem could possibly be addressed by expanding existing institutions like APEC to include India, or the East Asia Summit to include the United States and Russia. However, that leads only to another problem — the matter of cross-memberships. Currently, there are several countries that are members of one of the existing regional institutions, but not of others. Consider, for instance, Hong Kong, Taiwan, Mexico, Chile, and Peru who are all part of APEC (which is a conglomeration of economies rather than governments), while Papua New Guinea, Bangladesh, Sri Lanka, Pakistan, and the European Union are all members of the ARF. Any new regional architecture, including the APC, will almost certainly leave out some, perhaps even all, of these countries even as they, in turn, would most likely claim a legitimate right to be represented.

Second, there is the matter of the relationship between the APC and existing regional security institutions. It remains unclear whether the intention is for the APC to supplement or replace them. Notwithstanding its admittedly considerable structural and procedural limitations, the ARF remains the linchpin institution for security dialogue in the region. This being the case, the creation of an APC might dilute the commitment of regional states to the ARF, a situation that many ASEAN states view with concern given their centrality in the latter institution.

This dovetails into the third issue, which relates to leadership. Since the end of the Cold War, ASEAN countries have taken the lead in several regional multilateral institutions, the most prominent being the ARF and later the East Asia Summit. Not only has this given ASEAN a reinvigorated sense of purpose that was urgently required after the successful resolution of the Kampuchean conflict in the early 1990s, it also provided the major regional powers a neutral venue where confidence and mutual trust could be established. It is against this backdrop that the APC is viewed in several quarters within ASEAN as a direct threat to the association's pivotal role in regional initiatives. Moreover, it is not clear who is envisaged to, or can, take on the role of leadership in the APC. While it is clearly an Australian initiative, major powers such as the United States and China remain lukewarm in their response.

Finally, it is unclear from the current proposal what manner of decision-making mechanism is being considered that would not only be efficient, but also accommodative of smaller states' views and concerns.[21]

Having identified potential obstacles to the establishment of the APC, it is important to also note that not all ASEAN states have been categorical in their opposition to the initiative. Indonesia, in particular, had initially expressed interest, as did Thailand. Whether or not this signals the emergence of yet another point of contention within ASEAN though, remains to be seen.

Notwithstanding these reservations, the upshot of the APC proposal is that it has catalyzed critical thinking and vibrant debate over the matter of regional architecture. Taking the cue from the fundamental premise to Rudd's proposal — the perceived incapacity of existing regional institutions to deal decisively with the challenges confronting the region — some have argued that rather than create yet another institution, the region should explore ways of rationalizing and improving existing structures. One example put forward was to advance a more open and inclusive ASEAN-driven ARF, as well as the development of a "synergistic relationship between APEC and ARF to nurture a new security architecture."[22] Another counter-proposal suggested that in order to create a more coherent and consolidated regional system, the region should consider "a revitalized APEC with a strong ASEAN Plus Three (APT) as its core in East Asia and a transformed East Asia Summit (EAS) that is supported by the ARF at the working level."[23]

As for the responses of the region's major powers, the United States, China, Japan, and India have all been lukewarm with regards to the APC concept. U.S. Assistant Secretary of State for East Asian Affairs Kurt Campbell was noted as saying that "greater interest in finding appropriate forums from China, Japan and the U.S., as well as Australia, was a healthy thing."[24] He went on to add, however, that it would ultimately be the United States and not Australia who would be taking on the role of "harnessing and directing any large new institution that involved China and Japan."[25] Moreover, the move by the Obama administration to sign the Treaty of Amity and Cooperation with ASEAN was illustrative of American commitment to existing regional norms and paved the way for its entry into the East Asia Summit, thereby raising questions on the relevance of the APC in Washington circles.[26] China's response was far more categorical. Assistant Foreign Minister Hu Zhengyue was quoted as saying that "China is open to proposals that strengthen cooperation in the region, but East Asian cooperation is an incremental process... The conditions aren't ripe to put this [APC] mechanism on the agenda right away."[27] Preoccupation with domestic political and economic affairs meant that Tokyo gave little consideration to the APC proposal when it was articulated.[28] Indeed, Japan itself has presented its own version of a reinvigorated regionalism in the form of Prime Minister Hatoyama's East Asian Community concept. As for India, New Delhi's interest, albeit from a distance, is hardly surprising given its recent engagement with the East Asian region. Nevertheless, this interest fell short of full-fledged endorsement as Indian leaders expressed the view that they "would watch with interest" Rudd's move to build the new institution for cooperation in security, political and economic affairs."[29]

In short, after nearly a year since the APC was first proposed, there seems limited regional backing for the creation of a new regional institution. That being said, one desirable effect has been the climate of introspection it has fostered towards existing regional arrangements with the aim of creating a more effective regional architecture.[30]

East Asian Community

In his first summit meeting since becoming the new Prime Minister of Japan, Yukio Hatoyama expressed during his discussions with Chinese President Hu Jintao hopes that Sino-Japanese relations could transcend bilateral disputes and form the basis for a new East Asian Community.[31] Using the European experience of integration as his point of entry, Hatoyama's initial vision for the configuration of the East Asian Community consisted of China, Japan, South Korea, and ASEAN, which he suggested should work towards the creation of a common currency. Other Japanese officials, however, most notably Foreign Minister Katsuya Okada, have opined that the East Asian Community would need to include India, Australia, and

New Zealand as well. Beyond disagreements over the membership configuration, there was also a discernible lack of consensus within the Japanese establishment on the matter of the utility of the European blueprint, with Okada opining that "a situation like the European Union cannot be quickly created. What we can do now is to uphold the big vision of an East Asian community and work on what we have in front of us step by step."[32]

As with the APC, responses to the East Asian Community proposal have been lukewarm. With the leaders of Japan, China, and South Korea reaffirming ASEAN as the core for regional cooperation in the 2008 Trilateral Summit, it is unclear if the three northeast Asian powers can reach consensus on a vision for an East Asian Community. Moreover, despite the present upturn in Sino-Japanese relations, the traditional rivalry between Japan and China over primacy and leadership in East Asia, not to mention Beijing's comfort and clear preference for the ASEAN Plus Three as its institution of choice for regionalism, is likely to weigh down any efforts towards an East Asian Community.[33] Indeed, it did not take long for this rivalry to surface in direct reference to the East Asian Community, for insofar as Beijing has responded positively to the concept they have been quick to remind that it was China that first advocated such an idea.[34] Subsequently, when the idea was raised during the October 2009 ASEAN-Japan Summit, it was met with caution by ASEAN, which went no further than to record in the Chairman's Statement its "appreciation" for Japan's efforts to reinvigorate regionalism through the East Asian Community initiative. Likewise, while India has not closed the door on Hatoyama's initiative entirely, it has indicated that it saw the East Asia Summit as the foundation of any East Asian community.

Finally it remains to be seen whether the East Asian Community would be held hostage to American reservations. It is clear from Hatoyama's statements thus far that the United States falls outside of the geographical footprint of the East Asian Community. Many see this as part of a larger attempt by the Hatoyama administration to fashion a foreign policy outlook independent from the traditional reliance on Washington. Indeed, Hatoyama has also been quoted as saying "it could be said that we have so far depended on the United States too much. While the Japanese-U.S. alliance is important, I want to devise policies that focus more on Asia, as a member of Asia."[35] Be that as it may, since the end of the Cold War the United States has been the proverbial elephant in the room when discussions of the geographical boundaries of East Asian (as opposed to Asia-Pacific) regionalism arise. This being the case, it is likely that Washington will harbour misgivings about yet another attempt to exclude it from regional affairs, and this time all the more so given that the impetus towards its exclusion is coming from a traditional, and erstwhile staunch, ally.

Conclusion

Southeast Asian regionalism is at a crossroads. With the signing of the ASEAN Charter and the birth of the ASEAN Intergovernmental Commission on Human Rights, recent years have witnessed significant advances in regional integration. Further to that, it is clear that relations between ASEAN and major dialogue partners have also progressed over the past year, albeit at a different pace. The salience of these developments, however, has to some extent been eclipsed by the emergence of major trends over the past twelve months. The challenges that Thailand encountered while serving as ASEAN Chair have been illustrative of how ASEAN remains captive to the domestic affairs and sovereignty of member states, to the extent that regionalism was at various points in the year held hostage to the domestic politics of a single ASEAN country. This state of affairs was further compounded by the diplomatic vitriol in several bilateral relationships in Southeast Asia that threatened to undermine the spirit of ASEAN regionalism. Finally, ASEAN's model of inclusive regionalism has come under threat from two alternative, and competing, visions of regional order — the Asia-Pacific Community of Australian Prime Minister Kevin Rudd and the East Asian Community of Japanese Prime Minister Yukio Hatoyama. While both initiatives are undoubtedly a long way from materializing, they are nevertheless indicative of the fact that extra-regional players are not only uncomfortable with ASEAN's centrality in regional institutions, they are actively thinking up alternatives to the ASEAN-centred order.

Time and again, it has been forces beyond the control of Southeast Asian states that have forced their hand on matters of regional integration. This appears to be happening once more. As ASEAN faces up to the challenge, not only of rising Indian and Chinese power, but also the emergence of alternative visions of regional order that threatens the "ASEAN Way" with irrelevance, the members of the forty-two-year-old regional organization must yet again set aside their differences and apprehensions towards one another — and these are deep-seated apprehensions indeed — in order for the organization to remain relevant.

Notes

[1]   Previously, the ASEAN Chair would hold that position for a year, from mid-year to mid-year. Under the ASEAN Charter, however, the tenure of the chair would follow

the calendar year. In order to facilitate the transition, the first chair under the new charter, Thailand, was appointed to serve as chair for eighteen months in order to bring the process in line with the new calendar year rotation.

2   See, for instance, "China's State Council Approves Development Plan for Guangxi to Foster New Growth Pole", Xinhua News Agency, 28 October 2009.

3   "Cambodian PM Orders Troops to Shoot Any Thai 'Trespassers' in Border Feud", Agence France-Presse, 28 September 2009.

4   Ibid.

5   Chiep Mony, "Cambodia Turns to ASEAN in Border Dispute", VOANews.com, 12 October 2009.

6   "Cambodia Warned on Ex-PM Thaksin," *The Nation*, 7 April 2009.

7   "Spat between Thai and Cambodian Prime Ministers Continues", Thai News Service, 26 October 2009.

8   "Burmese Not Happy with Hun Sen", *Bangkok Post*, 26 October 2009.

9   "Activists Conduct Sweep of Malaysians on the Streets", *Jakarta Post*, 8 September 2009.

10   See Joseph Chinyong Liow and See Seng Tan, "Southeast Asia", in *From Superpower to Besieged Global Power: Restoring World Order after the Failure of the Bush Doctrine*, edited by Edward A. Kolodziej and Roger E. Kanet (Athens: The University of Georgia Press, 2008).

11   Robert M. Gates, "America's Security Role in the Asia-Pacific", The 8th IISS Asia Security Summit — The Shangri-La Dialogue, The International Institute for Strategic Studies, IISS, 30 May 2009 <http://www.iiss.org/conferences/the-shangri-la-dialogue/shangri-la-dialogue-2009/plenary-session-speeches-2009/first-plenary-session/dr-robert-gates> (accessed 16 October 2009).

12   See "Clinton Speaks of Shielding Mideast from Iran", *New York Times*, 23 September 2009.

13   As a matter of fact China already signed currency swap agreements with Malaysia and Indonesia this year.

14   "End is Nigh for Era of U.S. 'Hero Worship', says Yukio Hatoyama of Japan", *The Times*, 24 February 2009.

15   Baladas Goshal, "India, Southeast Asia, and the FTA: Strengthening Economic Integration", *IPCS Issue Brief*, no. 114, August 2009.

16   "Indonesia Asks India to Help Maintain Malacca Strait Security", Antara News Agency, 5 March 2009.

17   Ian Storey, "China-Vietnam's Year of Friendship Turns Fractious", *Straits Times*, 26 May 2009.

18   Kevin Rudd, "Address to the Asia Society AustralAsia Centre, Sydney: It's Time to Build an Asia Pacific Community", Prime Minister of Australia Website, 4 June 2008 <http://www.pm.gov.au/node/5763> (accessed 16 October 2009).

[19] Kevin Rudd, "Keynote Address", The 8th IISS Asia Security Summit — The Shangri-La Dialogue, The International Institute for Strategic Studies, IISS, 29 May 2009 <http://www.iiss.org/conferences/the-shangri-la-dialogue/shangri-la-dialogue-2009/plenary-session-speeches-2009/opening-remarks-and-keynote-address/keynote-address-kevin-rudd/> (accessed 16 October 2009).

[20] Richard Woolcott, "An Asia Pacific Community: An Idea Whose Time is Coming", East Asia Forum, 18 October 2009 <http://www.eastasiaforum.org/2009/10/18/an-asia-pacific-community-an-idea-whose-time-is-coming/> (accessed 20 October 2009).

[21] Jia Qingguo, "Realizing the Asia Pacific Community: Geographic, Institutional and Leadership Challenges," East Asia Forum, 28 July 2009 <http://www.eastasiaforum.org/2009/07/28/realizing-the-asia-pacific-community-geographic-institutional-and-leadership-challenges/> (accessed 16 October 2009).

[22] Goh Sui Noi, "A Challenge to Asean Centrality", *Straits Times*, 20 March 2009.

[23] Hadi Soesastro, "Insight: Kevin Rudd's Architecture for the Asia Pacific", *Jakarta Post*, 11 June 2008 <http://www.thejakartapost.com/news/2008/06/11/insight-kevin-rudd039s-architecture-asia-pacific.html> (accessed 16 October 2009).

[24] Brad Norington, "Barack Obama's Man Kurt Campbell Junks Kevin Rudd's Asia-Pacific Plan", *The Australian*, 12 June 2009 <http://www.theaustralian.news.com.au/story/0,25197,25623798-2702,00.html> (accessed 16 October 2009).

[25] Ibid.

[26] "Smith Spruiks Pacific Scheme at ASEAN", Australian Associated Press Bulletins, 23 July 2009.

[27] Lee Spears, "Conditions 'Not Ripe' for Asia-Pacific Community, China Says", Bloomberg.com, 8 April 2009 <http://www.bloomberg.com/apps/news?pid=20601081&sid=ayq3w9mW2hZw&refer=australia#> (accessed 16 October 2009).

[28] Charles Prestidge-King, "Japan's Unsurprising Silence on the Asia-Pacific Community", East Asia Forum, 3 August 2009 <http://www.eastasiaforum.org/2009/08/03/japans-unsurprising-silence-on-the-asia-pacific-community/> (accessed 16 October 2009).

[29] Sachin Parashar, "Despite Snub, India Backs Oz 'Community' Plan with China," *Times of India*, 25 June 2008.

[30] Carlyle A. Thayer, "Kevin Rudd's Multi-layered Asia Pacific Community Initiative", East Asia Forum, 22 June 2009 <http://www.eastasiaforum.org/2009/06/22/kevin-rudds-multi-layered-asia-pacific-community-initiative/> (accessed 16 October 2009).

[31] "Hatoyama Pushes East Asian Community", *Asahi Shimbun*, 23 September 2009 <http://www.asahi.com/english/Herald-asahi/TKY200909230045.html> (accessed 25 October 2009).

[32] "Specifics of East Asian Community Difficult to Work Out", Bernama.com, 30 September 2009 <http://www.bernama.com/bernama/v5/newsindex.php?id=443235> (accessed 16 October 2009).

[33] Aurelia George-Mulgan, "Hatoyama's East Asia Community and Regional Leadership Rivalries", East Asia Forum, 13 October 2009 <http://www.eastasiaforum. org/2009/10/13/hatoyamas-east-asia-community/comment-page-1/#comment-67254> (accessed 16 October 2009).

[34] "Japan, China to Work Together on Creating 'East Asia Community'", *Japan Times Online*, 29 September 2009 <http://search.japantimes.co.jp/cgi-bin/nn20090929a3.html> (accessed 16 October 2009).

[35] "Clarifying the Idea of Community," *Japan Times*, 16 October 2009.

REVIEW OF SOUTHEAST ASIAN ECONOMIC DEVELOPMENTS

Manu Bhaskaran

Introduction and Summary

Southeast Asian economies are integrated into the world economy through multiple channels and remain sufficiently exposed to the G-3 (European Union, Japan, United States) economies that they could not escape a substantial hit from the global financial crisis. Our views can be summarized as follows:

- What is striking about the regional economies then was their surprising resilience — GDP growth is on track for a robust rebound, reversing the global impact fairly quickly. We believe that this improved resilience springs from important structural changes in the region since the Asian financial crisis of 1997–98. In particular, policy changes have strengthened macroeconomic frameworks and banking sectors while also allowing some degree of diversification of the economic base.
- The regional economies are thus poised for a strong rebound, even with a global environment that is likely to remain troubled and occasionally subject to financial stresses. However, these global level risks are not likely to result in a double-dip slowdown in Southeast Asia — external demand is recovering and the lagged effects of monetary and fiscal easing will support growth.
- The real challenge in Southeast Asia is to build economic resilience and prepare for a global economy that will be substantially different from the pre-crisis era.

Manu Bhaskaran is Partner, Centennial Asia Advisors Pte Ltd, Singapore.

Impact of the Global Crisis

(a) Global Crisis Hurt but Region Displayed More Resilience Than Expected

Two features of the performance of Southeast Asian economies in 2009 stand out: First, the crisis showed how intricately integrated the region is with the global economy and, in particular, with the United States, European Union, and Japan. Second, despite this, their economies have developed greater resilience to external shocks as seen in the speed with which their economies have rebounded.

As Table 1 shows, most Southeast Asian economies suffered a sharp deceleration in economic growth as the global crisis spread. However, the recovery came fairly quickly, meaning that the recessionary impact of the global crisis on Southeast Asia was mostly limited in duration.

This initially severe impact of the crisis suggests little evidence for the decoupling that many had hoped for. This is seen in the multiple transmission mechanisms through which the global crisis hurt Southeast Asia:

• The first and immediate impact was felt through the financial channel. As the enormity of the financial crisis in the United States and European Union became evident, there was a sharp fall in risk appetites among global investors which precipitated a withdrawal of funds deployed to bonds and equities in "riskier" emerging markets. This in turn led to sharp falls in asset prices (Figures 1 and 2 for example) as well as a liquidity crunch in several economies as capital flowed out. Exchange rates came under pressure as well. Trade financing weakened sharply as well; much of the trade finance in the region was provided by European banks which had been hurt by the

TABLE 1
Economic Growth during the Global Financial Crisis

GDP growth y/y %	2008	4Q08	1Q09	2Q09	3Q09
Indonesia	6.3	5.1	4.5	4.0	4.2
Malaysia	6.3	0.1	−6.3	−3.9	−1.2
Philippines	3.9	2.8	0.6	1.5	0.8
Singapore	1.2	−4.2	−9.5	−3.5	0.6
Thailand	2.5	−4.2	−7.1	−4.9	−2.8
Vietnam	6.2	5.5	3.1	4.4	5.8

Source: Collated by Centennial Group using CEIC Database and official sources.

FIGURE 1
Sharp Falls in Assets Markets ...

Source: Collated by Centennial Group using CEIC database.

FIGURE 2
... Reflected Immediate Financial Impact of Crisis

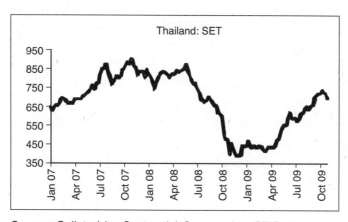

Source: Collated by Centennial Group using CEIC database.

crisis. Risk-averse banks became wary of engaging even in the relatively less risky funding of export and import transactions.

- Second, as businesses in developed economies became alarmed at the credit crunch in their economies, they did everything they could to conserve cash, including retrenching workers, liquidating inventories, and slashing orders for imported goods from developing economies. Not surprisingly, Southeast Asian exporting nations saw a precipitous fall in export orders from late

FIGURE 3
Exports Plunged ...

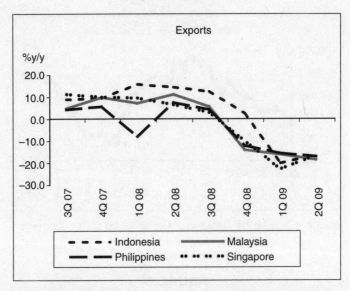

Source: Collated by Centennial Group using CEIC database.

2008 onwards, causing exports to fall sharply (Figure 3). Intra-Asian trade also fell sharply, bringing out clearly that a large proportion of intra-Asian trade was really trade in components that were eventually assembled in Asia for final consumption in the G-3.

- Third, as global demand fell, other factors affecting household incomes in Southeast Asia also came under pressure. Export-oriented manufacturing companies and companies affected by the financial turmoil, such as banks, reduced payrolls while also cutting back on overtime pay. Commodity prices fell and the growth of remittances also slowed. Local business and consumer confidence took a hit, leading to restrained spending by both businesses and consumers.

- Fourth, tourist arrivals fell as more consumers in the major tourism markets became cautious in their spending habits (Figure 4). Southeast Asia as a major tourist destination suffered as a result.

- Fifth, as the global crisis spread, foreign investment — another key driver of growth in the region — also slowed. Multinational companies in developed economies focused immediately on protecting their short-term profitability and cash reserves while deferring long-term capacity expansion.

FIGURE 4
... and Even Tourist Arrivals Slowed or Fell

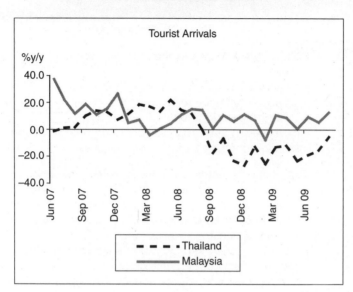

Source: Collated by Centennial Group using CEIC database.

In short, there were too many active channels of transmission of a global shock into the domestic economies of Southeast Asia for the region to have decoupled from the developed economies.

(b) What Explains This Resilience?

As discussed above, Southeast Asian economies are mostly highly open economies that are exposed to substantial flows of trade, portfolio capital, direct investment, and tourists as well as sensitive to global factors such as commodity prices and business confidence. Yet, Southeast Asia demonstrated a capacity to absorb shocks better than in previous crises, containing the downside and bouncing back after the initial hit. This economic resilience comprised five sets of factors that are explained in more detail in Table 2.

The final outcome of the resilience analysis is described in Figure 5, which shows that regional economies enjoyed some improvement, albeit small, in their economic resilience during the course of this decade.

Table 3 outlines how our estimate of each country's resilience changed between 2000 and 2008 and what factors accounted for the change.

TABLE 2
What Drives Resilience?

Factor	Comments
Political factors	Political weaknesses in the region in the past amplified external shocks: • Intra-elite conflicts, such as in Malaysia in 1997–98. • Substantial uncertainty over the longevity of a key leader, as in Indonesia in 1998. Conversely, a strong government can help to absorb shocks by inspiring confidence and acting decisively.
Financial vulnerabilities	The financial sector is a critical factor in resilience: • A high ratio of financially-mobile capital to foreign exchange reserves reduces resilience; the flight of capital induced by footloose investors can be disruptive for currencies, domestic liquidity, and the external accounts. • Currency and maturity mismatches can compound an external shock; this was a major problem in 1997. • Banking sector balance sheets: strongly capitalised, prudently managed domestic banks will lend resilience. • Corporate sector balance sheets are also important; the stronger these are, the better resilience is.
Diversity of the economic base	A more diverse economic base avoids concentration risks: • Economy's dependence on domestic demand versus external demand. • Economy's dependence on external actors such as investors or providers of funds. • In trade, whether there is disproportionate dependence on particular geographic markets or products.
Flexibility of an economy	Whether an economy has spontaneous domestic adjustment mechanisms/automatic stabilisers that help the economy to respond effectively to a shock. • A large social safety net, including unemployment benefits. • A flexible labour market that, say, adjusts wages down when economic conditions worsen so that unemployment does not rise sharply. • A floating exchange rate usually helps to absorb shocks better.
Capacity of policy to respond effectively	Swift and effective policy actions can help to absorb shocks. • Strength of the monetary anchor in an economy and credibility of the central bank helps to prevent speculative attacks or sudden and disruptive changes in inflationary or exchange rate expectations. • The amount of fiscal space the government has available to use to stimulate the economy.

Source: Prepared by Centennial Group.

TABLE 3
Changes in Economic Resilience in Southeast Asia 2000–8

	Resilience Index		Remarks
	2000	2008	
Thailand	46.6	48.9	• Increase in public debt • Significant reduction in non-performing loan (NPL) ratio • Growing tax mobilization relative to rise in gross domestic product (GDP) • Higher export diversity by destination
Vietnam	55.5	58.3	• Higher public debt • Political/regulatory improvements • Significant reduction in NPLs • Higher domestic demand due to massive increase in gross fixed capital formation (GFCF)
Malaysia	49.8	51.5	• Lower public debt • Political/regulatory improvements • Reduction in NPLs • Higher export diversity by destination
Indonesia	46.6	46.6	• Lower public debt • Lower average inflation • Political/regulatory improvements • Significant reduction in NPLs • Higher dependence on foreign energy • Higher domestic demand due to massive increase in private consumption expenditure (PCE) and GFCF • Significant loss in export diversity by destination • High external vulnerability due to surge in financially mobile capital and shrinking current-account surplus
Philippines	36.0	35.4	• Increase in political/regulatory risk • Significant reduction in NPLs • Slightly improved export diversity by commodity, significant rise in export diversity by destination • Reduction of domestic demand due to significant fall in GCE and GFCF
Singapore	63.6	59.7	• Reduction in NPLs • Loss in export diversity by commodity • Faster tax mobilization relative to GDP growth • Higher external vulnerability due to 400 per cent increase in financially mobile capital

Source: Calculated using CAA model.

FIGURE 5
Some Improvement in Southeast Asian Resilience

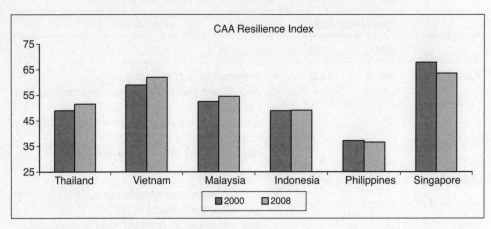

Source: Calculated using CAA model.

Some important conclusions emerge from this analysis. Essentially, Southeast Asian economies have built more shock absorbers and reduced the number of shock amplifiers in their economies:

- Financial sectors have become much stronger. Whereas in 1997–98, financial sectors in many parts of the region amplified the initial shock of currency depreciations, the region's finance sectors were generally quite robust, avoiding the sharp rise in non-performing loans which undermined the capital bases of the banking sector and produced a financial crisis in 1997. Most economies have done especially well to reduce their NPL ratios and substantially strengthen their banking sectors after the Asian financial crisis (Table 4).

TABLE 4
Non-Performing Loans

(% of commercial bank loans)	2000–4 Average	2004	2005	2006	2007	2008	2009
Indonesia	10.2	4.5	7.6	6.1	4.1	3.2	3.8
Malaysia	8.9	6.8	5.6	4.8	3.2	2.2	2.1
Philippines	14.8	12.7	8.5	5.7	4.4	3.5	3.5
Singapore	5.3	5.0	3.8	2.8	1.5	1.4	—
Thailand	13.5	10.9	8.3	7.5	7.3	5.3	5.3

Source: ADB *Asia Economic Monitor December 2009*; Data for Indonesia, Malaysia, and Thailand are as of September 2009; for Philippines as of August 2009; For Malaysia and Philippines, the reported NPLs are gross classified loans of retail banks.

• With a better track record of managing inflation, central banks in the region were more credible and were able to pursue monetary policy responses more effectively than before.

• Political systems proved to be more durable, unlike in 1997–98 when political problems in countries such as Indonesia and Malaysia compounded the effects of the currency crisis.

Second, increased diversity of demand helped some Asian economies as well. The share of domestic demand to GDP in several Association of Southeast Asian Nations (ASEAN) economies has increased from 2000 to 2008, coinciding with increased wages and consumer behaviour (Figure 6).

Third, policy responses were far more quickly implemented and more effective than before. Interest rates could be cut swiftly since central banks were more credible as explained above. Governments put together fiscal packages and implemented them more quickly than in previous downturns.

Fourth, there appear to be more automatic stabilizers in regional economies than before. More flexible exchange rates have clearly helped (Figure 7) — unlike in 1997 when the collapse of rigid exchange rates amplified the initial shock. Tax reforms have also improved the correlation of tax revenues with economic activity, meaning that as the economy slows, the tax automatically falls more than before, helping to stabilize demand.

FIGURE 6
Flexible Exchange Rates Helped

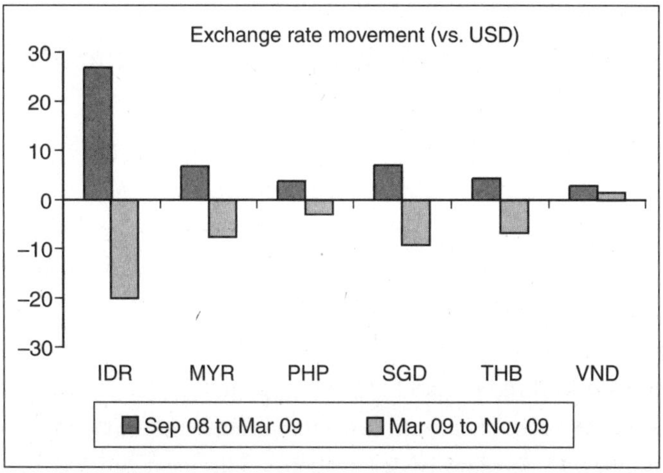

Source: Collated by Centennial Group using CEIC database.

FIGURE 7
Domestic Demand — Bigger Role in Some Cases

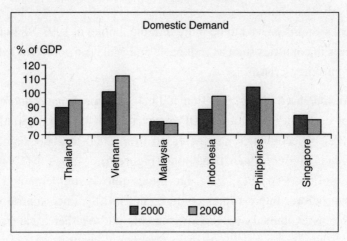

Source: Collated by Centennial Group using CEIC database.

Fifth, although we do not have the data to incorporate this into the resilience analysis, we also believe that supply-side forces unleashed by new economic reforms or by other structural improvements have lent substantially greater economic growth momentum to many economies. This is especially the case for Indonesia and Vietnam. Indonesia is enjoying the fruits of the economic and political stabilization of recent years while Vietnam is reaping the benefits of economic opening and entry into the World Trade Organization. This higher momentum makes it more difficult for an external shock to throw an economy off a growth track.

(c) Prospects for 2010: Strong Rebound but Need to Manage Turbulence

Improving prospects in the global economy will support the region's recovery. Recent data for manufacturing and service sector activity in the larger developed and emerging economies of the world show that the global economy has stopped contracting. More encouragingly, the available lead indicators suggest that this rebound in global economic growth is likely to be sustained into early 2010. Figure 8 shows the Organisation for Economic Co-operation and Development's (OECD) composite lead indicators for the G-3 economies — these indicators point unequivocally to the recovery continuing for at least the next six to nine months. A recovery in external demand bodes well for Southeast Asia as exports that are particularly sensitive to the global economic cycle such as electronics recover (Figure 9).

FIGURE 8
Lead Indicators for G-3 Rising, Allowing ...

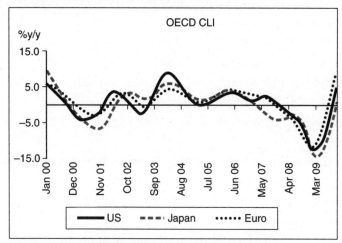

Source: Collated by Centennial Group using CEIC Database and the OECD website.

FIGURE 9
... Cyclically Sensitive Electronics to Recover

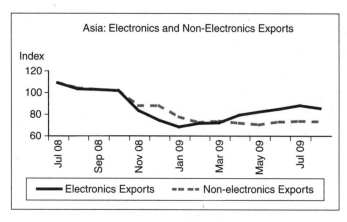

Source: Collated by Centennial Group using CEIC Database and the OECD website.

Despite this recovery, it is also clear that the recovery in Southeast Asia's major economic partners will be fragile and likely marked by turbulence. While global demand for ASEAN exports will probably be better in 2010, several unresolved stresses in the larger developed economies will probably make for an unsettled global environment:

- **Property-related loans in developed economies remain a risk:** Fitch estimates that U.S. banks can expect to see ten per cent of their US$1.1 trillion portfolio of direct commercial real estate loans default. The regional banks will bear the brunt of this problem, leading to a higher rate of bank failures in the United States.
- **Bank debts need to be refinanced:** Moody's estimates that close to US$7 trillion of global bank debt will mature by 2012 and a total of US$10 trillion by 2015. Banks will struggle to achieve this scale of refinancing. If there are further financial stresses, raising capital on this scale would prove difficult.
- **Many smaller European economies remain highly vulnerable to crisis:** Although financial investors have become more discerning, the risk remains that serious financial stresses in Europe would have a contagion effect on Asian emerging markets.
- **Public debt in the United States or Japan is likely to be in focus in 2010, precipitating new pressures:** Confidence in the United States could take a severe hit, for instance, if it transpired that large government agencies which are already under financial stress such as the Federal Deposit Insurance Corporation, Federal Housing Administration, the Pension Benefit Guarantee Corporation, and others required large scale re-capitalization.
- **Protectionism risks remain:** As unemployment continues to rise and the political mood in developed economies sours in 2010, the risk of more protectionism will rise.
- **Adjustment processes will hinder growth:** Companies in the United States and Europe have to adjust to a period of lower growth where the patterns of demand are shifting. This means more restructuring, including layoffs and cost cutting, which could hinder the recovery in labour markets in developed economies.

The net effect is that ASEAN economies are likely to bounce back fairly strongly in 2010, even if that recovery will be marked by occasional bouts of financial turbulence or uncertainty in developed economies. Indeed, recent lead indicators indicate that a recovery is under way. The available lead indicators for Asian economies are showing clear signs of a rebound. Other regional lead indicators are similarly showing signs of recovery (Figures 10 to 13).

There are reasons for confidence that ASEAN economies can sustain economic recovery into 2010 and 2011:

- First, the global recovery — even if it is uneven — will mean stronger export growth.

FIGURE 10
Region's Lead Indicators Are Recovering...

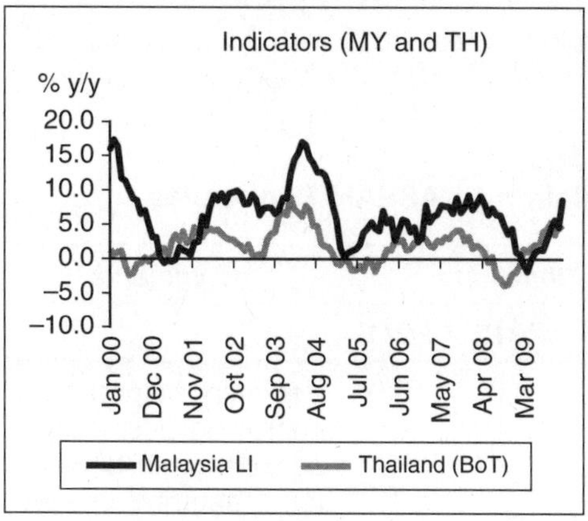

FIGURE 11
... Certainly in Indonesia

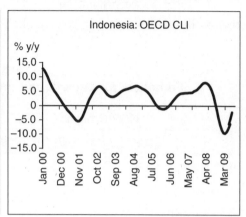

Source: CEIC and OECD.

FIGURE 12
... and the Philippines and ...

FIGURE 13
... in Highly Export-oriented Singapore

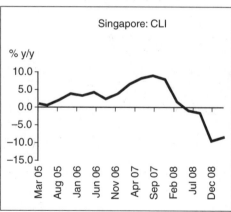

Source: CEIC.

- Second, this recovery in exports will coincide with the continued and lagged effects of monetary and fiscal easing. Malaysia and Thailand for example will see substantial parts of their fiscal stimulus packages implemented in the course of 2010. Singapore has also pledged to keep fiscal policy supportive.

- Third, some economies are enjoying supply-side boosts to economic growth as a result of previous policies or developments. For example, Singapore will see mega-projects in tourism and manufacturing come on stream — its massive integrated resorts will open in the course of 2010 while several large manufacturing plants are also set to start production.

In Table 5, we present our views on growth and inflation prospects for the region. In other words, the greater likelihood is that 2010 will be a substantially

TABLE 5
Forecasts for Growth and Inflation in ASEAN Economies

	GDP Growth			Inflation			Comments
	2009	2010	2011	2009	2010	2011	
Indonesia	4.6	7.1	7.5	5.0	6.0	5.0	Recovery helped by improving business confidence in longer term, spurring invest-ment as government acts to improve infrastructure and business environment.
Malaysia	−1.8	4.8	5.0	1.1	3.3	2.5	Moderate recovery helped by continued fiscal support. Reforms could spur further upside.
Philippines	1.4	4.5	4.5	3.2	5.5	4.5	Moderate growth close to potential.
Thailand	−2.7	4.5	6.5	−0.5	2.0	2.5	Benefits of global recovery balanced against domestic confidence concerns in 2010 with a stronger recovery in 2011.
Vietnam	4.5	6.5	7.5	6.8	8.5	10.0	Economic growth likely spurred by rising investment and lagged effects of WTO accession. Risks are mainly to price stability.
Singapore	−1.9	7.0	4.5	0	2.0	2.5	Strong rebound in 2010 spurred by exports plus new projects (e.g., integrated resorts) coming on stream.

Source: Forecasts by Centennial Asia Advisors.

better year for economic activity than 2009. The global environment will certainly provide a turbulent backdrop, but the shocks we can expect are not the sort that will hurt economic growth severely. The global stresses — mostly in the G-3 economies — will have a greater impact on financial markets than on aggregate demand and real economic activity in the region.

Longer Term Trends and Challenges

(a) Shape of the Post-crisis Global Economy

As the region exits the crisis, it needs to move away from crisis containment to focusing on adjusting to a post-crisis global landscape that will be quite unlike the pre-crisis one. The key dynamics which will confront Southeast Asian policy-makers, investors, businessmen, and workers include:

- **Noticeably slower global economic growth:** While recovering, growth in the G-3 economies will be dragged down by continued de-leveraging by households and banks, while the need to tighten excessively-loose fiscal and monetary conditions will also act as a brake on the pace of recovery. Chinese economic growth will also probably slow over time as China shifts focus to the quality of growth rather than just high growth per se. In addition to these major drags on global growth, other headwinds include the likelihood of higher oil prices as the demand-supply balance shifts unfavourably and costs of accommodating climate change become more material to growth. Southeast Asian economies will find it hard to avoid a long period of slower economic growth.

- **Changes to fundamental assumptions as the patterns of global growth shift:** Global growth will be slower and more dependent on large developing economies rather than the G-3 economies. Changes in global currencies, China's move up the value chain, India's emergence in global manufacturing, the consolidation of global supply chains, and the backlash in the West against the use of tax and other incentives by developing countries will all change the structure of competitiveness. What is more, the larger Asian economies such as China and India can no longer behave as passengers in the global economy, reacting to global changes: they will have to share responsibility with the G-3 for global economic governance. This means that they will be less able to shield their exchange rate and other macro-economic policy approaches from critical scrutiny by other powerful stakeholders in the global economy.

- **A more volatile global economy:** A far riskier world is emerging where financial stresses and outright crises are likely to be more frequent. This is probably especially so in the early phase of the post-crisis period when the costs of the policy steps taken to end the crisis begin to affect markets and economies. But these stresses will continue as we begin to adjust to the step changes that will occur such as the downshift in the role of the U.S. dollar.

(b) New Economic Policy Frameworks are Therefore Necessary

ASEAN governments are responding to the crisis and the changing shape of the global economy. Both Malaysia and Singapore are scheduled to announce important changes to their economic models in 2010. While each country will pursue its own particular models of development, the following areas will have to be addressed.

Increase the Role of Domestic Demand versus External Demand

Policies to boost the role of domestic demand in regional economies, such as allowing currencies to appreciate and expanding social safety nets, are important but will not suffice in themselves. Currency appreciation may not even be a feasible option — if China is not willing to allow its yuan to appreciate, ASEAN economies are unlikely to allow their currencies to rise. China has emphasized that it will not be pressured into currency appreciation. In all likelihood, the Chinese yuan will only rise gradually and China will probably complement such a policy with administrative measures and indirect subsidies that help its export sector preserve competitiveness. Hence, the incentive for China's Asian competitors to allow their currencies to rise sufficiently to produce an expenditure switch to imports is not that strong. Neither is it likely that more extensive social safety nets will be deployed very quickly — these reforms take many years to materialize. Consequently, ASEAN policymakers will need to try other policies to boost domestic demand:

- **Boosting housing sectors with easy monetary policy:** A more active housing market also spurs construction, real estate services, and financial services linked to housing.
- **Boost infrastructure spending:** A particularly potent area for infrastructure spending will be improving transport linkages in archipelagic countries such

as Indonesia and the Philippines where improved road/rail/bridge links among the islands could help integrate what are now fragmented local economies with sub-par economic scale into larger markets with better scale economies.

Increase Intra-regional Trade and Reduce Dependence on G-3 Demand

ASEAN economies know that they should not rely on domestic demand alone to grow rapidly. Since exports to G-3 economies are unlikely to grow fast, there is an urgent need for new impetus to boost intra-Asian trade. There are several ways this could be done:

- **Summoning the political will to create more effective regional trade arrangements:** So far, regional trade agreements such as the ASEAN Free Trade Agreement have only had limited success in creating a single market because there was not enough political will to overcome non-tariff and other barriers. With G-3 demand growing slowly but Asian economies performing well, there will now be greater incentive to fortify the existing agreements. We also see greater interest in expanding sub-regional integration in areas such as the Greater Mekong Sub-Region (GMS).

- **Improving connectivity within the region:** One way to improve the sub-regional integration would be through improved transport connectivity. We see more efforts to build road and rail networks spanning the sub-regions such as the GMS or the Iskandar Region straddling the Malaysia-Singapore border.

Build Greater Economic Resilience

Asian economies need to build up resilience. Since there is not likely to be any escape from frequent shocks and stresses in the global economy, policymakers will decide that the best they can do is to improve resilience. This means building greater diversity, increasing economic flexibility, and strengthening shock absorbers in the system while reducing the shock amplifiers in the system:

- **Diversity in export structures:** Apart from having more diverse domestic demand drivers, ASEAN countries are also likely to try to diversify the geographic concentration as well as product concentration of their exports. Some degree of industrial policy may be needed to achieve this.

- **Creation of more automatic stabilizers:** As social safety nets are extended, domestic demand would tend to become less volatile — since unemployment benefits and related social payments would tend to increase in an economic downturn.

- **Reduction of shock amplifiers:** This crisis has highlighted the role that financially mobile capital plays in amplifying an external shock. A disproportionate amount of foreigners' holdings of short-term debt and equity instruments in relation to the financial depth of the economy or in relation to its foreign exchange reserves amplifies shocks because the abrupt withdrawal of such capital forces precipitate currency weakness that arouses investor concerns. It also causes a sudden drying up of liquidity in the financial system. We suspect ASEAN policymakers will implement policies to limit the inflow of short-term capital during periods of financial market hubris such as we saw in 2006–7.

Build New Engines of Growth

With currency and cost differentials with developed economies narrowing, there will be particular pressure on the more successful economies such as Singapore to change economic strategies. While the previously less dynamic or poorer economies can still rely on catch up with the successful economies and will benefit from China vacating areas of lower value add, the more successful economies will now depend more on innovations in business processes and adopting new technology which can then raise productivity and boost competitiveness. ASEAN policymakers are likely to be pragmatic about how they go about achieving this.

- **Massive investment in human capital development:** East Asian economies and Singapore have invested heavily in tertiary education. We are likely to see countries such as Thailand and Malaysia step up efforts in this area — expanding the number and quality of tertiary institutions.

- **Increasing competition in the domestic economy:** Innovation is best spurred when companies in the domestic economy are forced to compete against one another. Many countries in Asia are beginning to introduce legislation to improve the competition frameworks in their respective economies. Moreover, as regional trade agreements become more ambitious, as argued above, we are likely to see more regional companies allowed to compete in domestic markets.

TABLE 6
Employment Conditions in Asian Economies

	Rigidity of Employment Index	Firing Cost (Weeks of Salary)
Indonesia	40	108
Philippines	29	91
Malaysia	10	75
Thailand	11	54
Vietnam	11	87
East Asia and Pacific Average	19.2	42.4
OECD Average	26.5	26.6

Source: World Bank Doing Business 2010.

Policymakers in smaller Asian economies to create policies to attract such labour intensive manufacturing:

- **Reform labour laws:** Many ASEAN economies still suffer from archaic labour laws which prevent any flexibility in the system, and rigidity is a major disincentive. Issues such as difficulty in hiring, rigidity of hours, and high firing costs are among the main problems (Table 6).
- **Loosen up the business environment:** The time and costs involved in registering a company should be reduced. Costs could be associated with fees, taxes, stamp duties etc.
- **Improve law and order:** Better law and order cannot be ignored. Countries could gain an advantage over others if they improved business conditions, including the law and order situation.

Reap Benefits of Increased Tourism

- **Create packages to suit new tastes:** Package tourists would be an important tool to attract attention. Unlike earlier packages, they should be directed towards Chinese and Indian tourists. Restaurants catering to this new clientele should be encouraged. There should be some coordination between airline operators, hotels, and travel agents. For example, offering special packages with options of vegetarian food will help attract Indian tourists.
- **Marketing and advertising:** Increasing the awareness of tourist locations can be done through advertisement and marketing campaigns in target countries.

Attract Foreign Direct Investment from These Markets

Besides being appealing locations for foreign direct investment, India and China have also become large outward investors. While historically these investments have been targeted toward the developed world, the slow growth forecast for the coming years in the United States and Europe indicates that returns on investment in these markets will be low. Investors could look towards countries in ASEAN for new investment opportunities.

Fill Gaps in Domestic Excess Workers

With the exodus of remittance workers from abroad and a shortage of new job opportunities, there will be a sudden excess in job markets in ASEAN economies like the Philippines, Indonesia, Thailand, and Vietnam. These countries should try and redirect these workers to development in China and India. It will be a slow process and cannot happen immediately, as India and China also have excess supply of labour and low labour costs, as well as tough regulations for hiring foreigners.

New Efforts in Regional Financial Integration Also Needed

ASEAN financial integration has progressed in recent years but remains well below its potential. The volume of intra-regional flows is relatively small, and intra–ASEAN Plus Three portfolio capital flows have grown more slowly than all global flows as well as external flows into ASEAN. Additionally, intra–ASEAN Plus Three flows have declined as a percentage of total flows into ASEAN countries and remain a small percentage of market capitalization in both equities and bonds. Integration so far has also been limited in range. Recipients of intra-regional flows are concentrated in a few countries, with only Malaysia in ASEAN Plus Three receiving a significant share of flows. Similarly, host countries, where the flows originate, are also limited. Singapore generates two-thirds of all intra–ASEAN Plus Three flows, with Japan as the next largest point of origin.

There are several possible reasons for the limited success in regional financial integration. Intra-regional trade is not as large as it seems since much of it is intra-firm trade within the production networks of transnational companies — hence the spin-offs from trade flows into financial flows within the region do not occur. Financial sectors in the region are still immature and lack financial depth. Moreover, savings institutions are underdeveloped in most countries in the region. With the exception of Singapore and to some extent Malaysia, household savings are consequently fragmented.

Nonetheless, ASEAN is making gradual progress towards regional integration with the expansion of the Chiang Mai Initiative Multilateralization (CMIM), the ratification of the ASEAN Charter, and the establishment of the ASEAN Integrated Food Security framework. A major sign of progress will be the CMIM. This US$120 billion pool of reserves will help to reduce the region's vulnerability during a crisis. Although this was actually an ASEAN Plus Three effort, expanding CMIM still helped to boost ASEAN integration.

THE UNITED STATES AND CHINA IN SOUTHEAST ASIA
Conflict or Convergence?

Robert Sutter

The year 2009 witnessed important initiatives by the United States and China in Southeast Asia. Evidence of some sharpening of Sino-American competition to protect interests and project influence in Southeast Asia grew amid a broader pattern of mixed divergence and convergence in Sino-American relations over such important international concerns as the global economic crisis and recession begun in 2008, climate change, the armed conflicts, instability in Afghanistan and Pakistan, and Iran's and North Korea's nuclear weapons development.

On balance, the leaders of both countries remained committed to a path of constructive engagement that has marked Sino-American interchange since early in the decade. Differences over various issues, including respective efforts to improve influence and protect interests in Southeast Asia, have tended to be dealt with through various private channels or formal "dialogues", out of the public limelight. Neither side has taken steps in their respective foreign policy initiatives that would seriously jeopardize the positive stasis that has developed in relations between the American and Chinese governments.

Many significant differences and strongly competing interests remain in U.S.-China relations, including in Southeast Asia. They feed deeply rooted mutual suspicions and impede progress in developing closer U.S.-China relations based on mutual trust. But the positive benefits of Sino-American engagement, ever closer mutual interdependence in U.S.-Chinese interests, especially in economic development, and massive preoccupations of both leaderships with other problems at

ROBERT SUTTER is Visiting Professor of Asian Studies in the School of Foreign Service, Georgetown University, Washington, USA.

home and abroad mean that neither the United States nor the Chinese government appear to see its interest well served with a disruptive confrontation with the other. This balance of interests foretells continued careful management of Sino-American differences in Southeast Asia as the United States and China pursue initiatives and compete for influence in the region.

RECENT SOUTHEAST ASIAN DEVELOPMENTS

U.S. Initiatives and China's Response

The incoming administration of President Barack Obama wasted little time in notifying the region and the world that the United States was "back" in Southeast Asia, pursuing active engagement. Secretary of State Hillary Clinton committed to attending regularly the annual ministerial meeting of the Association of Southeast Asian Nations (ASEAN) Regional Forum (ARF), which her predecessor had missed as often as not. The United States joined ASEAN's Treaty of Amity and Cooperation in a step that improved U.S. relations with Southeast Asian countries and offered possible U.S. participation in the Asian Leadership Summit conveyed by the ASEAN-anchored East Asia Summit forum.[1]

A shift toward greater official U.S. engagement with the reclusive military junta in Myanmar modified the seemingly ineffective U.S.-supported pressure and isolation on account of the junta's repression of democracy and human rights. The engagement also saw greater U.S. official contact with leading political oppositionist and Nobel Laureate, Ang San Suu Kyi, who seemed to support greater U.S. contact with the military regime. And it permitted President Obama's meeting with leaders of the ten ASEAN countries during his trip to Singapore for the annual Asia-Pacific Economic Cooperation (APEC) leaders meeting in November.

Avoiding prominent opposition to the U.S. moves, Chinese official commentary nonetheless showed ambivalence in reaction to stepped up U.S. activism in Southeast Asia. Official Chinese media placed the spotlight on U.S. Secretary of State Hillary Clinton during the ARF foreign ministers' meeting in Thailand in July, with a Chinese official expert in Southeast Asian matters saying that this year's foreign ministers' meeting gained "global attention" when the U.S. Secretary of State attended the meeting and signed the Treaty of Amity and Cooperation with ASEAN members; the U.S. visit marked "the return of the superpower" to the region. By contrast, the activities of the Chinese foreign minister and Chinese initiatives toward Southeast Asia received comparatively less attention.[2]

Chinese commentary saw an underlying U.S. effort to balance China. Chinese experts predicted that intensified U.S. competition with China in Southeast Asia would not upset overall U.S.-China relations as "both countries have more important things to do such as tackling the economic crisis and global warming". It also cited Secretary Clinton's remark that she hoped for a "positive framework" in working with China in Southeast Asia as the United States strengthens ties with "a lot of China's neighbours" who have "expressed concerns" regarding China.[3]

Chinese commentary reflected on the strengths and weaknesses of the Chinese position in Southeast Asia as it faced the prospect of greater American activism in the region. On the plus side were cited Chinese bilateral trade with ASEAN worth US$231 billion surpassing U.S.-ASEAN trade of US$178 billion, while Chinese-ASEAN investment was US$60 billion versus U.S.-ASEAN investment of US$100 billion. On the other hand, China was seen as having suffered a negative impact as a result of the recent disputes over territorial issues in the South China Sea, while greater U.S. activism could bring the unspecified challenges of "hegemonism" back to the region.[4]

As the year wore on, low-level Chinese commentary continued to offer negative assessments of U.S. motives as well as those of the new Japanese Government that was pressing initiatives for Asian regionalism that could broaden the U.S. role in the region. Chinese experts claimed in November that "China's presence in Southeast Asia is insulated from the US apparent renewal of interest in the region." The account also criticized a speech by Singapore leader Lee Kwan Yew on 27 October, where Lee said that the United States should maintain a strong balance in Asia against rising China. A tougher attack against Lee's views came in Beijing's *Global Times* on 4 November. Another *Global Times* commentary on 19 November advised that U.S. interest in joining Asian multilateral groups is suspect and the United States needs to prove its good intentions through a process of "socializing itself into Asia".[5]

Chinese ambivalence also greeted the proposal of the new Japanese Government of Prime Minister Yukio Hatoyama to promote an East Asian Community that, among other things, could be open to membership by the United States. Chinese officials on the one hand at times showed general support for the concept, but on the other hand Chinese wariness about Japan's expanded activism showed in the cool and sometimes critical reception the Japanese initiative received in official Chinese media. Chinese experts in late September said the idea cannot be realized in the near future and poses too many difficulties. A Chinese academic expert in October said "a conceptual gap exists between Beijing and Tokyo as China prefers the East Asian Community to be restricted to the Southeast Asian nations plus China, Japan, and the Republic of Korea. Japan wants to involve some other countries, even the United States."[6] A researcher in the Chinese Ministry of Commerce endeavoured to undermine Hatoyama's initiative by pointing to Japanese reluctance to conclude free trade agreements with ASEAN and by Japan catering to alleged U.S. pressure in pursuing a community of sixteen nations that "was not a truly East Asian community".[7] A commentary in November charged that Japan has split loyalties and interests between the United States and Asia, whereas China was seen as truly aligned with Asian interests.[8]

The U.S. and Japanese activism came at a time when official Chinese behaviour and commentary showed uncertainty and apparent reduced interest regarding Southeast Asia and ASEAN as focal points of Chinese foreign policy attention. The Chinese administration was slow in appointing an ambassador to ASEAN, doing so only after the United States followed through with its long announced intention to do so in 2008. ASEAN as a convener of Asian multilateralism lost Chinese support to some degree as Beijing appeared to split the "plus three" from the ASEAN Plus Three grouping as it actively pursued summit meetings with Japan and South Korea, separate from ASEAN. Chinese commentary appeared to underline the reasons for the shift in emphasis. Typically, *China Daily* in August noted slow progress in ASEAN-led multilateralism because of "long intractable" problems in ASEAN and among Southeast Asia nations regarding integration, development, and security. Citing postponed summits and graphic signs of instability in various Southeast Asian nations, the commentary saw few easy solutions. China's more sober view of Southeast Asian weaknesses has been accompanied by less frequent media and high-level leadership attention to ASEAN and its members — a contrast with the years of Chinese activism in the region at the end of the 1990s and throughout most of this decade.[9]

South China Sea Issues

China's harder line and military, diplomatic, and other manoeuvres regarding disputes over territorial and resource issues in the South China Sea tarnished its image in Southeast Asia as it raised the specter of Sino-American military confrontation. Tension was higher at the start of the year with strong and overt Chinese challenges to U.S. naval patrols in Chinese-claimed exclusive economic zones and stronger assertions of Chinese territorial and resource claims. March saw the confrontation between five Chinese Government ships and the U.S. surveillance ship *USNS Impeccable* in the South China Sea near China's Hainan Island. China's media highlighted a pattern of U.S. surveillance of China's growing military, and China's unwillingness to tolerate such actions.[10]

China also firmly defended territory in the South China Sea claimed by Southeast Asian nations. Looking back at the end of the year, one assessment concluded that China's "more accommodating and flexible attitude" regarding South China Sea issues in the first half of the decade had been put aside as China pursued a recently "more assertive posture in consolidating its jurisdictional claims, expanding its military reach and seeking to undermine the claims of other states through coercive diplomacy". In addition to Chinese ships confronting U.S. naval vessels, it cited as evidence increased Chinese naval patrols in the South China Sea, pressure on foreign oil companies to cease operations in contested waters, the establishment of administrative units to oversee China's claims to the disputed Paracel and Spratly Islands, the unilateral imposition of fishing bans, and the harshness of Chinese responses to the outer continental shelf submissions to the United Nations by other claimants.[11]

Economic Trends

Economic data showed the importance of the United States and China, along with several other economic partners, for ASEAN development. The broad trend in this decade was a rapid rise in Chinese trade with Southeast Asia, with China surpassing the United States in 2008 to become ASEAN's third most important trading partner, after Japan and the European Union. ASEAN figures on trade and investment differ from those cited by Chinese sources noted earlier. In 2008, they show China-ASEAN trade valued at US$192 billion and ASEAN-US trade valued at US$181 billion. That year, ASEAN trade with Japan was valued at US$211 billion and trade with the European Union was valued at US$202 billion. South Korea, Australia, and India were also important trading partners in ASEAN's highly diversified trading patterns, where no foreign power has more than a twelve per cent share of regional trade.[12]

Chinese-ASEAN trade more often than not involves foreign invested enterprises and so-called processing trade. This means that much of the trade is controlled by foreign enterprises and is dependent on production webs involving facilities in China and exports from China to international, mainly Western, markets.[13] ASEAN trade figures show the prominent trade surplus China runs with the region, valued at over US$22 billion in 2008. By contrast the United States ran a trade deficit with ASEAN of about the same size, as ASEAN exports to the United States surpassed ASEAN exports to China by US$16 billion in 2008.

Investment data for China is difficult to assess in part because much of Chinese investment abroad goes to Hong Kong and other tax havens, and an uncertain portion of this money is reinvested back into China. ASEAN data for the net inflow of foreign direct investment to ASEAN in the period 2006–8 showed US$12.7 billion for the United States and US$3.6 billion for China. Much higher figures were shown for the European Union (US$42.1 billion) and Japan (US$25.7 billion), while South Korea came in at (US$5.7 billion).[14]

The sharp decline in Chinese, U.S., and other international trade figures at the end of 2008 and early 2009 foreshadowed serious distress for Southeast Asian traders and manufacturers integrated with China-based enterprises involved with the widespread processing trade that has made up about half of Chinese trade with Southeast Asia. One option for Southeast Asian manufacturers and traders was to wait out the crisis, making ready to resume once the markets for these products revive. Since that day seemed distant, attention was sometimes directed to regional solutions or remedies to ease the pain of the slowdown.

Chinese commentary and actions placed Asian regional solutions low in Chinese priorities. China focused on three paths in dealing with the crisis: stimulating the domestic Chinese economy; participating in global cooperation efforts; and regional cooperation. Chinese leaders gave clear primacy to the first path, and their international attention was focused on interactions with developed and larger developing economies. In Asia, a China-Japan–South Korea currency swap arrangement was broadened in 2009 to include ASEAN countries. China also offered in April a US$10 billion China-ASEAN Investment Corporation Fund, US$15 billion in credit to support ASEAN nations, and US$40 million of special aid to underdeveloped ASEAN nations. At the same time, ASEAN manufacturers were girding for more difficult competition with Chinese manufacturers as the latter were using stimulus funds and loans from state-controlled banks to create ever greater modern manufacturing capacity that will guarantee that China sustains and advances its share of exports to slowly reviving U.S., European, and other international markets.[15]

Cooperation amid Differences in U.S.-China Relations

The recent overt and opaque competition and differences in Sino-American relations in Southeast Asia reinforced other signs of divergence between the two powers. China's military power was clearly developing beyond a focus on stopping Taiwanese independence and posed serious problems for U.S. security leadership in Asia. The Obama administration was privately disappointed with Chinese refusal to assist substantially in dealing with the escalating U.S.-led military efforts against the Taliban in Afghanistan and to support stability in

Pakistan. There was more cooperation between the United States and China in dealing with North Korea's second nuclear weapons test, but differences continued over such issues as the utility of international pressure on North Korea. Similar divergence limited Sino-American cooperation in dealing with Iran's suspected development of nuclear weapons.[16]

Stark differences between the United States and China on climate change broke into public view during the U.N.-sponsored meeting in Copenhagen in December. Media accounts showed that the meeting was headed to failure and collapse, with China and the United States on opposite sides, until President Obama undertook extraordinary last minute personal efforts to get China, India, Brazil, and South Africa to join in support of the limited accord that was agreed to.[17] Regarding the global economic crisis and recession, Chinese leaders and commentators complained frequently about U.S. stewardship in the world economy and made repeated references to diversifying from the U.S. market, investment in U.S. Government securities, and use of the U.S. dollar. American complaints and moves to restrict Chinese imports and other actions through World Trade Organization agreed paths prompted Chinese trade retaliation and loud charges of protectionism.[18]

Although Taiwan was a less urgent issue in U.S.-China relations as cross strait tensions had eased under the leadership of Taiwan President Ma Ying-jeou, Chinese officials pressed hard to curb U.S. arms sales, which seemed likely to occur in 2010 and to damage U.S.-China relations to some degree. Chinese pressure to isolate the Dalai Lama has reached unprecedented intensity in recent years. President Obama deferred seeing the Nobel Laureate until after the President's China visit in November, but when the meeting happens, U.S.-China relations probably will be affected negatively to some degree.[19]

Meanwhile, U.S. and Chinese decision makers remain privately wary and distrustful of one another despite the numerous Sino-American dialogues and positive public meetings; there reportedly has been little improvement in the mutual suspicion between the two leaderships in recent years.[20]

U.S. Leadership and Positive Stasis in U.S.-China Relations

While limiting forward movement in U.S.-China relations, the Sino-American differences over sensitive issues noted above appear insufficient to substantially offset enduring patterns of pragmatic decision making among the Chinese and American leaders. Enduring strengths of sustained U.S. leadership in Asia also argue for continuation of the positive equilibrium that has prevailed recently in

U.S.-China relations into the first years of the Obama government and possibly longer.

Chinese Calculations

The Chinese administration of Hu Jintao has set a central foreign and domestic policy goal for the next decade focused on China fostering a continuation of the prevailing international situation, seen generally advantageous for China in order to allow for expeditious modernization of the country. Exploiting this period of perceived "strategic opportunity" in international affairs requires keeping U.S.-China relations moving in a positive direction. The Hu Jintao administration worked hard in fostering business-like and constructive relations with the George W. Bush administration.[21]

More recently, the Chinese administration has ensured that its initiatives and probes do not seriously disrupt the advantages for China in sustaining generally positive relations with the United States. Thus, Chinese probes against U.S. military surveillance in the South China Sea have subsided. Despite public complaints and threats, Chinese investment in U.S. securities continues and Chinese reliance on the U.S. dollar remains. Chinese entrepreneurs seem determined to sustain and expand their shares of the reviving U.S. market. China has acceded to U.S. arguments on North Korea, Iran, and climate change. It resumed active military contacts cut off because of U.S. arms sales to Taiwan in 2008.

Meanwhile, the incentive for the Hu Jintao administration to sustain generally positive Sino-U.S. relations is reinforced by the pending generational leadership succession due to take place at the Eighteenth Chinese Communist Party Congress in 2012. Preparations for this decennial event are under way and involve behind-the-scenes bargaining over policy, power, and appointment issues that are best carried out in an atmosphere where Chinese leaders are not diverted by serious controversy in Sino-American relations.[22]

Against this background, if change is to come in the U.S.-China relationship, it is more likely to emerge from the U.S. side. However, the U.S. President and his administration seem unlikely to deviate from the positive engagement with China that characterized the latter years of the Bush administration. The U.S. Government remains in a strong leadership position in Asia, where engagement with China adds to U.S. beneficial relationships throughout the region. Meanwhile, American preoccupation with other problems at home and abroad will continue to place a premium on keeping Sino-American relations positive despite differences, suspicions, and possible difficulties.

U.S. Policy in Asia and China

President Obama found that the global financial crisis and economic recession[23] overshadowed what had been expected to be the new U.S. Government's most salient foreign policy preoccupation — the wars in Iraq and Afghanistan and the violence and instability in the broader Middle East–Southwest Asian region, including Iran's suspected development of nuclear weapons. U.S. relations with the rest of the Asia-Pacific region seemed likely to be a matter of comparatively less immediate urgency for incoming U.S. policymakers.

North Korea ascended to the top of the Obama government's policy agenda through a string of provocative actions in 2009.[24] Longstanding U.S. concern with the security situation in the Taiwan Straits declined.[25] Meanwhile, U.S. efforts to curb greenhouse gases appeared ineffective without the participation of China, reinforcing U.S. Government dialogue with China to arrive at mutually acceptable approaches.[26]

Status of U.S. Leadership in Asia

The new U.S. Government would be more inclined to shift policy toward China if it judged that prevailing policy and trends were not working well to nurture American interests, notably in the Asia-Pacific region. Media and specialist commentary as well as popular and elite sentiment in Asia tended to emphasize the shortcomings of U.S. policy and leadership in Asia throughout much of the twenty-first century.[27] By contrast, Asia's rising powers and particularly China seemed to be advancing rapidly.[28] A common prediction was that Asia was adjusting to an emerging China-centred order and U.S. influence was in decline.[29]

Over time, developments showed the reality in the region was more complex. Bush administration officials increasingly rallied around the public position first articulated by Deputy Secretary of State Robert Zoellick in 2005 arguing that China's rise was not having a substantial negative impact on U.S. interests. This line of approach was continued during the Obama administration. It reflects a more balanced and sophisticated assessment of U.S. and Chinese strengths and weaknesses in Asia, coming to the conclusion that enduring U.S. strengths mean that the United States has less to fear from China's rise in Asia than some would believe and that recent policies sustaining U.S. leadership in Asia should be continued.[30]

U.S. security strengths[31] rest on Asian governments. Most are strong, viable, and make the decisions that determine direction in foreign affairs. The officials make decisions on the basis of their own calculus. For the most part, the officials see their governments' legitimacy and success resting on nation building and economic development, which require a stable and secure international environment. Unfortunately, Asia is not particularly stable and most governments privately are wary of and tend not to trust each other. As a result, they look to the United States to provide the security they need to pursue goals of development and nation building in an appropriate environment. They recognize that the U.S. security role is very expensive and involves great risk, including large scale casualties if necessary, for the sake of preserving Asian security. They also recognize that neither rising China nor any other Asian power or coalition of powers is able or willing to undertake even a fraction of these risks, costs, and responsibilities.

Economic factors are also important determinants of enduring U.S. influence and leadership in Asia. The nation-building priority of most Asian governments depends importantly on export-oriented growth. Most recognize that the highly interdependent patterns of Asian trade involving China mean that Chinese and Asian trade remains heavily dependent on exports to developed countries, notably the United States. In recent years, the United States has run a massive and growing trade deficit with China, and a total trade deficit with Asia valued at over $350 billion at a time of an overall U.S. trade deficit of over $700 billion. Asian government officials recognize that China, which runs a large overall trade surplus, and other trading partners of Asia are unwilling and unable to bear even a fraction of the cost of such large trade deficits, that nonetheless are very important for Asian governments. Obviously, the 2008–9 global economic crisis is having an enormous impact on trade and investment. Some Asian officials are talking about relying more on domestic consumption, but tangible progress seems slow as they appear to be focusing on an eventual revival of world trade that would restore previous levels of export-oriented growth involving continued heavy reliance on the U.S. market.

A third set of factors working to sustain U.S. influence and leadership in Asia involves extensive and ongoing U.S. government engagement in the region and the tendency of Asian governments to engage more closely with the United States as they develop contingency plans (so-called "hedging") in the face of changing power relations in Asia prompted by the rise of China. The Obama administration inherited a U.S. position in Asia buttressed by generally effective Bush administration interaction with Asia's powers. It is very rare for the United States to enjoy good relations with Japan and China at the same time, but the Bush administration carefully managed relations with both powers effectively. It is unprecedented for the United States to be the leading foreign power in South Asia and to sustain good relations with both India and Pakistan, but that has been the case since relatively early in the Bush administration. And it is unprecedented for the United States to have good relations with Beijing and Taipei at the same time, but that situation emerged during the Bush years and strengthened with the election of President Ma Ying-jeou in 2008.

The U.S. Pacific Command and other U.S. military commands and security organizations have been in the lead regarding wide ranging and growing U.S. efforts to build and strengthen webs of military, security, intelligence, and other relationships throughout the region. In an overall Asian environment where the United States remains on good terms with major powers and most other governments, building security ties through education programmes, on-site training, exercises, and other means enhances U.S. influence in generally quiet but effective ways. Part of the reason for the success of these efforts has to do with active contingency planning by many Asian governments. As power relations change in the region, notably on account of China's rise, Asian governments generally seek to work positively and pragmatically with rising China on the one hand, but on the other hand they seek the reassurance of close security, intelligence, and other ties with the United States in case rising China shifts from its current generally benign approach to one of greater assertiveness or dominance. The U.S. government sees its interests well served by balancing U.S. engagement with China with active contingency planning with a wide variety of partners in the Asia-Pacific.[32]

A sometimes overlooked source of enduring U.S. influence in Asia has to do with non-governmental American interaction with the region, and the role immigrants to the United States play in that process. Active American non-government interaction with Asia through business, religious, educational, and other interchange has continued to put the United States in a unique position where the American non-government sector has such a strong and usually positive impact on the influence the United States exerts in the region. Meanwhile, the end of discriminatory U.S. restrictions on Asian immigration in 1965 has resulted in the influx of millions of Asian migrants who interact with their countries of origin in ways that generally undergird and reflect well on the U.S. position in Asia. No other country, with the exception of Canada, has such an active and powerfully positive channel of influence in Asia.

In sum, U.S. strengths show that the United States at the start of the Obama administration is deeply integrated in Asia at the government and non-government levels. U.S. security commitments and trade practices meet the fundamental security and economic needs of Asian government leaders and those leaders know it. The leaders also know that no other power or coalition of powers is able or willing to meet even a small fraction of those needs. And Asian contingency planning seems to work to the advantage of the United States, while rising China has no easy way to overcome pervasive Asian wariness of Chinese longer term intentions. On balance, the Obama administration can work to deal with various issues in U.S. policy in Asia, including U.S. relations with China and dealings in Southeast Asia, with confidence that U.S. leadership in the region remains broadly appreciated by Asian governments and unchallenged by regional powers or other forces. The fundamental directions of U.S. relations with Asia, including U.S. relations with China, seem sound, with no need for major change.

Obama's Positive Relations with China

Specialists in China and the United States have identified a pattern of dualism in U.S.-China relations that has emerged as part of the generally positive equilibrium which developed in the post Cold War period. The pattern involves constructive and cooperative engagement on the one hand and contingency planning or hedging on the other.[33] Chinese and U.S. contingency planning and hedging against one another sometimes involves actions like the respective Chinese and U.S. military buildups that are separate from and develop in tandem with the respective engagement policies the two leaderships pursue with each other. At the same time, dualism shows as each government has used engagement to build positive and cooperative ties while at the same time seeking to use these ties to build interdependencies and webs of relationships that have the effect of constraining the other power from taking actions that oppose its interests.

The Obama government and the Chinese administration have continued a pattern that characterized Sino-American relations during the later years of the George W. Bush administration. That is, differences between the two countries usually continue to be dealt with out of the limelight in over sixty dialogues and other high-level interaction between the two administrations. Public discourse between the two administrations tends to emphasize the positive in the relationship. Nonetheless, the differences between the two countries are readily apparent on the U.S. side, where they are repeatedly highlighted by U.S. media and U.S. interest groups concerned about various features of Chinese governance and practice, and where the majority of Americans give an unfavourable rating to the Chinese government. They are less apparent in the more controlled media environment of China, though Chinese officials and government commentaries clearly state opposition to U.S. efforts to support Taiwan and the Dalai Lama and to foster political change in China, as well as key aspects of U.S. alliances and U.S. security presence and arrangements around China's periphery, and U.S. positions on salient international issues ranging from the military use of space to fostering democratic change.[34]

The positive features of the relationship tend to outweigh the negatives for practical reasons. Both governments gain from cooperative engagement — the gains include beneficial economic ties, as well as cooperation over North Korea, terrorism, and even Taiwan. The gains also include smaller progress on Iran and even less on Sudan and Myanmar. Both governments recognize that, because of ever closer U.S.-China interdependence and other major policy preoccupations they both have, focusing on negative aspects in U.S.-China relations would be counterproductive to their interests.

Conclusion

At bottom, it seems fair to conclude that the recent U.S. relationship with China rests upon a common commitment to avoid conflict, cooperate in areas of common interest, and prevent disputes from shaking the overall relationship.[35] Against this background, the Obama government seems most likely to advance relations with China in small ways. It probably will show sufficient restraint and resolve to avoid serious conflict with China over trade, currency, environmental, security, Taiwan, Tibet, human rights, and other issues that appear counterproductive for what seem to be more important U.S. interests in preserving a collaborative relationship with China and avoiding frictions with such an important economy at a time when international economic cooperation seems of utmost importance.[36] The Sino-American overt and opaque competition for influence in Southeast Asia is a secondary priority for both governments; available evidence shows it is likely to continue, albeit with neither leadership allowing for serious disruption of the overall U.S.-China relationship.

Notes

[1]   The source of information on recent U.S. relations with Southeast Asia is the quarterly review of U.S.-Southeast Asian relations in *Comparative Connections* <www.csis. org/pacfor>.

[2]   Zhai Kun, "On the Road to Development with ASEAN", *China Daily*, 21 August 2009, p. 9.

[3]   "Treaty a Move to Balance China's Rise? News Analysis", *China Daily*, 23 July 2009, p. 12; "China-Southeast Asia Relations", *Comparative Connections* 11, no. 3 (October 2009): 72–73.

[4]   Wen Jia, "New Era of China-ASEAN Tie-up", *China Daily*, 22 October 2009, p. 8; Li Xiaokun, "China's Strengths in SE Asia to Stay", *China Daily*, 5 November 2009, p. 2, "China-Southeast Asia Relations", p. 73.

[5]   Li, "China's Strengths"; Chan Cheow Pong, "'Balance' Gets Lost in Translation", *Straits Times*, 5 November 2009 <www.straitstimes.com> (accessed 10 November 2009); "China-Southeast Asia Relations", *Comparative Connections* 11, no. 4 (January 2010) <www.csis.org/pacfor>.

[6]   Reviewed in "China-Southeast Asia Relations", *Comparative Connections* 11, no. 4 (January 2010) <www.csis.org/pacfor>. Cited in Tan Yingzi, "Trilateral Meeting to Boost Relations", *China Daily*, 10–11 October 2009, p. 2.

[7]   Reviewed in *Comparative Connections* article cited above. The researcher's article appeared under his name in Xu Changwen, "In Search of a Truly Regional Community", *China Daily*, 28 October 2009, p. 9.

[8]   Reviewed in "China-Southeast Asia Relations", *Comparative Connections* 11, no. 4 (January 2010) <www.csis.org/pacfor>.

[9]   Zhai Kun, "On the Road"; "China-Southeast Asia Relations", p. 73.

[10] "China-Southeast Asia Relations, p. 71.

[11] Clive Schofield and Ian Storey, *The South China Sea Dispute: Increasing Stakes and Rising Tensions* (Washington DC: The Jamestown Foundation, 2009), p. 1.

[12] Figures from ASEAN Trade Database (accessed December 2009).

[13] "China-Southeast Asia Relations", *Comparative Connections* 11, no. 1 (April 2009): 66.

[14] Figures from ASEAN Foreign Direct Investment Statistics Database (accessed December 2009).

[15] Zhao Cheng and Liao Lei, "Chinese Premier Wen Makes Six-Point Proposal", Xinhua 24 October 2009 <www.xinhuanet.com> (accessed 28 October 2009); Michael Wines, "Uneasy Engagement: China's Economic Power Unsettles the Neighbours", *New York Times*, 9 December 2009 <www.nytimes.org> (accessed 31 December 2009); "China-Southeast Asia Relations", p. 66.

[16] Salient events in U.S. policy toward China are reviewed quarterly in "United States-China Relations", *Comparative Connections* <www.csis.org/pacfor>.

[17] Charles Babington and Jennifer Loven, "Obama Raced Clock, Chaos, Comedy for Climate Deal", Associated Press, 19 December 2009 <www.ap.org> (accessed 21 December 2009).

[18] "US-China Relations", *Comparative Connections* 11, no. 3 (October 2009): 35–36; "US-China Relations", *Comparative Connections* 11, no. 4 (January 2010) <www.csis.org/pacfor>.

[19] "US-China Relations", *Comparative Connections* 11, no. 4 (January 2010) <www.csis.org/pacfor>.

[20] Kenneth Lieberthal, "How Domestic Forces Shape the PRC's Grand Strategy and International Impact", in *Strategic Asia 2007–2008*, edited by Ashley Tellis and Michael

Wills (Seattle, WA: National Bureau of Asian Research, 2007), p. 63; Kenneth Lieberthal and David Sandalow, *Overcoming Obstacles to US-China Cooperation on Climate Change* (Washington, DC: Brookings Institution, 2009), p. ix. Chinese and American officials and other specialists privately confirm this observation, noting the concerns of each side over differences on salient issues, especially those discussed above.

21   David Michael Lampton, *The Three Faces of Chinese Power* (Berkeley, CA: University of California Press 2008), pp. 1–2.

22   Willy Lam, "CCP Party Apparatchiks Gaining at Expense of Technocrats", *China Brief* 9, no. 25 (16 December 2009) <www.jamestown.org>.

23   Rupert Neate, "Markets Tumble on World Bank's Global Economy Fears", 22 June 2009 <telegraph.co.uk>.

24   Ralph Cossa and Brad Glosserman, "Old Challenges, New Approaches", *Comparative Connections* 11, no. 2 (July 2009): 1–5.

25   The Obama administration indicated little change from Bush administration efforts to support the more forthcoming approach of Taiwanese President Ma Ying-jeou and to avoid U.S. actions that would be unwelcome in Taipei and Beijing as they sought to ease tensions and facilitate communication. National Committee on American Foreign Policy, *Making Peace in the Taiwan Strait* (New York: National Committee on American Foreign Policy, 2009).

26   David Pierson and Jim Tankersley, "US, China Try to Reach Accord on Green House Gas Emissions", *Los Angeles Times*, 15 July 2009 <www.latimes.com>.

27   Morton Abramowitz and Stephen Bosworth, *Chasing the Sun* (New York: Century Foundation, 2006).

28   David Shambaugh, "China Engages Asia: Reshaping the Regional Order", *International Security* 29, no. 3 (Winter 2004/2005): 64–99; Joshua Kurlantzick, *Charm Offensive: How China's Soft Power is Transforming the World* (New Haven, CO: Yale University Press, 2007); David Kang, *China Rising: Peace, Power and Order in East Asia* (New York: Columbia University Press, 2007).

29   Robert Sutter, "Assessing China's Rise and U.S. Leadership in Asia — Growing Maturity and Balance", *PacNet 6*, 29 January 2009 <www.csis.org/pacfor>.

30   Evelyn Goh, "Southeast Asia: Strategic Diversification in the 'Asian Century'", in *Strategic Asia 2008–2009*, edited by Ashley Tellis, Mercy Kuo, and Andrew Marble (Seattle: National Bureau of Asian Research, 2008), pp. 261–96; Ralph Cossa, Brad Glosserman, Michael McDevitt, Nirav Patel, James Przystup, and Brad Roberts, *The United States and the Asia Pacific Region: Security Strategy for the Obama Administration* (Washington, DC: Center for Strategic and International Studies, 2009) <www.csis.org>.

31   Robert Sutter, *The United States in Asia* (Lanham, MD: Rowman and Littlefield, 2009); David Shambaugh and Michael Yahuda, eds. *International Relations of Asia* (Lanham, MD.: Rowman and Littlefield, 2008); Cossa et al., *The United States and the Asia Pacific Region: Security Strategy for the Obama Administration.*

[32] Evan Medeiros, *Pacific Currents: The Responses of US Allies and Security Partners in East Asia to China's Rise* (Santa Monica, CA: RAND Corporation, 2008).

[33] Evan Medeiros, "Strategic Hedging and the Future of Asia-Pacific Stability", *The Washington Quarterly* 29, no. 1 (2005–6): 145–67; Rosemary Foot, "Chinese Strategies in a US-Hegemonic Global Order: Accommodating and Hedging", *International Affairs* 82, no. 1 (2006): 77–94.

[34] *China's National Defense in 2008* (Beijing: Information Office of the State Council of the People's Republic of China, 2009).

[35] Edward Gresser and Daniel Twining, "Shock of the New: Congress and Asia in 2009", *NBR Analysis* (February 2009), p. 21.

[36] C. Fred Bergsten, "A Partnership of Equals: How Washington Should Respond to China's Economic Challenge", *Foreign Affairs* (July–August 2008) <www.foreignaffairs.org>.

THE YEAR IN ASEAN
The Charter, Trade Agreements, and the Global Economic Crisis

Rodolfo C. Severino

In the past year, the mass media have highlighted three developments in Southeast Asia, which thus became the subjects of public attention. One was the start of the implementation of the new Charter of the Association of Southeast Asian Nations (ASEAN), particularly the establishment of the ASEAN Inter-governmental Commission on Human Rights (AICHR). Another was the scheduled elimination on 1 January 2010 of tariffs on most goods traded among China and the six older, and more advanced and heavily trading, ASEAN members — Brunei Darussalam, Indonesia, Malaysia, the Philippines, Singapore, and Thailand (the other ASEAN members are Cambodia, Laos, Myanmar, and Vietnam). The third was the response of Southeast Asian countries to the regional impact of the global economic crisis.

The media spotlight on these developments has led the public to expect some dramatic, overnight changes in the region because of them. As an academic, I have sought to dampen such expectations, called for caution, and urged the media and the public to refrain from rash predictions and speculation. As the Americans say, "the jury is still out" on these three questions.

The ASEAN Charter

The drafting of the ASEAN Charter by a task force of senior ASEAN officials, its signing by the ASEAN leaders in November 2007, and its entry into force in December 2008 were significant for six reasons. For the first time, after forty years

RODOLFO C. SEVERINO is Head, ASEAN Studies Centre at the Institute of Southeast Asian Studies, Singapore.

of existence, ASEAN has adopted a charter for itself, comprehensively placing it more firmly on a rules-based path.

If one looks closely at the Charter's contents, this is more than a matter of form. For the first time, the ASEAN countries have committed themselves in a formal document to norms having to do with the internal behaviour of states. As first enshrined in the 1976 Treaty of Amity and Cooperation in Southeast Asia, norms for inter-state conduct had guided ASEAN and other countries related to it — the peaceful settlement of disputes, the rejection of the threat or use of force, and non-interference in the internal affairs of nations. This is important in itself, but the Charter goes beyond that. In it, the ASEAN countries have declared their aspiration for such goals as democracy, human rights and fundamental freedoms, the rule of law, good governance, constitutional government, and social justice.

The Charter seeks to expedite decision making in the association, more clearly defining responsibilities for it. It lays squarely on the shoulders of the ASEAN leaders the responsibility for arriving at decisions, including voting if necessary, to resolve issues on which consensus cannot be reached at lower levels. It has established a Committee of Permanent Representatives resident in Jakarta to accelerate the process of decision making on many issues requiring member-states' agreement.

At the same time, and this is the fourth reason, the Charter seeks to cultivate among its members a "culture of compliance". It assigns to the ASEAN National Secretariats at the ministries of foreign affairs the tasks of coordinating the implementation of ASEAN decisions and agreements as well as promoting knowledge and awareness of ASEAN at home. It calls upon the Secretary-General to submit regular reports on compliance and non-compliance with ASEAN agreements and decisions to the leaders, who would be expected to act on them. The Charter calls for the inclusion of dispute-settlement mechanisms in all ASEAN agreements in addition to the one already in place for the economic agreements. It reiterates the aim of the ASEAN Economic Community as the creation of a "single market and production base", re-affirming ASEAN's commitment to regional economic integration.

It seeks to clarify the diplomatic privileges and immunities of ASEAN Secretariat officials and of the permanent representatives and their staffs in Indonesia and in other ASEAN countries in accordance with the 1961 Vienna Convention on Diplomatic Relations or the national law of the ASEAN country concerned.

Lastly, the Charter confers legal personality on ASEAN. What this means exactly is still being worked out. In any case, it enables ASEAN to receive ambassadors from non-ASEAN states and other intergovernmental organizations.

In the one year in which it has been in force, implementation of the Charter has been surprisingly rapid. The Committee of Permanent Representatives is busily functioning in Jakarta. An additional two Deputy Secretaries-General have been appointed, raising the total to four. The ASEAN leaders now meet twice a year, as called for by the Charter, once to make decisions on moving ASEAN forward and the other time to conduct summit-level meetings with their counterparts from outside the region. The ASEAN chairmanship now coincides with the calendar year, with a single chairmanship for most ASEAN bodies. The economic ministers have devised a "scorecard" to keep track of compliance with ASEAN agreements and decisions.

A High-level Legal Experts Group is hard at work on the meaning and implications of ASEAN's legal personality, on the details of the dispute-settlement mechanisms, and on the question of privileges and immunities.

According to the ASEAN Secretariat, twenty-five ambassadors have been accredited to ASEAN (as of 4 January 2010) — those of Australia, Austria, Bulgaria, Canada, China, the Czech Republic, Denmark, the European Union, Finland, France, Greece, India, Italy, Japan, the Republic of Korea, Libya, Luxembourg, Norway, Peru, Portugal, Romania, Russia, Spain, the United Kingdom, and the United States. Of these, those of Australia, China, India, Japan, the Republic of Korea, and the United States are separate from their ambassadors to Indonesia. The United States has announced its desire to establish a resident embassy to ASEAN in Jakarta this year.

Not least, pursuant to the Charter, the terms of reference of the AICHR, something not envisioned even by the bold-thinking Eminent Persons Group on the ASEAN Charter, have been adopted and its members appointed. The members are:

- Brunei Darussalam — Pehin Dato Hamid Bakal, former Syar'ie Chief Judge, State Judiciary Department, formerly with the Ministry of Religious Affairs;
- Cambodia — Om Yentieng, Senior Minister, President of the Cambodian Human Rights Commission and of the Anti-Corruption Unit at the Council of Ministers;
- Indonesia — Rafendi Djamin, prominent human-rights advocate and activist;
- Lao PDR — Bounkeut Sangsomsak, former career diplomat and Vice Minister of Foreign Affairs, former member of the National Assembly;
- Malaysia — Dato' Sri Muhammad Shafee Abdullah, practicing lawyer arguing human rights cases among others and legal adviser to Malaysian prime ministers and the leading political party, the United Malays National Organisation;
- Myanmar — U Kyaw Tint Swe, career diplomat, former Permanent Representative to the United Nations, New York;

- Philippines — Rosario Gonzalez Manalo, retired career diplomat, member of the faculties of several prominent Philippine universities, Philippine representative to the task forces that drafted the ASEAN Charter and the terms of reference of the AICHR;
- Singapore — Richard R. Magnus, retired senior district judge, Chairman of the Casino Regulatory Authority, the Political Films Advisory Panel, the Public Guardian Board, and Temasek Cares TLG Ltd.;
- Thailand — Sriprapha Petcharamesree, Center for Human Rights Studies and Social Development, Mahidol University, of which she is a former Director; and
- Vietnam — Do Ngoc Son, career diplomat, Ambassador to Spain.

The diverse backgrounds of these members, their varied personalities, and the different degrees of their links with and independence from their governments place a question mark on how precisely the commission will function. Having been negotiated by governments, the commission's terms of reference are a product of many compromises.

Several things are clear, however. As noted above, the Charter and the Commission on Human Rights to which it gave rise place human rights, for the first time, on the ASEAN agenda. The commission is to meet twice a year, once at the ASEAN Secretariat and the other time at the country of the ASEAN chair. It cannot but discuss human rights and expose itself to the human rights situations in member countries. These may not necessarily give the commission the independence and "teeth" that some advocates and activists wish. However, it is a significant step forward.

At the same time, it is also clear that, in the continuing absence of a strong and authoritative regional institution, whether and how the provisions of the Charter will be carried out depend on the collective will of the member states and on their perception of how implementing those provisions will serve the interests of the nation, the regime, or even, politically or personally, the leaders themselves. In this sense, the Charter remains like other regional associations of sovereign states, except only for the European Union.

Nevertheless, the Charter does move ASEAN closer to being rules-based and institutionalized, although to what extent remains to be seen.

ASEAN Free Trade Agreements

The second ASEAN-related focus of media and public attention in the past year has been the "effectivity" of ASEAN-China "free trade", supposedly on 1 January

2010. What exactly happened at the beginning of this year? In the Framework Agreement on Comprehensive Economic Cooperation (CEC) that they signed in November 2002, the leaders of ASEAN and China committed themselves to the phased reduction of tariffs on goods traded among China and ASEAN's six older members so as to create a "free trade area (FTA)" among them by 2010. In November 2004, China's Commerce Minister and the Economic Ministers of the ten ASEAN countries signed the trade-in-goods component of the CEC agreement which set 1 January 2010 as the date for the elimination of all tariffs on trade among China and the ASEAN Six. However, up to 150 tariff lines could still be protected by tariffs up to 2012.

Even on the basis of these paper commitments, nothing really dramatic took place at the beginning of 2010. The process of tariff reductions was supposed to have begun in the middle of 2005, with tariffs dropping to no more than five per cent by 2009 on trade among China and the ASEAN Six. Moreover, it remains to be seen whether traders will actually undertake the expense and effort to apply for the preferential — or zero — tariff rates provided for in the CEC and trade-in-goods agreements. Those same traders will say — if they are honest — that what really matters is the ease of doing business in a particular country rather than the tariff rates, that tariff rates are less important than factors like product standards, customs procedures, the state of infrastructure, transportation links, and their cost, taxation, the time it takes for goods to be released from customs or for businesses to be registered, and, of course, corruption. On these things, the ASEAN-China trade-in-goods agreement has nothing to say. In other words, there is nothing to get excited about on ASEAN-China trade simply because of the advent of 2010.

It is probably for this reason that the Indonesian Government, through its Industry and Trade Minister, Mari Elka Pangestu, announced in January 2010 that it had no intention of seeking a re-negotiation of the ASEAN-China agreement. Minister Pangestu correctly pointed out that Indonesia had enough tools to wield against unfair trade practices, like anti-dumping measures. She might have added that the Indonesian business sectors that were so vocal — the most vocal in ASEAN — in denouncing the ASEAN-China agreement as placing Indonesian firms at a competitive disadvantage had had five to seven years to make their views known. Presumably, the Indonesian Government conducted extensive consultations with the business community before sending its negotiators to the conference table with China and the rest of ASEAN. Indeed, Indonesia designated 263 product groups, the most in ASEAN, for the postponement of zero tariffs from 2010 to 2012.

In the case of trade with China, the cause for legitimate complaint is not competition, which is what trade is all about, but the Chinese Government's possible or actual use of state power to support Chinese trading firms, many of which are state-owned. Possible tools are the manipulation of exchange rates, access to credit, and other forms of direct or indirect subsidy to exporting firms. If so, defensive measures ought to be targeted at these instruments and practices rather than at trade and competition themselves.

The broad purpose of FTAs is not only the liberalization and facilitation of trade and investments but to affirm to the world the parties' good relations with one another and their determination to improve and strengthen those relations. It is also to send a signal to the business community that their markets are full of opportunities for one another. In the case of ASEAN and China, this process began long ago. The 2002 CEC framework agreement and the 2004 trade-in-goods agreement were merely steps, albeit important ones, in the process. In this respect, there is nothing magical about 1 January 2010.

Similarly, the trade-in-goods agreement among South Korea and the ASEAN countries, signed in August 2006 (except by Thailand, which acceded to it two and a half years later), called for the abolition of tariffs on trade among South Korea and the ASEAN Six by 1 January 2010. This deadline, however, came and went without attracting the media's attention.

ASEAN signed its trade-in-goods agreement with India in August 2009. The agreement provided for the start of the reduction of tariffs on 1 January 2010 with a view to their eventual elimination. Again, the media took no note of the start of this process.

In the meantime, Japan had signed a "comprehensive partnership agreement" with ASEAN as a group in April 2008, having concluded individual free trade area or comprehensive economic partnership agreements, which differed in their provisions, with the ASEAN Six over the 2000–7 period. Tokyo subsequently signed such an agreement with Vietnam.

ASEAN's free trade area agreement with Australia and New Zealand, negotiated off and on since 2000 and signed in February 2009, is the most comprehensive of the lot, covering not only tariff cutting and elimination, rules of origin, and customs procedures, but also sanitary and phytosanitary measures, product standards and technical regulations, trade in services, the movement of people, electronic commerce, investments, intellectual property, competition, and dispute settlement.

Although the ASEAN-Australia–New Zealand agreement is the broadest and most comprehensive that ASEAN has concluded with external partners, it has received meager public attention, if any. Only the scheduled elimination of tariffs on ASEAN-China trade has attracted attention.

The Global Economic Crisis

The third ASEAN-related question that has been frequently asked over the past year or so has to do with the impact on Southeast Asia of the global economic crisis and what Southeast Asia as a region and as individual countries are doing about it.

Because of the lessons learned from the Asian financial crisis of 1997–98 and for other reasons, Southeast Asia's major financial institutions were, relatively speaking, cushioned from the impact of the global economic crisis that still has to play itself out. However, because market demand in the developed economies has shrunk, many Southeast Asian — and East Asian — countries, their economies dependent on exports and foreign direct investment, have been hit by the contraction of their major export markets and the reduction in investments and tourism. How hard the ASEAN economies have been hit has been, ironically, in direct proportion to the extent of their openness to and reliance on the international economy.

In addition to what Asian governments are already doing — lowering interest rates, fiscal stimulus packages, social safety nets — the usual response from economists both Asian and Western has been to call for a re-structuring of international economic relations, principally between Asia and the West, with Asia increasing its domestic and/or regional consumption and reducing its exports and the West reducing its consumption, especially of imported goods, and its private and public debt.

There are two things to be said about this proposal. The first is that East Asian countries' imports from one another are already increasing, leading to the growing integration of the East Asian economy in terms of regional trade. Trade within East Asia including Japan, that is, ASEAN Plus Three, is now more than fifty-five per cent of total trade, which approaches the equivalent figure for intra-EU trade and exceeds that for the parties to the North American Free Trade Agreement. China's share in East Asian trade is rapidly expanding. There are indications that Southeast Asia's exports to China are increasingly less for assembly in China and re-export to the developed countries than for ultimate consumption in the Chinese market. However, much of East Asia's intra-regional trade is largely accounted for by the growing trade among the three Northeast Asian economies.

The second is that, nevertheless, the proposal's realization and effectiveness, including the economic re-structuring that it entails on both sides, will take time, despite their steady march. New niches have to be found, factories have to be re-tooled, fresh markets have to be cultivated, training in new skills has to be conducted, investment decisions have to be made. We must keep in mind that, in the early stages of their development, North America, Western Europe, and Japan engaged in massive investments in the construction of infrastructure, the extraction of natural resources, and the education and training of human resources, and then went on from there to mass consumption, including eventually of imported goods.

China and India, on the other hand, are currently largely at the investment phase. Although an expanding middle class is at the same time raising somewhat the capacity and propensity of these countries to consume end products, commodities, food, energy, construction materials, and services of many kinds, rather than a broader range of finished goods for direct consumption, are expected to continue to dominate Southeast Asian countries' exports to the two large Asian economies for some time. Thus, to shift from the developed-country to regional, emerging-economy markets would take time and single-minded effort. To take an extreme example, Cambodia's manufactured exports are almost entirely accounted for by garments bound for the European Union. How long will it take Cambodia to find new markets and develop new products? Those markets will certainly not be in Cambodia itself, which the United Nations categorizes as one of the world's least-developed countries. Nor can the Chinese, Indian, or ASEAN markets completely take the place of the old developed-country markets for Southeast Asian exports anytime soon.

One thing is clear. The global economic crisis is no reason for a retreat into national protectionism and other nationalistic political gestures. Rather, it is a reason for accelerated regional economic integration in Southeast Asia and East Asia, as well as the closer regulation of financial institutions. Regional economic integration would both enlarge the "domestic" market and, in the long run, reduce dependence on developed markets. However, the run is long, although it has begun.

Conclusion

The implementation of the ASEAN Charter, the abolition of tariffs on ASEAN's trade with China or other countries, and the response of Southeast Asia to the impact on it of the global economic crisis should not be expected to lead to quick, overnight, and dramatic changes in ASEAN or Southeast Asia. Rather, they should be viewed in perspective, as part of a long-term trend whose effectiveness or ultimate outcome remains uncertain and unpredictable. They may be important, but, like all products of human decision or governmental agreement, should not be the subject of rash predictions or self-confident speculation.

Brunei Darussalam

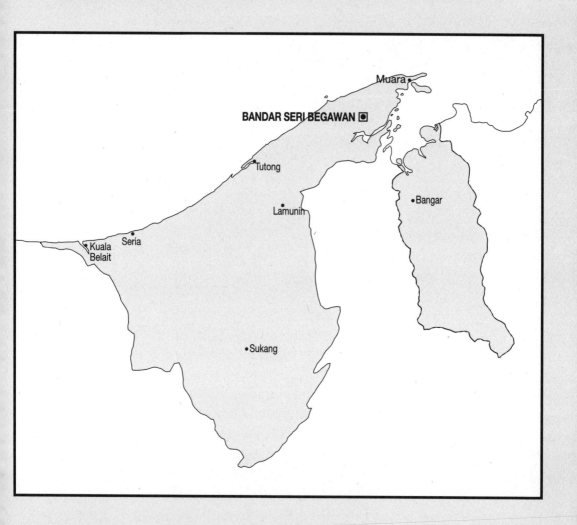

BRUNEI DARUSSALAM IN 2009
Addressing the Multiple Challenges

Pushpa Thambipillai

While the full impact of the global recession of 2008 and early 2009 spared Brunei Darussalam, it nevertheless had to tread cautiously and avert any negative consequences from the economic fallout on the socio-political landscape. Brunei Darussalam — the abode of peace — is often characterized by outsiders as a place where life is easy and nothing much ever happens. To the casual observer it may appear that no dramatic events upset this state of affairs. But Brunei Darussalam has had its share of significant issues, and 2009 will be seen as an eventful year in the socio-political annals of the state.

Maturing Nation

Brunei entered its twenty-fifth year of statehood with the theme *Kedewasaan Bernegara* (maturity of the nation) for its national day celebrations. The aspirations of a maturing nation were emphasized in leaders' pronouncements and policy implementations. Although a modernizing monarchical system with an appointed cabinet, the system has nevertheless become entrenched for ministers and civil servants to follow a well trodden behavioural system established over the decades. This particular attitude and work ethic finally drew a hard hitting speech from the monarch, Sultan Haji Hassanal Bolkiah. He berated the state's ministers and officials for their lack of initiative and failure to be proactive in a number of areas that required appropriate action plans, and remarked his abhorrence of the practice of acting like robots. Although welcoming his frank observations, the nation was taken aback by such a forceful speech by the Sultan. Moreover, it became a recurrent theme in his addresses throughout the year; he has been expressing his deep concern over the state of affairs through a few other equally

Pushpa Thambipillai teaches at the Department of Public Policy and Administration, Faculty of Business, Economics and Policy Studies, University of Brunei Darussalam.

intense remarks, for instance, on the issue of unspent zakat money in the face of prevalent poverty within certain sections of the community, the direction the newly created Islamic University was pursuing against the original intentions that it was established for, and the lack of obligatory religious education in the revamped syllabus for public schools.

As in previous years, the legislative council met for its annual deliberations in March. As expected, the Sultan highlighted a number of national concerns and strategies; he announced the formation of a sustainability fund to ensure the long term viability of the state's finances (heavily dependent on the volatility of hydrocarbon revenues tied to global markets), and a supplementary national budget of B$30 million for repair and reconstruction following damages from one of the worst floods and landslides to hit Brunei in early 2009. The legislative sessions continue to be one of the important venues where details on development and other matters are aired publicly and debated. Certain issues relating to budget allocation and the responsibilities of the various ministries were highlighted by the ministers in their statements and responses to queries, giving the public a clearer insight.

In keeping with the progressive intent of the government, a number of new policies were announced. The retirement age for Brunei's public sector employees is to be increased from the present fifty-five to sixty years as of the next calendar year. A new supplemental pension scheme was introduced especially for the lower income category, in addition to the existing Employee Provident Fund for the public and private sectors. Workers were also provided with a better work environment with the enactment of the Employment Order 2009, that takes into account standards set by the International Labor Organization, of which Brunei has been a member for the past two years. Previously, the Labor Act 1955 set the guidelines on employment issues and was deemed to be out of sync.

In line with national aspirations, the welfare of Brunei's citizens is a priority, including land and housing allocations. A new programme had been introduced a year earlier which tasked the Brunei Economic Development Board (BEDB) with constructing low cost houses for a long list of eligible recipients registered several years earlier. The BEDB had in turn engaged the private sector which would potentially accelerate the construction process. It was reported that the waiting list of people for the housing and land ownership schemes would reach 30,000 by 2012. It was also reported that one of the proposed solutions was to build multi-storey residences for the recipients, a concept not well received till lately because of the long wait by the applicants.

The new enactment related to housing, the Land Code Strata Act Chapter 189, came into force in July 2009. The act refers to strata titles issued to units in a multi-story building; the units may be owned by citizens, permanent residents, or foreigners on a ninety-nine-year lease. This may enliven the property market and the construction industry which has seen a glut in multi-unit buildings, especially shop houses, ownership of which was not attractive to locals except as rentals to foreigners. It also enables private individuals and foreign businesses to purchase units which was not possible previously.

Another issue that saw a positive outcome was the termination of the month-to-month service appointment of married female officers at certain lower levels of the public service, like clerks and general staff. Unlike their graduate colleagues, for decades these officers had lost out on certain benefits of employment until they were placed in a permanent service category under a new administrative policy. This was also in recognition of the Convention on the Elimination of All Forms of Discrimination against Women, signed by Brunei in May 2006. Not only did it eliminate discrimination in the workplace, it has also provided better incentives to the lower level women employees by recognizing their contributions and allaying fears of unfair retrenchment.

A significant development in the domestic legal environment was the appointment of Brunei's first local Chief Justice, Dato Awang Haji Kifrawi, who has had a long association with the legal service, his previous appointment being that of the attorney general with ministerial rank. Until his new appointment the Chief Justice's post had been filled by senior legal personalities from Commonwealth countries. Subsequently taking over as the Attorney General was the first woman officer, Datin Hajah Hayati, the former high court judge. The latter is a well regarded local personality, active in both government and non-governmental organizations, and a sought after public speaker at seminars.

Economic Activity

According to the report of the Finance Minister II to the Legislative Council, the 2009–10 budget would incur a deficit of B$1.65 billion with only about B$4 billion in expected revenue. Of the total revenue, only 19 per cent came from the non oil and gas and government services sectors, underscoring the dependence on an income susceptible to globally volatile price fluctuation in the oil and gas sector. According to the Department of Economic Planning and Development the gross domestic product (GDP) growth for 2009 was initially predicted to be between 1.3 per cent and 3.1 per cent compared to a negative growth in 2008. However, later estimates indicated another year of negative growth, caused mainly by a decrease in oil prices and a slow down in global market demand as major economies were still recovering from their deep recessions of 2008–9. Forecasts for 2010 are providing a more positive outlook for Brunei's economy with a number of initiatives in the industrial and agricultural sectors seeing implementation. Nevertheless, the GDP per capita was about B$51,000 dollars at current prices (US$1=B$1.40), making Brunei's GDP one of the highest in Asia.

According to the latest statistics, Brunei's estimated population is 406,000 — of which 263,000 are citizens — an increase of about 6,000 from the previous year. There is a steady figure of around 33,000 permanent residents, their growth offset by either emigration or when they are upgraded to citizens. In short Brunei typifies the resource-dependent economy with a small population base, relying on a major export while trying to diversify and attract foreign investment. At the same time the government continues to fund its social responsibility through infrastructure development and welfare services.

While hydrocarbon revenue is the predominant source of export income, the government continues to be the largest single employer, accounting for about 46,000 out of the total 181,800 people employed. The private sector employs about 127,000, of which only 31,500 are citizens and 8,000 permanent residents. Thus more than half of those employed in the private sector are foreigners. This is in spite of the fact that about 7,000 locals are unemployed with about 4,600 actually registered with the Labor Department seeking suitable employment. The situation of unemployment in the midst of jobs held by a large number of foreigners is not peculiar to Brunei — in areas where locals do not want to or are unable to be hired. The unemployment rate, around 3.7 per cent, is small by global standards, but enough to cause concern within the local environment for its negative social consequences. The implementation of the diversification policy and emphasis on the food and agro industry has provided more job opportunities for interested and qualified locals.

In a study on global competitiveness, the World Economic Forum, in its latest assessment for 2009–10, ranks Brunei at 32 out of 133 surveyed, ranking it slightly higher than it did a year earlier when Brunei was at 39/134. The index is based on published data as well as information gathered from expert opinions. Brunei generally tends to score well on multi-factor surveys as its political and social systems support a stable and peaceful environment. However, the latest results from a World Bank study on the "Ease of Doing Business" has given Brunei a low rank of 94 out of 183 economies. Some of Brunei's worst scores were in: starting a business (153/183 as it required eighteen procedures and 116 days), enforcing contracts (160/183), and registering property (183/183), but the country achieved better scores when it came to "employing workers" and "paying taxes". While the overall scores were not a surprise as fairly similar rankings have appeared in earlier years, the administration has been slow in introducing reforms that would make it attractive to foreign investment that could support its developmental goals of diversification. Observers have often acknowledged that foreign investors venturing into Brunei have had to deal with the issues on a case-by-case basis, without proper codification of regulations, and at times have abandoned their interests in despair.

Nevertheless, the government has supported some of the private sector activities to spur the diversification plans; for example, in tourism, the government has been financing promotional tours by the Tourism Development Board to potential customer markets during international and regional tourism exhibitions. Tourist arrivals have slowly increased over the last three years to about 140,000, mostly by air and some by cruise ship. Brunei's eco-tourism potential and promotion of its historical, cultural, and Islamic traditions are being explored for their special appeal, especially through joint promotions with the neighbouring Malaysian states. But it appears to be an uphill task, given Brunei's limited products and tourist-related infrastructure, as well as competition from well-established destinations like Sabah and Sarawak. Still, with the tireless efforts of the Tourism Board and local tour operators introducing new tourist sites (like the Ulu Ulu Resort by a local company in the heart of the Temburong jungle), there is keenness to be involved in underdeveloped but potentially attractive sectors.

The global commodity price hikes in 2008 and the threat of diminished grain supplies, especially rice, have had a positive effect on local agricultural activities. The government has added more land for rice cultivation with adequate drainage and irrigation; facilities like free seeds and fertilizer have also been provided as incentives, while existing cooperatives have been encouraged to engage members in rice farming. Consultants from China and the Philippines have also been invited to advise on hybrid rice cultivation. Targeting self-sufficiency in stages, the Hybrid Rice Development Research Centre was launched to identify fast growing breeds suitable for local conditions. A special variety of rice was named "Laila" after a nationwide name selection competition. Later, the first commercial crop was harvested with equal fanfare, with participation of the Sultan. The national aim is to increase domestic rice supply from 3 per cent to about 20 per cent in the next two years and then to gradually increase it to 60 per cent in the coming years. Similarly there was also renewed interest in aquaculture as there appears to be foreign demand for locally produced prawns and fish. A significant development was the renaming of the Department of Agriculture to the Department of Agriculture and Agro Industry to signify the efforts towards the twin strategy of food security and economic diversification. A new agro-technology park has also been established. The first day of November has been declared as Farmers Day to recognize the role of farmers, livestock breeders, fishermen, and agro-entrepreneurs. Regular agriculture and agro-industry exhibitions and sales have also contributed to understanding the issues associated with food security.

Learning from foreign experiences has always been on the agenda of Brunei's development strategies; for instance, a new partnership with Singapore was reflected in a memorandum of understanding signed between the two countries to promote collaboration in food and agro-technology, fisheries, and research into biodiversity. Promoting community involvement has also been the target through the "one village one product" concept, successfully practiced in some other countries. Another area that saw significant increase was the halal food industry and in national efforts to promote the Brunei Halal Brand that is favourably recognized by Brunei's fellow Muslim countries. The global halal market in various products has been reported at about US$2 trillion a year, and the food market alone could command US$630 billion. The Fourth International Halal Market Conference held in Bandar Seri Begawan was told that Brunei hoped to grab a portion of the vast opportunities available through its halal products.

Sharing the Dues of the MIB State

As a Malay Islamic Monarchy (*Melayu Islam Beraja*, MIB) state, Brunei Darussalam adheres to the tenants of Islam and its deep-rooted Malay reverence to its ruler. Two related issues that surfaced during the year were that of poverty eradication and zakat distribution. It is not widely realized that despite being a high per capita income country, there are still a few thousand households living in poverty. Some of these had been receiving regular assistance from the state's welfare agencies. During a meeting of the Islamic Religious Council, the Sultan queried the millions of dollars accumulated under the zakat collection and why it had not been distributed to the deserving recipients. Deserving parties are identified according to certain criteria in Islam; they include the poor and needy and those under certain forms of debt. Tithe collection is an annual obligation under Islam, and the Sultan reminded the council that the money collected was for rightful distribution and not for accumulation. This led to a "Run on the Zakat Millions" as a local daily termed it, when thousands of aspiring recipients turned up to apply for a share of the money. It took another nine months before the actual beneficiaries were selected and their share of the cash allocated, to be collected periodically from their financial institutions according to certain stipulations. Some 4,000 heads of households from the four districts received a total of B$90 million. Other deserving cases were also expected to be assisted under a following phase. The Sultan himself distributed the award certificates, proclaiming that Brunei could be free from poverty if all the monies in the tithe could be effectively given to the deserving, and provided the recipients utilized their shares wisely. The issue also generated discussions on how the poorer members of society could be helped in ways that could permanently get them out of the poverty syndrome so that they are not dependent on cash assistance from the government. Part of the zakat collection was also given to tenants for repaying outstanding loans to the Housing Department, for funding special housing schemes for the needy, and for distribution to new converts to the Islamic faith.

Education was another issue that became a national concern. Religious education coexists with other secular forms of education in Brunei's curriculum, but it became evident that some of the reorganized educational programmes for schools did not give adequate emphasis to Islamic education. Thus the educators are now assessing the reintroduction of compulsory religious education from secondary to tertiary levels.

While the leadership hopes that Brunei would be a model Islamic state, negative influences and activities continue to tarnish the abode of peace. The nation was shocked to learn that their own citizens were now branded as "drug mules" when at least four individuals in various parts of the world had been arrested and charged for smuggling drugs, including large quantities of heroin. The offenders included both men and women and have been apprehended in Australia, Chile, and China. They, especially the women, appear to be susceptible to foreign contacts either personally or through the Internet and willingly become "drug mules" in exchange for cash. In another development, a foreign woman, identified as a drug courier, was arrested in the capital, supporting the belief that Brunei may be on the map of international drug syndicates. Another man was arrested after he arrived by ferry from Labuan with half a kilo of marijuana concealed in his suitcase. In previous years efforts were only directed at apprehending trans-border drug distributors and their local accomplices, but now the threat appears more complex. Brunei's Narcotics Control Bureau address the challenges through various methods, including drug prevention education in schools and public symposia, such as the one during the International Day Against Drug Abuse and Illicit Drug Trafficking, and the World Conference of the International Federation of Non-Governmental Organizations for the Prevention of Drugs and Substance Abuse.

Defence and Security

Brunei showcased its interest in military-related hardware and defence issues by hosting the second Brunei International Defence Exhibition and Conference (BRIDEX) in August 2009, which assembled some of the leading manufacturers and specialists in the field. It also brought together leaders from within and outside the region, including King Abdullah of Jordon, for an informal meeting with Brunei's defence establishment that included the Sultan, who is also the Defence Minister and Supreme Commander. The BRIDEX Conference also heard expert views on defence and security and on the changing demands on the new armed forces, which would have to multitask to cope with these challenges. Brunei's Deputy Minister of Defence revealed that Brunei's next defence white paper covering both traditional and non-traditional security would be released in 2011 to coincide with the armed forces' golden anniversary. Besides the usual air displays, a number of navies, including those from France, India, Japan, and the United States were also in port and entertained officials and the public during their goodwill visits.

Throughout the year there were joint exercises with visiting foreign military, for example, the Cooperation Afloat Readiness and Training (CARAT) 2009 exercise with the United States to strengthen the defence and humanitarian assistance roles that both navies may have to perform if required. It was the fifteenth anniversary of the CARAT, and the event emphasized the new roles for the navies in view of increasing participation in international disaster relief. It exposed Brunei's armed forces to the emerging challenges of non-traditional security that had not been given enough attention in the past. There were also media reports that new patrol vessels built in Germany may be joining the Royal Brunei Navy to secure its maritime borders.

Meanwhile, the Sultan and the British Prime Minister Gordon Brown held talks in London on the continued stationing of the British Gurkha Brigade in Brunei. The Exchange of Notes provides for the stationing of the troops for another five years from September 2009 and furthering cooperation between the British brigade and Brunei's Armed Forces that has existed since the early 1960s when the Gurkhas first arrived to help put down a rebellion against the monarchy.

Transnational crimes appear to have increased over the past year and Brunei's Armed Forces and the marine police were actively involved in monitoring the borders for piracy, drug trafficking, and smuggling. The police forces of Malaysia, Indonesia, and Brunei have formed a tripartite alliance to fight such crimes. International terrorism was also being monitored through cooperation with Interpol and Aseanapol.

International Affairs

Brunei actively pursued its interests at the bilateral and multilateral levels, both regionally and globally. Diplomatic relations have been established with a number of countries in Africa and Eastern Europe, signaling Brunei's interest in forging ties with a wide range of states. Exchange of visits has become the preferred practice for strengthening bilateral ties and for extending political and cultural interests.

The Sultan, on a state visit to the Philippines, noted the close links between the two countries, one manifestation of which were the 20,000 Filipinos working in various sectors of Brunei's economy and contributing to Brunei's development. Brunei had also over the years supported Islamic education for the Filipinos in the south by offering training in institutions of higher learning, and as another gesture has donated funds for the building of a large mosque in Cotabatu. In addition, since 2004 Brunei has been participating in the international monitoring team assigned to monitor the peace process in Mindanao. The current ten-man team of Brunei observers is rotated on a yearly basis and may be increased to thirty on the request of President Gloria Macapagal Arroyo. Peace talks between the Philippine government and the Moro Islamic Liberation Front are ongoing under the chairmanship of Malaysia, but no new settlement has been reached, with reported ceasefire violations by both parties.

Bilateral relations with Indonesia were strengthened with the Sultan's attendance at the inauguration ceremony of President Susilo Bambang's second term of office. Further afield, the Sultan witnessed the signing of several agreements between Brunei and Kuwait during his state visit to the Gulf state. They included bilateral cooperation in oil and gas, air transport, and investment promotions. The reciprocal establishment of embassies has only taken place within the past year, and could assist in facilitating the implementation of the agreements. Another emerging link is with Russia, ASEAN's dialogue partner and APEC (Asia-Pacific Economic Cooperation) member. The Sultan's state visit followed the earlier one in 2005. Areas of interest converge on energy and military cooperation. While Brunei has maintained an embassy in Moscow for the past decade, the Russians will be establishing an embassy in Brunei in the coming months to facilitate further bilateral cooperation, which is presently insignificant.

Significant official visits have been from Malaysia — one by the outgoing Prime Minister Abdullah Ahmad Badawi in March and another in August by incumbent premier Najib Abdul Razak. Abdullah's visit saw the signing of the Exchange of Letters that would determine the maritime boundaries between the two countries, establish the Commercial Agreement Areas in oil and gas, and demarcate the land boundaries between Brunei and Malaysia. A furor ensued the following day when the media in both countries announced that an agreement on the long standing dispute over Limbang had been reached and that Brunei would drop its claim. Swiftly, spokesmen for both sides denied the stories and set the record straight that Limbang per se had not been part of the bilateral discussions. During another visit by the new Malaysian premier, further cooperation was discussed on the implementation of the points in the earlier Exchange of Letters and the possibility of joint maritime oil explorations.

The close ties with Singapore were enhanced through the exchange of numerous bilateral visits by both sides. The special relationship with the Singapore leadership was illustrated by the honour given to Minister Mentor Lee Kuan Yew to deliver the first Sultan Haji Omar Ali Saifuddien Memorial Lecture at the International Convention Centre to a packed hall of cabinet ministers, civil servants, students, and invited members of the public, chaired by the Crown Prince.

Participation in regional and international organizations has given Brunei the opportunities for enhancing its national interests and prestige as it gets ready to chair ASEAN in 2011 after a ten year period. Under ASEAN's Charter, the frequency of the summits have been increased to two per year, and with other summits like those of APEC, the Asia-Europe Meeting, and CHOGM (Commonwealth Heads of Government Meeting), it has taken a toll on the human resources of the small state that has to support the ongoing ministerial and senior officials meetings at the regional and global levels. In keeping with the new ASEAN structure, Brunei appointed its permanent representative to ASEAN in Jakarta. The Crown Prince and Senior Minister in the Prime Minister's Office, Prince Al-Muhtadee Billah, attended CHOGM, the Commonwealth Summit in Trinidad and Tobago, in line with his increasing role in deputizing for the Sultan, both at home and abroad. The Foreign Minister, Prince Mohamed, a twenty-seven-year veteran in representing Brunei's external affairs, is regarded as the bedrock of the small state's friendly and peaceful relations, frequently leading his team from bilateral to multilateral meetings in different parts of the world.

Brunei is a committed partner in the four-party Brunei-Indonesia-Malaysia-Philippines East ASEAN Growth Area (BIMP-EAGA) initiative and has supported various programmes in the sub-regional grouping. The Asian Development Bank is a regional supporter of EAGA and has backed Brunei's EAGA role in coordinating the regional transport connectivity by focusing on sea and air communication. Brunei is also actively involved with two other EAGA countries, Indonesia and Malaysia, in the Heart of Borneo tropical forest protection and management programme, and with the Coral Triangle initiative to protect the marine ecosystem. Under the EAGA priority infrastructure plan, Brunei will carry out feasibility studies on two projects: the Kuala Lurah Border Crossing Facility (between Brunei and Malaysia) and the Pandaruan Bridge (also between the two members). No decisions have been taken on the hosting of the BIMP-EAGA Facilitation Centre (the proposed coordinating and monitoring office), though there is strong expectation for Brunei to take up the offer.

The Global State

As a responsible member of the international community, Brunei has had occasions to prove its mantle. Brunei's armed forces have been participating in a peacekeeping mission in Lebanon, embedded with the Malaysian Contingent in the United Nations Interim Forces in Lebanon (UNIFIL). As the first five men returned another seven were dispatched to Lebanon after they had completed joint training with the Malaysians. Although Brunei's own armed forces are relatively small in size, it values its international contributions that not only recognize Brunei's commitment to the United Nations and world peace, but also affords experience that contributes to the development of the armed forces. The peacekeeping commitment is thus expected to continue.

It has not only been the leadership or public officials that have been increasing their involvement in the international community. Some members of the Brunei public have also done their part in putting the nation on the map. For instance, as part of the sixtieth anniversary celebrations of the Commonwealth, a women's expedition team selected from different Commonwealth countries set out on a mission to reach the South Pole. Brunei's selected participant was part of the team and successfully completed her mission along with her six team mates. Spurred by her determined example, for the first time a Brunei team is planning to scale Mount Everest, even if it is only to the base camp. However, on a disappointing note, football-mad Brunei fans had to see their national and league teams withdraw from regional competitions because of the decision by the International Federation of Association Football (FIFA) to ban Brunei's participation following the government deregistering the long-standing national football association on technical grounds. Attempts to get another association registered with FIFA to give the players another chance are still being pursued.

The global H1N1 pandemic did not spare Brunei. However, as the number affected was small, the health authorities were able to cope with the outbreak, mostly among school children. By the end of the year vaccination was encouraged for all and made available to anyone who wanted it. The health pandemic also tested the nation's preparedness in the face of disasters since a well organized multi-tasked disaster management committee was already in place after the major floods that hit Brunei in early 2009. In recognition of such calamities and from a humanitarian perspective, the government and peoples of Brunei continued to donate funds for other victims elsewhere, for example, those affected by the devastating earthquakes in Indonesia and the floods in the Philippines. Donations were also collected for the Palestine Humanitarian Fund.

On the whole, 2009 was a year of mixed economic fortunes as Brunei looked beyond recovery from the global recession and focused on its socio-economic development strategy to 2035 — its long term goals — by restructuring its education for better human resource development and protecting its environment for a sustainable future.

Note

The main sources of information for this chapter were the *Borneo Bulletin*, the *Brunei Times*, *Brunei Darussalam Key Indicators 2009* (Department of Economic Planning and Development, Prime Minister's Office, Brunei Darussalam <www.jpke.gov.bn>), <www. abd.org>, <www.doingbusiness.org>, and <www.weforum.org>.

Cambodia

CAMBODIA IN 2009
The Party's Not Over Yet

Caroline Hughes

The year 2009 began in Cambodia with a party. The Cambodian People's Party (CPP) celebrated thirty years of Cambodia's liberation from the Khmer Rouge regime with a spectacular event in Phnom Penh's Olympic Stadium and broadcast across the country by the Cambodian television stations. Thousands of civil servants and party officials attended the event, taking part in elaborate tableaux involving the holding up of coloured cards to make pictures and slogans. Party leaders were feted in speeches, dancers and marching bands performed, and boy scouts released white doves into the air.

The anniversary was indeed something for the CPP to celebrate. It followed close on the heels of a landslide election victory in 2008 which finally, after thirty years of struggle, allowed the CPP to form a government which controlled the whole country, without the need for bargaining with coalition partners. The anniversary also coincided with the crest of Cambodia's five-year economic boom, and the successful repositioning of its relations with donors to balance lingering Western dreams of conditionality with Chinese "soft power". The CPP had never been so popular or so powerful.

Subsequently, the picture has looked less rosy, as the ripples from the global financial crisis hit Cambodia's shores. Layoffs at garment factories and construction sites in Phnom Penh and around the region entailed that fewer remittances reached rural villages. But expectations of a good harvest cushioned the impact on the CPP's rural support base, and reduction in the high level of inflation of 2008 gave poor farmers and public sector workers some relief. The contraction of the economy in 2009 has not brought about significant social or political unrest; indeed, ongoing administrative reform entrenches CPP rule further into the institutional structure

CAROLINE HUGHES is Associate Professor Governance Studies at the School of Social Sciences and Humanities, Murdoch University, Australia.

of government and there seem to be few possibilities for contenders for power to make any headway against the CPP's formidable machinery of control.

Political Issues

Cambodia's programme of administrative decentralization rumbled on this year, with the election of councils at the provincial and district level across the country in May. These councils represent the latest phase of Cambodia's long-running decentralization and deconcentration reform programme, which began with the holding of elections at the commune level in 2002. The Law on Administration and Management of Capital, Province, Municipality, District, and Khan, passed in 2008, mandated that councils should be elected at all these levels of government for the first time, in preparation for a future deconcentration of functions from central ministries to these layers of government.

As yet, the precise functions to be deconcentrated have not been decided, so the substance of what these councils will do has yet to be determined. Throughout the year, the Ministry of Interior held a series of meetings with the various ministries in Phnom Penh in an attempt to establish concrete plans for deconcentration. The outcome of these meetings has yet to be published, suggesting a certain degree of reluctance on the part of the various ministries to commit themselves to devolving functions and, therefore, power and income. However, the structure of sub-national governance outlined in the law was put into place as a result of the elections. Now, Cambodia's provinces and districts, as well as its communes, have councils elected through proportional representation on the basis of party lists, which have the task of overseeing the day-to-day work of government conducted by boards of provincial and district governors.

According to the 2008 law, the purpose of this is to "establish, promote and sustain democratic development."[1] However, the democratic potential of the reform is equivocal, due both to the nature of the electoral procedures for selecting sub-national councils and to the continued significance of the Ministry of Interior's role. The elections held in 2009 were "indirect elections" in which the electorate comprised, not the totality of Cambodia's eight million plus registered voters, but the 11,353 commune councillors who were themselves directly elected in local elections in 2007. The landslide victory of the Cambodian People's Party in the 2007 local election entailed that the party also enjoyed a landslide victory in the 2009 sub-national elections, since seventy per cent of the voters in 2009 were elected to their own positions in 2007 via the CPP party list.[2]

Interestingly, the result of the 2009 elections suggested that some non-CPP commune councillors voted for the CPP list in the provincial/district council elections. The opposition Sam Rainsy Party (SRP), which has ostensibly controlled just over twenty-three per cent of commune council seats since 2007,[3] estimated that ten per cent of its councillors had voted against their own party, in favour of the CPP. According to the Sam Rainsy Party, this reflects a CPP vote-buying campaign, in which SRP commune councillors were offered US$1,500 each to vote for the CPP party list at the provincial and district level.[4]

The indirect election process entrenches the hold of the Cambodian People's Party over Cambodian politics. All elected positions in Cambodia, aside from the National Assembly itself, are now determined by the commune councils: commune councils appoint village chiefs, elect the national upper house, and now elect provincial and district level appointments also. The CPP enjoys a significant advantage at the commune level, since it has over the past ten years perfected the functioning of a mighty patronage machine, which provides millions of dollars of funding for local level development projects every year. According to one estimate, the level of party funding for commune level development outstrips state funding by a factor of two or three to one, thus entrenching the CPP as the only party which, to quote its own campaign slogan, "Gets things done". The party's ability to get things done in this impressive fashion is a result of the large donations it is able to mobilize from business tycoons who are dependent upon the Cambodian state for the award of land concessions, licences, and contracts.

The dominance of the CPP at the commune level is such that it controls ninety-eight per cent of commune chief positions, and controls all the seats on the council in ten per cent of communes. Consequently, the reorganization of the sub-national administrative structure in a manner which makes the commune level the key to the election or appointment of other levels permits the party to capitalize on its greatest strength: its dominance of the development landscape of rural villages and its impressive level of organization nationwide.

It is as yet unclear, however, whether the role of the commune in electing other layers of government will contribute to a "bottom-up" style of decision making and development planning. The text of the law takes pains to reassert the principle of "unified administration" as opposed to federalism in the Cambodian state, and therefore the extent to which elected local governments can challenge the centre is limited. Indeed, the Ministry of Interior retains the powers to dissolve councils with no right of appeal from councils themselves; and boards of governors are accountable to the Ministry of Interior, as well as to the councils that are supposed to oversee them. Furthermore, beyond the actual indirect election, the law does not mandate any specific mechanisms or procedures by which commune councils remain informed about the activities of the councils operating above them in the administrative pyramid. Consequently, the ability of directly elected commune councils to actively monitor higher levels, and hold them to account, would appear to be constrained.

The broad structure and procedures of sub-national councils is enshrined in the law. The councils will work alongside a board of governors, appointed by the Ministry of Interior, who will oversee the day-to-day work of government. The board will have a duty to report regularly to councils, and the councils will have to approve the board's annual budget. Supporting the work of the councils will be committees overseeing the specific issues of procurement and women's affairs.

However, the exact nature of the relationship between the board of governors and the sub-national councils will not become clear until the latter have settled into their roles and begun to tackle matters of substance. Anecdotal evidence suggests that many of the councillors elected at provincial and district level this year are older party cadres and retired officials, but systematic research into their motivations, experience, and attitude has yet to be undertaken, but may be crucial in determining whether decentralization will produce the "democratic development" to which the law refers.

Overall, the elections this year have an equivocal effect on Cambodian democracy. The institutional reforms associated with deconcentration of function and decentralization of power have in fact significantly bolstered the power of the CPP, already the dominant party. The extent to which they also allow empowered participation of the rural population in setting development policy and monitoring its implementation is yet to be seen. Research into local development practices since the initial election of commune councils in 2002 suggests that local government has become less coercive and more consultative, albeit with continued widespread practices of exclusion of particular marginalized groups, but that in a significant number of communes, the connivance of local authorities in landgrabbing and corrupt practices is a serious issue.[5] The entrenchment of party discipline through the use of party lists to determine candidates for all these positions is a significant constraint to the potential for reorienting local officials at all levels in Cambodia towards a representative and accountable role vis-à-vis the rural population.

A further development in administrative reform came with the approval of a long-awaited anti-corruption bill by the Council of Ministers. At time of writing, the bill was reported as having been passed to the National Assembly for debate towards the end of December, but its provisions had not been made public. The bill has been in the process of being drafted since 1994, reflecting the highly politicized nature of corruption in Cambodia and its entrenchment in the systems of both the state and major political parties. Sudden movement on the issue reflects both the pressure that has been mounting on this issue from Cambodia's major donors, and to some extent from local non-governmental organizations; and, presumably, a calculation by the CPP that even with the law, its key income streams will be secure. The dramatic expansion of the private sector and, in particular, domestic direct investment, has allowed more financing of party campaigns and development projects by donations from tycoons, entailing less reliance on the skimming of state budgets, although the latter practice continues notwithstanding some progress on public financial management reform. Furthermore, domestic activism on the issue of corruption has been mainly focused on petty graft, such as the practice of poorly paid teachers charging fees from students. Focus on these kinds of practices would give the government a popularity boost and distract attention from larger-scale misappropriation of resources.

At the level of national politics, the year saw continued pressure on the opposition Sam Rainsy Party, whose leader, Sam Rainsy, was twice stripped of his parliamentary immunity in order to face prosecution over various issues. Another senior party member, Mu Sochua, also lost her immunity after being prosecuted for defamation by Prime Minister Hun Sen. Although these incidents ultimately blew over, they exemplify a continuation of tactics of low level harassment against popular anti-government politicians.

These activities also indicate the continued weakness of the opposition movement in national politics. Following the virtual demise of the royalist movement in the 2008 elections, the Sam Rainsy Party remains the only significant party other than the Cambodian People's Party. In the 2008 elections, the SRP did less well than some of its supporters had hoped, failing to pick up votes from disenchanted royalist supporters, although holding its ground in terms of its overall vote share. To some extent, this reflected the highly favourable environment in which the 2008 elections were held, at the height of the economic boom and in the grip of a military confrontation on the Thai border over ownership of the ancient temple of Preah Vihear, which stands in disputed territory. But to some extent, it reflects the sophisticated manner with which the CPP has honed its patronage practices, to the long-term detriment of the prospects for any Cambodian opposition. To some extent also, it reflects the fact that little public protest or dissent, that could raise the opposition's profile, is tolerated in contemporary Cambodia.

The Khmer Rouge Tribunal

In the third year of its establishment, the Extraordinary Chambers of the Courts of Cambodia (ECCC), or Khmer Rouge Tribunal, saw its first two cases this year. The case against Kaing Guek Eav, commonly known as Duch, the former Chief of the Special Branch or S-21 jail at Tuol Sleng in Phnom Penh, began in February and reached closing arguments by the end of the year. More than 12,000 prisoners died of ill-treatment, torture, or execution at the jail between 1975 and 1979, under the Democratic Kampuchea regime. Duch is charged with crimes against humanity, grave breaches of the Geneva Convention of 1949, homicide, and torture and is alleged to have personally overseen the torture of the most important prisoners at the jail.[6]

Duch initially entered a guilty plea at the tribunal, acknowledging his guilt and offering an apology to his victims and their families. However, in a dramatic twist at the end of the case, and amid some confusion among the defence team, Duch asked for an acquittal on the basis of mitigating factors. The defence team had argued throughout the hearing for a number of mitigating factors to be taken into account. First, they argued that Duch acted under superior orders and under duress, and did not make the policy of elimination of enemies of the revolution, even though he implemented it. Second, they argued that Duch's cooperation with the prosecution should be taken into account. Third, they argued that Duch had shown remorse and contrition. Fourth, they argued that psychological assessments indicated the process of dehumanization which they claimed transformed Duch into a torturer and murderer during the period of Khmer Rouge rule. The defence also drew attention to the fact that no other prison guards or interrogators from other Khmer Rouge prisons are currently under indictment, suggesting that Duch, even though guilty, should not become a scapegoat for the entire system. In short, they argued that the crimes were committed by the Communist Party of Kampuchea (CPK), and that the CPK therefore bore ultimate responsibility. The last day of closing arguments saw some of the defence team asking for mitigation of sentence on these bases, while others asked for acquittal in the light of these factors. When asked directly for clarification, Duch himself said that he sought an acquittal.

The legal basis for such an acquittal is a jurisdictional one. The ECCC was established to try individuals "most responsible" for the crimes of the Democratic Kampuchea era. In arguing that he was not "most responsible" and that therefore the charges should be dropped, Duch effectively challenged the jurisdiction of the court to try him for his actions. The prosecution rejected this claim on the basis that it was entered eighteen months too late, as well as on the basis that as supervisor of the S-21 prison, Duch had opportunities to mitigate CPK policies which he did not choose to take. They also argued that the request for acquittal reflected the disingenuous nature of Duch's previous guilty plea, and of his apology to his victims.[7]

The outcome for Duch is yet to be determined, but the trial raised larger questions about the rationale for the ECCC and its impact on Cambodian politics. For much of its functioning, the ECCC has been met with a lack of interest by the broader Cambodian population. The last weeks of the Duch trial were, however, broadcast on national television, raising the profile of the case, and animating wider public discussion. Throughout the trial, the ECCC ran free bus services for groups wishing to attend the trial, and more than 12,000 people did so. Furthermore, the trial operated a system for victims' participation which is groundbreaking in terms of such tribunals; victims were represented in court by their own counsel with a view to assisting in establishing the guilt of the defendant and in pursuit of claims for reparations.

The new system caused some problems: for example, the victims were divided into four different groups, and represented by four different teams of lawyers. The division was an arbitrary one, dependent on which non-governmental organization had initially encouraged the participation of the particular victim, and resulted in overlapping and poorly coordinated representation in court. Some of the victims' claims to be victims were challenged at a late stage of the trial, and some of these challenges were upheld as documentation was frequently found to be incomplete when reviewed. Also, the victims themselves protested their exclusion from having a say over sentencing, as opposed to the issues of guilt and reparations. At one stage, the victims groups boycotted the hearing in response to the judges' ruling that they could not question character witnesses, since issues of character related to sentencing rather than guilt and reparations. Conflicts such as this reflected the difficulty of developing new procedures on the run and caused disappointment among victims' groups; but they also had the effect of keeping the victims in the public eye and in the news, widening the impact of the trial.[8]

A further controversy was a request by prosecutors to pursue further investigations as a means to provide more defendants for the court to try. At present, a second case, against former Khmer Rouge leader Nuon Chea, is in pre-trial hearings; while three other leaders, Ieng Sary, Ieng Thirith, and Khieu Samphan have been charged with crimes under ECCC jurisdiction and are in detention. The request to widen the basis for prosecution has been criticized by Prime Minister Hun Sen, who claims that it could cause civil unrest and a return to civil war within the country. This claim has also been made by Cambodian members of the prosecution team, leading to charges that the prosecution, and the ECCC more broadly, is politically influenced.

Overall, the move to actual trial has increased the level of awareness of and interest in the tribunal in Cambodia. Resistance from the Prime Minister to expanding the list of persons charged reflects a longstanding reluctance, on the part of the Cambodian Government, to submit itself to rule-based proceedings that are beyond its ability to control — a reluctance which manifests itself not only in relation to justice proceedings, but also in relation to most other areas of governance. Like many other international tribunals, the ECCC seems set to deliver a handful of punishments to a group of evil former leaders; but fears that it could destabilize contemporary Cambodia, as much as aspirations that it could reform contemporary Cambodia into a state governed by the rule of law, appear overblown.

Economic Issues

The global financial crisis took its toll on Cambodia in the form of slumping demand for exports, reduction in private sector credit, and a burst bubble in the domestic property market. Cambodia's banking sector is both young and small, with private banks only really making headway in the past five years as property prices increased and the private sector expanded. As such, the sector had no significant exposure to the sub-prime lending market. However, the percentage of non-performing loans increased as the real economy suffered from recession elsewhere in the world, and the bursting of the domestic property bubble left the balance sheets of those banks that had invested heavily in the relatively young mortgage market looking fragile. The youth of the sector entails a lack of experience in monitoring and oversight, and Cambodian banks operate with a low level of transparency. The International Monetary Fund (IMF) expressed concern about the health of the banking sector and the ability of the authorities to monitor banks' compliance with banking regulations at the end of the year, but there have been no dramatic collapses.

Nevertheless, tight credit in the region and the reduction in consumer demand elsewhere in the world resulted in the real economy suffering a serious blow, contracting by 2.5 per cent following five years of dramatic growth. Part of the reason for this dramatic deterioration in performance is dependence on exports. Cambodia's industrial sector remains heavily specialized in garment manufacturing; garments comprise about 65 per cent of Cambodian exports, and about three quarters of the garments produced in Cambodia are headed for the United States.

At the same time as U.S. consumer demand was plunging, agreements with the United States which safeguarded Cambodian exports against Chinese competition expired in December 2008, exacerbating the impact on Cambodian manufacturers. Furthermore, the garment industry is based upon foreign direct investment rather than domestic investment, and consequently was hard hit by the credit crunch in the region. Garment manufacturing expanded by an average of 13.2 per cent per year between 2005 and 2007; this slowed to only 2.2 per cent in 2008, and contracted by 15 per cent in 2009. In the first half of the year, forty factories closed, with another twenty-five suspending operations and 40,000 workers lost their jobs. The income of remaining workers dropped by about 20 per cent due to reductions in overtime.[9] Similar effects in the rest of the region entailed that opportunities for Cambodians to seek work as migrants abroad contracted sharply also.[10] A United Nations report released mid-year suggested that one response to unemployment was an increase in women engaging voluntarily in sex work.[11]

Similarly, work on some of the prestige construction projects that had begun to dominate Phnom Penh's skyline over the past two or three years ground to a halt as the companies concerned similarly found their credit lines drying up. Expansion of the construction industry averaged more than 16 per cent per year between 2005 and 2007, falling to 5.8 per cent growth in 2008, and 8 per cent contraction in 2009. Tourism, which had expanded by an average of 15 per cent between 2005 and 2007, dropped to 9.8 per cent growth in 2008 before contracting by 10 per cent in 2009.

Foreign direct investment fell by more than a quarter from US$815 million in 2008 to a projected US$595 million in 2009.[12] The main sources of foreign investment were Cambodia's ASEAN neighbours, specifically Thailand, Singapore, Indonesia, and Vietnam, with other Asian investors following.[13] Key areas for investment were tourism, construction, and agro-industry, with the largest investors, Thailand and Vietnam, investing respectively in sugar cane plantations to the west of the country, and rubber plantations in the east.[14] Cross-border trade with Thailand remained relatively stable, despite a military stand-off in Cambodia's north over disputed ownership of the ancient temple at Preah Vihear.

The main bright spot in a gloomy economic picture was agriculture, which is dependent mainly on good weather conditions. The weather this year was conducive to a good harvest, and the decline in the inflation rate, which had hit the poor hard in 2008, is good news for the rural population. However, a combination of the effect on wealth of the dramatic price rises in 2008 and the significant reduction of flows in remittances from urban and migrant workers in 2009 means that the poor will be hit by the recession. The World Bank estimates that over the next three years the poverty headcount could rise by between 1 and 4 per cent as a result of the downturn, making Cambodia one of only four countries in the Asia Pacific in which poverty is expected to rise as a result of the global financial crisis.[15]

Cambodia's economic strategy is heavily based upon its integration into the region, upon which it relies for investment and other inputs. Since 2001, the Cambodian Government has prioritized agro-industry, awarding land concessions on degraded forest land around Cambodia's periphery to companies wishing to establish plantations. This has attracted significant investment from Cambodia's Asian neighbours, as well as from more distant investors from countries such as Kuwait, although it has been the subject of contestation at home as villagers are displaced from land which they had customarily enjoyed access to the resources of. A second economic strategy that is dependent upon flows from the region is the heavy investment in Special Economic Zones since 2006. A total of twenty-one Special Economic Zones are either completed or under construction; most are located on Cambodia's borders with Thailand and Vietnam, intended to take advantage of better infrastructure and utilities across the border.

Foreign Affairs

Cambodia's political relationships with its powerful north-east Asian neighbours continued to strengthen this year, although economic relations were hit by the crisis. In October, South Korean President Lee Myung-bak visited Cambodia to sign a range of bilateral agreements, reaffirming a longstanding relationship with Hun Sen, for whom Lee worked as a special economic advisor before being elected to the South Korean presidency in 2008. The close relations between Hun Sen and Lee Myung-bak appear likely to promote South Korean investment in Cambodia: South Korea is already the second biggest investor behind China. However, the impact on the South Korean economy of the global financial crisis has damaged its interests in Cambodia. Work stopped on a number of construction projects in Phnom Penh, and the opening of a Hyundai car assembly plant currently under construction in Koh Kong province appears likely to be delayed as a result of the depreciation of the Korean currency.

With respect to China, investment also fell dramatically in the first half of the year, by more than 90 per cent from the US$4.3 billion level of 2008.[16] But political relations ended the year on a high note, with a visit from Chinese Vice-President Xi Jinping. The day before the Vice-President's arrival in Cambodia, authorities deported a group of twenty Uighur asylum seekers who had sought refuge in Cambodia following the crackdown on demonstrations in Xinjiang province earlier in the year. The deportation occurred over the protests of human rights groups and apparently took place in response to a note sent by Beijing to the Cambodian Government a week earlier. The affair exemplifies the influence China has been able to buy after six years of "soft power" during which it invested more than any other country in Cambodia.

Cambodia's relations with its immediate neighbours, Thailand and Vietnam, have always been fraught, but there was evidence this year that the significance of investment and trade from these sources has changed the nature of political relations with them too. There has long been a pronounced tendency on the part of Cambodian politicians to regard dissent at home as evidence of interference from abroad, and to deal with it via tirades or outright attacks against one or other of the neighbours. The significance of trade and investments along the border makes this a strategy to which politicians are far less inclined, but the availability of populist nationalism as a strategy for criticizing government action makes it difficult on occasion to resist.

In 2008, Cambodia's military came to blows with the Thai military over a dispute relating to the temple of Preah Vihear which stands on the border between the two countries. Ownership of the temple has long been disputed, but an appeal to the World Court in 1962 found in Cambodia's favour. For decades the issue was largely moot, since the area was cut off by warfare, landmines, and the destruction of infrastructure; but since 2003 it has been accessible again, raising once more the issue of ownership.

In 2008, the Cambodian Government, with the support of the Samak government in Thailand, made a bid to have the temple listed as a World Heritage Site. The attempt was successful, prompting dancing in the streets in Phnom Penh, and this was very welcome news to a government gearing up to fight a national election. However, subsequently the issue became entangled with the internal dynamics of Thai politics, with the anti-Thaksin movement in Thailand seeking to undermine the government of Thaksin's successor Samak by claiming that his support for the Cambodian bid was unconstitutional and a betrayal of Thailand's national interest.

Subsequently, a group of anti-Thaksin protestors travelled to the Preah Vihear temple to hold a demonstration, prompting the appearance of the Thai military in the temple, ostensibly to control the demonstrators. For the Cambodian Government this represented an incursion onto national soil, and a counter-mobilization by the Cambodian army was ordered. Soldiers from the two sides faced one another across the temple as politicians held a series of talks that have failed to resolve the problem. The stand-off is currently entering its eighteenth month, but appears to have settled into a stalemate. Significantly, it does not appear to be having much effect on cross-border trade between the two countries. The border was not closed, even at the height of the dispute, and Thai companies have continued to operate in Cambodia. There has been no repeat of the 2003 riots which saw both Thai businesses and the Thai embassy razed to the ground in Phnom Penh.

In fact, the stand-off came at a very good time for the Cambodian military, which was able to squeeze a budget increase out of the government in the light of the confrontation, and which received large public donations via a fundraising campaign conducted by television and radio stations on behalf of the soldiers on the front line. The military also began a campaign of conscription to provide soldiers to hold off the Thais. The need for conscription in a notoriously bloated military to handle the crisis raised the question again of the pressing need for military reform and for rationalization of the large numbers of "ghost soldiers" that still apparently populate the personnel lists maintained by the Ministry of National Security. However, the fighting never really took place, leaving a suspicion that the two governments are less interested in actually claiming the temple than in using the issue to incite predictable emotions among their followers.

Towards the end of 2009, however, a new issue complicated Thai-Cambodian relations: namely, a new close relationship between Prime Minister Hun Sen and deposed former Thai Prime Minister Thaksin Shinawatra. During a visit to Thailand for the ASEAN summit in October, Hun Sen made a speech in which he compared Thaksin to the Burmese dissident Aung San Suu Kyi and proposed employing Thaksin as an advisor. Evidently Thaksin took him up on the proposal, and a royal decree formalizing the offer was signed at the end of October. In response, Thailand withdrew its Ambassador and Cambodia followed suit. The row worsened when Thaksin arrived in Cambodia in November, and Thailand demanded his extradition — a demand the Cambodian government rejected. Meanwhile, Cambodian police arrested a Thai flight engineer working at Phnom Penh's airport for leaking information about Thaksin's flight details. The engineer was imprisoned to await trial on charges of espionage. The leak was apparently solicited by the First Secretary of the Thai Embassy in Phnom Penh, prompting his expulsion from Cambodia. This precipitated the retaliatory expulsion of the First Secretary of the Cambodian Embassy in Bangkok. Subsequently, the flight engineer — a Thai man named Sivarak Chutipong — was convicted of spying and sentenced to seven years in prison. But Thaksin then intervened to broker a royal pardon for Sivarak and, in a bizarre scene on the day of his release, Sivarak was invited to a party at Hun Sen's house in Phnom Penh to celebrate his pardon.[17]

The release of Sivarak lowered tensions to an extent, but the affair raises a number of questions about the relationship between Cambodia and Thailand. In a speech made in Cambodia, Thaksin accused the Abhisit government in Bangkok of "false patriotism" in its relations with its regional neighbours, and argued that Thailand's and Cambodia's economic futures were inextricably linked.[18] Yet the internal instability that has prompted the emergence of nationalist rhetoric in Thailand at the expense of processes of regional integration promoted by the Thaksin government between 2001 and 2006 has not seriously affected trade between the two countries.

What is Thaksin doing in Cambodia? Unconfirmed reports surfaced that Thaksin plans to invest heavily in a resort complex in Koh Kong province on the Thai border, creating a power base from which he would be able to wield considerable influence in Eastern Thailand. Hun Sen's motivations in reaching out the hand of friendship are less clear. Some analysts suggest that Hun Sen is interested in using Thaksin's expertise in dealing with the rural poor. Thaksin's electoral strategy shares much in common with Hun Sen's, since both focused on promoting development programmes, infrastructure, and services in rural areas. One report speculated that Hun Sen's interest in Thaksin's expertise is more related to the increasing number of bad debts in the Cambodian banking system.[19] Other reports suggest that Hun Sen's overtures to Thaksin represent retaliation towards the Thai Government for a speech that opposition leader Sam Rainsy was permitted to make at the Foreign Correspondent's Club of Thailand in Bangkok, about Cambodia's human rights record, in advance of the inauguration of the ASEAN Human Rights Commission.

Whatever the reason, the strategy is a high-risk one, given the level of existing Thai investment on the Thai border and across Cambodia. Thailand cancelled a memorandum of understanding (MOU) relating to exploration of maritime oil reserves during the row, a move which could potentially delay the onset of oil revenues to Cambodia. As yet, the amount of revenue that could accrue from exploitation of reserves in the Gulf of Thailand is unclear, but there has been considerable excitement within Cambodia over the potential for oil exploitation, and therefore the cancellation of the MOU represents a cost to the Cambodian government.

However, like the preceding dispute over Preah Vihear, this diplomatic row does not seem to have adversely affected everyday Thai-Cambodian business relations. Unlike the situation in 2003, when remarks made by a Thai actress over Thai claims to be the builders of Angkor Wat sparked riots in Phnom Penh, the situation inside Cambodia remains calm, and there has been no evacuation of

Thai nationals or attacks on Thai businesses. The odd ceremony in which Hun Sen presented Sivarak with his royal pardon appears to have been designed to avert, rather than stir up, any popular anti-Thai emotions in the Cambodian population, and thus safeguard Thai business investments.

The opposition Sam Rainsy Party responded to the affair by attempting to recall public attention to Cambodia's relations with its other neighbour, Vietnam. Relations on this border are also complicated by disputed land claims, but a border deal signed by Hun Sen in Hanoi in 2006 has allowed scope for development, including special economic zones and a growth triangle. According to the Sam Rainsy Party, the 2006 border deal has not stopped Vietnamese encroachment onto Cambodian soil, and the party has long conducted activist campaigns in the area, including mass "invasions" by unarmed crowds of SRP supporters into supposedly Vietnamese territory. The tension on the Thai border overshadowed these activities, and Sam Rainsy responded by raising the stakes. In December, he was arrested for pulling up Vietnamese border posts which, he claimed, had been moved onto Cambodian land. It was this transgression that led to the loss of his parliamentary immunity; yet the stunt was ultimately unsuccessful in refocusing attention away from Thailand and towards Vietnam. Hun Sen's rapport with Thaksin underlines the populist stance of both leaders and their ability to undermine the aspirations of cosmopolitan urban populations through vast patronage schemes in rural areas. Whereas the Thai urban middle class had the King and the military on their side, the Cambodian middle class have no such allies, and therefore the prospects for the SRP achieving more than a toehold in Cambodian politics appear limited in the foreseeable future. Yet these incidents indicate the continued significance of regional relations in Cambodian domestic political identities.

Notes

[1]   Royal Government of Cambodia, *Law on Administration and Management of the Capital, Provinces, Municipalities, Districts and Khans*.

[2]   Committee for Free Elections in Cambodia, *Final Report and Assessment on the 2007 Commune Council Elections* (Phnom Penh: Comfrel, 2007) <http://www.comfrel.org/images/others/1188360503COMFREL%20CCE%20Report%20Final%20without%20Pictures.pdf> (accessed 13 December 2009), p. 58.

[3]   Ibid.

[4]   Mu Sochua, "The District-Province Council Election", Sam Rainsy Party website <http://www.cambodiatribunal.org/blog/2009/11/civil-party-participation-at-eccc.html> (accessed 14 December 2009).

5 See for example, Joakim Ojendal and Kim Sedara, "Korob, Kaud, Klach: In Search of Agency in Rural Cambodia", *Journal of Southeast Asian Studies* 37 (2006), pp. 507–26; Caroline Hughes, Eng Netra, Thon Vimealea, Ou Sivhuoch, and Ly Tem, "Local Leaders and Big Business in Cambodia", paper presented at the workshop on Cambodia's Economic Transformation, Phnom Penh, 6 January 2009.

6 Case Information Sheet, ECCC, Phnom Penh, 2009 <http://www.eccc.gov.kh/english/cabinet/files/Case_Info_DUCH_EN.pdf> (accessed 14 December 2009).

7 David Scheffer, "Duch Seeks an Acquittal and Immediate Release", The Trial Observer weblog, 27 November 2009 <http://www.cambodiatribunal.org/blog/2009/11/duch-seeks-aquittal-and-immediate.html> (accessed 14 December 2009).

8 Michael Saliba, "Civil Party Participation at the ECCC: An Overview", The Trial Observer weblog, 6 November 2009 <http://www.cambodiatribunal.org/blog/2009/11/civil-party-participation-at-eccc.html> (accessed 14 December 2009).

9 Figures are taken from International Monetary Fund (IMF), *Staff Report for the Article IV 2009 Consultation* (Phnom Penh: IMF, 2009) <http://www.imf.org/external/pubs/ft/scr/2009/cr09325.pdf> (accessed 13 December 2009).

10 May Kunmakara, "Migrant Worker Jobs Hit by Regional Unemployment", *Phnom Penh Post*, 4 February 2009.

11 Katrin Redfern, "Voluntary Sex Work on the Rise: UN Report", *Phnom Penh Post*, 16 July 2009.

12 Figures are taken from IMF, *Staff Report for the Article IV 2009 Consultation*.

13 "Cambodian FDI Down 73pct in First Half of 2009", Xinhua News Agency, 16 July 2008 <http://www.sithi.org/landissue/source/SEZ/090716_Global%20Times_Camb%20FDI%20down.pdf>.

14 "Vietnam Fixed Asset Investment Increases", *Phnom Penh Post*, 20 August 2009.

15 Steve Finch, "Cambodia to Face Worst Increase in Poverty in Asia Pacific", *Phnom Penh Post*, 7 April 2004.

16 Nguon Sovan, "China's Investment in Cambodia's Fixed Assets Dives amid Downturn", *Phnom Penh Post*, 11 August 2009.

17 Cheang Sokha and James O'Toole, "Thai Spy Released from Jail", *Phnom Penh Post*, 15 Decembe 2009.

18 Cheang Sokha and James O'Toole, "Thaksin Accuses Abhisit of 'False Patriotism'", *Phnom Penh Post*, 12 November 2009.

19 Jared Ferrie, "'Advisor' Thaksin Hits Out at Protests", *Asia Times Online*, 13 November 2009 <http://www.atimes.com/atimes/Southeast_Asia/KK13Ae02.html> (accessed 13 December 2009).

Indonesia

INDONESIA IN 2009
Democratic Triumphs and Trials

Edward Aspinall

In 2009, national affairs in Indonesia were dominated by elections that were held in two rounds: legislative elections on 9 April and presidential elections on 8 July. A second round of presidential elections was scheduled for September, but proved unnecessary because the incumbent, Susilo Bambang Yudhoyono, won a landslide victory in the first round, with just over sixty per cent of the vote. With his political party also coming first in the parliamentary elections, 2009 was President Yudhoyono's year: he becomes the first post-Suharto president to serve more than one term, and the first Indonesian president to be democratically re-elected. Moreover, in 2009 his government could also claim other significant achievements, including continuing positive economic performance which largely spared Indonesia from the worst effects of the global financial crisis, and, after two bombings in Jakarta in July, the killing by police of key Islamist terrorists. His government also demonstrated an increasingly confident posture and high profile on the world stage. With the third successful elections since Indonesia's transition from authoritarian rule began in 1998, the year also marked a milestone in democratic consolidation.

Yet amid the triumph, both for President Yudhoyono and for Indonesian democracy, there were also stumbles, some of which point toward future dangers. The administration of the elections was bungled — so badly that had the margin of Yudhoyono's victory been narrower, the very legitimacy of his victory may have been in doubt. In the final months of 2009, the President's efforts to form a new government and set out an agenda for a second term were overshadowed by a series of interconnected corruption scandals, exposing serious misdeeds

EDWARD ASPINALL is a Senior Fellow in the Department of Political and Social Change, Australian National University.

and a culture of mendacity in the bureaucracy that not only cast a pall over the President's much-vaunted achievements on the anti-corruption front but also pointed to underlying systemic problems in Indonesian democracy.

The Legislative Elections: Yudhoyono's Dominance and Party Realignments

The year 2009 dawned with all political forces concentrating on preparations for the April legislative polls. Approximately 171 million voters were to vote in over half a million polling booths around the country, for 560 seats in Indonesia's national parliament, the DPR (Dewan Perwakilan Rakyat, People's Representative Council), 132 seats in the less powerful DPD (Dewan Perwakilan Daerah, Regional Representative Council), and for several thousand seats in the thirty-three provincial legislatures and about 500 district legislatures around the country. In many ways, the legislative elections are thus a multitude of separate local polls fought out by individual candidates mobilizing local networks and appealing to local concerns. They are also, as in any democracy, an important moment of nationwide political participation and an opportunity for voters to pass judgment on their national government and leaders.

President Yudhoyono was the dominant national political figure entering the election year, and the ease and magnitude of his victory, and that of his party, Partai Demokrat, were the striking features of the whole electoral cycle in 2009. Up to the middle of 2008, public opinion polls had shown that Yudhoyono's popularity was in decline, and for a time his predecessor and chief rival, Megawati Soekarnoputri, was ahead. It seemed that Yudhoyono would be the latest victim of the mood of cynicism and disenchantment through which the Indonesian public has viewed most of their political leaders since the new democratic era began in 1999.

Several factors combined to put Yudhoyono in a commanding position as the election year dawned, including the paucity of credible opposition and the relative health of the economy, despite the global financial crisis (see below). Most important were a number of economic policies by which the government made direct payments to poorer Indonesians. In particular, a direct cash assistance (BLT, Bantuan Langsung Tunai) programme was launched in mid-2008 to compensate over eighteen million poor families with payments of 100,000 rupiah (US$10) per month when fuel prices increased due to rises in the world price of oil. These payments continued, despite the subsequent decline in fuel prices, with the third and final round made in March 2009, just weeks before the legislative election. Along with other measures benefitting the poor (notably, credit programmes and education subsidies) this programme amounted to US$2 billion between mid-2008 and February 2009.[1] Analysts have noted how it was precisely at the time that these measures were introduced that Yudhoyono began to experience a turnaround in his electoral fortunes, indicated by opinion poll approval ratings that increased from 25 per cent in June 2008 to 50.3 per cent in February 2009.[2]

Not surprisingly, the campaign themes of Partai Demokrat and Yudhoyono made much of the government's economic achievements and policies, in areas such as reduction of fuel prices, increased funding for health and education, reduction of foreign debt, and the like. Campaigning was also heavily focused on the person of Yudhoyono, summed up in the main slogan: *Lanjutkan!* which can be translated as "continue" or "proceeding as before". By the time of the parliamentary elections in April, opinion polls had made it clear that Partai Demokrat, which is little more than a personal electoral vehicle for Yudhoyono and does not represent a coherent party machinery or ideology in its own right, was in a leading position. In the end it won 20.9 per cent of the vote, almost tripling its 2004 result and making it the only party of government to achieve an improved vote since the introduction of democratic elections in 1999. This result also made it one of the most successful parties in post-Suharto Indonesia (only Partai Demokrasi Indonesia Perjuangan [PDIP] in 1999 and GOLKAR in 1999 and 2004 have done better).

The other side of the coin of the increased Partai Demokrat vote was the declining popularity of virtually all established political parties. Most major parties that won seats in the first post-Suharto elections in 1999 experienced a decline in their support in 2009, adding to earlier falls in 2004, and pointing to widespread and underlying disillusionment with established political forces (the only exception was Partai Keadilan Sejahtera [PKS], see below). One result of this pattern was a continuation of a trend of fragmentation of the political map. Thus, whereas the two biggest parties in 1999 (then PDIP and GOLKAR) had between them won 56 per cent of the vote and then 40 per cent in 2004, in 2009 the two largest parties (now Partai Demokrat and GOLKAR) achieved only 34 per cent. In 1999, the five largest parties between them won 86 per cent of the vote, in 2004 they won 66 per cent, and in 2009 only 61 per cent. Moreover, at the national level a little over 18 per cent of voters chose small parties that failed to meet the new electoral threshold of 2.5 per cent, and which would thus not be represented in the national parliament, the DPR.[3]

Particularly noteworthy was the decline of Islamic parties, which collectively gained a little over 29 per cent of valid votes, down from 37 per cent in 1999 and 38 per cent in 2004. Many Islamic parties had suffered from the same maladies that affected most major parties over the last decade, including internal conflicts, weak leadership, and corruption scandals. Unlike PD, Islamic parties did not benefit from

TABLE 1
Election Results
Parties reaching the 2.5% electoral threshold for representation in the DPR

Party	1999	2004	2009
Nationalist parties			
Partai Demokrat (Democrat Party)	—	7.5%	20.9%
PDIP, Partai Demokrasi Indonesia Perjuangan (Indonesian Democracy Party of Struggle)	33.7%	18.5%	14.0%
Partai GOLKAR (GOLKAR Party)	22.4%	21.6%	14.5%
Gerindra, Partai Gerakan Indonesia Raya (Greater Indonesia Movement Party)			4.5%
Hanura, Partai Hati Nurani Rakyat (People's Conscience Party)	—	—	3.8%
Islamic parties			
PKS, Partai Keadilan Sejahtera (Prosperous Justice Party)	1.4%	7.3%	7.9%
PAN, Partai Amanat Nasional (National Mandate Party)	7.1%	6.4%	6.0%
PPP, Partai Persatuan Pembangunan (Unity Development Party)	10.7%	8.2%	5.3%
PKB, Partai Kebangkitan Bangsa (National Awakening Party)	12.6%	10.6%	4.9%

close association with a popular president, and they suffered from voters' growing interest in economic policy and performance. As Greg Fealy has pointed out, public opinion polls "show an inverse correlation between the perceived 'Islamic-ness' of a party and its capacity to bring prosperity to the country", with negative results for the Islamic parties.[4] Similar trends also limited the increase in support for the PKS, a party with its roots in a puritanical campus-based movement inspired by the Islamic Brotherhood of the Middle East and which in 2004 had been seen by many analysts as a rising force in Indonesian politics due to the dramatic increase in its vote that year to 7.3 per cent, up from 1.4 per cent in 1999. By 2009, however, "The party's 'clean' and reformist image has been tarnished by several of its prominent figures being implicated in corruption scandals";[5] the party was now increasingly viewed as behaving just like other mainstream parties, and it faced more determined opposition from mainstream Muslim organizations. It achieved only a modest increase to 7.9 per cent, far short of its goal of 20 per cent.

In fact, the decline of the Islamic parties was part of a wider weakening of an old political pattern known by the Indonesian term of *aliran* (stream), by which ordinary voters identified with various social-cultural groups in Indonesian society. The decline of *aliran*-based voting and the rise of a new model drawing on modern campaigning techniques, the media, image-building, and (to a lesser extent) promises of economic and policy performance was already apparent in 2004.[6] It became even more obvious in 2009, with traditional *aliran*-style parties (if we include PDIP) now winning less than 50 per cent of the vote and some (such as PKB, National Awakening Party, which appeals to traditionalist Muslim voters) suffering a cataclysmic drop in support. Parties and candidates put much more emphasis on the design of slick campaign materials and advertisements. AGB Nielsen Media Research estimates that government and political party spending on advertising in the first half of the year alone was 2.154 trillion rupiah, (US$224 million), largely due to elections,[7] and pollsters and consultants played an important role in designing and running most campaigns.[8] At the grassroots, the decline of appeals based on cultural loyalties is reflected more in the continuing and expanding role of "money politics" in campaigning, including promises or transfers of cash or other material benefits in exchange for votes, and in the role of political brokers in mediating relations between candidates and voters.[9]

Another sign of the declining role of collective identities in voting was the fact that the only parties to experience large increases in votes this year were parties that were effectively personal vehicles of prominent politicians (who also happened to be former generals). The most important was Partai Demokrat, the other two were Partai Gerakan Indonesia Raya (Greater Indonesia Movement Party, Gerindra), led by ex-President Suharto's former son-in-law, Prabowo Subianto, and Partai Hati Nurani Bangsa (National Conscience Party, Hanura), led by former Commander-in-Chief of the Armed Forces, Wiranto. Winning 4.46 per cent and 3.77 per cent of the vote respectively, these were the only two new parties to exceed the 2.5 per cent electoral threshold and gain seats in the national parliament. Prabowo and Gerindra were especially important, partly because Prabowo's Suharto-era credentials and poor human rights record (he was found guilty by a military tribunal for his role in the 1998 disappearance of student activists) stoked fears among Indonesian liberals about the political resurrection of authoritarian political actors. He was also important because of the nature of his campaign: adopting fiery nationalist oratory and running well-produced television commercials, he condemned government policies for neglecting the poor, selling out to foreign interests, and being enslaved by "neo-liberalism". By doing so, he largely set the terms of the whole election debate, requiring President

Yudhoyono and his aides to repeatedly reject the neo-liberal label and emphasize economic policies of their own that benefited the poor. However, as Marcus Mietzner has pointed out, both Wiranto and Prabowo poured tens of millions of dollars into their campaigns and must have been disappointed with results that were "disproportionately low to that investment".[10] Even so, their role points to the growing electoral influence of powerful individuals rather than massive party machines or social constituencies. More significantly, Prabowo's campaign points to a space for populist challenges to establishment politics that has opened in Indonesia after a decade of democratization, and which may be important in the next elections in 2014.

The rise of more individuated voting patterns was reinforced by the increased prominence of individual *candidates* in the legislative elections as a result of a change to Indonesia's electoral system produced by a Constitutional Court decision in December 2008. This decision had the effect of introducing an open party list system, by which voters had a choice of voting for a party only or for an individual party candidate. Parties that won a seat in a particular electoral district were then required to allocate that seat to the candidate with the most individual votes (previously a candidate's position on the party's list of candidates was most important). This decision radically altered the nature of campaigning, with legislative candidates now pouring their resources and efforts into promoting their own individual candidacies, rather than those of their parties. Wealthy candidates were reportedly pouring up to 4 or 5 billion rupiah (US$420,000–530,000) into their campaigns. Indeed, in many places the new system effectively led to the important axis of competition being between candidates of the same party. Candidates were also forced to invest large sums in paying for teams of scrutineers at polling booths to ensure that there was no manipulation in vote counting (for example, by switching votes of an individual candidate to count for his or her party instead), and there were many reports that precisely this sort of manipulation was rampant. The new system also resulted in some established politicians, such as the DPR speaker and prominent leader of GOLKAR, Agung Laksono, losing to candidates who had greater name recognition, and an increase in the number of celebrities (film, television, and music artists) who won legislative seats.

Presidential Elections and Their Aftermath

In the weeks that followed the April legislative elections, as is by now becoming a tradition in Indonesia, national political dynamics were dominated by bargaining and jockeying leading to the announcement of presidential and vice-presidential tickets. After considering a number of potential candidates, in the end President Yudhoyono chose as his running-mate Boediono, a modest and widely-respected technocrat who had previously served the President as Coordinating Minister for Economic Affairs and Governor of Bank Indonesia, the central bank. Yudhoyono's choice of a non-party technocrat re-emphasized the role economic management would play in his election campaign and second term, but also pointed to the difficulties that had previously arisen in his relations with his former Vice-President, Jusuf Kalla, who as Chairperson of GOLKAR had political interests of his own that did not always coincide with those of Yudhoyono. The nomination of Boediono also indicated Yudhoyono's confidence in his chances of electoral victory, because Boediono had no party machine with which to campaign, nor was he a popular figure among some nationalist and Islamic parties. The President's main contender, Megawati Soekarnoputri, eventually chose to run with Prabowo, integrating Prabowo's populist critique of neo-liberalism into her own campaign. Jusuf Kalla, who had been effectively spurned by Yudhoyono, also ran, though he must have known he had little chance of success, choosing Wiranto as his running-mate. In the end, the presidential campaign was an anti-climax, with opinion polls consistently showing Yudhoyono far ahead of his rivals. Some spice was added to the campaign by the vigor with which Prabowo pressed his populist critique, and by some underhanded campaigning questioning Boediono's Islamic credentials. In the end, however, these efforts were minor distractions for the Yudhoyono juggernaut, with the President winning an unprecedented first round victory with 60.8 per cent of the vote, as well as absolute majorities in twenty-six of Indonesia's thirty-three provinces and pluralities in two others. Megawati came a distant second with 26.8 per cent and Jusuf Kalla secured only 12.4 per cent.

As part of what has become another established pattern in Indonesian politics, immediately after the presidential election the political elite refocused its attention on the formation of a cabinet and the opportunities for power-sharing this presented. As is also conventional, President Yudhoyono announced he would form a cabinet that combined both professionals and party representatives, with parties that had supported him in the presidential elections especially set to be rewarded. All of Indonesia's post-Suharto cabinets have been broadly-inclusive affairs, in which most major parties strive to be included in order to have access to the policymaking powers and resources that come with government. As the founder of Partai Amanat Nasional (PAN), Amien Rais, had explained earlier in the year, "forming a coalition with the losing side, and not with the winning side, that's a waste."[11] Thus, GOLKAR, which had supported Jusuf Kalla in the presidential election, quickly reoriented itself under a new leader, mining magnate and former Minister Aburizal Bakrie, and announced that it would support the government. Even an important group in PDIP, led by Megawati's husband Taufiq Kiemas, tried to bring the party into cabinet, but Megawati resisted. In the end, when Yudhoyono announced his cabinet in October, only three out of the nine parties in the DPR (PDIP, Hanura, and Gerindra) were not represented. In a cabinet of thirty-four, twenty posts were filled by party representatives, with the parties gaining the most seats being Partai Demokrat (six posts), PKS (four), and GOLKAR (three). Again following established patterns, most of the key economic ministries went to non-party technocrats and key security positions went to former military or police men. The overall shape of the cabinet thus continues the pattern of broadly-based "rainbow coalition" cabinets that is a tradition of post-Suharto politics. Many liberal commentators were disappointed that the cabinet contained relatively few strong reformers, and its composition seemed to put paid to the predictions of many that Yudhoyono would be bolder in his second term. However, such disappointments are also part of the post-Suharto political norm.

Poor-quality Elections

Before moving on, it is necessary to examine another aspect of the elections: the administrative and technical problems that plagued them, producing a much lower-quality election than in 2004. In part, the problems were due to the nature of the KPU (General Elections Commission). After 2004, a large number of KPU commissioners and staff were imprisoned for corrupt dealings in the procurement process for election supplies, leading to loss of expertise and institutional memory in the commission. The new KPU commissioners were mostly undistinguished bureaucrats, in part because "the KPU recruitment committee had disqualified several respected academics and NGO activists in the first round of the selection process".[12] Moreover, both government and donor financial support for the election was much reduced.

Space does not permit full consideration of the administrative failures that affected the elections. One key problem involved the voter registry. Compilation of the registry had been taken over by the Ministry of Home Affairs in 2006. The budget for this programme was enormous, and many experts suspect that the patronage opportunities it provided was a major incentive for officials at the ministry. The population data the ministry eventually provided to the KPU was outdated and contained many errors. Door-to-door verification of the registry by the KPU did not go as planned, because funds were running late, and only limited time was allowed for voters to check for themselves whether they were listed, and this process itself was hardly publicized. The upshot was that large numbers of voters — perhaps many millions — were simply not on the list and could not vote in the parliamentary elections. Then, with the list still not properly updated days before the presidential election, Kalla and Megawati met to demand that the KPU allow unregistered voters to take part. At this point, potential disaster was averted by a last-minute decision by the Constitutional Court allowing people to vote merely by showing their national ID cards. There was a plethora of other problems with the administration of the polls, including problems with the printing and distribution of ballot papers, and delays and breakdown in the counting process and allocation of seats.

Both Kalla and Megawati challenged the results of the presidential elections in the Constitutional Court, alleging that the voter lists had been deliberately manipulated, their supporters disenfranchized, and (implausibly) the counting subject to political interference. Megawati was characteristically blunt, saying the elections had produced only "a fake appearance of democracy".[13] In fact, as argued by Rizal Sukma, it was "the incompetence of the KPU, rather than any demonstrated systematic fraud or manipulation... that provided the basis for contestation of the election results."[14] Even so, these failures were significant: had the margin of Yudhoyono's victory been narrower there would have been serious doubts about its legitimacy, and a political crisis could have ensued. Overall, the near-debacle of the 2009 elections provides a salutary lesson about the dangers of taking Indonesia's democratic progress for granted, or of assuming that institutional achievements reached in the past have been locked in.

Security and Violence

Early in Indonesia's democratic transition, no annual survey of political events in the country would have been complete without a major focus on communal and separatist conflicts and political violence. Such violence has steadily declined in Indonesia since the early 2000s, as democracy has consolidated, and 2009 provided further evidence of this trend. Even the one obvious exception — terrorist bombings in Jakarta in July — is best seen as part of a long-term downward trajectory rather than marking a new upswing.

The first major bombings in Indonesia in almost four years occurred when terrorists detonated two bombs in adjacent luxury hotels in Jakarta on 17 July, killing nine people and injuring over fifty. The bombings indicated a high degree of planning and coordination: one of the plotters was a florist who was placed in one of the hotels three years earlier, and one of the suicide bombers successfully targeted an informal breakfast gathering of mostly foreign businesspeople (the most successful terrorist attack so far on a "high-value" target). Security officials immediately blamed Noordin Mohammed Top, a Malaysian jihadist who has been a key player in all the major terrorist attacks targeting Western interests in Indonesia since 2003, and who broke away from the radical Islamist organization Jemaah Islamiyah (JI) in 2004. He had since helped to establish a loose network of militants, including former JI supporters, followers of other splinter groups, and even more diffuse networks.[15] While the bombings were thus a reminder of the regenerative powers of jihadist terrorist networks in Indonesia, in fact these bombings may in the long run be a turning point because they provided police with crucial new information that allowed them to break open Noordin's network. In a series of bloody raids over the following months, police shot dead most organizers of the bombings, with their chief prize being Noordin Top himself who was killed on 17 September in Central Java. Most of the senior jihadists are now dead, imprisoned, or eschewing terrorist activity.

It would be premature to conclude that terrorist violence in Indonesia will end. Many members of the networks who have supported previous attacks are still at large, or are in jail and will eventually be released. Even so, another important effect of the bombing was to underline the illegitimacy of such actions in Indonesia. After the first Bali bombings in 2002, many ordinary Indonesian Muslims and opinion-leaders appeared, if not sympathetic to the bombers, at least ambivalent about them, with many expressing skepticism that Muslims were responsible. After the 2009 bombings, there were numerous signs that public opinion had decisively shifted. For example, local residents in a village in Central Java demonstrated to oppose the burial of Urwah, one of the Jakarta bombers, and there were similar protests or localized reactions against suspected Islamist extremists elsewhere.[16] Public discourse in the media also had become almost unreservedly hostile to the bombers.

As for the other conflicts that characterized Indonesia's early transition, most have faded. The year 2009 marked another step in the stabilization of one of the worst-afflicted areas, Aceh. As part of a peace deal reached in Helsinki in 2005, the former rebels of GAM (Free Aceh Movement) agreed to give up their arms and their independence goal, and were in exchange offered the chance to compete in elections. Former guerillas and their allies had from 2006 already won important executive government elections in the province, including for the governorship; in 2009 they had the chance to compete for seats in legislatures, by dint of an exception to Indonesia's national legal framework allowing local parties to run in elections in Aceh (elsewhere, only parties that have a broad national presence can do so). Partai Aceh, the party formed by former GAM members, emerged as by far the most important party, winning a near-majority in the provincial parliament and becoming the largest party in sixteen of twenty-three district parliaments. In the presidential election, President Yudhoyono won an astonishing 93 per cent of the vote in Aceh, by far the best result for him throughout Indonesia, and indicating strong appreciation among Acehnese voters for the role played by the president in bringing peace there, itself a hopeful sign for the consolidation of the peace process.

At the other end of the archipelago, in the two provinces of Papua and West Papua, the elections also passed mostly peacefully. However, sporadic outbursts of political unrest continued throughout the year, such as a series of protests in the town of Timika after security forces announced they had shot dead Kelly Kwalik, the most famous leader of the separatist Free Papua Movement, in December. There is no reason to believe that Kwalik's killing will represent a breakthrough in the campaign against Papuan separatism, as might the shooting of Noordin Top in the campaign against terrorism, but neither did developments in Papua point toward a dramatic upswing in violence or political tension. Instead, Papua will continue to be a chronic, unresolved but low-level political and security problem for Indonesia into the future.

Corruption Controversies

Throughout 2009, a series of interconnected corruption scandals and investigations had important implications for President Yudhoyono's government and for Indonesian democracy. At the centre of them was the Corruption Eradication Commission (Komisi Pemberantasan Korupsi, *KPK*), a special body with extraordinary powers to investigate and prosecute corruption cases. In the final months of 2009, just as Yudhoyono should have been celebrating his re-election, public attention was riveted to the dramatic developments in an apparent high-level conspiracy to undermine the KPK. For weeks on end, reports about the commission and corruption dominated the front pages of the nation's newspapers and received blanket coverage on the round-the-clock television news channels, galvanizing public opinion (especially in the middle classes) in a way that arguably has not happened since the protests that felled Suharto in 1998. A popular movement to defend the KPK grew in the media, the Internet, and the streets. The credibility of Indonesia's political elite, its law enforcement bodies, and even its newly re-elected president were severely tested.

Corruption has been the Achilles' heel of Indonesia's democratization from the start, with repeated scandals having damaging effects on public confidence in government institutions. In recent years, however, the public has been delighted by the KPK's work in investigating and prosecuting legislators, ministers, and other senior officials, and for using sting operations and wiretaps to expose many of their more sordid dealings.[17] President Yudhoyono, too, has made much of his anti-corruption credentials, for example emphasizing that he did not prevent the KPK from successfully prosecuting the father of his own daughter-in-law, a Bank Indonesia official, in 2008. Through 2009, the KPK continued to play a significant role in corruption eradication, continuing public investigations against prominent persons. By November 2009 the Commission was reporting that it had salvaged 139.8 billion rupiah (US$14.5 million) of state funds throughout 2009, as a result of 31 successful convictions.[18] Partly as a result of KPK activities and the institution's high public profile, Indonesia's place in global rankings of corruption continued to improve: in 2009 it ranked 111 out of 180 countries on Transparency International's Corruption Perception Index (back in 2001 it was equal third from the bottom, in a list that then included 91 countries).[19]

However, the KPK, too, became infected with the taint of criminality after a sensational murder case early in the year implicated its chairperson, Antasari Azhar. The victim, Nasrudin Zulkarnaen, was the director of a subsidiary of a state-owned company, PT Rajawali Nusantara Indonesia (RNI), whose director was himself being tried (and was later convicted) for a 4.4 billion rupiah (US$418,000) corruption case involving a sugar importing scheme. Nasrudin was killed in a drive-by shooting in South Jakarta on 14 March 2009. Before long, police investigators accused Antasari of being behind the murder, and also arrested the alleged hitmen and middlemen. In making their case, police and prosecutors focused on a love triangle involving Nasrudin, Antasari, and an attractive female golf caddy, Rhani Julianti. It was alleged that Nasrudin was using evidence of sexual liaisons between Antasari and Rhani to intimidate and blackmail Antasari, possibly in connection with the investigations into RNI. Another theory was that the murder was a by-product of corrupt dealings between the two men (at the trial Nasrudin's first wife testified that Antasari and her husband had unspecified business dealings and that Nasrudin had earned a 1.5 billion rupiah (US$156,000) commission from "a business project he had handled with Antasari".[20]) Antasari and his associates' trial is still proceeding as this chapter is being finalized, and many aspects of the case remain murky.

The Antasari case might have been only an unsavoury footnote in the history of Indonesian anti-corruption efforts but for the fact that it provided an opportunity for numerous members of the national political elite (many of whom had been targeted by KPK investigations) to try to undermine the commission. Some politicians called for the KPK to be dissolved, others argued that its powers should be curtailed. President Yudhoyono himself publically warned that the KPK had become an "extraordinary powerholder, accountable only to Allah", and that such "power must not go unchecked".[21] A new anti-corruption bill was being debated in the DPR (because a decision of the Constitutional Court had earlier invalidated sections of the original law) and most parties appeared determined to strip the KPK of key powers to prosecute and to wiretap (in the end these reductions of KPK powers were dropped).

Adding to the intensity of the campaign, and further complicating the picture, the KPK was at the same time investigating another major scandal with the potential to implicate senior government officials. This scandal involved a bailout of Bank Century, a private bank that had been under Bank Indonesia supervision since 2005 and had tottered on the brink of collapse when the global financial crisis hit in late 2008. The government propped up the bank, saying that it threatened the stability of the financial system, with the cost eventually blowing out to 6.76 trillion rupiah (US$716 million). Investigations revealed serious malfeasance in the management of the bank, resulting in the conviction and imprisonment of its director, Robert Tantular, in September 2009. According to an investigation by the Supreme Audit Agency, made public in November, around 91 per cent of the bailout funds were "aimed at covering losses stemming from fraud and irregularities committed by shareholders."[22] Moreover, the media publically speculated that many politically-connected big depositors in the bank had been able to withdraw their money after the bailout, in violation of a regulation by which the government guaranteed only small deposits. Many of President Yudhoyono's political foes believed that by this and other means, much of the bailout funds ended up financing political allies of the president and supporting his re-election campaign (it should be stressed that no evidence had been publically presented to support such claims by the time of writing). By late 2009, the DPR had launched an investigation, with many legislators focusing their opprobrium on Finance Minister Sri Mulyani and Boediono (ironically, two of the government officials with the strongest reputations for personal probity).[23]

Back in mid-2009, when many of the details of the Bank Century scandal were still unknown to the public, the KPK was already investigating the case. It was later revealed to have tapped the telephone of Susno Djuadi, the head of the National Police's Criminal Detective Body, who had allegedly been involved trying to broker a deal, for a fee, by which a tycoon could have US$18 million released from the bank. Susno told the press his telephone was being tapped, and gave an angry interview in *Tempo* magazine where he likened the KPK's conflict with the police to an ineffectual *cicak* (gecko) trying to fight a *buaya* (crocodile), a nomenclature that was enthusiastically embraced by supporters of the commission.[24] Around the same time, events in the Antasari case took a serious turn when police announced that Antasari had revealed a case of bribery involving other KPK commissioners (Susno Djuadi himself was involved in the investigations). They said that they had uncovered a plot by KPK commissioners to extort money from another graft suspect, Anggoro Widjojo, a businessman involved in corruption in the supply of radio equipment to the Forestry Ministry who was a fugitive from justice in Singapore.

At first, this allegation looked like it might deal a serious blow to the credibility of the KPK, but before long there were signs of a frame-up. In late October, extracts of transcripts of more KPK phone taps began to circulate, this time of conversations between Anggoro's brother, Anggodo Widjojo, and various officials and third parties pointing to a conspiracy to fabricate evidence against the two KPK commissioners, Bibit Samad Riyanto and Chandra Hamzah, whom the police were accusing of being behind the extortion. With the public increasingly skeptical of the case, the police pressed ahead and detained the two KPK commissioners on 29 October, provoking a massive public outcry. Within forty-eight hours 110,000 persons had joined a Facebook group defending the pair, with a million signing up within nine days. The media exploded into a frenzy of condemnation of the police, prosecutors, and government, and there were large demonstrations. Responding to the pressure, the President formed a team to investigate the case and, to the delight of the public but to Yudhoyono's chagrin, the Constitutional Court publically played the wiretapped conversations between Anggodo and a colourful cast of characters, including police officers and prosecutors. The recordings not only exposed how Anggodo and his associates had tried to frame the two KPK commissioners, but also turned a harsh light on to the culture of corruption and "case brokerage" that pervades the justice sector. After a delay, the public outcry forced the release of the two commissioners, and President Yudhoyono ordered stern action against the "legal mafia", though without offering much by way of specifics.

Throughout the affair, President Yudhoyono acted in a manner that was widely criticized not only for being hesitant and ineffectual (a charge frequently levied against him in the past), but also for effectively giving the green light to the campaign against the KPK. He was slow to stop the prosecution against the KPK commissioners or to take action against the officials implicated in the conspiracy. In fact, the only times Yudhoyono seemed to become personally animated was when his own name was blackened. Thus, when it was first leaked that in the taped Anngodo conversations Yudhoyono was mentioned as supporting the conspirators, his tone was typically personal: "I'm hurt, terribly hurt." At the same time, however, he also pointed his finger at the KPK: "Is wiretapping in line with the law? Imagine if people can buy bugging devices and wiretapping as they please."[25] When anti-corruption campaigners planned demonstrations in early December he warned darkly about character assassination and a conspiracy to topple him.[26] DPR members enthusiastically defended the police and their investigation even as its credibility crumbled in the eyes of the public, while Yudhoyono's new Information Minister prepared a government regulation that would restrict wiretapping. Added to other events during the imbroglio, such as the mobilization of thugs and kampung-dwellers in counter-demonstrations to condemn the KPK, and attempts by the national police chief to call in media editors and warn them against negative coverage, it is little wonder that some commentators spoke of a return to authoritarian habits associated with the Suharto era.

The snarled thicket of corruption investigations, allegations, and counter-allegations exposed through 2009 was complex and even confusing for many members of the public. Yet it provided extraordinarily graphic evidence of the penetration of a culture of corruption throughout government and law enforcement agencies. It also took some of the gloss off President Yudhoyono's election triumph. At the same time, the massive public response, as well as the powerful media and civil society campaign to expose and condemn the attack on the KPK, were testimony to the continuing depth of hostility to corruption that animates Indonesian society.

The Economy

An important part of the context for the re-election of Susilo Bambang Yudhoyono was the relative health of Indonesia's economy, despite the impact of the global financial crisis that plunged some of Indonesia's neighbours, including Singapore, Malaysia, and Thailand, into serious economic contractions forecast to be in the range of 6–10 per cent. In Indonesia, the crisis did have immediate negative effects, such as causing a (temporary) depreciation of the rupiah of about 25 per cent, a decline in the value of the stock market by 56 per cent, as well as dramatic falls of investment in crucial sectors such as manufacturing and transport.[27] By mid-2009, however, it was already clear that Indonesia was being spared the worst effects of the crisis. The growth rate of the economy declined, from 6.4 per cent year-on-year in the second quarter of 2008 to 4 per cent in the second quarter of 2009, but it kept far from negative territory. Crucially, too, the effects on the poor of the crisis were limited; if anything their situation improved somewhat. Unemployment fell, from 8.4 to 7.9 per cent between August 2008 and August 2009.[28] The poverty rate also declined, from 15.4 to 14.1 per cent in the year to March 2009.[29] Inflation, after peaking at 12 per cent in late 2008, fell to below 3 per cent by late 2009 because of the central bank gradually tightening the money supply, with the result that price rises did not have a negative impact on the poor, traditionally a very politically-sensitive issue in Indonesia.[30] When we add the effects of the direct cash transfers discussed above, it is perhaps not surprising that attempts by President Yudhoyono's electoral rivals to denigrate his economic achievements failed to make an impression on voters.

Economists have suggested several reasons for the light impact of the global financial crisis on Indonesia. These include Indonesia's relatively low exposure to international trade, with only about 17 per cent of Indonesian output being exported.[31] The government also launched a major fiscal stimulus package in early 2009, amounting to 71.3 trillion rupiah (about US$7.5 billion), almost 80 per cent of which consisted of cuts in taxes and duties (reflecting the bureaucracy's limited ability to quickly deliver programmes involving new spending), with the remainder being directed at increases in subsidies and government spending, especially on infrastructure[32] The cash transfers to poorer Indonesians also had a stimulatory effect on the economy, as did the formal and informal spending associated with the elections themselves.

Given the robustness of Indonesia's economy amid such difficult global circumstances, and other signs of growing economic weight (such as Indonesia's entry into the ranks of middle-income countries several years ago), it is perhaps not surprising that many Indonesian and international commentators are pointing to Indonesia as an emerging economic power, even as a new BRIC (the term used to describe the emerging Brazil, Russia, India, and China high-growth and high-population economies).[33] In fact, when viewed over the term of Yudhoyono's government, the performance of the Indonesian economy has been solid, but not spectacular. Growth rates have averaged at 5.7 per cent, lower than the president's target of 7 per cent, and the government has persistently failed to reach its employment and poverty-reduction targets.[34] Key problems have included continuing low investment in infrastructure, as well as stagnation or slow growth of the manufacturing sector, with the result that improvements in employment and poverty figures have been limited. At the outset of his second term, Yudhoyono has re-emphasized many of his former economic goals, including a target of

7 per cent growth by 2014, further reductions in poverty and unemployment, improvements in infrastructure development, and bureaucratic reform. Economists, however, question whether the poverty reduction goals can be achieved if growth does not hit the 7 per cent rate well before 2014.[35]

Indonesia on the World Stage[36]

In terms of foreign policy, the most striking trend in 2009 was Indonesia's increasing international profile. A hallmark of the Yudhoyono presidency has been an aspiration for Indonesia to play a more prominent international role matching its status as a consolidating democracy, an emerging economy, and the third most populous country, with the largest number of Muslims. Moreover, President Yudhoyono enjoys the limelight of international politics and gives every sign of wanting to make diplomacy a bigger priority in his second term.

Following from Indonesia's role in hosting the United Nations Climate Change Conference in Bali in December 2008, during 2009 Indonesia had several further opportunities to demonstrate its growing weight in world affairs. For example, in November, Indonesia signed a "Partnership and Cooperation Agreement (PCA)" with the European Union, prioritizing trade and investment, environment, education and human rights, making Indonesia the first Asian country to sign such an agreement with the EU.[37] The most significant indication of Indonesia's ability to access the big players was probably President Yudhoyono's participation in the G-20 summit in Pittsburgh in September, when it was announced that the G-20 would replace the G-8 as the main council for economic coordination between the world's wealthy nations. Immediately after the summit, President Yudhoyono gave a well-publicized speech at Harvard University where he noted that Indonesia was pleased that "the G-20 has been institutionalized, and looks set to be the premier forum for international economic cooperation." The main theme of the speech was inter-civilizational harmony, and Indonesia's role as a "bridge between the Islamic and the western worlds."[38]

Despite gaining access to more important global forums, President Yudhoyono's government is still struggling to articulate a foreign policy role concomitant with its increased profile. The President himself has at times promoted sometimes unrealistic goals when addressing global audiences, for instance in the past suggesting that Indonesia could play a role as mediator in the Palestine conflict or between Iran and its critics on nuclear policy. At Pittsburgh he similarly announced that Indonesia would reduce its carbon emissions by 26 per cent by 2020, with that figure rising to 41 per cent if the country received international assistance. While apparently placing Indonesia at the forefront of the international fight against global warning, and gaining much sympathetic international media coverage as a result, the President's goal was immediately questioned by experts who knew it was unrealistic given Indonesia's continued rapid rate of deforestation and its reliance on coal-powered electricity plants. Marty Natalegawa, appointed as Foreign Minister in Yudhoyono's new cabinet, has a more modest assessment of Indonesia's global role, telling *Tempo* magazine soon after he was sworn in, for example, that Indonesia would be the "last to say that we will be a part of the solution" to the Palestinian problem, describing this conflict as better left to the "big players" such as the United States and Russia.[39]

One part of the explanation for the Yudhoyono government's desire to play a more significant global role has been its growing frustrations closer to home, especially in the Association of Southeast Asian Nations (ASEAN), which has been traditionally central to Indonesia's foreign policy. Adding to frustration in recent years over issues such as the new ASEAN Charter or attempts to urge Myanmar to pursue meaningful democratic reform, in 2009 Indonesia lobbied for the establishment of a relatively powerful ASEAN human rights commission, but ended up with a largely toothless "ASEAN Inter-governmental Commission on Human Rights", as a result of objections from all other ASEAN member countries. As an unnamed source close to the process told the *Jakarta Post*, "At the end it was a case of one against nine", prompting the journalist to ask "is it any surprise then that there is a growing narrative here questioning the sustainability of ASEAN as a cornerstone of Indonesia's foreign policy when such a divergence of values is so evident?"[40] One influential foreign policy thinker to propose such a position was Rizal Sukma of the Centre for Strategic and International Studies who has argued that "Indonesia has always been forced into compromise or into a corner by other members for the sake of ASEAN" and that it was time for the country to break out of this "golden cage" and develop a "post-ASEAN foreign policy".[41]

Adding to Indonesia's frustrations in the region in 2009 were a series of rancorous disputes with Malaysia, including renewed tension over incursions by Malaysian navy and coastguard boats into the Ambalat sea block off East Kalimantan, protests about mistreatment of Indonesian guest workers in Malaysia, and, most dramatically, a dispute about theft of Indonesian cultural property that was triggered by a Malaysian tourism television advertisement that featured a distinctively Balinese dance. All these issues led to the by now regular outraged nationalist condemnations of Malaysian perfidy and arrogance in the Indonesian media, and by prominent national figures (former leader of PAN, Amien Rais, for example, suggested that Indonesia should start practicing "military diplomacy" against Malaysia).[42] On the other hand, emphasizing Indonesia's growing weight in the region, at an ASEAN summit in Thailand in October, it was agreed that ASEAN finance ministers would in the future always meet before G-20 meetings to coordinate their positions, effectively meaning that other ASEAN countries are recognizing Indonesia's role as a channel for them to access major world powers.[43] Overall, although Indonesia experienced a further increase in its global profile in 2009, and a continuation of frustrations closer to home, the country still seems to be struggling to make use of that profile by articulating a coherent and powerful international vision. As Rizal Sukma put it, "it's all about form so far, now it's time to start thinking about content."[44]

Conclusion

The year 2009 provided further positive evidence of Indonesia's post-Suharto transformation. With over ten years of transition behind it, the democratic maturation of Indonesia's political institutions and population was demonstrated by the third set of national elections since the transition began in 1998. Despite the administrative glitches, the polls passed generally peacefully, and they had a routine and rather mundane aspect, failing to excite passions or even greatly arouse the expectations of most voters. The fact that President Yudhoyono was re-elected with such a large majority, in a poll that was not tainted by systematic manipulation or fraud, is itself an important sign that Indonesian voters are at least minimally satisfied with their political institutions and leaders. Political disorder and violence continued to wane, with the Jakarta terrorist bombings hardly affecting the country's overall stability, but instead significantly weakening the perpetrators. Moreover, the country also has a relatively successful economy, and has a growing international role and significance. These are no mean achievements, and they all point to the solid progress that Indonesia made in locking in its democratic progress during the first Yudhoyono term.

But some developments in 2009 show that Indonesia is not the unqualified democratic success story it is sometimes portrayed as being. Its third post-Suharto elections were very badly organized, and could have sparked a real political crisis had the results been closer. Such severe problems in such a crucial democratic institution point not toward democratic learning and consolidation, but toward backsliding and indifference. The modest electoral successes of Wiranto and, especially, Prabowo show that authoritarian political actors are not persona non grata in Indonesian democracy, and point to a political space that might be occupied by non-democrats in the future. Moreover, there are signs of slippage in the campaign against corruption, with recalcitrants in national politics, the bureaucracy, and law enforcement agencies showing a new confidence, not only by continuing to engage in corrupt practices and evade prosecution, but by trying actively to sabotage the chief institution that has led the corruption eradication campaign, the KPK. And there were also causes for concern in the behavior of a president who is showing, if not authoritarian tendencies, at least increasingly narcissistic ones, and who was at best strikingly complacent in responding to the attacks on the KPK and in reading the effect they were having on public opinion.

It would be wrong to over-dramatize these problems. Each of these negative stories also had its positive side. In the debacle of the administration of the elections, we can point not only to the maturity of Indonesia's voters but also to the positive role played by the nation's Constitutional Court as the arbiter of contentious political disputes and its ability to defuse political tensions before they reach a critical point. In the election campaigns of Wiranto and Prabowo we can see stories of failed authoritarian comebacks. In the ferocity of the attacks on the KPK, we can see the protestations of a ruling caste which has been seriously discomfited by the campaign to eradicate corruption, and in the street protests, media tumult, and Internet activism that followed those attacks there was visible evidence of the continuing energies of a vigilant citizenry and its determination to force greater integrity in public life.

It is therefore far too early to talk about a crisis of Indonesian democracy, with the events of 2009 in many ways pointing to the continuing robustness of the country's democratic system. But it would be equally wrong to ignore the problems and adopt a merely celebratory tone. The first Yudhoyono term, 2004–9, was not a period of dramatic forward movement in democratic reform. Neither Parliament nor the President concentrated on further grand restructuring of Indonesia's political architecture. Instead, it was a period in which the new institutions established in previous years — such as the Constitutional Court and the KPK — began to function. Viewed favourably, as most Indonesian voters apparently do, the first Yudhoyono term was a period of consolidation, and of modest progress. Viewed in another light, it was a period of stasis and perhaps even stagnation. Yudhoyono's next term in office promises to be — quite literally — more of the same. In the composition of his cabinet, and in the nature of his announced policy goals, President Yudhoyono has demonstrated an orientation to a programme of continued but highly cautious democratic, institutional, and economic reform. So far, this has been a recipe for neither democratic triumph nor calamity for Indonesia. But in 2009 there were signs that the long-term effects of such an approach might fall short of what many Indonesians desire out of their democracy, even if they expect little more from it.

Notes

The author thanks his colleagues Greg Fealy and Marcus Mietzner for their very helpful comments on this piece. Of course, they are not responsible for the views expressed in the piece, and any errors of interpretation or fact in it remain the sole responsibility of the author.

[1] Marcus Mietzner, *Indonesia's 2009 Elections: Populism, Dynasties and the Consolidation of the Party System* (Sydney: Lowy Institute for International Policy, 2009), p. 4.

[2] Ibid., p. 4.

[3] The nineteen million voters who voted for parties that did not make the electoral threshold, plus the seventeen million votes that were declared invalid, meant that about 22 per cent of individuals who cast votes in the legislative election did not end up with their votes being represented in the DPR: "Representasi DPR Lebih Rendah", *Kompas*, 13 November 2009.

[4] Greg Fealy, "Indonesia's Islamic Parties in Decline", Inside Story website, 11 May 2009 <http://inside.org.au/indonesia%E2%80%99s-islamic-parties-in-decline/>. Fealy cites polls conducted by the Lembaga Survei Indonesia, LSI. See also Bernhard Platzdasch, "Down But Not", *Inside Indonesia*, no. 97 (July–September 2009) <http://insideindonesia.org/content/view/1210/47/>.

[5] Anthony Bubalo, Greg Fealy, and Whit Mason, *Zealous Democrats: Islamism and Democracy in Egypt, Indonesia and Turkey* (Sydney: Lowy Institute, 2008), p. 50.

[6] See Edward Aspinall, "Elections and the Normalization of Politics in Indonesia", *South East Asia Research* 13, no. 2 (July 2005): 117–56; R. William Liddle and Saiful Mujani, "Leadership, Party, and Religion: Explaining Voting Behavior in Indonesia", *Comparative Political Studies* 40, no. 7 (2007): 832–57.

[7] "Advertising Spending to Increase in Second Half of 2009, Survey Predicts", *Jakarta Globe*, 16 July 2009.

[8] On this trend see Marcus Mietzner, "Political Opinion Polling in Post-authoritarian Indonesia: Catalyst or Obstacle to Democratic Consolidation?" *Bijdragen tot de Taal, Land- en Volkenkunde (BKI)* 165, no. 1 (2009): 95–126; and Muhammad Qodari, "The Professionalisation of Politics: The Growing Role of Polling Organisations and Political Consultants", in *Problems of Democratisation in Indonesia: Elections, Institutions and Society*, edited by Edward Aspinall and Marcus Mietzner (Institute of Southeast Asian Studies, Singapore, 2010).

[9] Two revealing local studies are Blair Palmer, "Services Rendered: Peace, Patronage and Post-conflict Elections in Aceh", in *Problems of Democratisation in Indonesia:*

Elections, Institutions and Society, edited by Edward Aspinall and Marcus Mietzner (Institute of Southeast Asian Studies, Singapore, 2010); and Achmad Uzair Fauzan, "Winning the Villages", *Inside Indonesia*, no. 97 (July–September 2009) <http://insideindonesia.org/content/view/1219/47/>.

[10] Mietzner, *Indonesia's 2009 Elections*, p. 8.

[11] "Amien Rais Arahkan PAN ke Yudhoyono", *Koran Tempo*, 20 April 2009.

[12] Marcus Mietzner, "Chaos and Consolidation", *Inside Indonesia* 97, July–September 2009 <http://insideindonesia.org/content/view/1221/47/>.

[13] "Dia Lagi", *Koran Tempo*, 9 July 2009.

[14] Rizal Sukma, "Indonesian Politics in 2009: Defective Elections, Resilient Democracy", *Bulletin of Indonesian Economic Studies* 45, no. 3 (2009): 325.

[15] *Indonesia: Noordin Top's Support Base*, International Crisis Group, Asia Briefing no. 95 Jakarta/Brussels, 2009.

[16] "Warga Demo Tolak Jenazah Urwah", *Suara Merdeka*, 24 September 2009; "Terrorism Feared, Jama'ah Tabligh Members Expelled", *Jakarta Post*, 19 August 2009.

[17] For a useful summary of the KPK's work, see Gerry van Klinken, "Indonesian Politics in 2008: The Ambiguities of Democratic Change", *Bulletin of Indonesian Economic Studies* 44, no. 3 (2008): 371–77.

[18] "MK, KPK Provide Hope For Rule of Law", *Jakarta Post*, 5 November 2009.

[19] See <http://www.transparency.org/policy_research/surveys_indices/cpi/2009>. My thanks to Marcus Mietzner for this point.

[20] "Nasrudin had close connection with Antasari: Witness", *Jakarta Post*, 4 November 2009.

[21] "Berbahaya, Kekuasaan yang Terlalu Besar dan Tanpa Kontrol", *Kompas*, 25 June 2009.

[22] "Bank Century Rescue Audit Puts Boediono Against the Wall", *Jakarta Post*, 24 November 2009.

[23] Both had been the key decision makers approving the original bailout. Key parties in the DPR had their own reasons to oppose these two, including because they eyed their positions. Sri Mulyani, meanwhile, publically accused Abdurizal Bakrie, the new head of GOLKAR, former Coordinating Minister for people's welfare, and the owner of massive mining and other business interests, of being behind the moves to oust her. She had been responsible for a number of decisions that had harmed Bakrie companies: "Jakarta Official Defends Bailout, *Wall Street Journal*, 10 December 2009.

[24] *Tempo*, 6–12 July 2009.

[25] "SBY Urges Publication of Tapes, Decries Wiretaps", *Jakarta Post*, 31 October 2009.

[26] These comments were similar in their tone of self-absorption bordering on paranoia to remarks the president made immediately after the July bombings in Jakarta, when he linked the bombings to alleged plots to sabotage his re-election and prevent his inauguration as president: "SBY's Speech on the Jakarta Bombings: Full Text", *Jakarta Globe*, 17 July 2009.

27 Mudrajad Kuncoro, Tri Widodo, and Ross H. McLeod, "Survey of Recent Developments", *Bulletin of Indonesian Economic Studies*, 45, no. 2 (2009): 155, 158.

28 "Jobless Rate Falls Below 8%, BPS says", *The Jakarta Post*, 2 December 2009.

29 Budy P. Resosudarmo and Arief A Yusuf, "Survey of Recent Developments", *Bulletin of Indonesian Economic Studies* 45, no. 3 (2009): 303.

30 Ibid., p. 300.

31 Ibid., p. 289.

32 Anton H. Gunawan and Reza Y. Siregar, "Survey of Recent Developments", *Bulletin of Indonesian Economic Studies*, 45, no. 1 (2009): 31.

33 Christian Nolting, "Indonesia: Another 'I' in the BRIC story?", *Business Times* (Singapore), 29 July 2009.

34 Resosudarmo and Yusuf, "Survey of Recent Developments", p. 304.

35 Ibid., p. 304.

36 My thanks to Rizal Sukma for his insights and input to this section.

37 "Indonesia, EU Sign Partnership Agreement", *The Jakarta Post*, 9 November 2009.

38 "Towards Harmony Among Civilizations", speech by Susilo Bambang Yudhoyono President of the Republic of Indonesia at the John F. Kennedy School of Government, Harvard University, Boston, 29 September 2009.

39 "M. Marty Muliana Natalegawa: Tidak Ada Urut Kacang di Deplu", *Tempo*, 2 November 2009.

40 Meidyatama Suryodiningrat, "ASEAN 9, Human Rights 1", *Jakarta Post*, 24 July 2009.

41 Rizal Sukma, "Indonesia Needs a Post-ASEAN Foreign Policy", *Jakarta Post*, 30 June 2009.

42 "Pakai Diplomasi Militer untuk Hadapi Malaysia", *Republika*, 15 June 2009.

43 "ASEAN Seeks Stronger G20 voice", *Jakarta Post*, 25 October 2009.

44 Interview with Rizal Sukma, 11 November 2009, Jakarta.

THE IMPACT OF DOMESTIC AND ASIAN REGIONAL CHANGES ON INDONESIAN FOREIGN POLICY

Dewi Fortuna Anwar

The past decade has seen fundamental and dramatic changes in Indonesian national politics which have affected all aspects of public life. The forced resignation of President Suharto amid the Asian financial crisis in May 1998 ended the stranglehold of the authoritarian New Order regime which had ruled Indonesia for thirty-two years, and ushered in a new *reformasi* era characterized by rejection of many key features of the New Order. In a zeal to outlaw authoritarianism and build a more pluralistic democracy, Indonesia carried out four successive amendments to the 1945 constitution which, among others, abolished the social-political role of the armed forces, ensure a clear separation of power between the executive, the legislative, and the judiciary, enshrine the principles of human rights in the constitution, and allow the development of a truly multiparty system. To prevent the rise of another long-term leader like Suharto who was able to manipulate the Consultative Assembly to elect him for seven consecutive five-year terms, the presidential term has been limited to two non-renewable five-year terms while the president and vice-president are to be directly elected by the people. As a reaction to the overt centralization under the New Order which gave little room for regional initiatives, the post-Suharto governments have also introduced sweeping regional autonomy.

After difficult early years of transition, marked by various internal conflicts and political instability, relative normalcy and political stability seemed to have been restored by 2004 as Indonesia succeeded in holding its first direct presidential election, affirming its status as the world's third-largest democracy. The newly

DEWI FORTUNA ANWAR is Deputy Chairman for Social Sciences and Humanities at the Indonesian Institute of Sciences (IPSK-LIPI), Jakarta.

democratic Indonesia recognizes freedoms of expression and association as key principles, giving rise to a vibrant and increasingly critical civil society, free-wheeling media, and numerous political parties. These fundamental changes in Indonesia's political landscape have led to a re-structuring of relations between the state and society, between the central government and the regional governments, and between the various institutions of the state, which in turn has transformed the ways that decisions are made. One of the key areas affected by these political changes is in the making and implementation of Indonesian foreign policy, which during the previous era had been the prerogative solely of the predominant executive.

Besides the political transformation which has changed some of the ways that Indonesia looked at itself and the world, including new foreign policy priorities and strategies, Indonesia's economic development in the aftermath of the Asian financial crisis has also affected its regional and global standing. After several years of turning inward to deal with its myriad domestic problems, Indonesia's recent economic recovery — though its growth has been well below the pre-crisis level — and its relative ability to weather the latest global financial meltdown which started in the United States in early 2008, has helped to improve Indonesia's international image and also injected a new sense of self-confidence in the articulation and implementation of its foreign policy.

While domestic political changes have influenced the way decisions are made, introduced new national priorities, and influenced how these priorities are expressed, the changing regional dynamics have also led to some re-alignments in Indonesia's external relations. The rise of major regional powers, China and India, has re-focused Indonesia's attention on these two countries, particularly on the former, reviving memories of the particularly close relations between Jakarta and Beijing throughout the 1950s till the mid 1960s under President Sukarno. At the same time relations with other key regional and global powers have also reached new heights, including with Australia and the United States, indicating that Indonesia's "Free and Active" foreign policy principle could in fact only really be implemented in the post–Cold War international political climate. While reaching beyond the region, ASEAN has also continued to be a major factor in Indonesia's foreign policy, through which Indonesia tries to promote its core national values as well as enhance the ability of the regional members to shape policies in the wider East Asian region.

This chapter will examine how Indonesia's transition to democracy has had an impact on the way that decisions related to foreign policy are made, how democratization has introduced new priorities and attitudes, especially in Indonesia's relations with its ASEAN (Association of Southeast Asian Nations) neighbours, and how Indonesia has adapted to the rise of China.

Making Foreign Policy under Multiple Centres of Power

Throughout the New Order period most strategic decisions were made by the executive dominated by President Suharto at the top supported by the military-bureaucratic elites. No other power centres existed, and while the House of Representatives (DPR) had the sole power to ratify treaties and was supposed to be consulted on major policies, the DPR for the most part acted as a rubber stamp for the government. It is true that except during special circumstances, such as when a country is involved in external conflicts, foreign policy does not usually engage the interests of the general public even in well-established democracies. In Indonesia under Suharto the crafting and implementation of foreign policy remained largely in the hands of the Department of Foreign Affairs, which received a large infusion of senior military figures who often occupied ambassadorial positions in key foreign capitals. With a tame DPR, repressed countervailing forces, and media that practiced self-censorship to avoid closure, Indonesia's foreign policy throughout the New Order period was quite insulated from forces outside of the bureaucracy. Except on issues related to the Israeli-Palestinian conflict, which usually attracted the interest of Islamic groups who supported the Palestinians and opposed any moves by Indonesia to have relations with Israel, public interest on foreign policy as a whole was low. The fall of Suharto brought this government monopoly over the decision-making process, including in foreign policy, to an end.

One of the most significant outcomes of the *reformasi* has been the amendment of the 1945 Constitution — four times since 1999. With the constitutional amendments, the power of the DPR has increased exponentially, fully matching that of the executive. Although Indonesia has a presidential system with a powerful presidency, new checks and balances have been put in place, with a fully independent judiciary and an equally powerful DPR which is quite eager to flex its muscle.

The first constitutional amendment stipulates in Chapter 13, Article 1 that the DPR must be consulted on ambassadorial appointments, which in practice has in fact given the DPR the right to approve or reject the government's ambassadorial candidates. This provision was introduced to prevent the recurrence of old practices such as when Suharto used ambassadorial postings either as rewards for senior military figures for services rendered or as a means of getting rid of rivals,[1] and to ensure that the ambassadors sent overseas are of sufficiently high quality.

The DPR has exercised this power over ambassadorial appointment with great enthusiasm, often rejecting the candidates who have been carefully selected by the Department of Foreign Affairs for trivial reasons, such as being unable to sing the national anthem properly, or being unable to fluently translate *Pancasila*, the state ideology, into English. The DPR has also switched the placements of candidates from those originally put forward by the Foreign Ministry, such as when the nominee for ambassador to Moscow was considered by the DPR to be better suited to serve in the more difficult post in Canberra. The upshot was that the ambassadorial candidate originally intended to head the Indonesian Embassy in Moscow was given the post in Canberra, and vice versa.[2]

Carried away by the zeal for reform and the desire to curtail the prerogatives of the president, the reformers have also included a provision in the first constitutional amendment which gives the DPR the right to approve the ambassadors being sent to Jakarta by other countries. This is in fact quite unique and contrary to common diplomatic practices, as the names of ambassadors are usually kept secret until official agreement by the host country has been received. The important roles played by the DPR in both the appointment of Indonesian ambassadors overseas and the approval of incoming ambassadors have sometimes resulted in long delays in filling these posts.

According to the 1945 constitution the DPR has always had the authority to ratify international treaties, but throughout the New Order period every international agreement signed by the government had been ratified by the DPR without exceptions. Under the current democratic setting, however, the process of treaty ratification is no longer just a formality since the DPR can as easily refuse to ratify a treaty if it believes that the treaty is not in the best national interest. Such a refusal became a reality in 2007 when the Defence Cooperation Agreement (DCA) signed by the Indonesian and Singaporean governments was met by public resistance in Indonesia who lobbied the DPR to reject the agreement. The failure of the DCA to get through the DPR was illustrative of the challenges of making foreign policy in a political setting where the views and aspirations of the general public can no longer be ignored with impunity. At the same time the DCA debacle also demonstrated the growing power of the regions, although under Indonesia's far reaching decentralization policy introduced in 1999 defence and foreign policy remain in the domain of the central government.

In February 2007 the governments of Indonesia and Singapore signed the Defence Cooperation Agreement (DCA) in Bali, in tandem with another agreement, a bilateral extradition treaty. Indonesia has long sought to secure a bilateral extradition agreement with Singapore, which became more urgent since the Asian financial crisis when it was alleged that several economic criminals from Indonesia had taken refuge in Singapore. For its part Singapore wished to renew its defence cooperation with Indonesia, particularly to gain access to Indonesian territory for its military to conduct exercises. In Indonesia the two negotiations were conducted separately, the extradition treaty led by the Ministry of Foreign Affairs, and the DCA by the Ministry of Defence, and given the sensitivities and complexities of both issues the public had mostly been kept in the dark about the details contained in the agreements. It was generally perceived in Indonesia that the Indonesian Government agreed to the signing of the DCA as a quid pro quo for Singapore agreeing to the extradition treaty. The two agreements were tied up and sent to the DPR for ratification in tandem, clearly in the hope that support for the extradition treaty would help to smooth the ratification of the defence cooperation agreement.

When details of the DCA became public however there were howls of protest from various quarters, particularly from the three provinces directly affected by the DCA. The terms of the DCA allowed Singapore to conduct military exercises in three separate areas; in Siabu (Kampar, Riau Province), Natuna waters (Riau Islands Province), and Baturaja (South Sumatra Province). All three regions protested that the Singaporean military exercises would have an adverse impact on the people's livelihood and called on the DPR to reject the DCA.[3] A number of political parties, such as the Islamic United Development party (PPP) and the National Mandate Party (PAN), also openly opposed ratification of the DCA. In the end both the DCA and the extradition treaty failed to pass through the DPR.

The making of foreign policy in Indonesia, therefore, just as in other democracies, must increasingly involve wider public consultations and participation and become more sensitive to popular sentiments. Failure to do so can lead to embarrassment to the government as in the case of the DCA or, even more serious, the president may be openly called to account by the DPR if Indonesia adopted an international stance that is contrary to the prevailing opinions in the DPR. For instance, in March 2007, as a non-permanent member of the United Nations Security Council, Indonesia supported UNSC Resolution No. 1747 imposing sanctions on Iran for its nuclear programme, which had been suspected of violating the nuclear non-proliferation treaty (NPT). Public perception in Indonesia, however, shared by a significant number of the DPR members, was strongly opposed to this as the resolution was regarded as being driven by the United States, which was seen to be unfairly targeting Iran, a fellow Muslim country. At the time the United States under President George W. Bush was still highly unpopular due to the American invasion and occupation of Iraq and Washington's war on terror, which was mostly perceived by Muslims as a war against the Islamic world.

The DPR, therefore, employed its right of interpellation by calling President Susilo Bambang Yudhoyono to come to the DPR to be questioned over Indonesia's support for the resolution. A stand-off occurred when the President did not come in person to the DPR but only sent a delegation of ministers, comprising the Coordinating Minister for Political and Security Affairs, the Foreign Minister, and the State Secretary Minister in July 2007, whom the DPR refused to meet. It was only after intensive lobbying of the DPR leadership by the President that the DPR softened its position and was willing to hear the government's explanation from another delegation of ministers.[4] It is to be expected that after this incident in which the President was put through a difficult political position over a relatively minor vote at the UN Security Council, Indonesian diplomats and the Indonesian foreign ministry as a whole must become much more circumspect in adopting an international position, especially on issues that attract public attention. On the Iranian nuclear issue henceforth Indonesia abstained every time the UN Security Council voted on another sanction against Iran.

Besides having to defer more closely to the wishes of the DPR, notably to Commission I in charge of defence and foreign policy, the Foreign Ministry has also recognized the importance of involving other stakeholders so as to ensure a wider sense of ownership towards Indonesian foreign policy. There was a conscious effort by Foreign Minister Nur Hasan Wirajuda (2001–9) to democratize the process of foreign policy making by actively consulting and engaging with think tanks, academics, religious groups, the media, and civil society organizations as well as with members of Parliament. The Foreign Ministry frequently commissioned papers from leading academics which would be openly discussed in workshops to provide policy inputs to the ministry. It also held regular closed briefings with these opinion makers through forums such as the "foreign policy breakfasts".[5] In one of his speeches soon after being appointed as Foreign Minister, Wirajuda's successor, Marty Natalegawa, reiterated that he will continue the democratization of Indonesia's foreign policy making, both in terms of substance as well as in terms of process.[6] Even then the Foreign Ministry has to accept more public scrutiny and criticism for every perceived shortcoming than ever before.

Democracy as the New Foreign Policy Agenda

In his first foreign-policy speech in 2005 President Susilo Bambang Yudhoyono outlined what he considered to be Indonesia's "international identity", comprising three key elements. These are the fact that Indonesia is the world's fourth most populous nation, that it is the home to the world's largest Muslim population, and that it is the world's third largest democracy. Yudhoyono took pride in the fact that Indonesia is "also a country where democracy, Islam and modernity go hand-in-hand".[7] The themes of Indonesia being the world's largest Muslim nation and the third largest democracy with a modern outward looking society have been emphasized over and over again as Indonesia projects itself onto the international stage, including in the newly formed forum of the major world economies, the G-20, in which Indonesia is the only member from Southeast Asia. In his first annual press briefing Indonesia's new Foreign Minister Marty Natalegawa stated that "As G-20 confirms its status as the premier forum on economic issues, Indonesia is challenged to carve a niche within the Group that is unique to itself as the world's third largest democracy, the country with the world's largest Muslim population and a voice of moderation."[8]

Indonesia has always been the home to the largest Muslim population, who are predominantly moderate, yet this fact was not considered as of any special value to the country's external relations before. It was the emerging problems of international terrorism linked to extremist Islamic movements, and the perceived clash of civilizations between Islam and the West, which drew international interest to the new phenomenon of Indonesia, where democracy is taking root in the world's largest Muslim nation. Indonesia has, therefore, been quick to seize the opportunity to project this new international identity and to capitalize on its unique position to try to act as a bridge between the Islamic world and the West. Promoting dialogue between civilizations and interfaith dialogues have become an important part of Indonesia's foreign policy agenda, which is also regarded as important in overcoming religious extremism at home.

The most important impact of Indonesia's political transformation on the substance of its foreign policy in the past decade, however, has been the mainstreaming of democracy and human rights issues in its foreign policy agenda, particularly in its policy towards ASEAN. Since its establishment ASEAN has been regarded as the cornerstone of Indonesia's foreign policy, and Jakarta had been a staunch supporter of the "ASEAN Way", which includes non-interference in each other's internal affairs, decision making by consensus, and a minimalist approach towards regional integration. With the dramatic political transformation at home, however, the foreign-policy establishment came under increasing pressure to align Indonesia's external stance with its core values at home, which now include respect for democracy and human rights. Indonesian pro-democracy activists have become increasingly critical of ASEAN's traditional non-interference policy which has prevented the association or its members from taking a critical stance when a fellow member committed gross violations of human rights. ASEAN is popularly perceived as an elitist regional organization with little relevance to the lives of the common people and the issues that matter to them most. The political situation in Myanmar, particularly the long imprisonment of the democratic leader Aung San Suu Kyi who had won the general elections in 1990, has long been a focus of pro-democracy activists around the world, and lately also in Indonesia. The result is that the Indonesian Government has been under considerable domestic pressure to push for the promotion of democracy and human rights as one of the key political agendas for ASEAN.

When Indonesia took over the chairmanship of ASEAN in 2003 it proposed the establishment of an ASEAN Security Community (ASC) — later renamed as ASEAN Political-Security Community (APSC) — to complement the ASEAN Economic Community which had been put forward by Singapore earlier as one of the three pillars of the ASEAN Community. Besides re-emphasizing the key treaties and agreements of ASEAN which have governed interstate relations since the establishment of ASEAN in 1967, the APSC for the first time also talks about democracy and human rights as being part of the core values of ASEAN as well as goals to which all members aspire. The third pillar, the Social-Cultural Community has been put forward by the Philippines. The Declaration of ASEAN Concord II (Bali Concord II) of 2003 formally agreed to the establishment of an ASEAN Community comprising the three pillars by 2020, later brought forward to 2015. The ASEAN Community initiative is envisioned to transform the primarily intergovernmental regional organization into a more people-oriented one.

The correlation between Indonesia's democratic transition and ASEAN's move towards a more people-oriented organization has recently been highlighted by the new Foreign Minister, which is worth quoting at length: "Almost mirroring Indonesia's democratic transformation over the past decade, the period since 2003 when Indonesia last held the Chairmanship of ASEAN has witnessed ASEAN's own evolution towards an ASEAN Community. This development has not been an accident. For Indonesia, the evolution of an ASEAN that is more alert to democratic principles and good governance is critical to ensure that there would not be a disconnect or divide between the transformation that has taken place in Indonesia and the regional milieu."[9]

Given the existing political differences within ASEAN it is to be expected that not all of the suggestions put forward by Indonesia, with many of the initiatives coming from civil society, will be accepted by the other ASEAN members. While the Indonesian Government has in fact been accommodative to the domestic demands that democracy and human rights take centre stage in Indonesia's policy towards ASEAN, and ASEAN has adopted some of the key proposals put forward by Indonesia, Indonesian public discontent towards ASEAN has continued to grow in the past years. Important elements of Indonesian civil society were deeply dissatisfied that the ASEAN Charter, which was finally adopted by the ASEAN governments in December 2007, was a watered down version from the original draft, with a much weaker provision for the protection of human rights and no provision for sanctions in the case of non-compliance.

A number of influential opinion-makers who in the past had been most active in promoting ASEAN regional cooperation, such as Rizal Sukma who was commissioned by the Foreign Ministry to help draft the ASEAN Security Community proposal in 2003, had in fact called on the Indonesian Parliament not to ratify the ASEAN Charter.[10] After intensive lobbying by the Foreign Ministry the DPR finally ratified the ASEAN Charter in late 2008, with Indonesia among the last ASEAN members to do so.

The establishment of the ASEAN Intergovernmental Commission on Human Rights (AICHR) in July 2009, which is a much weaker body than that initially envisioned by its champions, with no real power to monitor and protect human rights in the region, has also caused general disappointment. The former Minister of Foreign Affairs, Hasan Wirajuda, admitted that it was a case of one against nine between Indonesia and the rest of the ASEAN members as Indonesia's proposal to give real teeth to the ASEAN human rights commission was overwhelmingly outvoted, resulting in a fairly weak commission.[11] The Foreign Ministry has, however, appointed Rafendi Djamin, a well known human rights activist to represent Indonesia in the AICHR, so far the only commissioner in the AICHR who is from an NGO. This appointment clearly reflects Indonesia's seriousness in trying to develop the AICHR into a credible human rights body in ASEAN.

Members of the Indonesian Government, particularly the President and the Foreign Minister, have in recent year repeatedly reiterated the importance of ASEAN to Indonesia, that it remains the cornerstone of Indonesia's foreign policy. Marty Natalegawa in his speech at the Seventh CSAP General Conference quoted earlier said that "Indonesia's engagement in ASEAN is not optional in its nature. ASEAN is a fact of life."[12] The frequency of government pronouncements that ASEAN remains central to Indonesian foreign policy interests in part may be seen as a response to the growing call that Indonesia should not be investing so much of its time and energy in ASEAN. For instance, Rizal Sukma and Jusuf Wanandi from the Center for International and Strategic Studies (CSIS)

— CSIS is a member of the long-established ASEAN-ISIS network which had actively promoted regional integration — have in the past year been agitating for Indonesia not to allow itself to become a hostage of ASEAN. In one of his many articles on the subject, Sukma wrote, "Indonesia has always been forced into compromise or into a corner by other members for the sake of ASEAN". Among his litany of complaints against ASEAN, Sukma listed Indonesia's bilateral dispute with Malaysia over Ambalat, Indonesia's failure to convince fellow ASEAN members to have a credible human rights body, and the fact that Indonesia's views on the ASEAN Charter were largely ignored. Sukma wrote that "there is nothing more irritating than being ignored" and then went on to say "that enough is enough. It is enough for Indonesia to imprison itself in the 'golden cage' of ASEAN for more than 40 years." Sukma concluded that "Indonesia, therefore, needs to begin formulating a post-ASEAN foreign policy. ASEAN should no longer be treated as the only cornerstone of Indonesia's foreign policy."[13]

The frustrations expressed towards ASEAN and the nationalist calls for Indonesia not to be held hostage by ASEAN within certain quarters reflect a combination of factors. The first is clearly the growing divide in core values between Indonesia, which is now in the midst of trying to consolidate its undoubtedly still messy democracy, and some of the other ASEAN members which still limit political freedom and have resisted Indonesia's efforts to give ASEAN the authority to enforce democratic and human rights principles through a more binding ASEAN Charter and a stronger human rights body. The second is that after recovering from several years of crisis, Indonesia's confidence has been restored and with it a certain assertiveness, which had been deliberately suppressed throughout the New Order period when Indonesia adopted a low profile foreign policy in ASEAN. With the existence of multiple actors seeking to influence foreign policy it is no longer possible for Indonesia to adopt a low profile in ASEAN if this conflicts with public opinion at home. The third is the reality of ASEAN, that it is after all an association of sovereign states in which decision making is made through consensus; and while Indonesia is by far the largest member, it is not able to force its will on the association without fatally damaging ASEAN, which has been the lynchpin of peace and stability in Southeast Asia over the past four decades.

While continuing to emphasize the importance of ASEAN to Indonesia and accepting compromises on its proposals on democracy and human rights, which have disappointed so many activists at home, the Indonesian Government has in fact not limited its promotion of the democratic agenda to ASEAN. In December

2008 Indonesia launched the Bali Democracy Forum as the first governmental or first track forum for dialogues on democracy in Asia. The Bali Democracy Forum (BDF) is part of Indonesia's public diplomacy which tries to showcase Indonesia's attainments in democracy as well as promote an inclusive dialogue about democracy by inviting not only countries that are already democracies but also those "aspiring to be democracies". While the BDF was the initiative of the Foreign Ministry, the President has taken a direct interest in the matter and presided over the two BDFs held in 2008 and 2009.

The Bali Democracy Forum has four stated goals and objectives.[14] First, to establish a regional cooperation forum that promotes political development, through dialogue and sharing of experience, aiming at strengthening democratic institutions. Two, to initiate a learning and sharing process among countries in Asia as a strategy towards the maintenance of peace, stability, and prosperity in the region and beyond. Three, to initiate and build a platform for mutual support and cooperation in the field of democracy and political development. Four, to establish a working institution which would function as a resource base and information centre for research and study as well as a pool of expertise in the various sectors relevant to democracy. To prepare and support the BDF the foreign ministry, in collaboration with the Udayana University in Denpasar, Bali, has established the Institute for Peace and Democracy (IPD), which acts as the secretariat of the BDF.[15]

When it was first launched on 10–11 December 2008 the BDF received mixed reviews. On the one hand it was warmly received, as could be seen by the numbers of countries that sent high-level delegations. Australia, Brunei, and Timor Leste were represented by their respective heads of government while many countries sent delegations led by cabinet ministers. In 2008, thirty-one countries from Asia and observers from outside of the region attended. There was, however, also scepticism, especially from well-established democracies, at the inclusive nature of the dialogue, which also included countries that cannot be categorized as democratic, like China and Myanmar. However, interest in the BDF has grown since to date it is the only forum in Asia where government officials can talk openly about issues related to democracy and the political development in their respective countries and the region as a whole. As part of its programme, Indonesia invited the BDF participants to observe Indonesia's 2009 presidential election, with the expectation that inviting outside observers to watch elections, which can help ensure electoral fairness and transparency, would become generally acceptable in Asia. In the second Bali Democracy Forum in 2009, thirty-six countries sent delegations, including the Sultan of Brunei, the Prime Minister of Japan, and the

Prime Minister of Timor Leste. The number and rank of observers from outside the region also increased, with the United States sending the Under Secretary for Political Affairs, Williams J. Burns, to attend.

Adapting to the Rise of China

Like other countries in the region, Indonesia has had to adapt its foreign policy to the changing regional dynamics, in particular the rise of China and India. As far as Indonesia is concerned the biggest transformation in its external relations in the past decade has been in its relations with China. It is worth remembering that after very close relations between Jakarta and Beijing throughout the 1950s and early 1960s under President Sukarno, from 1966 to 1990 Indonesia froze diplomatic relations with China. The strongly anti-communist New Order government under President Suharto not only banned any direct contact with mainland China, it also prohibited Chinese cultural influences, including Chinese language and writings. China was seen as the primary external threat to Indonesian security. After the end of the Cold War Indonesia normalized diplomatic relations with China, but interactions between the two countries were still strictly regulated. Yet by 2005 Indonesia and China had signed a strategic partnership agreement and the top leaderships of the two countries had exchanged state visits. The strict visa control for visiting Chinese nationals has been lifted and Chinese visitors can now obtain visas on arrival. Past suspicions of China's intent have clearly diminished as Indonesia also granted concessions and permits to Chinese companies to be involved in Indonesia's strategic industries, such as oil and gas and the construction of power plants.

Indonesia has clearly come to realize that it cannot afford to ignore China's huge economic potential, which other countries are also eager to tap. China's "charm offensive" towards Southeast Asia, including coming to Indonesia's assistance during the 1997–98 economic crisis and the December 2004 tsunami in Aceh, has also helped to remove some of Indonesia's earlier suspicions of China. China's technological prowess has also attracted Indonesia's attention, with moves to develop closer science and technology cooperation between the two countries, including in the area of defence. The last few years have, therefore, witnessed increasing interaction between Indonesia and China in almost all fields.

At the same time that Jakarta's relations with Beijing have blossomed, Indonesia has also intensified its relations with other regional powers, such as with Australia, Japan, South Korea, and with India. Indonesia's sometimes volatile relations with Australia, mostly due to political and security differences, have been anchored with the signing in 2006 of the Agreement on the Framework for Security Cooperation (Lombok Treaty), which came into force in February 2008, a wide-ranging security cooperation agreement replacing an earlier framework security agreement (which Indonesia unilaterally revoked in 1999 in the wake of Australia's role in East Timor after the ballot). Indonesia has also signed a strategic partnership with India and South Korea and an economic partnership agreement with Japan. With the improvement of the United States' international standing after the election of President Barack Obama, Jakarta is also seeking to finalize a comprehensive partnership agreement with Washington.

In his annual press briefing quoted earlier, the Foreign Minister stated that Indonesia's foreign policy is multi-directional with the aim of having a thousand friends and zero enemies. The proclivity of Indonesia's strategic or comprehensive partnership agreements clearly point in that direction. Taking a more realist perspective and using the rise of China as the backdrop, however, it can also be argued that Indonesia, like many of its ASEAN neighbours, is pursuing a multi-hedging policy of both engaging China and counterbalancing it by engaging several other regional and extra-regional powers at the same time. Indonesia's support for an enlarged East Asia Summit to include Australia, India, and New Zealand, rather than simply accepting the transformation of the ASEAN Plus Three (China, Japan, and South Korea) into a new East Asian regional architecture, is clearly indicative of Jakarta's policy of "the more the merrier", hence preventing any one regional power from becoming overly dominant. Indonesia's support for ASEAN continuing to be in the driver's seat of wider regional initiatives also reflects Indonesia's unchanging attitude regarding the importance of regional resilience and ASEAN as a regional actor. Lately the Indonesian Foreign Minister has voiced support for the inclusion of Russia and the United States in the East Asia Summit, a forum still primarily driven by ASEAN, while rebuffing the initiatives from Australia and others to form a wider supra-regional architecture such as the Asia Pacific Community which will not be anchored in ASEAN.

It should be noted, however, that voices critical of ASEAN in Indonesia have also cast doubts about the ability of ASEAN to continue to aspire to be in the driving seat of various regional fora or to provide the necessary support to Indonesia in the face of various challenges. Thus, contrary to the official stance of the Foreign Ministry, there has also been some support in Jakarta for the establishment of a wider East Asian forum to include the United States. Jusuf Wanandi for instance wrote, "It may be necessary for the East Asian region to establish an overarching summit to deliberate on strategic issues, including traditional security issues, with the participation of the United States."[16] Even here, however, there is clearly no support for an East Asian regional architecture that is exclusively Asian in nature.

Conclusion

Indonesia's foreign policy since the fall of President Suharto has shown both continuity and change. The basic doctrine of an independent and active foreign policy, of commitment to ASEAN, supporting multilateralism, and the central role of the United Nations in maintaining international security has not changed. The role of foreign policy in serving Indonesia's national interests, particularly its economic development, has also remained the same. At the same time there have also been major changes, as consequences of domestic political transformations, both in the process and substance of Indonesian foreign policy. In terms of process, the making of foreign policy has been democratized, with the existence of multiple power centres and a diversity of stakeholders, which present both constraints and opportunities to the traditional foreign policy establishment. On the one hand, the government has to defer increasingly to the DPR and listen to the aspirations of the various opinion-makers. On the other hand, the foreign ministry is greatly assisted by the inputs provided by independent scholars and think tanks in formulating foreign policy, who together with the media and other civil society actors also help in disseminating foreign policy issues to the wider public.

In terms of substance Indonesia's transition to democracy has also influenced its foreign policy agenda. Issues related to democracy and human rights now occupy an important position in Indonesia's foreign policy agenda, particularly towards ASEAN as support for the development of an ASEAN Community grows. Indonesia is also actively projecting its image as the world's largest Muslim democracy as a national asset in the wider international fora.

With the end of the Cold War and the concurrent rise of China as a global economic power, Jakarta's formerly aloof attitude towards China has also changed. In the past five years in particular, relations between Jakarta and Beijing have intensified in almost all fields. Nevertheless, Indonesia remains wary of China or any other regional power becoming too dominant within an overarching East Asian regional architecture. Indonesia's position that ASEAN should be in the driving seat of any wider regional initiatives has remained unchanged, though there are already voices in Indonesia which, dissatisfied with ASEAN, support the establishment of a new East Asian or Asia Pacific architecture.

Notes

1   During much of the New Order period key diplomatic posts, such as ambassadors in the major ASEAN capitals, Washington, Tokyo, and Canberra, were held by senior military figures, mostly from the army. Powerful members of the elite whom Suharto could not simply dismiss were often sent overseas as ambassadors, popularly known by the term, *di Dubeskan*, or to be made an ambassador as a punishment rather than an achievement.

2   In July 2003 the DPR rejected the nomination of Susanto Pudjomartono, a former chief editor of the English daily, the *Jakarta Post*, as the new Indonesian Ambassador to Australia. The soft spoken Javanese was considered to be unsuited to be Indonesia's chief envoy in Australia, where the media were often highly critical of Indonesia. The outgoing Ambassador, Sabam Siagian, who was also a former chief editor of the *Jakarta Post* and regarded to have been a fairly successful Ambassador, is a blunt outspoken Batak from North Sumatra. The DPR instead preferred Imron Cotan, a career diplomat who had served as the Deputy Chief of Mission in Canberra and was nominated to be the new Ambassador to Russia, to return to Canberra as the new Ambassador. Imron Cotan is also a straight-talking Batak. In the end the DPR's views prevailed and the ambassadorial appointments for Canberra and Moscow were switched.

3   Since the onset of *reformasi* it has become increasingly common for delegations from the regions to put their aspirations or demands directly to the relevant commissions in the DPR, something that did not really happen in the earlier New Order period when the DPR had little control over legislation. In the case of the DCA, for instance, members of the legislative assembly of the affected districts came to Jakarta to lobby DPR Commission I in charge of foreign affairs and defence.

4   The president invited the top leaders of the DPR to the palace for consultations and a briefing on Indonesia's vote at the UN Security Council on UNSC No. 1747. The DPR then agreed that another delegation of ministers comprising the Coordinating Minister for Political and Security Affairs, the Minister of Foreign Affairs, and the State Secretary Minister will be allowed to explain the government's policy to the DPR Commission I <http:www.tempointeraktif.com/hg/timeline/2007/03/20070330-01.id.html>.

5   The writer has participated in these workshops and foreign policy breakfasts several times.

6   Remarks by H.E. Dr Marty Natalegawa, Foreign Minister of the Republic of Indonesia on the occasion of the 7th General Conference of the Council for Security Cooperation in the Asia Pacific, 16 October 2009, Grand Hyatt Hotel, Jakarta <http://www.cscap. org/uploads/GeneralConfReport/7GenConfMinistersRemarks.pdf>.

7   Speech by President of the Republic of Indonesia before the Indonesian Council on World Affairs (ICWA), Jakarta, 19 May 2005 <http://www.presidensby.info/index. php/pidato/2005/05/19/332.html>.

8   Annual Press Briefing, Minister for Foreign Affairs of the Republic of Indonesia, H.E. Dr R.M. Marty M. Natalegawa, "Indonesia and the World 2010". Indonesian Ministry of Foreign Affairs, Jakarta, 8 January 2010.

9   Ibid.

10   Rizal Sukma, "To Be Responsible, Indonesia Should Not Ratify ASEAN Charter", *Jakarta Post*, 22 July 2008.

11   Rakaryan Sukarjaputra, "Badan HAM ASEAN Jauh di Bawah Standar", 9 August 2009, Kompas.com <http://m.kompas.com/xl/read/data/2009.08.09.06163052>.

12   Remarks by H.E. Dr Marty Natalegawa, 7th General Conference of the Council for Security Coopearation.

13   Rizal Sukma, "Indonesia Needs a Post-ASEAN Foreign Policy", *Jakarta Post*, 30 June 2009.

14   See The Bali Democracy Forum website <http://balidemocracyforum.org>.

15   The writer is a member of the Board of Governors, later named Board of Advisors, of the Institute of Peace and Democracy.

16   Jusuf Wanandi, "The ASEAN Summit and Indonesia's National Interests", *Jakarta Post*, 19 March 2009.

Laos

LAO PEOPLE'S DEMOCRATIC REPUBLIC IN 2009
Economic Performance, Prospects, and Challenges

Omkar Lal Shrestha

With an area of 236,800 square kilometres, the Lao People's Democratic Republic (PDR) is a landlocked country sharing 5,083 kilometres of borders with five countries, namely Thailand, Myanmar, Cambodia, Vietnam, and China. It is rich in natural resources like timber and minerals (including copper, gold, tin, and gypsum), and has significant hydropower potential (in the range of 18,000 to 21,000 megawatts). With a population of 6.6 million, it is one of the most sparsely populated countries of Southeast Asia, with a population density of only twenty-three people per square kilometre. The country falls under the United Nations Development Programme (UNDP)'s list of Landlocked Least Developed Countries (LLDC) and is clearly among the weakest economies in the ASEAN group. Two-thirds of its households go without access to electricity, half with no safe water supply, and about half of all villages are not reachable by road during the rainy season. The infrastructure remains constrained with a mere 7,141 kilometres of national roads (as of 2004) of which only 56 per cent are paved. There are no railways and only a very limited telecommunications system. Nearly half of the population (46 per cent) lived below the poverty line in 1992.

Aimed at bringing poverty down, the country prepared its National Growth and Poverty Eradication Strategy in 2003. Accordingly, the ongoing Sixth National Socio-Economic Development Plan 2006–10 (NSEDP) has placed a strong focus on poverty reduction, targeting a high growth rate in the range of 7 to 7.5 per cent. The country has achieved an annual average growth rate of over 7 per cent

Omkar Lal Shrestha is Visiting Senior Research Fellow at the Institute of Southeast Asian Studies.

over the past several years as envisaged in the plan. The gross domestic product (GDP) per capita has increased from \$581 in financial year (FY) 2006/07 to \$810 in FY 2007/08, and commendable progress has been made in reducing poverty from 46 per cent in 1992, to 33 per cent in 2003, and to around 27 per cent in 2008. The country is also aiming to graduate from LLDC status and enter the ranks of the middle income countries by the end of the Eighth NSEDP in 2020; a vision considered attainable by the World Bank.

The country is making a gradual transition to a market economy, promoting the role of the private sector and opening the economy to external trade and foreign investment. It applied for World Trade Organization (WTO) membership in 1997. It is also engaged in a series of reform measures in various sectors to obtain WTO membership by the end of the current Sixth NSEDP in 2010. Improvements in bilateral relations with neighbouring countries are facilitating cross-border trade and regional integration with Thailand, Vietnam, and China. There is an increased level of foreign direct investment (FDI) interest in the country's hydropower and minerals. In the agriculture sector, public investment in irrigation and more land under cultivation have led to a healthy agricultural sector growth of 4.7 per cent annually over the past decade.

Economic Performance in 2009

The impact of the global economic crisis on the Lao PDR has been milder than on many of the other regional economies because of its relative isolation from the global economy; however, it has not been fully spared from it. The impact of the global crisis affected the Lao PDR in the form of a reduction in FDI in mining and hydroelectricity, a drop in exports, and reduced earnings from tourism. Accordingly, in 2009 the economy was estimated to have grown by 6.5 per cent compared to 7.2 per cent in 2008. However, this growth rate, though slightly lower than its past rates, is still considerably healthy by regional standards and much higher than the 5 per cent growth projection made by the multilateral agencies in the earlier part of the year. The economy's relatively healthy performance was the result of strong performance by the mining sector (copper and gold), manufacturing (cement, metal industries), as well as other sectors — including construction, agriculture, and services — which all performed better than expected. Their strong performance was the result of the recovery in world commodity prices and the resurge in regional demand (in particular from China). The recovery in the international prices of minerals helped renew foreign investors' interest in the mining sector, especially from China. The mining and power sectors alone contributed 3.3 percentage points to the overall growth of 6.4 per cent in 2009. The construction industry's strong contribution to growth was due to the surge in construction activities following the country's hosting of the Southeast Asia (SEA) Games in December 2009 and the large scale of physical facilities built for the celebration of the 450th anniversary of Vientiane in early 2010. Furthermore, under the government's expansionary fiscal policy to stimulate the economy, civil service wages were given a good raise. Small and medium enterprises (SMEs) were provided with credit and other support, and power tariffs were temporarily reduced to ease the financial conditions of the mining companies. All these factors helped support relatively healthy growth in 2009.

Increased public expenditures (including off-budget spending) relating to the SEA Games and other public events combined with the government stimulus expenditure resulted in a budget deficit of 6.8 per cent of GDP in FY 2009 compared with the deficit of 1.8 per cent in 2008. The increased level of public expenditure was not matched by a commensurate increase in government revenue. The fiscal revenue indeed was placed under strain following reduced tax collection from mining and hydroelectricity investments as foreign investors delayed their expansion and/or new plans due to tighter global financing conditions. Government revenue in fact showed a modest decline from 13.9 per cent of GDP in FY 2008 to 13.8 per cent of GDP in FY 2009.

Driven by the decline in the global prices of food and fuels, the country experienced its first ever deflation in April 2009, with consumer prices falling by 0.2 per cent in year-on-year basis. However, with the recovery of prices in the last several months of 2009, the annual average inflation in 2009 is estimated at 0.7 per cent (vis-à-vis 7.6 per cent in 2008).

In the external sector, the country's main exports include copper, gold, clothing, power, and coffee. In 2009, exports were estimated to have declined due to weak economic growth in the country's major export market (Thailand) and lower prices of commodities like copper, gold, and other minerals. Exports were estimated to have dropped by about 7.2 per cent in 2009, bringing down the share of exports to GDP from about 26 per cent in 2008 to about 22 per cent in 2009. Imports were estimated to have declined even more — by 9.6 per cent vis-à-vis 2008 — reflecting the declining prices of capital goods and fuels and delayed and deferred investments in the mining and hydropower sectors. World Bank figures indicate that the trade deficit declined from $222 million in 2008 to $204 million in 2009 and the current account deficit from 12.7 per cent in 2008 to 7.9 per cent. The capital account balance is also estimated to have recorded a lower surplus, from $771 million in 2008 to $614 million in 2009. This was due to the global-crisis-connected drop in FDI inflows for new hydropower and mining projects. The official external reserves were projected to have shown a modest decrease from $630 million in 2008 to $600 million in 2009.

Growth Prospects in 2010

The growth prospects of the Lao PDR in 2010 are expected to remain strong. With the projected growth of the world economy at 4 per cent in 2010, led by emerging countries in the region, the demand for the Lao PDR's exports of goods and services to neighbouring countries is expected to register a healthy growth. Tourism, which had slowed in 2009, is expected to recover, and with it an expansion of hotels, restaurants, travel agencies, and other affiliated services. The implementation of several transportation and power projects, which had been temporarily slowed in 2009, is expected to resume with the increased inflows of FDI. With the recovery of commodity prices, the mining sector is also expected to see a rise in the export of minerals and increased investment activities. Nam Theun II (NT2), with a total capacity of 1,088 megawatts and costing $1.2 billion, is expected to operate at full capacity in 2010. Accordingly, the electricity export earnings from NT2 are expected to generate $300 million to $340 million in 2010. The economy is projected to grow at 7 per cent in 2010.

Government revenue is projected to increase in 2010 as the global prices of copper and gold recover from the earlier drop. NT2 is also expected to generate more revenue for the government during the year. Furthermore, the government is expected to take some additional steps — such as the reintroduction of value-added tax (VAT) after a ten-month suspension and the imposition of a new tax on luxury goods — to augment government revenue. The government off-budget expenditures on the other hand are expected to be phased out following the completion of the construction activities relating to the 2009 SEA Games events and the Vientiane 450th capital anniversary celebration. However, substantial expansion in capital spending may result in increased fiscal deficit in 2010.

The expansionary monetary policy adopted in 2009 to stimulate domestic demand through lowering of interest rates had resulted in the acceleration of credit growth by 98 per cent in June 2009, compared with 84 per cent in 2008. A large part of credit expansion was on account of direct lending by the Bank of the Lao PDR (BOL) to the local governments and state-owned banks to finance public infrastructure projects. The government is expected to slow the credit growth as it adopts a more restrictive monetary policy.

Exports are expected to perform strongly in 2010 as the Lao PDR's major export market, Thailand, and other regional economies recover from the effects of the global economic crisis. However, imports of capital goods are expected to expand even more rapidly as foreign mining and other companies renew their interest in the Lao PDR's resource and non-resource projects, ranging from coal-fired power plants to hydropower projects. These expanded imports could widen the trade deficit in 2010. There could also be repatriation of profits and dividends by the foreign mining companies. Thus the country's current account deficit in 2010 is expected to be somewhat bigger than in 2009.

Considering foreign investors' renewed interest in the economy, continued low cost concessional assistance from bilateral and multilateral agencies, and the country's own foreign exchange reserves accumulated over the years, the ability of the Lao PDR to service external debt in the immediate to medium term is not a major concern. Although external debt is projected to remain high, the concessional assistance will keep public debt service manageable. While there may be a slight increase in debt stock over the near term, the government's policy of maintaining the debt on a downward path will continue over the medium term.

Constraints and Challenges

The government has been able to manage the economy and its natural resource endowments with efficiency and prudence, thereby securing macro-stability over the years and receiving commendation from donor agencies. Notwithstanding this, the Lao PDR remains a country whose development is constrained by inadequate infrastructure, insufficient capital, shortage of skilled human resources, a limited telecommunications system, and an overwhelmingly large proportion of its population subsisting on agriculture. Some eighty per cent of the population still depend on farming for their livelihood. The country continues to remain heavily dependent on external sources for its capital investment and remains vulnerable to any fall in world commodity prices.

The country's quest for securing a poverty-free economy would critically hinge on its ability to sustain high growth in agriculture. Improvement in the agricultural sector's performance in the past has been achieved more through increased land brought under cultivation than through improved land productivity. To improve both agricultural productivity and rural livelihoods, various measures will be necessary. These include the provision of quality agricultural extension services, rural roads to enable farmers to bring their products to market, and providing farmers with timely market information. These measures will help towards the commercialization of agriculture and will give farmers better returns for their agricultural products. They will also help farmers to move beyond being simply suppliers of raw commodities. In a country like the Lao PDR, where the use of natural resources is keenly contested, the government will need to skilfully manage its land, forest, and water resources to ensure proper valuation of them and appropriate care for the environment.

With the country's increasing integration with regional and global economies, managing its banking and financial sectors and conducting monetary and fiscal policies will be more complex and challenging. The BOL will be required to shift away from its legacy of direct intervention and rely more on indirect policy instruments. It will need to convert itself into a lender of the last resort as it engages in the management of domestic liquidity. Five new commercial banks have begun operations in the past five years, bringing the total number of financial institutions in the Lao PDR to twenty. As the number of financial institutions increase, the oversight capacity of BOL will need to be considerably strengthened. BOL's risk management capacity in the banking sector will also need to be significantly improved. Considering that the state-owned enterprises account for only one per cent of employment and that the greater part of employment opportunities are generated by small and medium sized enterprises and joint ventures in the private sector, it will be important for BOL to help create a banking and financial environment in which banks feel safe to lend to the SMEs and that the SMEs feel assured of access to finance on commercial terms. The challenges in public financial management will be similarly complex, with the broadening of the tax base as increased numbers of large-sized projects like NT2 come on stream. Building institutional capacity and overcoming the shortage of human capital will be critically important as the country forges ahead with its outward-oriented growth strategy.

In essence, the country's major development challenges will include, among others, the need for diversifying sources of growth, maintaining macroeconomic stability, strengthening institutional and human capital, creating an attractive business investment climate, ensuring financial sustainability, and strengthening good governance.

Policy Options and Medium-term Prospects

As the country readies itself for the implementation of its Seventh Plan (NSEDP 2011–15), beginning in 2011, the policymakers will need to bear in mind that the economy's sources of growth at present are heavily focussed on a narrow base of natural resources, primarily mining and hydropower. Such a narrow base tends to enhance the economy's vulnerability to the vagaries of world prices of a few commodities. It is therefore essential to diversify the growth base in order to achieve sustained stable high growth. A broadened growth foundation will also help to create more productive employment opportunities in multiple sectors, thereby helping to reduce poverty.

Policymakers will also need to continue their focus on pro-poor high growth, with priority placed on employment generation through private sector initiatives. The transition to commercial agriculture will call for the government to take steps to benefit from the emerging cross-border roads and highways that are being funded under regional cooperation activities by multilateral agencies like the Asian Development Bank and the World Bank. As these cross-border projects gain increased momentum, the Lao PDR will have the potential to convert itself from being a landlocked country to one that is land-linked to its five surrounding neighbours. The scale of development dividends to the Lao PDR from such a conversion will be immense.

The country will need to improve its investment climate to retain and further enhance the interest of foreign investors as well as to promote the domestic business sector. Domestically, ninety-seven per cent of manufacturing units are of small and medium size, primarily owned by the private sector and joint ventures with foreigners. Considering that the country's population is projected to double in less than twenty-five years, the private sector will need to play an instrumental role in absorbing the young labour force by generating more gainful job opportunities, otherwise poverty reduction is going to be much more challenging. Broader structural reforms will be necessary in multiple sectors as the country aims at graduating from LLDC status by 2020.

The recent reform measures taken by the government clearly indicate its seriousness in tackling development challenges. It has taken a series of steps in the correct direction. These include recent legislative measures such as the Enterprise Law, Mining Law, draft Investment Law, Commercial Bank Law, and revised Tax and Customs Law. Cumulatively, these measures are aimed at reducing the degree of discretion in regulations, helping establish a level playing field for private and state-owned enterprises as well as for domestic and foreign investors, streamlining and simplifying business procedures, and helping improve the overall business climate. Response to these reform measures from donor agencies and foreign investors alike have been positive. Commendable progress has been made towards poverty reduction, and clearly more such initiatives need to be undertaken. If the government continues reform measures in tackling the issues identified above, the medium-term growth prospects for the Lao PDR are encouraging.

Note

The main sources of information for this chapter were *Asian Development Outlook 2009* (Manila: Asian Development Bank [ADB], 2009); *Lao People's Democratic Republic, 2009–2011, Country Operations Business Plan* (Manila: ADB, 2008); *Background Paper: Greater Mekong Subregion, Mobilizing Aid for Trade: Focus on Asia and the Pacific* (Manila: ADB, 2007); *Key Indicators for Asia and the Pacific*, 40th edition (Manila: ADB, 2009); *Economist Intelligence Unit Country Report*, various issues (London: Economist Intelligence Unit); "Lao People's Democratic Republic, Report on Round Table Implementation Meeting" (Vientiane: Ministry of Planning and Investment, Department of International Cooperation, 2009); *Lao PDR Recent Economic Developments, Lao PDR Economic Monitor, End-Year Update, 2009* (Vientiane: World Bank, 2009); "Lao People's Democratic Republic: 2009 Article IV Consultation — Staff Report" (Washington, DC: 2009); and *Lao PDR, Poverty Reduction* (UNDP, 2009).

LAOS
Crisis and Resource Contestation

Holly High

Laos in 2009 must be understood in terms of the broader context of ongoing crises that affected not only Laos, but also the region and indeed the globe. These include, primarily, the global financial crisis, the environmental crisis, and the food crisis, as well as Typhoon Ketsana and international outcry over the treatment of Hmong asylum seekers. While many of these critical situations have been developing for some time now, their cascading coalescence in 2009 gave this year a particular poignancy. They highlighted through stress and pressure not only Laos's deep engagements in regional and global dependencies, but also fractures and weaknesses in the Lao political, economic, and social setting. In particular, they highlighted the potentials but also dangers associated with resource exploitation. While resource exploitation is now Laos's main strategy for achieving development goals, the process is marked by unusually public conflict over associated rights and responsibilities. While this is unlikely to significantly undermine existing political arrangements, it is demonstrating the contradictions of political authority in contemporary Laos.

Resourcification

In recent years there has been a discursive shift towards describing Laos in terms of "resources". In contemporary development reports and investment brochures, Laos is described as "resource rich". The vision for development here is that abundant resources, in the form of mountains, waterways, and forested areas, will attract foreign direct investment, primarily in mining, agri-business, and hydroelectricity.[1] There are, of course, attendant concerns, such as that Laos may fall victim to the "resource curse", resources will be over-exploited, or the exploitation of one resource will compromise another. Nevertheless, these concerns, like the

HOLLY HIGH is Research Associate in the Department of Anthropology, The University of Cambridge, United Kingdom.

strategies that they critique, are framed within the language of resources. This language is not particularly new: interest in Laos as a source of raw materials was an aspect of the colonial endeavour, and recent radiocarbon dates suggest that copper-smelting and long-distance trade took place in Laos at least 2000 years ago (ongoing archaeological work may well push this back further into the Bronze Age). While the concept may not be radically new, it is ascendant in the current era and is particularly defining of contemporary understandings of Laos, both in terms of Laos's potentials and her vulnerabilities. The language of an enticing store of resource wealth is all the more striking in a context where, not so long ago, it was more common to read descriptions of Laos as problematically inaccessible, "isolated", and a backwater characterized by inhospitable mountain wildernesses. Now, however, those self same tracts of land are being revalued as they fall under the hungry gaze produced by resourcification.

In contemporary "resourcified" understandings of Laos, mining plays a particularly prominent role. At present there are 132 mining companies operating in the nation. Mineral surveys suggest that Laos holds large reserves of ores, including gold, silver, copper, lead-zinc, tin, aluminium, and iron. Of course, it is not uncommon for the earth's crust to contain minerals. What varies across contexts is not merely the combination and concentration of minerals but crucially also the combination and concentration of socially produced conditions. Regulatory frameworks, the cost of the "social license" to operate (including costs of resettlement of local inhabitants, environmental mitigation, and hearts-and-minds winning corporate social responsibility activities) as well as transport and energy infrastructure have a significant impact on the profitability and probability of mining. Thus, the rush to locate and extract minerals in Laos must be understood not only in terms of a wealth secreted under the Lao soil but also in terms of these manmade conditions. The Lao Government has made significant moves towards attracting foreign direct investment, including simplifying paperwork and attempting to install clear regulations (it should be noted that many foreign investors still find these steps less than satisfactory, but progress has been made). Some observers have been concerned, however, about how the social license to operate mines is obtained in authoritarian Laos, where public debate is severely curtailed.

Another key plank of the national Lao development strategy is hydro-power. The Lao government has signed a staggering seventy memoranda of under-standing on proposed hydropower projects.[2] Fifteen of these are currently under construction or operational. Laos has committed to exporting power to Thailand, Vietnam, and Cambodia by 2015, and also has plans to use hydropower to provide electricity domestically. Perhaps the most famous and certainly the largest of Laos's hydropower constructions is the Nam Theun II hydropower scheme. A joint venture between a Lao state enterprise, a French company, and two Thai companies, the hydropower scheme is expected to produce 1,088 megawatts, 95 per cent of which is to be exported to Thailand. The hydropower scheme is scheduled to enter full production in 2010. Like mining ventures, hydropower schemes are large consumers of land and water and have a potential social and environmental impact not only locally but also downstream. The stakes are high: large profits can be made, but at significant cost. These are inherently political projects because often those who are asked to bear the costs are not those who directly stand to reap the profits, especially when these projects are privately owned and run for the profit of shareholders. Like mines, then, dams are particularly catalyzing sites for opposition. The question of how these political questions are answered is pertinent not only to local populations and their governments, but also the foreign investors and multilateral banks that enable these projects.

A third plank of Laos's resource-driven development strategy is concerned with land itself. Perhaps unsurprisingly, land is viewed as the state's ultimate resource in Laos. Under current law, all land belongs to the state (land titling has so far occurred only in a small amount of urban areas). The right to pay land tax on a plot is established by demonstrating use and improvements on the land. Recent years have seen a controversial land classification scheme set boundaries to those places claimable under this usufruct system. Land to be preserved amounts to some 73.48 per cent of the nation's land mass, while land to be developed makes up the remaining 26.5 per cent. This second category is to hold all subsistence farming and gardening, agri-business, livestock, dwellings and urban centres, and mining. Disuse of land classified as productive is discouraged through higher taxation or threats of reallocation to other users. In rural areas, there have been moves to resettle people out of areas zoned for "preservation" and into areas zoned as productive. When food prices spiked in 2008, Gulf States indicated their interest in Southeast Asian agricultural lands generally, and significant deals have been struck in Cambodia and the Philippines. In Laos, China and Vietnam continued to be the main foreign investors in this sector. This attracted some controversy, because land concessions were viewed as open to corruption and as having a negative impact on local livelihoods and National Protected Areas. Land concessions were officially suspended in 2007; they resumed in May 2009 only to be suspended again in July 2009. The central government attempted to curb ongoing abuses by announcing a Decree on State Land Lease or Concession, but it is unclear what effect this central decree will have in heavily (and de facto) decentralized Laos.

Despite these controversies, in 2009 the Lao Government continued to use land to lure foreign investment and assistance. A new law was debated that would allow foreign investors the same rights as domestic citizens to own or access land. This suggestion was met with some disquiet and subsequent formulations suggested that foreign ownership only be allowed in a select array of geographical sites, and only in exchange for significant (US$500,000) investment. Even the Southeast Asian Games ended in a dispute over resources, and more particularly, the use of land as collateral in international deals. The biennial sporting event, hosted by Laos from December 7 to 18 in 2009, brought together eleven Southeast Asian nations to participate in local and international sports. Concerns sprouted early about Laos's ability to provide the required stadiums and housing for athletes. In 2008, a rare debate broke out over an announcement that the stadium would be funded by a Chinese consortium in return for a fifty-year concession to develop land in the That Luang Marshes in Vientiane. When Martin Stuart-Fox wrote about these events for this publication last year (2009), he noted the rumours that the authorities might be forced to back down in the face of widespread discontent.[3] As 2009 unfolded, however, it became clear that the deal remained in place. In addition, it emerged that the athletes' dormitories were built with Vietnamese funds, reportedly in exchange for 10,000 hectares in south-eastern Laos to plant rubber trees. These events very clearly demonstrated a wider logic where resources are offered in exchange for development. But they also demonstrated another element: resource conflict. The kind and level of discontent demonstrated in the That Luang Marshes affair is becoming more common.

These examples illustrate that Laos is undergoing a process of "resourcification". Her population and territory are increasingly being reinterpreted as resources available for profitable exploitation in exchange for the radical transformations imagined in developmentalist dreams. Encased in the logic of resourcification is a very particular view of the relationship between humans, between humans and their natural environment, and the politics of appropriation and benefit. Resources do not pre-exist human interest, waiting merely to be stumbled upon in a chance "discovery". Instead, resources are the result of human appraisal: it is when natural features are judged as useful in relation to human wants that resourcification occurs.[4] A resource-development regime of value implies notions of community benefit (in the case of Laos, typically national benefit), where some members of the community are asked or forced to sacrifice their access or livelihoods so that resources can be exploited for the profit of the greater collective. Resources, then, are intimately linked to issues of ownership, access, and governance.[5] The spread of resource-development regimes of value to include almost all of Laos heralds the arrival of a particular form of authority, and a particular form of politics, a point I shall return to below.

The Year of Crisis

Intriguingly, there were scattered reports from senior officials and academics claiming that the global financial crisis would have no effect in Laos at all. One economist from the National University of Laos, for instance, explained that Laos's economy was "immune" to the effects of the global financial crisis because of the agricultural sector: most people were subsistence agriculturalists, and others could merely return to agriculture if other sectors failed. The laconic New Mandala website summarized this view with the headline "Laos Too Poor to Get Any Poorer".[6] Informally in Laos, jokes circulated such as that perhaps because there was no economy there would be no economic crisis. But such comments — either from official media statements or everyday speculation — seem to have been bravado or gallows humour. Certainly, 2009 saw the economic crisis hit Laos. Economic growth slowed. Some foreign investments in mining and hydropower were suspended. Exports declined and tourism, another major driver for the economy, was hit hard. Prices for agricultural products also tumbled. For surplus-producing rice farmers, the sudden drop in the price of and markets for rice was very unwelcome news. Those who had invested in biofuel plantations saw their dreams of a bonanza shrivel as prices for crude oil tumbled from US$147 a gallon in July 2008 to just US$36 in December 2009. Rubber plantations came under similar pressure. While prices made a strong recovery throughout the year, a stern lesson had been delivered and the full effects of the crisis may not have yet been fully felt.

Perhaps the effects of the global financial crisis can be illustrated best by the case of the Sepon Gold and Copper Mine. Promoted as a "flagship" example of foreign direct investment in Laos at its establishment in 2003, the mine quickly became a pin-up story of pioneer exploration and get-rich-quick investment. Oxiana saw shares on the Australian Stock Exchange climb from under A$0.50 in the phase of exploration to a height of A$4.32 in November 2007. Very soon after a merger with Zinifex in 2008 (the combined companies became Oz Minerals) commodity prices and stocks tumbled and Oz Minerals found itself with combined debts that it could not service. Eventually the Sepon Gold and Copper Mine was purchased by the Chinese state-owned trading company Minmetals as part of a global sell-off of Oz Minerals assets. Minmetals' interest in purchasing Australian and Asian mining operations during the crisis was widely understood as part of an effort at obtaining resource security for China. Minmetals is China's largest importer of copper. The global financial crisis, then, had complex effects in Laos that extended beyond economic set backs and included shifts in the political control of resources.

It is worth noting too that 2009 saw world leaders meet at the UN Climate Change Conference in Copenhagen to discuss responses to the environmental crisis. The deputy prime minister of Laos, Asang Laoly, in his address to the conference acknowledged the severity of the environmental crisis. His suggested response was telling: legally binding regulations backed with sanctions. While this could be interpreted in terms of Copenhagen politics, it can also be interpreted as reflective of a more general tendency among Lao political leaders: the response to crisis is regulation, law-making, and the search for effective and implementable sanctions. This tendency can be seen in the resource conflicts unfolding domestically in Laos as resources continue to come under pressure.

Resource Contestation

The contemporary resourcification of Laos is perhaps one of the most openly and hotly contested issues in the country. Laos is an authoritarian state. As Martin Stuart-Fox has noted, there is no practical distinction between the ruling Lao People's Democratic Party and the bureaucratic apparatus of the Lao state.[7] Locally, they are glossed in one term: *pak-lad* (party-state). Open criticism of the party-state is said to attract violent punishment or systemic disadvantage. Amnesty International maintains a litany of examples of political imprisonment or the vanishing of peaceful political protesters.[8] In 2009, this international image of Laos was vigorously reasserted when over 4,000 asylum seekers were forcibly repatriated to Laos from holding camps in Thaliand. One hundred and fifty-eight of these had been assessed as registered refugees by the United Nations High Commissioner for Refugees (UNHCR), while the UNHCR had been denied access to another 4,000 asylum seekers to assess their status. This event unleashed a steady flow of news reports in the international English-language media decrying the lack of transparency and apparent disregard of refugee conventions and expressing fears for the safety of the refugees and asylum seekers.

Despite this reputation for repression, the latest events in the realm of resource politics demonstrate that Lao people do have some leeway to express at least some dissatisfaction: the That Luang Marshes incident is only one example of an emerging pattern of resource contestation.   , this contestation is not conducted openly and directly. Instead, it takes place obliquely, often phrased in terms that echo party-state language. For instance, the Lao party-state has announced frequently and vociferously its commitment to the eradication of poverty by 2020. Many policies, including those of resource appropriation like mining and hydropower, are justified and conceptualized under the encompassing language of poverty reduction. Yet claims to poverty are also a powerful tool for otherwise marginal people to evade state claims, or at least to claim a small stake in resource exploitation. For instance, failing to pay taxes or attend work events in rural villages is often rationalized by ordinary residents by claims to particular poverty.[9] Poverty also played a role in local explanations (in non-political terms) of what were essentially farmer-led policy reversals that saw the end of the collectivization of agriculture and the curtailment of ineffective state-backed irrigation projects.[10] The example of the That Luang Marshes is again representative. While Stuart-Fox pointed out that much of the concern in 2008 centred on the ethnic Chinese character of the proposed new settlement, news reports also related that much of the controversy was phrased in terms of concern over the level of compensation offered to residents. American news radio, for example, reported that local residents were demanding US$100 per square meter, while the government was offering only US$20. Using this discrepancy as a platform for opposition to the proposal, people had refused to move: a striking example of an apparent rejection of a direct order. Similar contours of debate are evident in the resettlement schemes that often accompany large resource reallocations, including mining endeavours or the recent decision to build a golf course and five-star resort on the fringes of Vientiane. In these debates, local residents are surprisingly outspoken, but what they speak of is most frequently the question of wealth sharing, not the question of rights. The language of poverty provides a relatively common and apolitical form of resource contestation because it does not present a direct threat to existing authorities, and indeed employs party-state terms.

The party-state has also engaged in numerous anti-corruption measures, many of them widely reported publicity events. In 2009 Laos signed the UN Convention against Corruption, and a national anti-corruption law is already in place. The UN anti-corruption day is observed annually in Laos with a media event and high-level official statements (in 2009 from Deputy Prime Minister Asang Laoly). Corruption has also become a kind of universal critique of all levels of the party-state. Ordinary people suspect the officials that they come into contact with and also suspect the central authorities. Vientiane leaders suspect district officials. Provincial officials suspect the centre and the district. Different state agencies suspect each other. While numerous reports suggest that there is some accuracy to this rampant suspicion, because corruption is a major challenge to Laos, it is also true that corruption has become embedded in the language of politics in Laos. Notably, it is a critical language. Given the lack of freedom in expressing political criticism in Laos, the ubiquity of this critical talk is striking. For instance, during the National Assembly in 2009 a discussion focused on the loss of forest resources to illegal logging. Representatives reported that their constituents were concerned about this issue and had pressed them to raise it at the Assembly. The Assembly's telephone hotline received calls from citizens accusing district officials of corrupt involvement in illegal logging. A top official from the Ministry of Agriculture and Forestry's Inspection Department confirmed to the Assembly that officials in positions of some authority were indeed involved in the illegal timber trade. A top prosecutor was asked to report on the issue to the Assembly and his comments reflected a sense of helplessness: he described illegal logging as "a chronic problem" and entreated the Assembly to decide if there was the political will in place to actually support prosecutions against corrupt offenders. Later in 2009 it emerged that one official response to this crisis in illegal logging was the plan to abolish the private quota system for timber extraction because it is thought to be open to abuse. It was to be replaced with state-owned enterprises that will have a monopoly on tree felling in Laos. The rhetoric of corruption has thus bred the contradictory situation where the culprit — the party-state, in the form of government officials — is also thought to be the cure, in the form of more regulations, more sanctions, and more official oversight. This reflects the significant fractures in the Lao party-state as central authorities remain in tension with provincial and district levels.

In summary, the resourcification of Laos is a political process. Answers to questions of who has rights over resources and who has responsibility for the costs and benefits of resource exploitation depend on the political authority to settle these questions. The party-state in Laos claims a monopoly on this authority, but this is authorized in turn by particular claims, especially that the party-state undertakes rule for the ultimate benefit of the populace (in the form of poverty reduction) without corruptly abusing that power. The possibilities of profit but also loss in the transformation of Laos into a field of enticing resources has brought this authorization into the realm of debate. The resourcification of Laos has brought with it not only new wealth, but very serious questions about how this wealth will be distributed. Alongside this, questions have been raised about the legitimacy of how such distribution is decided and achieved. This is a political debate, but this debate does not occur in direct terms. Instead it is marked by the indirect but nonetheless powerful language of poverty and corruption. This is powerful if oblique language because it harnesses the language used by the party-state to claim authority in order to bring into question the very authorization of that authority. While it is unlikely to lead to significant political change in Laos in the near future, it does reveal the complexities of the exercise of power in the country during a period of resourcification and crisis.

Notes

1   Keith Barney, "Laos the Making of a 'Relational' Resource Frontier", *Geographical Journal* 175, no. 2 (2009): 146–59.

2   Department of Energy Promotion and Development (EDP), "Operational and Planned Projects" <http://poweringprogress.org> (accessed 15 February 2010).

3   Martin Stuart-Fox, "Laos: The Chinese Connection", in *Southeast Asian Affairs 2009* edited by Daljit Singh (Singapore: Institute of Southeast Asian Studies, 2009), pp. 141–69.

4   Erich W. Zimmerman, *World Resources and Industries: A Functional Appraisal of the Availability of Agricultural and Industrial Resources* (New York: Harper and Brothers, 1933).

5   Thomas Sikor and Christian Lund, "Access and Property: A Question of Power and Authority", *Development and Change* 40, no. 1 (2009): 1–22.

6   New Mandala: New Perspectives on Southeast Asia, "Laos Too Poor to Get Any Poorer <http://asiapacific.anu.edu.au/newmandala/2009/01/28/laos-too-poor-to-get-any-poorer/> (accessed 15 February 10).

7   Martin Stuart-Fox, "Politics and Reform in the Lao People's Democratic Republic". Working Paper No. 126 (Melbourne: Asia Research Centre, Murdoch University, November 2005).

8   Amnesty International, "Human Rights in the Lao People's Democratic Republic" <http://www.amnesty.org/en/region/laos> (accessed 15 February 10).

9   Holly High, "The Road to Nowhere: Poverty and Policy in the South of Laos", *Focaal: European Journal of Anthropology* 53 (2009): 75–88.

10   Holly High, "Village in Laos: Poverty and Policy among the Mekong's Flows". Thesis submitted in completion of Ph.D. requirements. Canberra: Australian National University, 2005.

Malaysia

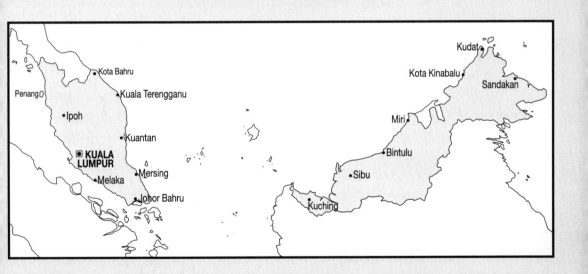

MALAYSIA
The Rise of Najib and 1Malaysia

James Chin

The year 2009 will be remembered for Malaysia's first political dynasty coming to fruition. Najib Tun Razak, the son of Abdul Razak who was Malaysia's second Prime Minister, became Malaysia's sixth PM. His predecessor paid the price for losing the March 2008 General Elections and was forced to resign. At the start of the year, the People's Pact (PR or Pakatan Rakyat) under Anwar Ibrahim appeared to still have the political momentum generated by the general elections. However, as the year progressed, it was clear that Najib managed to get the upper hand over Anwar and the opposition.

Perak Falls and Najib Takes Over

On 3 April, Najib took over as PM from Abdullah Ahmad Badawi, whose term as PM was widely seen as a colossal failure — in the 2008 General Elections (GE) the Barisan Nasional (BN) lost its two-thirds majority. Two months earlier, Najib showed his political skills when he engineered the fall of the PR-led Perak State Government. Three PR state assemblymen — Democratic Action Party (DAP)'s Hee Yit Foong (Jelapang), Parti Keadilan Rayak (PKR)'s Jamaluddin Mohd Radzi (Behrang), and Mohd Osman Jailu (Changkat Jering) — defected to the BN and it was enough for the PR to lose its majority. The PR *Menteri-Besar* (MB or Chief Minister) Mohammad Nizar Jamaluddin asked the constitutional monarch of Perak, Sultan Azlan Shah, to dissolve the State Assembly, but he refused. Under normal circumstances, the state ruler must follow the wishes of the MB, but in this case the Sultan refused and took the position that the BN had the majority now.[1] In an unprecedented episode, the PR Speaker of the Assembly was physically dragged out of the Assembly with the connivance of the Clerk of the Assembly, the police,

---

JAMES CHIN is Head, School of Arts and Social Sciences, Monash University, Malaysian campus.

and the State Secretary. It was clear that key institutions such as the civil service and the police were still loyal to the United Malays National Organisation (UMNO) and actively helped to undermine and remove the PR administration. A new BN state was duly installed along with a new speaker from the BN.[2]

Najib's ability to remove the PR government sent a clear signal to the PR alliance that unlike his predecessor he was no pushover and was willing to play hardball. This action destabilised the PR as there were rumours that Najib was close to overthrowing the PR-led Selangor State Government through defections as well.

1Malaysia's Triumph amid Economic Decline

Najib had plenty of time to plan for his ascension and he used the time well. He brought in a new team of public relations experts to help him create a new image.[3] The new image was the slogan and tagline "1Malaysia. People First, Performance Now". Although it was never defined properly, it was brilliant in that it appealed to the non-Malay population which had abandoned the BN in the 2008 GE. 1Malaysia sounded to them like political equality, inclusiveness, and an end to institutional racism since the introduction of the New Economic Policy (NEP) in 1971.[4] As part of the charm offensive, Najib told UMNO's General Assembly to be "champions of the rakyat" and toned down the rhetoric of Ketuanan Melayu (Malay supremacy). He also announced a liberalization of NEP rules and followed it up by announcing that the long-standing 30 per cent compulsory bumiputera shareholding would be reduced to 12.5 per cent for companies listed on the stock exchange, and the abolition of the Foreign Investment Committee (FIC) which had forced foreign investors to take bumiputera shareholders. Najib also announced that a new category of government scholarships would be given out purely on merit.[5] All these announcements were very well received by the Chinese community as they were effectively shut out of the public service scholarships by official and unofficial quota systems. He further reached out to the Chinese community by attending a dinner to commemorate the Ninetieth Anniversary of the Chong Hwa Chinese Independent High School. This was the first time a PM had visited the Chinese school. For the Malay population, especially the younger Malay youth, 1Malaysia sounded like a more inclusive form of government with less emphasis on race and religion. Many younger Malay voters had voted against BN-UMNO because of its racist politics. In reality, 1Malaysia was no different from all the earlier slogans and campaigns to promote a united polity — it was really just a slogan and it was clear that the preferential policies and special rights of the Malays and bumiputeras would stay in spite of 1Malaysia.[6]

As part of the "People First, Performance Now" component, Najib announced a Government Transformation Programme (GTP), consisting of six National Key Results Areas (NKRA): accessibility to quality and affordable education; crime reduction; battling graft; improvement of living standards; rural development; and improvement of public transportation. To show his seriousness, he brought in Idris Jala, an outsider and non-politician, as a Minister in charge of the NRKA. Jala, a Kelabit from Sarawak, was known as a turnaround specialist who had made a name for himself by successfully rescuing Malaysian Airlines from insolvency. The NKRA was popular with the polity and a poll showed Najib's popularity had risen despite constant attacks from political bloggers and the opposition.[7]

Like other economies in the region, the Malaysian economy was stagnant and estimated to contract by about 2 per cent in 2009. The most serious contraction occurred in the first half of the year with exports dropping by about 30 per cent. However, exports and the stock market recovered somewhat by the end of the year. The government's stimulus package, worth about RM 67 billion (US$18 billion) appears to be slowly working and the economy is expected to post growth of between 4 and 7 per cent in 2010. The new Najib administration also liberalized twenty-seven services sub-sectors, allowing for majority ownership without bumiputera shareholdings,[8] to improve economic competitiveness. Foreign corporate finance and financial planning companies will be allowed to set up operation in Malaysia without local shareholding. For unit trust segments, the foreign shareholding limit will be raised from 49 per cent to 70 per cent and foreign shareholding in existing stock broking companies will be increased from 49 per cent to 70 per cent. To the disappointment of many, Najib retained the 30 per cent cap on local commercial banks. A single foreign investor can now only own up to 20 per cent in a single stake in a commercial bank, while the overall limit stays at 30 per cent for foreign ownership.

To ensure that bumiputera interests were kept, a new vehicle, Ekuiti Nasional Berhad (Ekuinas), with an initial funding of half a billion ringgit (eventually going up to RM 10 billion), focusing on helping bumiputera entrepreneurs who have the potential and capability to develop into global players, was launched.[9]

Despite earlier optimism, Malaysia was unable to close the deal on the free trade agreement (FTA) with the United States in 2009. Najib's much talked about New Economic Model (NEM), based on innovation, creativity, and high-value-added activities, was also postponed to 2010. The NEM will help Malaysia avoid being caught in the middle-income country trap. The NEM was delayed probably because the government was unable to resolve the contradiction of making the economy more competitive and transparent while at the same time keeping the bumiputera-only business opportunities. As long as there is a need to keep the bumiputera (read UMNO-connected businessmen) happy, real structural adjustments to the economy may be impossible. Interestingly, one of the loudest voices for reforms of the pro-bumiputera NEP was Nazir Razak, the Prime Minister's younger brother and chief executive officer of CIMB, the country's second-largest bank.[10]

Although much was made of reforms under "Najibnomics",[11] his first budget speech did not impress the market. Among the key items were the introduction of a 4 per cent goods and services tax (GST), a lowering of the personal income tax by 1 per cent to 26 per cent, and a real property gains tax (RPGT). However, the GST has attracted much opposition from within his own party while he was forced to rescind the RPGT after negative feedback from property developers and foreign investors.[12] The budget deficit is expected to be running at 7.6 per cent of the RM 663 billion (US$195 billion) GDP in 2009. A far more serious problem during the year was the massive drop in foreign direct investments (FDI). In 2009, FDI was expected to go down by 50 per cent compared to 2008.[13] This drop follows a 21 per cent drop in 2008.

MIC And MCA Troubles

The year 2009 saw major changes in the Malaysian Chinese Association (MCA) and the Malaysian Indian Congress (MIC), the two most important parties in the BN after UMNO. The MCA crisis erupted when the President Ong Tee Keat engineered the sacking of his deputy Chua Soi Lek in July. Ong had refused to accept Chua as his deputy from the moment they were both elected in 2008, claiming that the latter's sex scandal meant that he was not morally fit to be a political leader.[14] With nothing to lose, Chua managed to get enough support to force an MCA Extraordinary General Meeting (EGM) to nullify his sacking from the party, restore him to the deputy presidency, and obtain a vote of no-confidence against Ong. The EGM held on 10 October 2009 surprised all when the delegates voted to give Chua back his membership of MCA but not the deputy presidency, and supported the no-confidence motion against Ong Tee Keat. Ong refused to resign despite an earlier public pledge that he would resign if he lost the vote. Chua, meanwhile approached Najib and UMNO for support, and this paved the way for the Registrar of Societies (ROS) to reinstate him to the deputy presidency. By this time, both Ong and Chua realized that the only way for both to stay in power was to join forces. They announced a "Greater Unity Plan" (GUP), but this was rejected by about a quarter of the central committee who wanted fresh elections to select a completely new leadership. This group was led by Liow Tiong Lai, a MCA Vice President and Wee Ka Siong and Chew Mei Fun, from the Youth and Women's wing respectively. With the crisis affecting BN's public persona and increasing pressure on UMNO to intervene,[15] Najib told the two MCA factions that fresh elections was the only option. The party election will take place in early 2010. UMNO's very public intervention is bound to affect MCA's credibility in the next GE, and confirms the critic's view that MCA is merely a political tool for UMNO to get Chinese support.

While MCA replaced its leadership after the 2008 GE, it was the reverse for MIC. Samy Vellu's feudal-like grip on the party saw him re-elected unopposed for his eleventh term as MIC President. First elected as President in 1979, he is the longest serving president in MIC and this feat can never be replicated. This is despite an open plea from Najib for the MIC delegates to replace Vellu with a new team of leaders.[16] While Najib was more diplomatic,[17] former PM Mahathir was blunt telling delegates to "throw out" Samy Vellu and his team and support a rival team led by S. Subramaniam.[18] Despite this, delegates voted for all of Samy Vellu's men. Samy's win gave him a new level of confidence and he announced that he will lead the "rebranding" of MIC. However, nobody seriously believed that the MIC could regain Indian support as long as Samy Vellu held on to power.

The inability of MIC to bring in new leadership forced Najib to look outside of MIC for Indian support. In October, Najib launched a new Indian-based party, Makkal Sakti,[19] hoping that the party would help the BN recover its Indian support. Unfortunately, the Makkal Sakti party imploded two months later in December when its central committee tried to sack its President for, ironically, behaving like Samy Vellu, that is, running the party like a feudal lord.[20]

By-elections, Cow Head, Ketuanan Melayu, Caning, and Back to Bahasa Melayu

The year opened with the Kuala Terengganu by-election, followed by Bukit Gantang, Bukit Selambau, and Batang Ai (in Sarawak) simultaneously, Penanti, Permatang Pasir, Manek Urai, and Bagan Pinang. PR won all, except for Bagan Pinang and Batang Ai, confirming that East Malaysia still remained the BN's stronghold.

In August, a group of fifty Muslims paraded a severed cow's head and placed it at the gates of the Selangor Government's state secretariat. They were protesting the relocation of a Hindu temple to Shah Alam, a Malay-majority residential area. This shocked the nation as the cow is sacred to the minority Hindus. Initially, the Home Minister, Hishamuddin Hussein, the first cousin of Najib, defended the protestors, many of whom were UMNO members. However, the huge public outcry compelled the Home Minister to order the ringleaders to be charged under the Sedition Act. To add insult to injury, one of the ringleaders, Ahmad Mahayuddin Abd Manaf, said this outside the court as a reminder to the non-Malay population: "It's proven historically that this is Tanah Melayu. Others are categorised as second-class citizens."[21]

The same month saw a young Malay mother, Kartika Sari Dewi Shukarno, sentenced to six strokes of the cane for drinking beer by the Pahang Syariah Court. In an unusual twist, she refused to appeal and said she wanted to be caned. It created a huge furore among women's groups around the world as no Muslim woman had ever been caned for drinking in Malaysia. The controversy forced the court to postpone the caning several times using all sorts of excuses, and the PM even asked her to appeal her sentence. At the year's end, the sentence had yet to be carried out.[22]

The rise of Islamic fundamentalism went beyond the cow-head issue as radical Muslims became bolder during the year. PKR's MP Zulkifli Noordin submitted a private member's bill to amend Article 3 of the Federal Constitution to clearly define Malaysia as an Islamic state.[23] Although the private member's bill had no chance to become law, it nevertheless gave comfort to the Islamists that there are fundamentalists among lawmakers. This was soon followed up by another controversy when Selangor PartiIslam Semalaysia (PAS) Commissioner Hasan Ali championed banning the sale of beer in Muslim-majority areas.[24] This has wide ranging implications given that there are very few locations where the Muslims are in a minority. In another blatant incident, two Muslim journalists acting on false information that the Catholic Church was converting Muslims into Christians and the word "Allah" was being used in church services, participated in a Catholic mass where they took the communion,[25] considered sacred by Catholics. The men later wrote about their experience in an article entitled "Tinjaun Al Islam Dalam Gereja: Mencari Kesahihan Remaja Murtad" (Observation of *Al Islam* in Church: Searching for the Truth About Apostasy among Muslim Youth) which was published in the May 2009 issue of the *Al Islam* magazine. Despite several police reports, no action was taken against the journalists or the magazine. If the reverse had occurred, if non-Muslims had taken part in an Islamic ritual in a mosque, the government would have taken action immediately.

There was also a dispute over the use of the word "Allah" by non-Muslims, with the government taking the position that only Muslims can use that word even though Christians in the Middle-East have been using "Allah" for many years without any problems. When a lower court ruled on 31 December 2009 that a Catholic newspaper could use the word "Allah" for its Bahasa Melayu section, Muslim groups promised demonstrations in the new year.[26] The increasing intolerance towards non-Islamic faiths in Malaysia is a trend that is worrying to many given that the government appears unwilling to confront the Islamists for fear of losing Malay support.

For most of the second half of the year, the opposition successfully put the government on the defensive over National Civics Bureau (BTN or Biro Tata Negara) courses. The Selangor Government started the assault by ruling that Selangor civil servants were banned from BTN courses.[27] The BTN courses were said to spread racism towards the non-Malays, promote the concept of *Ketuanan Melayu* (Malay Supremacy), and "brainwash" participants into supporting UMNO. Previously all civil servants, students in public universities, and holders of government overseas scholarships were required to attend BTN courses, usually held in a camp over several days. Despite overwhelming evidence that BTN courses catering to Malay-Muslim participants were encouraging racism,[28] the government refused to scrap the courses, arguing that BTN programmes were useful nation-building courses. Najib side-stepped the issue by ordering BTN to have more elements on 1Malaysia while his deputy, Muhyiddin Yassin, maintained that there was nothing wrong with the existing BTN.[29]

In July, after six years, the government reversed the policy of teaching science and mathematics in English. The policy was introduced by then Prime Minister Mahathir Mohamad to improve the standard of English in the country. The policy reversal was due to intense pressure from the unlikely alliance between Malay nationalist Gapena (Gabungan Penulis Nasional or National Writers Union) and Chinese educationists who argued that teaching science and mathematics in English would make no difference to the overall standard of English in the country. At a demonstration organized by the Abolish PPMSI (Pengajaran dan Pembelajaran Sains dan Matematik dalam Bahasa Inggeris or Teaching and Learning of Science and Mathematics in English) Movement in Kuala Lumpur on 7 March, the police had to use water cannons and tear gas to disperse thousands of protesters. Mahathir tried to reverse the decision by running a poll on his popular blog, Che-Det.com, which showed overwhelming support for the continuation of the policy.[30] But the government stuck to its decision and it is certain the standard of English in Malaysia, already low, will get worse with this decision. This was also the first reversal of a major policy put in place by Mahathir. Beginning in 2012 the teaching of both subjects in primary schools will revert to Bahasa Melayu for national schools and Chinese and Tamil in vernacular schools.

PKFZ Political Business and Missing Jet Engines

Despite Najib's ability to generate a new image, he could not escape from the perception among the middle class that it is business as usual when it comes to corruption. This was reflected in Transparency International's 2009 Corruption Perception Index (CPI) which saw Malaysia slide from number 47 to number 56 out of 180 countries. Two major corruption cases stood out in 2009: the Port Klang Free Zone (PKFZ) scandal and two "missing" jet engines.

In the PKFZ affair, Kuala Dimensi, a company linked to UMNO heavyweights and a politician allegedly overcharged the Port Klang Authority by several billion ringgit when it acted as the turnkey contactor for the PKFZ. A report claimed that cost overruns and interest payments could go as high as RM 12 billion (about US$3.4 billion).[31] The previous Minister of Transport had earlier issued letters of guarantees to the project, meaning that the government was liable if the project became insolvent. The scandal affected the MCA as all the guarantee letters were issued by MCA ministers. Public pressure caused the arrest of an engineer, project architect, and two former Port Klang Authority officials. However, the three senior BN politicians named in the report, former Transport Ministers Ling Liong Sik and Chan Kong Choy and BN Backbenchers Club's chair Tiong King Sing, were left out. This caused many to question the government's commitment to fight high-level corruption, although the Attorney General did announce that more arrests will take place in 2010. However, it is almost certain that no senior MCA figures will be charged given that senior UMNO members are involved in the deal.

In November, it was reported that the Royal Malaysia Air Force (RMAF) had "lost" one F5E jet engine worth RM 50 million in 2008. It was an inside job with several ranking officers involved. Two weeks later, after intensive media scrutiny, the RMAF was forced to admit that in fact two jet engines went missing, smuggled out of Malaysia and sold to a middleman in Argentina. It was also revealed that a Brigadier-General, who was a department head at the time, and forty other armed forces personnel were dismissed in 2008 over the incident. It was also clear that there was an attempt to cover-up as the Brigadier-General continued to receive his pension and other retirement benefits despite the sacking. The story gained currency primarily because Najib was Defence Minister in 2008 and any cover-up would require his sanction. By the end of the year, all that was promised was "no cover-up" and that an investigation was under way.[32]

MACC and Teoh Beng Hock

The government's credibility in combating corruption was left in tatters on 16 July 2009 when Teoh Beng Hock, a thirty-year-old political aide to a DAP Selangor State Executive Councillor, was found dead outside the office of the Selangor Malaysian Anti-Corruption Commission's (MACC) office in Shah Alam. The political aide had been interrogated overnight despite the fact that he was merely a witness and was not under arrest. There was immediate suspicion that he was pushed off the building although the MACC claimed that he fell out of a window. They also insinuated that he may have committed suicide as he was involved in corruption. Nobody believed the MACC's version of events and many felt insulted by the suicide insinuation.[33] Teoh would not have committed suicide as he was planning for his wedding and his fiancée was two months' pregnant with their child.

Rather, the DAP and the public believed that MACC was ordered by the BN federal government to find evidence of corruption in the PR-led Selangor State Government in order to bring down the state government.[34] This was quite clear as the MACC (and the police), controlled by the federal government, were openly biased in favour of the BN government.

The inquest into Teoh's death brought more political drama when the Selangor government engaged an external expert, Pornthip Rojanasunand, head of Thailand's Central Institute of Forensic Science (CIFS), as their consultant. Her testimony that there was an "80 per cent" chance that Teoh was murdered prompted the coroner to order Teoh's body be exhumed for a second autopsy.[35] At the time of writing, the inquest had been postponed to January 2010. Whatever the outcome of the inquest, it is clear that the majority of the public believed that Teoh did not die an accidental death and that foul play was involved.

Opposition Politics and Pakatan Rakyat's First Convention

The opposition, especially PAS, suffered from serious internal disputes for most of the year. Problems arose because one faction, led by Party President Abdul Hadi Awang, Deputy President Nasharuddin Mat Isa, Secretary-General Mustafa Ali, and Selangor PAS Commissioner Hasan Ali, wanted to talk to UMNO about a possible "unity" government. This faction believed that Malay/Muslim unity was paramount to ensure Malay/Muslim political dominance. The other faction, dubbed the Erdogan faction, was led indirectly by Nik Abdul Aziz Nik Mat, better known as Tok Guru, the *member-besar* of Kelantan.[36] Tok Guru was adamant that PAS must not form a unity government or pact with UMNO.[37] Matters came to a head when Tok Guru called for a special *muktamar* to sack what he called "problematic leaders" — meaning Hadi and his group. Hadi Awang and Isa were strong enough to stop the EM but agreed to a one-day "seminar". The seminar reaffirmed PAS's commitment to PR and no more "unity talks" with UMNO.[38] Towards the end of the year, the pro-UMNO faction launched an internal assault on Tok Guru using political blogs, attacking his deputy Husam Musa and his son-in-law.[39] They also forced Tok Guru to cancel a trip to Mecca which was sponsored by a businessman. However, given Tok Guru's personal popularity, it is unlikely that they can force him from office.

PKR had an eventful year primarily because Anwar Ibrahim, its defacto leader, faced his second sodomy trial. After several delays, the court refused to throw out the case but adjourned it to 2010. Internal politicking was intense and some saw Anwar losing control of the party during several internal spats. For example, Anwar could not control the internal criticism against Zaid Ibrahim, one of PKR's most prominent members. In the end, Zaid announced that he would go "on leave" from PKR and concentrate on PR's common platform (see below). In East Malaysia, Anwar was unable to quell a rebellion when his nominees, who were to lead the state PKR, were rejected by the locals. In the end Anwar was forced to appoint Baru Bian to lead Sarawak PKR, while in Sabah Jeffrey Kitingan emerged as a key power broker after challenging Anwar's nominee.

Among the three PR parties, DAP had a relatively quiet year politically. Other than the defection of its state assemblyman in Perak, which caused the downfall of the Perak PR government, the party was relatively united. Penang residents were generally happy with Lim Guan Eng's tenure as Chief Minister, although there were complaints that he had become more arrogant since assuming the post.

The common problem faced by the opposition-held states was the civil service and other state institutions. Many civil servants were still loyal to the BN and actively sabotaged the work of PR governments. The PR government had to be careful as the police and MACC were used to harass and investigate the PR governments. The year saw several high profile investigations against the Selangor MB and other executive councillors.[40] The MACC and police regularly investigate other PR politicians, and even threatened to charge Lim Guan Eng with sedition.[41] There appears to be a deliberate attempt to destabilize the PR-led state governments by constantly investigating its members for corruption and other offences.

On 19 December, PR made a significant political move forward when it held its first convention, with delegates from all three parties. A significant document, the Common Policy Framework (CPF), was adopted.[42] It explicitly rejects the racial politics of the BN and stresses on good governance and social justice. Although it was less detailed than the original draft submitted by Zaid Ibrahim, it was nevertheless a major achievement for the alliance given the completely opposite aims of PAS (which wants an Islamic state) and DAP (which wants a secular state). Although contentious issues such as an Islamic state were purposely left out, there was enough in the CPF to send a message to the polity that PR was capable of holding together if they were to win in the next GE.

Foreign Policy: Tracing the Father's Footsteps

The highlight of Najib's first year was his four-day official visit to China in early June which he described as "most fruitful". It was a sentimental journey given that it was Prime Minister Abdul Razak Hussein, Najib's father, who established diplomatic relations with China thirty-five years ago in 1974. China rolled out the red carpet for the visit and the event was reciprocated by President Hu Jintao, who flew into Kuala Lumpur on 10 November, the first visit by a Chinese head of state to Malaysia in fifteen years.

Najib also visited some of the ASEAN capitals, a ritual for all new prime ministers. He visited Indonesia on 22–23 April, followed by a trip to Brunei at the end of April. He visited Singapore on 21–22 May. In early December, he paid his first official visit to Thailand.

Najib's first official engagement with ASEAN turned out to be a non-event as the Fourteenth ASEAN Summit in Pattaya on 3 April was cancelled when Thai demonstrators stormed the conference centre.

There was some minor turbulence during the year in relations with Indonesia. The first issue was over a traditional dance. A Malaysian tourism commercial aired on Discovery Channel sparked uproar in Indonesia because it featured the Pendet dance, which the Indonesians claimed is unique to Bali. Indonesians vented their anger over the perceived cultural piracy, calling Malaysia a "nation of thieves". Large scale demonstrations were held in Jakarta and one firebrand legislator even urged the Indonesian government to declare war on Malaysia. It was later revealed that the advertisement was produced by Discovery (who admitted to the mistake and apologized) and the advertisement was quickly withdrawn. A similar spat erupted two years ago over the use of the folk song Rasa Sayang in another Malaysian tourism advertisement. The Indonesians claimed that Rasa Sayang "belongs" to them.

The second, and far more serious, issue was the treatment of Indonesian workers in Malaysia. It is estimated there are about two million Indonesian workers in Malaysia, employed as drivers, maids, and construction workers. There have been many horrific cases of abused Indonesian maids. In June, the Indonesian government enforced a temporary ban on sending domestic workers to Malaysia. The Indonesians also wanted Malaysia to set a higher minimum wage for maids and better working conditions. The ban has not been lifted officially.

In early December it was revealed that the Foreign Ministry had recalled the country's envoy to the United Nations in Vienna after he voted against an International Atomic Energy Agency (IAEA) resolution criticizing Iran for ignoring UN Security Council resolutions by continuing to build its uranium enrichment programme. Wisma Putra was concerned over international perceptions after Malaysia, along with Venezuela and Cuba, voted against the IAEA resolution.

In general, Malaysia's foreign policy did not change during Najib's first year in office. ASEAN and the Organisation of the Islamic Conference (OIC) remained the key areas of Malaysia's foreign policy, while maintaining good relations with the West and China. If anything, the perception was that Najib is more pro-Western than his predecessor Badawi.

The Rise and Rise of Najib

By year's end it was clear that Najib Tun Razak was a much more sophisticated and wily politician than his predecessor Abdullah Ahmad Badawi. A poll showed that Malaysians liked him and that the BN would probably win back the two-thirds majority if a GE was held.[43] More importantly, he had strong support in UMNO.[44] Najib and his advisors were able to project only the positives and discard the negatives. One simple explanation for this is that Najib is still on his honeymoon period with the polity as 2009 was his first year in office. His clever use of the slogan "1Malaysia. People First, Performance Now" appeared to have captured the people's imagination and the NKRA was designed to meet the major criticism of the government's delivery system. Najib' strategy was simple: as long as the government can deliver a better life and living standards, the public will support the BN despite issues with good governance, Islamization, ethnic politics, and high-level corruption.

As for the opposition, they will be glad to see the end of 2009. Although the opposition was able to unveil the CPF in December, for most of the year Anwar was unable to build any political momentum for the PR. In 2008, Anwar had all the political momentum and many believed that he would be in Putrajaya within a year of the March 2008 GE. This did not happen and by the end of 2009 there was no more talk of Anwar taking power through defections. In summary, 2009 was Najib's year.

Notes

1   There is a lot of controversy over the Sultan's decision. He was heavily criticized primarily because he was the former Lord President (Chief Justice) and had written that under normal circumstances the constitutional monarch must always accept the political advice of the incumbent political head. Read the opinion of BN Chan, a widely respected former court of appeal judge, "The pretended power of dispensing with the law by regal authority as perceived in the tussle between the Sultan of Perak and the Mentri Besar" <http://english.cpiasia.net/images/sultan_of_perak_mb.pdf> (accessed on 1 December 2009). Among the chattering class, the explanation for the Sultan's action was a threat from the BN that they would not guarantee that the Perak throne would pass to Sultan Azlan's son, Raja Nazrin Shah, as there are other claimants. This threat is credible given that in December 2008 a new ruler was elected as the Yang-di-Pertuan Besar of Negri Sembilan, bypassing the eldest son of the previous ruler.

2   "No Dissolution, New MB to be Sworn In", Malaysiakini, 5 February 2009; "Pathetic Police Play Politics in Perak", Malaysiakini, 3 November 2009; "Shame of the Decade: The Perak Power Grab", *Malaysian Insider*, 30 December 2009. The government told the mainstream media not to air any pictures or video of the Perak Speaker being dragged out of the Assembly.

3   Among the key PR people were an American company, APCO Worldwide. APCO's strategic role was confirmed when they opened an office in Kuala Lumpur in August 2009, five months after Najib became PM.

4   The NEP is hugely unpopular with the Chinese and other non-Malays as many feel that the NEP has rendered them as "second-class" citizens. See James Chin, "The Malaysian Chinese Dilemma: The Never Ending Policy (NEP)", *Chinese Southern Diaspora Studies* 3 (2009): 167–82.

5   "Najib: New Category of Merit-Based PSD Scholarships", *The Star*, 27 June 2009.

6   "Najib Assures Bumis, Malays of Their Rights", *New Straits Times*, 13 June 2009.

7   "Najib Popularity Surges in First 100 Days: Poll", Malaysiakini, 8 July 2009.

8   However, critics pointed out that there was no real "liberalization" given that there was no bumiputera participation in the twenty-seven subsectors in the first place.

9   "Ekuinas Aims for Double-digit Returns on Investments", Bernama, 4 September 2009.

10   "Why it is Time to Review the NEP", Malaysiakini, 24 April 2009.

11   "Harvard Business School to Study 'Najibnomics'", *The Star*, 25 September 2009.

12   "Property Tax Let-off for Owners", *The Star*, 23 December 2009; "Najib Plumps for GST to Fill Revenue Hole", *Business Times* (Singapore), 25 November 2009.

[13] "Najib Braces Country for Severe FDI Drop", *Malaysian Insider*, 11 June 2009.

[14] Chua Soi Lek was secretly videotaped having sex with his mistress, and the video was widely distributed to the public prior to the 2008 GE. Chua was forced to resign from the MCA vice-presidency as well as his post as Health Minister, and he did not stand in the 2008 GE.

[15] In two previous serious leadership tussles, UMNO intervened as MCA's "big brother" and imposed a peace plan. See James Chin, "New Chinese Leadership in Malaysia: The Contest for the MCA and Gerakan Presidency", *Contemporary Southeast Asia* 28, no. 1 (April 2006).

[16] "In MIC, Samy Vellu Shows Who's the Boss", *The Malaysian Insider*, 12 September 2009.

[17] "Najib: Party Leaders Must Be Popular with People, Not Just Party Members", *The Star*, 12 September 2009.

[18] See the exclusive interview with Mahathir in *Makkal Osai*, 10 September 2009. The interview was conducted two days before the MIC convention and it was clear Mahathir wanted to send a message to the MIC delegates.

[19] "Najib Launches Malaysia Makkal Sakti Party", *The Star*, 10 October 2009.

[20] "Revolt in Makkal Sakti over Samy Vellu-style Leader", *The Malaysian Insider*, 28 November 2009.

[21] "'Cow Heads' Launch Racist Rant", *Malaysian Insider*, 8 December 2009.

[22] "Kartika Spared Caning, But Only Until after Ramadan", *Malaysian Insider*, 24 August 2009; "Whipping Kartika", *Nut Graph*, 1 September 2009.

[23] "Zul Noordin Wants Constitution Amended to Clarify Country's Status", *Malaysian Insider*, 21 October 2009.

[24] "Hassan Ali's Religious Police to Nab Errant Muslims", *Malaysian Insider*, 24 August 2009.

[25] The men had consumed the "communion" which is a white wafer that is blessed by the priest. Catholics believe the blessing supernaturally transforms the white wafer into Jesus Christ's body.

[26] "PM Calls for Calm as Debate Rages On", *Malaysian Insider*, 4 January 2009.

[27] "Selangor Moves to Unveil BTN Inner Workings", *Malaysian Insider*, 30 November 2009.

[28] "Inner Details of BTN Reveal Past Transgressions", *Malaysian Insider*, 8 December 2009; "BTN's Stolen Malaysians", *Nut Graph*, 23 December 2009; "PKR to Dissect BTN with Aid of Insiders", *Malaysian Insider*, 27 November 2009.

[29] "BTN Course to Inculcate Nationalism Not Political Indoctrination Says Muhyiddin", Bernama, 26 November 2009.

[30] "Dr M: 80% of Poll Respondents Oppose PPSMI Abolishment", Bernama, 10 July 2009.

[31] See the report "Position Review of Port Klang Free Zone Project and Port Klang Free Zone Sdn Bhd", PriceWaterhouseCoopers (PWC), 3 February 2009.

[32] "PM: No Cover Up Over Missing Jet Engine", *The Star*, 21 December 2009.

[33] There was widespread disgust with the head of MACC, Ahmad Said Hamdan, when it was revealed that his son was found guilty of importing child pornography into Australia. When asked about it, he was quoted as saying "I can bet with you that it's something that you will find on most men's handphones." "Ahmad Said: Not Fair to Link Me to Son's Offence", *The Star*, 1 March 2009. In December, it was announced that Ahmad Said Hamdan would retire from MACC five months early. The government obviously felt that public confidence could not be regained with him at the helm of the MACC.

[34] One DAP member commented cynically to this writer that Teoh's death "saved" the Selangor government as the huge public outcry forced the BN to rethink its strategy of using corruption to bring down the Selangor government in 2009.

[35] "Thai Expert Says Teoh's Death '80pc' Homicide", *Malaysian Insider*, 21 October 2009.

[36] The Erdogan faction, named after Turkey's Islamist PM Recep Tayyip Erdogan, as a source of inspiration. They are known also as strong Anwar supporters in PAS. They believe that the only way to defeat the BN is to join forces with DAP and PKR.

[37] Nik Aziz's strong opposition to PAS-UMNO unity was due in part to his experience in the early 1970s when PAS joined the BN. In the mid-1970s UMNO caused a split in PAS Kelantan and engineered PAS's ouster from BN in 1978. "Nik Aziz Calls for EGM to Dispose Pas President and Problematic Leaders!" *Sin Chew Daily*, 23 October 2009.

[38] "Hadi: PAS Committed to Pakatan", *The Star*, 7 November, 2009.

[39] Nik Aziz's son-in-law held the position as CEO Kelantan Menteri Besar Incorporated, a company owned by the state government. He was forced to resign. See "Nik Aziz Tells Son-in-law to Step Down as Kelantan MB Inc's CEO", *The Star*, 23 November, 2009.

[40] "MACC Goes after Another Selangor Exco", *Malaysian Insider*, 5 August 2009; "Selangor MB Sues Govt, MACC and Its Chief, *The Star*, 28 April 2009; "MACC Quizzes Selangor Exco Member Ronnie Liu", *The Star*, 23 October 2009; "MB: MACC on Fishing Trip in Selangor", Malaysiakini, 8 September 2009.

[41] "Kit Siang Claims IGP [Inspector General of Police] Out to Get Him, Pakatan Leaders", *Malaysian Insider*, 2 August 2009; "DAP Backs Guan Eng against Cops", *Malaysian Insider*, 26 December 2009.

[42] A copy of the CPF can be downloaded from <http://dapmalaysia.org/repository/The_Policies_of_Pakatan_Rakyat-EN.pdf>.

[43] "BN Will Win Elections If Held Today", Malaysiakini, 15 November 2009.

[44] "Poll Shows Strong UMNO Backing For Najib", *Malaysian Insider*, 30 December 2009.

Southeast Asian Affairs 2010

THE LIMITS OF MALAY EDUCATIONAL AND LANGUAGE HEGEMONY

Lee Hock Guan

In Malaysia, the implementation of official policies to entrench Malay educational and language hegemony has prevented the growth of an inclusive multicultural educational system. The New Economic Policy (NEP) period, 1971–90, was characterized by the United Malays National Organization (UMNO) dominated state aggressively pursuing its educational and linguistic hegemonic objectives. In the 1990s, however, several developments forced the state to take a more conciliatory stance towards the educational and linguistic needs of the minority groups. The state claims that critical aspects of multiculturalism have been incorporated into the 1996 Education Act. But, in practice, it appears that official policies have not fully abandoned the hegemonic project, and minority languages and educational needs are still discriminated against in the national education system.

Malay Educational and Language Hegemony

During British rule, the colonial state's use of racial categories to classify and control the local population contributed to the emergence of a racially segmented society. Race-based discrimination policies set the British colonizers apart from the colonized, and, significantly, indigenous Malays from the immigrant Chinese and Indians. Race thus was constitutive of the state in colonial Malaya. Indirect rule, attained through various treaty agreements, recognized Malay States as sovereign states and treated Malays as the native group with a "special position". For this reason, the British positioned Malays at the top of the political hierarchy of ethnic groups in the colony. Selected Malays, then, were educated and recruited for high administrative positions in the colonial

LEE HOCK GUAN is Senior Fellow at the Institute of Southeast Asian Studies.

bureaucracy, which were denied to Chinese and Indians because of their immigrant status.

Partly to maintain the Malay character of the Malay States, the colonial state felt morally obliged to provide Malays with a Malay-medium education that would enable them to preserve and reproduce their culture and tradition. Colonial policies gave preferential treatment to the education of Malays and this resulted in the formation of a separate and unequal colonial educational system. For ideological and economic reasons, the colonial state funded a limited number of public English schools and financially assisted Christian missionary English schools. Enrolment in English schools was largely multi-ethnic as admission was open to students of all races. In contrast, the British refused to build mother tongue schools for Chinese and Indian students because of their immigrant status.[1] While Chinese medium schools were funded, established, and administered by the Chinese community, the plantation owners were tasked by the state to provide Tamil education for the Indians, most of whom were Tamils. In brief, in colonial Malaya, Malay and English schools were regarded as state educational institutions, while Chinese and Indian schools were treated as not just private — but in fact "foreign" — institutions in the colony.

The primacy of mother tongue schooling in colonial Malaya naturally reinforced the ethnic groups' primordial attachment to their languages such that language became an essential ethnic marker. Because Malay feelings of insecurity were intertwined with their attachment to their language, defending Malay as the national language of *Tanah Melayu* (Land of the Malays) appealed to most Malay individuals and nationalist groups. Malay emotive attachment to their language also coalesced with a nationalism that imagines a nation as a community of people sharing a common culture and language. However, although a majority of Malay nationalists clamoured to recreate multi-ethnic colonial Malaya into a linguistically homogenous nation, UMNO elites, in order to win the support of their Chinese and Indian political partners and the British, agreed to constitutionally define Malay(si)a as a monolingual polity where Malay is the sole national and official language, while also recognizing minority language rights. UMNO elites' language and educational concessions to the Chinese and Indians were met with strident criticisms from Malay writers, journalists and teachers, UMNO lower rank leaders and the grassroots, and, at that time, the "ultra-nationalist" Pan-Malaysian Islamic Party (PAS). Those who strongly championed the Malay language also disagreed with the compromise to include Chinese and Indian primary schools in the national education system.[2]

In the 1960s, Chinese struggles for a multilingual official language policy that would recognize Malay, Chinese, Tamil, and English as official languages were upended when the state categorically rejected it. Chinese and Tamil primary schools were also denied equality of status and treatment, and to denote their inferior status their designation as "vernacular schools" was maintained. As for the Chinese-medium secondary schools, the state refused to grant them official recognition and so excluded them from the national education system. Given the strident Malay voices calling for a Malay-medium-only educational system, the non-Malay ethnic groups, especially the Chinese, became increasingly suspicious of the real intent of Article 12 of the 1956 Razak Report on education:

> the ultimate objective of educational policy in this country must be to bring together the children of all races under a national educational system in which the national language is the major medium of instruction, though we recognize that progress towards this goal cannot be rushed and must be gradual.

Chinese educationists in particular came to suspect that the state's "ultimate objective" was to eradicate mother tongue primary schools in order to construct a single stream education system. They assumed this was the real reason why Section 21(2) in the 1961 Education Act gave the Education Minister the authority to convert the Chinese and Tamil schools into the Malay medium. Chinese distrust of the UMNO-dominated state's "ultimate objective" intensified after the 31 May 1969 ethnic violence when the state started to forcefully pursue policies to entrench Malay language hegemony while marginalizing the Chinese and Tamil primary schools.[3]

The mounting politicization of language and education issues from 1970 to 1990 led the linguist Asmah Haji Omar to criticize Malay politicians and "national language pejuang" (defenders) for incessantly exhorting that "national language is the tool for national unity."[4] Arguing against those who zealously championed the linguistic homogenization of society as a means to achieve national unity, she wrote:

> use of one and the same language in an ordinary social interaction does not guarantee that a nation will be united. This goes to show that language is not the only tool for the soldering of a multiracial nation. There are other tools for this purpose; among these are social justice, tolerance, unity of purpose, ideology, equal opportunity ... and so on.[5]

She reminded the *pejuang* of the national language:

> to comprehend well the Language Act in the Malaysian Constitution as
> well as the provision for foreign and local languages, as given in the
> Education Ordinance, before fighting any aspect of this issue. There
> is no indication in the Language Act that Malay is the one and only
> medium of instruction; rather it is the main medium of instruction in
> the national system of education. This provision in the Language Act
> again reflects the language tolerance that is practiced by the Malaysian
> government within a multilingual society. If the language pejuang do
> not ensure this tolerant attitude, then there is a danger that language,
> the so-called tool of unification, will turn into a tool for breaking-up of
> society.[6]

Moderate voices like hers were, however, ignored by official policies. Mixing
ethnocentric sentiments with the belief that only a single education stream can
facilitate national unity, the national language *pejuang* demanded the conversion
of Chinese and Tamil primary schools into the Malay medium. From 1970 to
1990, they were an influential force as their leadership and supporters came
from the Malay teachers, journalists, and writers, in short the Malay-educated
intellectuals who constituted the most powerful Malay social groups. In their
defence and promotion of the Malay language, they obtained fervent support from
Malay tertiary students and associations, as well as the main opposition Malay
political party, PAS.

Partly because Malay teachers formed a very powerful group within UMNO
in the 1970s and 1980s, championing the Malay language became an important
UMNO agenda. Crafting language and education policies that appealed to Malays
led to sizable Malay electoral support for UMNO over the years. With the party's
growing dominance, the education bureaucracy was soon transformed into an
entity subservient to UMNO's frequent interference. Conversely, Chinese and
Indian individuals and groups increasingly were excluded from official language
and education policymaking processes, which became monopolized by Malay
bureaucratic elites and UMNO leaders. Consequently, throughout the 1970s and
1980s the Education Ministry enacted and pursued policies to entrench Malay
language hegemony at the expense of marginalizing minority language instruction[7]
and Chinese and Tamil primary schools.

Can a largely ethnically homogenous education civil service and teaching
profession remain responsive to and serve the needs of a multi-ethnic society?
In theory, if an ethnically homogenous education civil service acts professionally,
it should be able to serve the diverse interests and needs of a multi-ethnic

society without prejudice. In the Malaysian case, regrettably, the mostly Malay education bureaucracy has rarely shown any capability of acting impartially on the language and educational needs of the different ethnic groups in society. In fact, more often than not, Malay education bureaucrats and teachers are imbued with deeply rooted ethnocentric sentiments, which has led them to denigrate the value of minority cultures and languages while privileging the Malay language and culture. Mohamad Ikhsan, a former director of Technical Teacher's Training College, Kuala Lumpur, wrote:

> Employment with the government, for example, is in favour of one racial group. Thus, in the domain of educational services, which is overseen by the government, the majority ethnic group, which is the Malays, predominates. Given this scenario, many educational leaders, whether inadvertently or purposely, develop and conduct programmes and activities that favour the majority and exclude the minority. Many educational institutions fail to capture the essence of multiculturalism or conduct leadership and decision-making as if homogeneity were the norm, even though the school or organization has a heterogeneous population. … Under present circumstances, many educational administrators and leaders in the system lack competencies to deal with the complexities presented by a pluralistic society.[8]

Indeed, the majority of Malay linguists, intellectuals, and educators probably would identify with the national language *pejuang*'s demand to convert the national education system into a single stream education system as a means to achieve national integration.

In brief, throughout the 1970s and 1980s, the UMNO-Malay dominated state implemented policies to entrench Malay language hegemony by greatly magnifying the role of the Malay language at all educational levels while marginalizing the minority languages. The state harboured an "ultimate objective" to linguistically homogenize the national educational system. But it has not pursued its "ultimate objective", and it still cannot do so, because UMNO is afraid of losing the vital Chinese and Indian votes. Unlike the Chinese and Tamil communities, which could protect and preserve their mother tongue schools, the situation of non-Malay bumiputra languages is rather dire, with many of them in varying stages of obsolescence. Since 1990, although the state has included selected aspects of multiculturalism in official language and education policies, in practice, however, official policies continue to be riddled with ambiguities and contradictions. Needless to say, the Chinese and Indian communities, and a growing number of non-Malay bumiputra groups as well, do not trust the Malay-dominated education bureaucracy to look after their language and educational interests.

Language, Schooling, and National Integration

In the early 1990s, several cases of alleged racial discrimination against Indian students in some national primary schools in the Klang valley forced the state to appoint K.J. Ratnam to lead a commission to investigate those allegations, and, more importantly, the general question of racial discrimination in schools. From the findings, Ratnam and his team concluded that there was no systematic racial discrimination in the national primary schools, but only isolated cases of it. The team's findings and conclusions were, however, fiercely contested and criticized by a broad range of Indian and Chinese individuals and groups. Since a majority of Chinese and Indian parents continue to believe that racial discrimination is deeply entrenched in the national schools, the ethnic polarization of primary schools has worsened over the years.

Several factors have contributed to the Chinese and Indian students' exodus from national primary schools. Since the implementation of the 1967 National Language Bill and 1971 National Culture Act, state efforts were directed towards entrenching Malay language and cultural hegemony in public educational institutions. Malay bureaucrats and school administrators and teachers would discriminate against minority languages and cultures such as not providing for pupil's own language (POL) classes even though there were more than fifteen non-Malay students in a class, practise selective or outright banning of non-Malay cultural symbols and celebrations, refuse to allow the registration of non-Malay and non-Muslim student societies, and indulge in negative stereotyping of non-Malay bumiputra, Chinese, and Indian students, and so on.

With the growing Islamization of Malay society and politicization of Islam, ethnocentric practices in the public educational institutions extended into the religious sphere as well. When UMNO and PAS became intensely embroiled in championing Islam, invariably public educational institutions were drawn into the heated tussle between the two parties. In the late 1980s, when Anwar Ibrahim was the Minister of Education, he initiated the Islamization of public educational curricula and institutions. A variety of Islamic practices and symbols thus were incorporated into school curricula and extramural activities. The end result was that the secular character of public educational institutions was incrementally usurped and displaced by an Islamization trend which constrained and proscribed behaviour, dress codes, symbols, and activities deemed "un-Islamic". For non-Muslim students, the increasing Islamization of national schools simply meant additional marginalization and discrimination against their cultures and religions.

The aggressive pursuit of policies to re-make the national primary schools into largely conservative Malay-Muslim institutions led Chinese and Indian parents to perceive the schools as at best unresponsive and at worst antithetical to their children's pedagogical and social, cultural, and religious needs. For the Chinese and Indians, the practical need to master the Malay language has also lost its value since non-Malay students' admission into local public tertiary institutions is curtailed by ethnic quota policies and employment opportunities in the public sector by ethnic preferential hiring policies. For the Chinese, there is also a perception that the quality of instruction in national primary schools is inferior to that of the Chinese primary schools. Naturally then, as the majority of Chinese and Indian parents would prefer to enroll their children in the Chinese and Tamil primary schools, ethnic segmentation at the primary school level has worsened over the years. For example, in 2000, more than ninety per cent of Chinese students were enrolled in Chinese primary schools and seventy-five per cent of Indians in Tamil schools.[9]

While the state is concerned with the worsening ethnic polarization of primary schools, it remains unable, or perhaps is unwilling, to sensibly deal with the push factors which have contributed to the exodus of Chinese and Indian students from the national schools. The prevailing belief in UMNO, and probably also the education bureaucracy, continues to be that ethnic polarization at the primary school level is harmful to national integration. Since politically UMNO cannot afford to eradicate the mother tongue schools so as to create a single stream education system, the education bureaucracy has introduced some measures to address the ethnic polarization problem. One of the measures was the Vision Schools project.

Proposed in the early 1990s by the Mahathir administration, the Vision Schools project was seen as a means to overcome the increasing ethnic segmentation at the primary school level.[10] In this project selected national and Chinese and Tamil primary schools would be housed in a common compound. To preserve their unique identity, each of the constituent schools would be independently operated with its own administration, teachers, headmaster, and classrooms. However, students from the three different schools would share common facilities such as the school canteen, courtyard, multi-purpose hall, library, and school field. The rationale was that the sharing of common facilities and co-participation in intramural activities, club activities, and games and team sports would facilitate ethnic interaction from an early age and help to inculcate cooperation, understanding, and tolerance. Thus, in theory, Vision Schools could promote "unity in diversity" since each school would be run independently and would maintain its own identity.

Mahathir's attempt to implement the Vision Schools project was strongly opposed by Chinese educationists, many Chinese associations, and probably a majority in the Chinese community. For them, as officially conceived, the national schools would be first among equals in the Vision Schools as the Malay language would be the language of communication for all the inter-ethnic extracurricular activities and communication outside of the classrooms. If Malay is the only language used outside of the classrooms, it would modify the school environment for the constituent Chinese and Indian schools. The Chinese thus felt that the Chinese schools might end up losing their Chinese identity; in fact, they feared that in the long-run the Chinese schools could become Malay medium schools. As such, suspicion abounds among the Chinese that the Vision Schools project is yet another underhand attempt by UMNO and the education bureaucracy to pursue their "ultimate objective" of eradicating Chinese schools. Unsurprisingly, since 2002[11] only five Vision Schools have been established even though in the Seventh Malaysian Plan (1996 to 2000) the Education Ministry had aimed to build twelve Vision Schools in different locations in the country.

If the ethnic, religious, and lingustic discriminatory practices in the national schools persist, the non-Malays will continue to prefer to enroll their children in their mother tongue schools. In fact, to make the national primary schools more attractive to the non-Malay students there is a need to move towards a multicultural education environment where minority students and their languages, cultures, and religions are given equal respect and treated fairly. UMNO and education bureaucrats need to see that the state of inter-ethnic relations in a multiethnic society is dependent on a variety of factors, including equal opportunity, equality of treatment, tolerance, and acceptance. Inter-ethnic communication in a common language in itself is not sufficient to guarantee better ethnic relations.

Teaching Mathematics and Science in English

On 11 May 2002, Prime Minister Mahathir announced that English would replace the Malay language as the medium of instruction for the teaching of science and mathematics in the national education system. In fact, as early as the 1990s Mahathir was already convinced that Malays needed to master the English language in order to upgrade their scientific and technical knowledge and skills and to stay relevant and competitive in the increasingly globalized knowledge economy.[12] The shift to English policy elicited passionate objections from a wide spectrum of both Malay and Chinese individuals and groups. The policy shift was hastily executed six months later in 2003 in a staggered fashion, beginning with primary one, secondary one, and lower six.

By the mid-1990s, the Malaysian manufacturing economy was gradually losing the competitive edge to other Southeast Asian countries and China. Thus there was a need to upgrade the economy from a manufacturing- to a knowledge-based one. But the shift to a knowledge economy encountered two major deficiencies: a shortage of skilled workers and the relative underdeveloped scientific knowledge and research competencies in the country. Without conducting any study, Mahathir asserted that the lack of progress of scientific and technological research and knowledge in the country was due to the use of the Malay medium to teach science and mathematics. Although considerable resources had been allocated to develop Malay as a language of science and technology, Mahathir felt that the language had not kept pace with the development of knowledge in these fields. The problem was further compounded by the fact that even as English was taught as a subject from primary one, English proficiency had deteriorated in Malaysia. Malaysian students' weak mastery of English had resulted in their having difficulties dealing with scientific and technical texts, especially at the tertiary levels where the majority of readings are in English. Rather than fast tracking the translation of scientific and technological knowledge into Malay, Mahathir decided that it would be more efficient and effective to revert to the English medium for teaching mathematics and science.

The government hastily implemented the shift to English policy without public debates or consideration of objections from the various segments of Malaysian society. Furthermore, no research was conducted to examine the utility, feasibility, and implications of the shift before the policy was implemented. For example, problems like the need to retrain teachers to teach in English and to translate adequate textbooks and other teaching materials into English were not addressed. Obviously, if teachers themselves are not competent in English, how can they competently impart content knowledge in English to the students? Unsurprisingly, the preliminary findings of student performance in mathematics and science after the shift to the English medium were not promising at all.

When the policy shift was announced, the Malay language *pejuang* and Chinese educationists publicly raised their objections; many in UMNO and the education ministry were also against the policy shift, but they did not dare to go against Mahathir. Both Malay language *pejuang* and Chinese educationists highlighted the claim that students learn mathematics and science more effectively when the subjects are taught in their mother tongue. Because children grow up in an environment where they are exposed primarily to their mother tongue, they would learn concepts and thinking skills faster in it.

The Malay language *pejuang* also alarmingly claimed that the language shift would undermine the Malay language's premier status as the national language and thus dilute Malay identity. At the functional level, the national language *pejuang* insisted that the switch to English would stifle the growth of the Malay language, especially as a language for science and mathematics. They also claimed that the switch would lead to English usurping the role of Malay as the medium of inter-ethnic communication. The generalized fear then was that the shift to English policy would undermine the Malay language's role in facilitating national integration, as the new policy would hold back the spread of the Malay language within the non-Malay communities.

On the other hand the Chinese educationists did not see why Chinese primary schools should also be subjected to the English-medium policy since the quality of science and mathematics instruction in Chinese schools was generally well regarded. Given that the subjects tested at the primary six assessment examinations are Malay, English, Chinese, Mathematics, and Science, it would mean that in the Chinese schools all subjects would be in English except Malay and Chinese. In other words, the policy shift would in effect transform the Chinese schools into English medium schools with Mandarin and Malay offered as language subjects. While the Chinese educationists could not prevent the implementation of the policy in the Chinese schools, because of their rigorous objections a compromise was struck in which both Mandarin and English would be used to teach mathematics and science in the Chinese schools. The formula used would maintain the dominance of Mandarin as the medium of instruction: for mathematics two hours were to be taught in English and six hours in Mandarin, and for science two hours in English and three hours in Mandarin; thus English as a subject would be reduced to four hours per week. In the end, Chinese educationists regarded the move to subject Chinese students to the English-medium policy as another insidious attempt by the UMNO-controlled state to dilute the schools' Chinese identity, and, in the long run, to eliminate it.

Predictably, the implementation of the shift to English-medium policy resulted in all sorts of deficiencies and problems. A study conducted by Universiti Pendidikan Sultan Idris (UPSI)[13] in 2008 raised a number of problems: a majority of teachers had problems teaching the subject in English, many students could not follow the lessons in English, the Standard Five science and mathematics results for their sample pioneer cohort were less than satisfactory, and there was no significant improvement in students' English proficiency.[14] The most important effect of the shift to English policy, the UPSI study claimed, was that it greatly widened the urban-rural and upper-lower income educational inequalities. Indeed, the UPSI study insists that only the urban middle and upper income group stood to gain from the shift to English-medium policy.

Unsurprisingly, when Mahathir stepped down as the prime minister in late 2003, the support for the shift to English-medium policy started to peter out. Education bureaucrats and UMNO politicians started to voice their objections and disagreements. The national language *pejuang* and their supporters, including the Chinese educationists, started to actively mobilize against the policy. On 31 January 2009, various opponents of the policy shift established the Movement for the Abolition of the Teaching of Mathematics and Science in English. Supporters of this movement included the political parties, PKR and PAS, student groups such as the National Union of Malaysian Muslim Students, and language groups such as National Writers Association Malaysia and Linguistic Society of Malaysia. Without Mahathir around to back the policy, the Najib administration quickly conceded and announced in late 2009 that the government would revert back to teaching mathematics and science subjects in Malay in 2012. Again, the latest decision was made by UMNO leaders and the education bureaucratic elite without any public debate or consultation, especially with segments of the Malaysian public that supported the shift to English-medium policy.

The Plight of Other Indigenous Languages

The situation of the non-Malay indigenous languages is very different from that of the Chinese and Tamil languages.[15] The preservation and reproduction of the latter are assured because they are used as media of instruction in the national-type primary schools. In theory, the other indigenous languages should be in good standing since the Malaysian constitution recognizes minority language rights. But, in reality, many linguists have acknowledged that a significant number of the around 140 other indigenous languages are in varying stages of obsolescence and, indeed, some are facing language death. Even though the 1996 Education Act stipulates that in national primary and secondary schools "indigenous languages shall be made available if it is reasonable and practicable to do so and if the parents of at least fifteen pupils in the school so request", the future of the other indigenous languages remains rather bleak. Official policies that entrenched Malay language hegemony had their most damaging effects on the languages of the smaller, weaker indigenous groups in both Peninsular and East Malaysia.

While language loss can be attributed to a number of factors, in the modern world of nation states a major threat to indigenous languages has come from the belief that an official language is necessary to facilitate national integration. In this contest, the preservation of minority languages is seen as antithetical to the fostering of an official language, and thus to facilitating national integration. In fact "states often operate under the questionable assumption that citizens will speak and write the national language only if they are prevented from using any other language".[16] Since the UMNO-Malay dominated state regarded the other indigenous groups as belonging to the "Malay peoples", it largely adopted a strategy of integrating and assimilating them into Malay society. Malay policymakers also tended to hold negative opinions about the other indigenous groups' language, culture, and religion precisely because they regarded the non-Malay natives as less advanced. Thus it was only in the 1990s that the Malay-centric state started to provide facilities to teach the other indigenous languages in the national schools. Otherwise, since official language policies systematically marginalized or excluded the non-Malay indigenous languages, their preservation and reproduction became very dependent on the efforts of civil society groups, local communities, and academics.

The role of academics is very important in the preservation and reproduction of the other indigenous languages because of the need to systematically record, codify, and develop the languages and to collect their oral stories and histories. During the colonial period, Christian missionaries and European scholars played key roles in the codification and teaching of indigenous languages; for example, the American-based Summer Institute of Linguistics (SIL), a Christian-based language research institute established in 1934, helped to preserve some of the Austronesian languages, including the indigenous languages in Sabah and Sarawak.[17] SIL has indeed produced several major publications on a number of the indigenous languages in Sabah and Sarawak. Even after independence in 1963, SIL linguists have continued to partner various individuals and groups from Sabah and Sarawak to record and codify the other indigenous languages and stories.[18]

Sadly, since independence, most research on other indigenous languages in Malaysia is still conducted by foreign scholars as Malaysian linguists, the majority of them Malays, "have been preoccupied with research on Malay and on the national language development and planning processes, and on strategies in the implementation of the language policy".[19] The majority of Malay linguists indeed would probably identify with the national language *pejuang* camp and thus it was not surprising that the Malaysian Linguistic Society played a very active role in opposing the 2003 shift to English-medium policy.

The Department of Orang Asli Affairs (Jabatan Hal Ehwal Orang Asli — JHEOA) has for years aggressively pursued measures to assimilate the Orang Asli into Malay society, such as conversion to Islam and language shift to Malay. Thus, even though eighteen Orang Asli languages are supposed to be protected by the JHEOA, in practice, instead of protecting the languages, it tried to linguistically assimilate the Orang Asli into the Malay language. Partly in response to the JHEOA's assimilationist policy and the increasing state appropriation of their ancestral land, the Orang Asli mobilized and formed organizations such as Peninsular Malaysia Orang Asli Association (established in 1976). In addition, various international and local civil society groups have linked up with Orang Asli communities and associations to fight for their interests and rights. In 1999, the state was thus pressured to consider introducing two Orang Asli languages, Semai and Temiar, as subjects in selected national primary schools in Perak. But, in the end only the Semai language was introduced as a subject in selected schools in Perak. In general, for a number of reasons, the future of a majority of Orang Asli languages remains depressing.

The twenty-point Agreement which the Federal Government signed with Sabah and Sarawak in 1963 stipulates that: (a) Malay should be the national language of the federation; (b) English should continue to be used for a period of ten years after Malaysia Day (i.e., 1963), and (c) English should be an official language of Sabah and Sarawak for all purposes, state or federal, without limitation of time. Yet, by the 1990s, English was no longer a functioning official language in Sabah and Sarawak; instead Malay had become the sole official language. The federal state, with the support of their Malay-Muslim supporters in Sabah and Sarawak, aggressively promoted Malay language hegemony. Consequently, several of the other indigenous languages are in varying critical obsolescence stages.[20]

In Sarawak, during British colonial rule, the Iban language was treated as one of the state official languages. Also, Christian missionaries established Iban vernacular schools in selected rural areas, and Iban was offered as a subject in primary and secondary schools. To facilitate the development of Iban culture and language, the colonial state established the Borneo Literature Bureau (BLB) in 1958. The BLB played an active and important role in promoting the Iban language and in collecting, recording, and publishing Iban oral literature and histories. Since 1970, however, the standing of the Iban language in Sarawak has declined precipitously; it has lost its official language status, and its presence in national schools has shrunk considerably. Indeed, when in 1977 the Dewan Bahasa dan Pustaka took control over the BLB, it started to actively promote Malay language hegemony while marginalizing the other indigenous languages, especially the Iban language.[21] In view of this, a number of individuals and civil society organizations have mobilized to struggle for Iban language rights. Three of the most prominent organizations are the Society for the Advancement of the Iban Language (established 1964), Sarawak Dayak Iban Association (established 1984), and Tun Jugah Foundation (established 1985). In the end, although the Iban language has been taught as a subject in selected schools in Sarawak for many years, the teaching of the language faces all sorts of obstacles and discriminations.[22]

Classes in Kadazandusun, the other indigenous language taught as a subject in selected national schools in Sabah, were only started in 1997. This was in spite of the fact that during colonial rule Kadanzandusun was taught in selected missionary schools and Native Voluntary Schools in the 1950s and 1960s. But, with the state actively promoting Malay language hegemony since 1970, the Kadazandusun language was dropped as a POL until its reinstatement in 1997. As with the Iban language, civil society organizations, such the Kadazandusun Language Foundation (established 1995), played a key role in preserving and reproducing the language as well as pressuring the federal government to recognize it as a mother tongue to be included in the POL programme. In 2003, although the state announced that the Murut language would be taught as a subject in four primary schools, the policy has yet to be carried out. The only other Sabahan indigenous language that has experienced any organized efforts at preservation is the Iranun language, with the assistance of the SIL.

Thus, in spite of the 1996 Education Act, official policies toward the other indigenous languages have yet to deviate from the state's aim to entrench Malay language hegemony. Only the larger minority groups such as the Iban and Kadzandusun have been successful in pressuring the federal government to include the teaching of their languages as subjects in the schools. In general, the Malay-centric state continues to devote only limited resources to support the preservation and reproduction of the other indigenous languages. Instead, it is civil society groups and local communities that are shouldering the burden of recording, codifying, and developing the other indigenous languages. Given their limited resources, lackluster state support, and the presence of a number of adverse factors,[23] the preservation and reproduction of the other indigenous languages are not assured in the long run.

Conclusion

The problem of education and language in Malaysia is that government policies are pro-assimilationist in that the primary aim is to construct a linguistically homogenous nation. As such the government has aggressively pushed policies to expand the role and presence of the Malay language and cultural symbols in the national education system. Although minority language rights are recognized in the constitution and the teaching of selected minority languages is stipulated in the 1996 Education Act, in practice the Malay-dominated education bureaucracy has discriminated against the minorities and their languages, cultures, and religions in the national education system. The majority of the other indigenous languages in the country need attention and, if effective policies are not implemented soon, some of them will become extinct. The Najib administration's decision to abandon the shift to English-medium to teach science and mathematics does not signify real progress but, rather, a return to the status quo. If there is demand for the teaching of mathematics and science in English, steps need to be taken to address that demand.

In the international arena, since the second half of the twentieth century, language and education policies increasingly have come under the influence of a multiculturalist vision which believes all languages are of great value and language rights are an integral part of human rights. Apart from the rising influence of multiculturalism, various globalization forces and the rise of English as the international language have also pressured monolingual polities and policies to move in the direction of bilingualism or multilingualism. In Malaysia, the trend has been in the opposite direction.

Notes

1   There were also Chinese and Tamil mother tongue schools established by Christian missionaries. In the 1930s, fearing the increasing politicization of Chinese schools, the British tried to exert control over them by promising financial assistance such that Chinese schools which accepted funds from the colonial state came under the latter's control.

2   They were also upset with the decision to keep English as an official language for ten years after independence.

3   Before 1970, the national education system comprised Malay, English, Mandarin, and Tamil primary schools; Malay and English secondary schools; and largely English-medium tertiary institutions. Chinese secondary schools which accepted government financial aid had to switch to English medium, while those which did not accept aid were excluded from the national education system and became the privately funded secondary schools or Independent Chinese Secondary Schools (ICSS).

4   Asmah Haji Omar, *Language and Society in Malaysia* (Kuala Lumpur: Dewan Bahasa dan Pustaka, 1982), p. 50.

5   Ibid.

6   Ibid., p. 51.

7   Importantly, in Sabah and Sarawak there was not much protest from the non-Malay
     bumiputera groups over the federal state's decision not to provide them with mother
     tongue education until the mid-1980s.

8   Mohamad Ikhsan, *Malaysia: From Traditional to Smart Schools, The Malaysian
     Education Odyssey*, edited by Ibrahim A. Bajunid (Shah Alam, Selangor: Oxford
     Fajar, 2008), p. 325.

9   Although there is less ethnic segmentation at the secondary school level, there are
     pockets of largely monoethnic secondary schools such as national-type Chinese
     secondary schools, ICSS, Islamic secondary schools, MARA colleges and sains
     secondary schools. At the tertiary level, since the privatization of this sector, growing
     ethnic segmentation at this level has emerged with the Chinese and Indian students
     making up the majority of enrolment in the private colleges (except for Malay-
     owned private colleges which enrolled mostly Malay students) and the public tertiary
     institutions being largely Malay enclaves except for University of Malaya and Universiti
     Sains Malaysia.

10   In the 1980s, the then Minister of Education, Abdullah Badawi, proposed the Student
     Integration Plan for Unity, or RIMUP, policy to facilitate racial integration in schools,
     but the policy was not really implemented.

11   In mid-2000, after the economy had already started to achieve healthy growth rates,
     Mahathir, with the support of the MCA and Gerakan, announced reviving the Vision
     Schools project.

12   In December 1993, then Prime Minister Mahathir declared that Malaysian universities
     would be allowed to use English as a medium of instruction in courses related to
     science and technology. Two years later in 1995, the Education Ministry issued a
     guideline that would permit public universities and higher institutions to determine the
     percentage of their courses to be taught in English and this should be in accordance
     with the relevance and needs of the use of the language, as well as with the ability
     of these institutions to conduct academic courses in the language. Apart from this,
     a hundred per cent use of English is allowed if the courses concerned are taught by
     foreign lecturers, or if the courses are postgraduate ones which are attended by foreign
     students as well. The guideline also proposed that these institutions should increase the
     use of English in tutorials, seminars, assignments, etc. Asmah Haji Omar, *Language
     and Language Situation in Southeast Asia: With a Focus on Malaysia* (Kuala Lumpur:
     Akademi Pengajian Melayu, Universiti Malaya, 2003).

13   It is important to note that the authors of the UPSI study most likely would identify
     with the Malay language *pejuang* camp. Indeed, many scholars affiliated with UPSI were
     actively involved in the Movement for the Abolition of the Teaching of Mathematics
     and Science in English.

14   Thus, of the 2003 pioneer batch who were taught mathematics and science entirely in English, in 2008 only 31.1 per cent of year six pupils elected to answer the Primary School Evaluation Test (UPSR) Science paper fully in English, while 68.9 per cent opted to use Malay, or vernacular (Chinese/Tamil), or a combination of three languages (English-Malay-vernacular).

15   The non-Tamil South Asian languages, such as Punjabi, Sindhi, Malayee, Telugu, and Chinese dialects, such as Hokkien, Cantonese, Teochew, Hainanese, have also been adversely affected. Within the Chinese and Indian communities, there is a great variety of dialects and languages. For the Chinese, the linguistic homogenization of the community started with the advent of modern Chinese nationalism in the early 1900s. After the 1919 Chinese Revolution in China, the language standardization in Chinese schools in colonial Malaya took place with a shift in the medium of instruction from various dialects, particularly Hokkien, Cantonese, Hakka, Teochew and Hainanese, to Mandarin or Putong Hua. Since independence, with Mandarin essentially achieving the status as the language marker defining Chinese identity, the in-group linguistic homogenization of the Chinese community has accelerated. For a number of reasons, increasingly the younger generation of Chinese Malaysians are losing their proficiency in their dialects while gaining fluency in Mandarin. Indeed, the dialect speakers and communication spaces are shrinking in numbers and size. A similar trend is observed with the non-Tamil language groups like the Punjabi, Sindhi, Bengali, Telugu, Malayalam and others, but in this case the shift is to English as their first language as few of them would enroll their children in the Tamil schools. For historical, economic, and social reasons, non-Tamil language groups have shifted from their mother tongue to English. During colonial rule, the non-Tamil groups would largely enrol their children in the English schools.

16   Geoffrey Benjamin, "Orang Alsi Languages: From Heritage to Death", in *Minority Cultures of Peninsular Malaysia: Survival of Indigenous Heritage*, edited by Razha Rashid and Wazir Jahan Karim (Penang: Academy of Social Sciences, 2001).

17   <http://www.sil.org/sil/> (accessed 9 December 2009).

18   In fact, SIL together with three local organizations — Kebudayaan Iranun, Kadazandusun Language Foundation, and United Sabah Bajau Organization — and UNESCO, organized the first Malaysian Indigenous Peoples' Conference on Education (MIPCE), in Kota Belud, Sabah in April 2007.

19   Asmah Haji Omar, *Language and Language Situation in Southeast Asia: With a Focus on Malaysia* (Kuala Lumpur: Akademi Pengajian Melayu, Universiti Malaya, 2003), p. 41.

20   See John Postill, *Media and Nation Building: How the Iban Became Malaysian* (New York: Berghahn Books, 2006) (chapters three and four) on the state Malayization of Sarawak while marginalizing Iban language and literature.

21   For an excellent summary of the plight of the Iban language see Jimbun Anak Tawai, in *Mother Tongue Education of Malaysian Ethnic Minorities*, edited by Kua Kia Soong (Kajang, Selangor: Dong Jiao Zong Higher Learning Centre, 1998).

22   Ibid.

23   Limited access to formal education, remote physical location, the concentration of speakers of particular languages, and low rates of exogamous marriage, among other relevant factors such as group cohesion and religious uniformity, have meant that so far there has been little threat to the maintenance of selected minority languages, despite little institutional support. However, encroachment of urbanization, easier access to urban centres, and rising enrollment in formal education have had a negative impact on language maintenance.

Myanmar

MYANMAR IN 2009
On the Cusp of Normality?

Robert H. Taylor

The year prior to the inauguration of Myanmar's first ostensibly civilian government chosen through multiparty elections since 1960 seemed remarkably ordinary after the alarums of the previous two *annus horribilis*. While 2007 saw public protests by Buddhist monks and 2008 the devastating Cyclone Nargis that resulted in approximately 140,000 deaths, despite various issues such as those discussed in Martin Smith's accompanying essay on relations between the military State Peace and Development Council (SPDC) government and various ethnically-designated organizations, the major political events of 2009 took place largely in meeting venues and courtrooms. The high drama that have marked so many of the years between the 1988 public protests which brought to an end the rule of the Burma Socialist Programme Party and 2009 was absent. Except for a few incidents, some verging on the tragic, others the farcical, Myanmar seemed rather similar to other ASEAN countries which are considered "normal" by most observers most of the time.

Daw Aung San Suu Kyi on Trial

The most bizarre event of the year was the arrest of a middle aged, unemployed, four-time married, fifty-four-year-old, student of trauma and religion, Mormon devotee, and former member of the United States Army, to whom, he claimed, God had spoken in regard to an alleged threat on the life of Daw Aung San Suu Kyi, the General-Secretary of the National League for Democracy (NLD).[1] Daw Aung San Suu Kyi's many years of house arrest since her first detention in 1989 were due to come to an end in May 2009, thus placing the ruling military

ROBERT H. TAYLOR, the author of *The State in Myanmar* (2009), is Visiting Professor in Asian and International Studies at the City University of Hong Kong.

council, whose Chairman, Senior General Than Shwe, ultimately makes major decisions, in a quandary. Should they release her and risk her generating both domestic and international attention, perhaps destabilizing the final stages of their seven-step road map to a constitutional government acceptable to the military in 2010, or contrive a means to keep her under detention and thus incur the wrath of exiled political organizations and most Western and some Asian governments? The antics of John William Yettaw, whether inspired by God or man, saved them from facing that dilemma.

Daw Aung San Suu Kyi, who had been under house arrest for the past six years at her late mother's house on University Avenue in Yangon, was to be released on 27 May under the terms of her detention order according to the 1975 Law to Safeguard the State Against the Dangers of Those Desiring to Cause Subversive Acts. However, on the morning of 6 May, at approximately half past five, Yettaw was arrested while swimming, with the aid of home made flippers and two empty five-litre water bottles, in Inya Lake, thirty yards from the residence of the United States Charge d'Affair's residence on Pyi Road, the opposite end of the lake from Daw Aung San Suu Kyi's abode. Upon arrest, he admitted he was coming from her home.

Daw Aung San Suu Kyi, Yettaw, and Daw Aung San Suu Kyi's two female companions were consequently placed on trial for a variety of offences surrounding the bizarre events of 3 to 6 May. According to the court record, Yettaw had arrived in Myanmar on a tourist visa on 2 May and checked into a small downtown hotel. The next evening he took a taxi to the vicinity of the NLD leader's residence, not far from the new American embassy building, walked through a drainage pipe toward the lake, and made his way along the bank to the rear entrance of her residence. It turned out that he had used this mode of access and egress the previous November during a twenty-six-day visit to Myanmar. During this visit he also called on various non-government organizations in Yangon, offering to work for them. In 2008, though not meeting Daw Aung San Suu Kyi, he left her a copy of the *Book of Mormon* which she subsequently gave to the police after his arrest.

The trial, which commenced on 14 May, was heard in the North Yangon District Court at Insein Prison where Daw Aung San Suu Kyi and the others were detained for the duration, she in special prison officers' facilities. In addition to an American consular official on behalf of Yettaw who attended all sessions of the trial, on two occasions, journalists and diplomats were able to witness the hearings, which concluded on 11 August with a verdict of guilty. Three diplomats were also allowed to meet with the NLD leader on one occasion after hearings concluded.

The length of the trial was in part determined by a number of procedural questions surrounding requests by the defence team to call the NLD Vice-Chairman, former General Tin Oo, and NLD executive committee member, recently released from detention, former journalist U Win Tin, as character witnesses for Daw Aung San Suu Kyi. The court eventually ruled that her character was not in question, but rather her action in allowing Yettaw to rest, take two meals, and leave a number of items, including two chador, at her residence. In his statement to the court, Yettaw stated that prior to entering Myanmar he had visited the Thai town of Maesot and met with, among others, several members of the exiled political activist community there. Never explained in the course of the trial was what Yettaw did between approximately midnight when he left Daw Aung San Suu Kyi's back garden on the fifth of May and his arrest five and a half hours later on the sixth, nor why he chose to swim rather than leave via a drain pipe as on the previous occasion. All four of those on trial were found guilty; the three Myanmar citizens were given three years' rigorous imprisonment and the American a total of seven years' rigorous imprisonment under three separate acts, including for swimming in the lake and violating the conditions of his tourist visa.

However, before the court had issued its verdict in front of fifty-one ambassadors and other diplomats and twenty-five local and foreign journalists, an order had been received from the Chairman of the SPDC to the Home Minister, remitting half of the sentence and suspending the remainder. The three women would therefore be held for eighteen months house arrest in acknowledgement of Daw Aung San Suu Kyi "being the daughter of Bogyoke Aung San who sacrificed his life for the independence of Myanmar, viewing that peace, tranquility, and stability will prevail, that no malice be held against each other, that there be no obstruction to the path to democracy", as an act of leniency on his behalf.

Daw Aung San Suu Kyi's lawyers, all of whom are leading members of the NLD, immediately appealed her conviction and by the end of the year the Supreme Court had yet to rule on the legality of the law under which she had been convicted or whether the trial itself had been fairly conducted. In the meantime, she and her companions were returned to her University Avenue home to sit out the next eighteen months, a term of house arrest which most likely would end after the 2010 elections. Yettaw was also soon removed from Insein Prison thanks to the intervention of United States Senator James Webb. Senator Webb, recently an articulate critic of the American policy of isolating Myanmar and applying economic and other sanctions to the disadvantage of American strategic interests — and to the great benefit to China — flew to Naypyitaw on 15 August where he met with the senior general and other top leaders of the SPDC. Senator Webb, who is the Chairman of the East Asia and Pacific Affairs Sub-Committee of the Senate Foreign Relations Committee, left Yangon by special United States military plane accompanied by Yettaw, who was subsequently returned via Bangkok to the United States. The Myanmar state media marked Senator Webb's visit as a "first step to promotion of the relations between" the United States and Myanmar. He is the highest-level American congressman or official to visit Myanmar in more than fourteen years. He also met with Daw Aung San Suu Kyi and they reportedly expressed differing views as to whether China posed a potential threat to American and Myanmar interests. Though Senator Webb's stopover to Myanmar as part of a tour of the region did precede more official diplomatic exchanges between the new Obama administration and Naypyitaw, the original Yettaw saga was seen by the government of Myanmar as a stunt designed by unknown sources to place an obstacle in the way of improved relations following the election of Barrack Obama as President of the United States.

The United States Rediscovers Myanmar

The new government of President Obama made it clear early on that the long-standing position of the former Bush administration, one which could be characterized as ever increasing economic sanctions and no dialogue except on American terms that amounted to capitulation by the SPDC, was inadequate to protect America's larger interests in Asia. Consequently, Secretary of State Hillary Clinton launched an immediate review of policy toward Myanmar. Her deputy, Kurt Campbell, as Assistant Secretary for East Asian and Pacific affairs, in an explanation which revealed his unfamiliarity with the recent history of Myanmar's approaches to the United States, articulated at a State Department press conference on 28 September the result of the review. The revised American approach, he said, was to "begin a direct dialogue with the Burmese authorities to lay out a path towards better relations." This would include democracy, human rights, cooperation on international security issues, including non-proliferation of nuclear and other weapons, as well as narcotics cooperation and the retrieval of the remains of American military personnel killed in Myanmar during World War II. However, until there was "concrete progress toward reforms", left unspecified, existing sanctions would remain in place. In any event, the administration had little choice over the lifting of sanctions as most are mandated by congressional legislation.

This new American agenda, which broadened United States interests from vague and ultimately unrealistic political demands linked to release of all political detainees, and the revision of the finalized constitution prior to elections, was actuated in early November when Campbell and his assistant, Scott Marciel, paid a two-day visit to Myanmar. In Naypyitaw, they met with Prime Minister General Thein Sein, and other senior SPDC officials, but not the Senior or Vice-Senior Chairmen of the SPDC. Senior General Than Shwe was pointedly touring the Nargis-hit areas of the delta at the time. The American delegation also met with representatives from a variety of former insurgent organizations that had reached ceasefire agreements with the government and some senior leaders of the NLD and other political groups.

The government also tried to arrange a meeting, at the request of the U.S. State Department, between the American team and Daw Aung San Suu Kyi and other members of the NLD Central Executive Committee. However, as the SPDC refused to allow former General and NLD Vice-Chairman Tin Oo, who was also under house arrest, to attend, Daw Aung San Suu Kyi cancelled the meeting. Arrangements were made for Campbell and Marciel to meet with other leaders of legally registered political parties, including the National Unity Party, which received twenty-five per cent of the vote in Myanmar's aborted elections in 1990, but they did not attend those meetings and arranged their own with ethnic spokespersons, officially unrecognized by the government, and others at the American Charge d'Affaires residence.

In reporting on their encounters in Myanmar to the press upon arrival in Bangkok, Marciel indicated that they covered much the same ground as previous Western and United Nations interlocutors had frequently assayed. The need for the 2010 elections to be inclusive, fair, and to take into account all actors in the political process as they defined it, including the NLD and its leaders and unspecified but presumably non-ceasefire ethnically-designated political or armed groups were the fundamental points. Unsurprisingly, given the high bar that the Americans had established as their goals, little had resulted from the November exchanges by the end of the year and once more spokespersons in Washington expressed frustration at what they called "the lack of progress" in Myanmar. However, the efforts did reveal that the United States had other interests in Myanmar than just the achievement of an American-certified democratic regime, and allowed for some degree of latitude to develop in United States–Myanmar relations after the eventual elections.

While the courts in Myanmar were dealing with the results of Yettaw's midnight swim, there was finally a settlement out of court in the United States of another case that had dragged on for fifteen years. In 1994 an official of the U.S. Drug Enforcement Administration, Richard Horn, sued the Charge d'Affaire of the

American embassy and the Central Intelligence Agency station chief for allegedly attempting to discredit him in order to undermine his reports on the government of Myanmar's anti-narcotics activities, and hence creating the conditions for the renewal of American support for these activities. Such support was terminated in 1988 and has yet to be resumed. While denying any admission of guilt, the United States Government settled with Horn in November with a payout of three million dollars.

European and UN Policy in Disarray

During the Bush years, the European Union and its member states often appeared to be pursuing a similar approach to Myanmar as the United States, but perhaps with a greater degree of finesse and subtlety. That impression collapsed during 2009, not only as a result of the more sophisticated approach of the Obama administration, but also as disagreements among the member states of the European Union and the European Commission became increasingly apparent. While British Prime Minister Gordon Brown published a letter he wrote to "Dear Sui [sic]" on 29 December, making it clear that in his view the likelihood of the forthcoming elections, failing revisions to not only the government's plans but also the previously agreed constitution, would result in "condemning Burma to more years of diplomatic isolation and economic stagnation." He clearly did not share the view of the French Foreign Minister, Bernard Kouchner, who told the National Assembly's Foreign Affairs Commission on 7 October that "Sanctions are useless and everyone recognizes that." Referring to the review of policy then under way in Washington, Monsieur Kouchner suggested that perhaps the Europeans should "show greater openness to this government."

The disarray in European policy was revealed by the contradictory signals sent to Naypyitaw by various European Commission institutions. Following the conviction of Daw Aung San Suu Kyi, sanctions were increased, allegedly targeted at those involved in the legal processes of her conviction. However, at the Copenhagen Summit on climate change, the Myanmar Foreign Minister was met on the side of the formal meetings by the Swedish Foreign Minister, Sweden then holding the presidency of the European Union, the Danish Foreign Minister, and the EU Special Envoy to Myanmar, a left-wing Italian politician. It is believed to have been the first meeting between the EU special envoy, Piero Fassino, and a Myanmar minister. As the new European Union treaty, the EU constitution in all but name, came into place in November, confusion over who made European policy on Myanmar was compounded. Ambassador David Lipman, the EU's first

Ambassador to Myanmar, presented his credentials to Senior General Than Shwe in early December and announced afterwards that the EU was commencing a "sustained political dialogue" with the SPDC. This was in addition to the existing policy of supporting community-based organizations in Myanmar and providing humanitarian assistance.

United Nations Secretary-General Ban Ki Moon made his second visit to Myanmar in as many years in July. The brief visit, which included two meetings with Senior General Than Shwe and a quick tour of the Ayeyawady Delta area to inspect reconstruction work following Cyclone Nargis, concluded with a major address at the Drug Eradication Museum in Yangon. Whereas his previous visit centred on the UN assistance following Nargis, the 2009 visit focused on UN efforts, previously spearheaded by the secretary-general's series of special envoys, the most recent being Nigerian Professor Ibrahim Gambari. None of them had had any success, despite various expressions of optimism and lots of globe trotting and high level consultations, to finding a way of reconciling the interests of the SPDC government with Daw Aung San Suu Kyi and the NLD, which has been the primary focus of UN efforts. The Secretary-General's personal intervention proved to be no more successful.

Despite it being made clear to him in advance of his arrival in Myanmar that a meeting between the Secretary-General and Daw Aung San Suu Kyi would not be possible as she was sub judice, Ban Ki Moon raised the matter again in his first meeting with the Senior General. His willingness to do so in two meetings with Senior General Than Shwe in Naypyitaw was taken as an affront and evidence of the pressure the Secretary-General was under from the Western powers which dominate United Nations affairs on Myanmar. The lack of what was seen as "even handedness" by the United Nations in Myanmar's internal matters led to subsequent criticism of the Secretary-General's visit. That he brought the matter up again in his speech in Yangon and subsequent briefing to the Security Council in New York merely served to underscore the lack of rapport between the UN Secretary-General and the SPDC.

The Governments of Russia and China, both of whom vetoed a joint United States–United Kingdom Security Council resolution on Myanmar in 2007, highlighted again their very different approaches from those of the West to the country during the year. In June the Russian Foreign Ministry issued a statement noting Moscow's continuing opposition to "attempts to internationalise the internal situation in Myanmar, because it does not endanger peace and security in the region and the world at large." The statement, issued to note Russia's position on the trial of Daw Aung Suu Kyi then under way in Yangon, coincided with a five-day visit to China by Vice Senior General Maung Aye as the guest of Chinese Vice President Xi Jinping. Xi, believed to be slated to be the next President of China, visited Myanmar later in the year as a state guest of the Vice Senior General. In the Security Council following the Secretary-General's briefing, the Chinese representative, Lui Zhenmin, said it was "unfair to turn a blind eye to the progress that Myanmar had made" and that China fully understood Myanmar's challenges. Lui's views were echoed by the comments of the Vietnam representative and of several others from Africa but roundly opposed by Western spokespersons.

Near the end of the year the Secretary-General's Special Envoy to Myanmar, Professor Gambari, was reassigned to head up the joint UN–African Union peacekeeping mission to the Darfur region of Sudan. Having visited Myanmar twice during the year, his feeble influence had further waned as had that of all his predecessors. During his first visit of the year in February, the SPDC demonstrated its distain by not even inviting him to Naypyitaw to meet top leaders. Similarly, Daw Aung San Suu Kyi also refused to meet with him. His second visit was to lay the ground for the Secretary-General's visit. No new special envoy was yet appointed and the UN, like the EU, were left floundering to find a political role for itself. Meanwhile, it and other international actors waited to learn if they would have a function in Myanmar in the future.

ASEAN, China, India, and Bangladesh Maintain Business as Usual

Despite occasional floundering efforts to put pressure on the Government of Myanmar to conform to Western demands in support of the NLD and its leader, such as a claim by the Thai Foreign Minister in August about a possible consensus among member states to ask the SPDC to pardon Daw Aung San Suu Kyi following her conviction, the lack of unanimity among the governments of the region meant that ASEAN remained incapable of effecting anything within Myanmar's domestic affairs. Even the signing of a joint declaration by the ASEAN states with President Obama in November failed to include a reference to her renewed detention even though this was high on the American's agenda and initially expected by many following the inclusion of the issue in a major address on Asian policy by the president in Tokyo prior to the meeting.

China, on the other hand, continued to develop its economic and strategic relationship with Myanmar completely separate from internal political issues. The China National Petroleum Corporation completed agreements on the construction and operation of an oil pipeline from Rakhine state to Ruili/Shweli on the China-Myanmar border and commenced construction of a port near Sittwe where the oil will come on shore. When completed, this will obviate the need for ships to negotiate the Strait of Malacca and sail to the east coast in order to supply western China's petroleum needs. A similar agreement to construct a gas pipeline from Myanmar's Shwe gas field in the Bay of Bengal will supplement western China's natural gas requirements. Trade and investment between the two countries also continued to grow; trade by 26.4 per cent in 2008–9.

As noted at the beginning of this article, and discussed more fully by Martin Smith in his accompanying essay, the most violent episode in Myanmar during the past year occurred near the border between China and Myanmar, at Laukkai, the headquarters of the Kokang ceasefire group, led by Phon Kya Shin. According to the Myanmar Government, the Myanmar Democratic Alliance Army that Phon Kya Shin had led for a number of years — following the collapse of the gambling and other businesses it had been pursuing — had taken up the manufacture of weapons and illicit drugs to supplement its income. When efforts by the police to halt these activities led to the detention of a number of law enforcement officers by the rebel group, conflict erupted on the border and the resulting insecurity led to approximately 37,000 persons fleeing into China. The Myanmar side made it clear that it had acted on the basis of information provided by the Chinese authorities in Yunnan and subsequently Chinese Foreign Ministry spokespersons in Beijing said that "safeguarding the stability of the China-Myanmar border is in line with the vital interests of both people and is the shared responsibility of both governments."

India too continued to develop relations with Myanmar and Myanmar cordially responded. Indian Vice President Harnid Ansari visited Naypyitaw in February and signed a number of agreements designed to encourage growing trade, investment, and technical exchanges between the two countries. Myanmar's military continued also to cooperate with India in its efforts to contain ethnic insurgency along their mutual border in the north-west. Despite occasional expressions of concern from Dacca stimulated by the ongoing saga of illegal immigration in both directions across the Bangladesh-Myanmar border — often referred to misleadingly as the "Rohingya question" — and a tussle over the sea boundary between the two countries which has an impact on the development of the gas fields of the Bay of Bengal, relations between the two countries remained remarkably cordial, with a number of bilateral exchanges and meetings throughout the year intended to increase their tiny trade relations and improve electronic communications.

NLD Stands Pat

As international diplomacy concentrated on the role of the NLD and its iconic leader, the party and Daw Aung San Suu Kyi continued to struggle to make themselves relevant within or in contrast to the ongoing plans of the regime's seven-step road map to "disciplined democracy". As the party General Secretary was under house arrest she was only rarely allowed to meet with other members of the party, and the aging Central Executive Committee (CEC) — most of whose members were in their 80s and 90s — came under pressure from dwindling party rank-and-file to do something in the face of imminent elections. Consequently, a major two-day party strategy meeting was held at NLD headquarters in late April and resulted in the issuance of the Shwegondine Declaration.

The declaration, issued on 29 April and named after the street on which the party headquarters are located, covered little new ground. It reiterated repeated calls from the NLD leadership since the 1990s for the unconditional release of all political prisoners, a more recent demand for the revision of the constitution finalized in 2008, and recognition somehow of the results of the 1990 elections. Failing the resolution of these points, the party made it clear that it was most uncertain whether it would participate in the 2010 elections. Those elections, they also insisted, must be held under international supervision, a demand that the SPDC, with its repeated assertion of the need to find home-grown solutions to problems in a manner which respected state sovereignty, would be unlikely to concede.

Given her isolation and infrequent meetings with either the minister appointed to conduct relations with her, Labour Minister U Aung Kyi, or senior members of her party, other than occasionally with her doctor and lawyers, Daw Aung San Suu Kyi had to chart her own path through Myanmar's politics largely unguided by advice from others. Perhaps sensing that the support that had been generated both domestically and internationally for her call for economic sanctions in the mid-1990s was waning in the face of the forthcoming elections, she apparently indicated to her Special Branch liaison officer on 12 September that she wished to work with the Senior General to find a way to lift the sanctions. About two weeks later she wrote to the Senior General requesting permission to meet with the American Charge d'Affaire, a European Ambassador, and the Australian Ambassador in order to understand the nature and impact of the sanctions as well as the policies of their respective governments toward them.

Such a meeting was arranged on 9 October but the results were inconclusive and little was learned of the content of the exchanges. However, a month later Daw Aung San Suu Kyi wrote again to the Senior General directly in regard to the sanctions. The letter was released over the Internet probably before it had arrived in Naypyitaw, suggesting to some that it was more a stunt to draw attention to her activities than a serious offer to work to end sanctions. In the letter, she thanked the SPDC for facilitating the visit of the American delegation in October and offered to work for the benefit of the country with the government. She also requested meetings with three unwell senior members of the NLD CEC, including party Chairman U Aung Shwe, at their homes, as well as a CEC meeting at her home. Finally, she requested a meeting directly between herself and the Senior General.

No response to the letter ever emanated from Naypyitaw but subsequently she was able to meet the three ailing CEC members at a government guest house and afterwards it was reported that she intended to revitalize the party leadership by revising the central executive committee membership; it had not been significantly changed since 1992. In January, 2010, nine additional members, including a second woman member other than Daw Aung San Suu Kyi, were appointed. However, the future of the party remained in doubt on a number of scores. After twenty years of coping with a variety of government pressures to limit, if not terminate, its activities, the party was in a very weak organizational position. Moreover, its chief achievement in its twenty-two years of existence was the 1990 election result which, as demonstrated by the Shwegondine Declaration, it still clung to two decades later. Unless the party was willing to accept the terms of the 2010 elections, it would be excluded from that process and then its fate would be sealed. At the beginning of the election year, the NLD faced cruel choices — abandon its previously stated positions and participate in the elections or accept its demise. That choice fuelled differences in the party, with some leaders, including U Win Tit, pushing to reject the electoral option, and younger members of the party who felt that ending organization on a point of principle would be foolhardy.

Other Opposition Activities

The looming elections and the inability of the international community to divert the SPDC from its chosen course caused mounting frustration from within other political groups allied with and in support of the NLD and various ethnically designated organizations. Several resorted to bombings and in particular seven small bombs were exploded over the night of 16 and 17 September in industrial suburbs of Yangon and blasts in Shwepyitha on 19 October. No one was injured and several men were arrested in January 2010 for the September attacks. Other bombs went off during the year such as at the Kayin New Year celebration in Pa-an which the regime attributed to the Karen (Kayin) National Union. Such acts evidenced the desperation that a number of groups felt that their end was nigh.

Non-violent groups abroad faced similar frustrations and concerns that the funding they had received from a number of Western governments and foundations might continue to decline caused several to issue ever more alarmist claims. These increasingly fell on deaf ears as more than two decades of exile politics had begun to undermine the credibility of many claims. The arrest of Kyaw Zaw Lwin, a student activist in 1988 who eventually went to the United States and became an American citizen, for violation of immigration regulations and conspiracy to commit terrorism in Myanmar was only the latest of a number of failed efforts by opposition groups to have an impact. Even the leader of the National Coalition Government of the Union of Burma, so-called Prime Minister Sein Win, issued a call for the year to compromise with the regime, though in terms which indicated that there was no likely meeting of minds between the military and their exiled compatriots.

The exile movement faced many difficulties in 2009, not least because of the declining levels of financial support they received from various governments and foundations. As many governments and other financial supporters of the exile groups had concluded that the exile movement had either outlived its usefulness, or was no longer effective or realistic in its increasingly disputatious organizational forms, their ability to generate news and attract international attention was in decline. In Thailand, though many thought the Abhisit government, compared to governments supported by followers of former Prime Minister Thaksin Shinawatra, might be more sympathetic to the activities of groups along the border, that proved not to be the case, and not only were the exile groups facing a financial crisis at the end of the year but were also finding it difficult to operate legally inside Thailand.

A new development during the year was the gradual emergence of groups and individuals within Myanmar who declared that they were willing to organize political parties and participate in the eventual elections. Prominent among them was the announcement of the re-formation of the Democratic Party. The party, and its now leader, U Thu Wai, participated in the 1990 elections. Its prominence comes from the fact that three of its key members are the descendants of the disputatious leaders of the Anti-Fascist People's Freedom League governments of the 1950s, including former Prime Minister U Nu's daughter Than Than Nu, and former Deputy Prime Ministers U Kyaw Nyein and U Ba Swe's daughters, Choo Choo Kyaw Nyein and Nay Yee Ba Swe. Their optimism that their names and the political records of their families would draw support to them was frustrated in 1990, but their emergence in 2009 encouraged the government to believe that its goal of multi-party elections would eventually be concretized.

The SPDC Marches On

Meanwhile, despite dire warnings that the Myanmar economy was crumbling, signs continued to be revealed of economic growth and development. Myanmar reportedly produced a rice surplus of five million tonnes in 2008–9 and exported approximately one million tonnes via thirty-five private companies to markets in the Middle East and Europe as well as traditional markets in Asia and Africa. Trade continued to grow with Thailand and other neighbours and at the end of 2009 tourism was so buoyant that getting a flight into or out of Yangon International Airport was almost impossible. Such a situation had never occurred before. The growing tourist industry consequently tempted foreign investors to once more look to the development of the hotel sector in Yangon and other tourist destinations. The sale or privatization of a number of government assets also continued during the year, in part to meet a state ambition to produce a fiscal year with greatly reduced inflationary pressures prior to elections. Myanmar remains, however, one of the poorest countries in Asia and ranks 138 on the United Nations *Human Development Report 2009*, a report that noted the large emigrant community that the country's years of civil war had spawned.

The past year also saw the usual range of rumours, reports, and alarums in the media about Myanmar and what, if anything, the SPDC was planning. Reports on mysterious tunnels, North Korean nuclear links, rice eating rats and the like occasionally prompted attention, but hard evidence was rarely, if ever, revealed. In the meantime, the military government pressed on doggedly with the plans that it laid out years ago as its seven-step road map to democracy. After more than twenty years of ceasefire deals with various insurgent armies patterns of relations have been established. The government has established a record with its domestic allies and clients. It renewed its ongoing agreements with international agencies, such as the International Labour Organisation. Many people feel they know where the government is going and give it the benefit of the doubt. The prospect of elections and a new government, looking sufficiently like the existing one, is enough for many to go along. What other choice is there realistically, most will ask.

Notes

[1]   Mormons believe that God speaks directly to them through revelations. See John Krakauer, *Under the Banner of Heaven: The Story of a Violent Faith* (New York: Random House, 2003).

ETHNIC POLITICS IN MYANMAR
A Year of Tension and Anticipation

Martin Smith

The year 2009 was marked by rising tension in ethnic politics as different parties and stakeholder groups began to position themselves in advance of the 2010 general election, pledged by the ruling State Peace and Development Council (SPDC).[1] The first general election in Myanmar in twenty years (and only third in fifty), the 2010 polls are an integral element in what could become the most defining year in a generation, setting the landscape for the introduction of a new constitution and system of government. No quantum leap of change is expected. Under the new constitution, the leading role of the Myanmar armed forces (Tatmadaw) in national politics will be maintained through reserved positions for military personnel in both parliament and government.

Nevertheless, as 2009 progressed, leaders on all sides of Myanmar's political and ethnic divisions recognized that the 2010 election is an eventuality that they cannot ignore. For while the success or failure of the 2010 polls is likely to prove historic judgment on the political road map of the military government, events during 2009 signalled that they also represent a landmark challenge for the country's different ethnic groups. Whether by contesting, boycotting, or confronting the polls, the fate of individual nationality movements could be decided for many years to come.

Adding pressure on the political actors in Myanmar were the activities of Asian neighbours. In a fast developing region, political and ethnic events in Myanmar were followed with ever greater interest. During 2009, economic engagement accelerated, with a host of major energy, trade, and infrastructure projects under way or in the early stages of planning that are likely to change the political economy forever. Many are located in the ethnic minority borderlands, meaning that stability in Myanmar and international progress are becoming closely

---

MARTIN SMITH is author of *Burma: Insurgency and the Politics of Ethnicity*.

interlinked. In the longer-term, Myanmar could be moving towards economic restructuring where the geopolitical consequences will also have an epoch-shaping impact on internal affairs.

There remains, however, a long way to go. One of the most ethnically diverse countries in Asia, the legacies of ethnic conflict have long underpinned state failure and humanitarian decline.[2] Developments in 2009 could only provide indications of the likely trends as the SPDC attempts to initiate its plans for the 2010 election and its political road map. A critical time has arrived, causing all political actors to respond.

The Ethnic Landscape

During 2009 the distinctions between the different groupings in ethnic politics began to blur. There have always been overlaps and links. But during the two decades of SPDC government (formerly State Law and Order Restoration Council: SLORC), a surprising stability developed among the different parties and factions that were, in part, strategic and, in part, a reflection of the country's long-standing politics of survival. In many borderland areas, armed opposition has been a way of life since independence in 1948, with large territories controlled by ethnic and political forces of varying persuasions and goals.

A radical shake-up of the conflict landscape did take place during 1988–89. A rapid series of benchmark events occurred: mass pro-democracy protests, assumption of power by the military SLORC from the Burma Socialist Programme Party of General Ne Win, formation of new electoral parties, collapse of the insurgent Communist Party of Burma (CPB), and subsequent ethnic ceasefire policy by the new SLORC government.

Any expectations, however, that pan-ethnic movements would develop to unite either above ground or as armed opposition organizations soon petered out. Instead, ethnic-based movements became characterized by three main groupings during the SLORC-SPDC era: new electoral parties that stood in the 1990 election; ceasefire groups that included both former CPB allies and members of the pro-federal National Democratic Front (NDF; formed 1976); and non-ceasefire groups, most of which were allied in such border-based fronts as the National Council Union of Burma (NCUB) and worked with dissident and exile Burman groups that emerged after 1988.[3] (A fourth group can also be mentioned: community-based and non-governmental organizations whose energy reflected the greater social changes taking place after the BSPP's demise. But such groups are not generally involved in political affairs.)[4]

During 2009, opposition groups generally continued within these structures, reflecting a long-standing paradigm in Myanmar politics of a contested but unified military government against locally popular but disparate ethnic movements. Pressures increased on all political and armed opposition organizations during the year, and by the end of 2010 it is quite possible that few ethnic opposition groups — whether electoral or armed — will survive any longer in their present forms. Few clear election plans were announced by the SPDC, making long-term strategizing more difficult. But ethnic parties were forced to start actions and prepare contingency plans. Gradually, the political writing was appearing on the wall.

Electoral Parties and Ceasefire Groups

Differences remained in organization and outlook between ethnic electoral parties and ceasefire groups throughout the year. But since both groupings have worked with the military government in various ways during the past two decades (i.e., the 1990 election, National Convention, or ceasefires), they face similar dilemmas in decision making over the 2010 election and introduction of a new system of government. In some cases, this is likely to see the emergence of new political parties through the conjunction of electoral and ceasefire supporters and consequent disappearance of former groups. But the diversity of responses also warned that volatility could lie ahead, reflecting the turbulence that occurred during earlier periods of political transition (1948, 1962, 1974, and 1988). As in any strife-torn state, the 2010 election is unlikely to resolve all political or conflict issues within the country.

Among the electoral parties, a division already exists between the fifteen remaining ethnic parties from the 1990 general election, of which six had continued attendance at the government-organized National Convention until its 2008 completion, while others had allied in the 1998 Committee Representing the People's Parliament with the National League for Democracy (NLD) and subsequently formed the 2002 United Nationalities Alliance (UNA).[5] Under constant security restriction, many of these parties have become shadows of their former sizes and long wanted to reorganize. But among groups close to the military government, the formation of a new ethnic Pao party to contest the polls is widely expected between the electoral Union Pao National Organisation and ceasefire Pao National Organisation (PNO) after the election law is announced.[6] At the same time, other new electoral parties may emerge that are organized by SPDC critics, such as veteran Shan politician Shwe Ohn who in September invited nationality parties to join a "Union Democratic Alliance Organization" so that the ethnic reform voice would be strong in the future parliament.[7]

In contrast, statements from leaders of the nine-party UNA indicated that none of these parties is likely to stand in the 2010 election under current conditions. Since the parties do not believe that the new constitution will establish "democracy" or ethnic "rights", they cannot take part in an election that will bring it into force.[8] For this reason, UNA spokesmen aligned their likely decision-making with their NLD ally,[9] which in its Shwegondaing Declaration of April 2009 said that the party could take part in the election on three conditions: the release of all political prisoners, constitutional amendments, and international monitoring of "inclusive free and fair" polls.[10]

Underpinning UNA distrust of the SPDC was the continuing imprisonment of Hkun Htun Oo and fellow leaders of a key UNA member, the Shan Nationalities League for Democracy (SNLD), who were serving jail terms of up to ninety-three years for alleged sedition. In December, SNLD members petitioned the SPDC for a meeting with their detained leaders on the grounds that 2010 will be a critical year in which all must cooperate in "democratization and national solidarity".[11] But there was no immediate response from the SPDC. Also remaining in prison was the ceasefire leader, General Hso Ten of the Shan State Army (North) (SSA-N), who had been arrested at the same time following a 2005 meeting with SNLD leaders and similarly charged.

Against this tense backdrop, different opposition groups accused the government of "divide and rule" rather than promoting reconciliation through the electoral process.[12] Events during 2009 warned that such divisive tactics could prove high risk, especially in dealings with the country's ceasefire groups, some of which have significant territories and support. Since its 1989 initiation, the ethnic ceasefire policy has been a key feature of the SLORC-SPDC era, bringing not only the first halt to hostilities in many borderlands for decades but also preventing ethnic opposition forces from joining other insurgent groups in anti-regime alliances. Without this policy, it is doubtful that the SLORC-SPDC could have endured and opened different borderlands to international visitors and trade.

By 2009, the borderland landscape had become ever more fragmented, with sixteen "official" or major forces and a similar number of smaller or breakaway factions having military agreements with the SPDC.[13] Individual truces varied, but all had been generally timed by the introduction of Myanmar's future constitution until when they would be allowed to maintain their arms and territories. Clear differences of opinion, however, existed over both political reforms and when ceasefire groups should militarily transform. Sooner or later, something would have to give in this "neither war nor peace" impasse.[14]

During 2009, arguments came to the surface over both political and military affairs. Under Myanmar's new constitution, more powers appear promised to the fourteen states and divisions (in future, "regions") under a bicameral legislature in which there will be three votes: "one for each of the two chambers of the union (national) legislature, and one for the region/state legislatures".[15] In an unusual innovation, there will also be new "self-administered" territories with certain local rights for the Danu, Kokang, Naga, Palaung, Pao, and Wa ethnic groups who have not previously been acknowledged on the political map. However, many ethnic leaders in all political groupings have reservations about the limitations of this new model. Not only will twenty-five per cent of all seats in parliament be reserved for candidates from the Tatmadaw, but the new system will be "unitary" rather than "union", with an executive system of government that, they fear, will continue pro-military choices in key positions.[16]

Despite these concerns, ceasefire representatives had attended the National Convention until its 2008 conclusion, where they put forward their demands in two main blocks: a thirteen-party group headed by ex-NDF members that seek a federal union and the other by a four-party ex-CPB group, known as the Peace and Democracy Front (PDF), which prefers autonomous regions similar to those in China. Even when it became clear that their proposals would not make it through to the final draft (SPDC leaders equate goals such as "federalism" with "disintegration"[17]), ceasefire delegates continued attendance, keen that their goals should appear in the record and thus, they argued, be retrievable for future debate and constitutional amendments. Furthermore, despite limitations in the constitution making amendments difficult, most ceasefire leaders stated that they would cooperate with the 2010 election and the SPDC's political road map since they believed that dialogue and reform processes were the only ways to resolve the country's conflicts.[18]

For its part, the SPDC was very quiet on these issues in early 2009 as the challenges of ceasefire transformation first began to attract attention. Older ceasefire groups, such as the Kachin Independence Organisation (KIO), New Mon State Party (NMSP), and SSA-N, privately took the view that, since they perceived themselves as armed "political" movements and their ceasefires "military", they should continue to hold their arms and territories until after the 2010 election when they wanted to negotiate transformation with the future government. Any complacency, however, was dispelled on 28 April when the SPDC unexpectedly announced a new Border Guard Force (BGF) plan under which ceasefire groups would have to break up their organizations by transforming into individual BGF battalions. Each would consist of 326 troops, with thirty soldiers from the Tatmadaw, including one out of the three commanding officers. Officers aged over fifty would have to retire and future salaries would be the same as for the Myanmar military.[19]

The fallout from this order dominated ethnic politics for the rest of 2009. The Military Affairs Security Chief Lieutenant-General Ye Myint and different regional commanders frequently met with ceasefire leaders, trying to persuade them to agree. Many initially refused. Groups such as the KIO and NMSP argued that their administrations were much more than military organizations, so the challenges of transformation could only be accomplished after the election.[20] In meetings with Tatmadaw officers, the KIO included leaders of its health, education, rural, and other departments to demonstrate the community basis of its structures. There was also local opposition to Burman troops and commanders coming in to ethnic minority areas, with veterans remembering with regret the disappearance of the Kachin Rifles and other ethnic-based units in the Tatmadaw after independence.

Distrust then further deepened in late August when the SPDC appeared to take advantage of disunity within the ceasefire Myanmar National Democratic Alliance Army (MNDAA) in the Kokang region by sending in troops to support a breakaway faction that agreed to its BGF plans. As many as 200 combatants and civilians were killed or wounded, and 37,000 refugees — including the Kokang leader, Pheung Kya-shin — fled into China, bringing a temporary halt to international aid projects in the area and a rare statement of concern from the Chinese authorities.[21] Subsequently, the SPDC accused the MNDAA of illicit arms and narcotics activities.[22] But since the MNDAA was the oldest ceasefire force and Pheung Kya-shin was previously close to the SPDC, the Kokang crisis cast a deep shadow over the landscape of ethnic politics.

Undeterred, the SPDC continued to pursue its BGF policy. In some respects, this was not new and appeared to complement a longer-term strategy to create local militia forces working with the Tatmadaw to manage conflict rather than expecting to defeat all ethnic resistance.[23] Such tactics date back to independence and have witnessed different models over the decades, such as the Ka Kwe Ye of the 1960s and 70s. Militarization was continuing rather than decreasing in restive border areas, despite the approach of the 2010 election.[24] Gradually, under a combination of inducements and pressure, most smaller ceasefire forces accepted the BGF orders, and ceremonies were held in November for the transformation of two groups, the New Democratic Army-Kachin (NDA-K) and Karenni Nationalities People's Liberation Front (KNPLF).[25] But by the year's end, six forces still appeared to reject full implementation of the BGF order: the KIO, NMSP, SSA-N, Kayan New Land Party, and two closely-linked allies on the China border, the United Wa State Army (UWSA) and National Democratic Alliance Army (Eastern Shan State).

As a compromise, the remaining ceasefire leaders privately communicated to the SPDC that they agreed, in principle, to the future formation of forces similar to the BGFs after the 2010 election when the political and reform landscape was likely to be more certain. In particular, the KIO told the SPDC that transformation would be acceptable as long as change was according to the historic Panglong Agreement of 1947 that determined the ethnic principles for the future union.[26] But leaders of the major forces still wanted to negotiate the re-organization of their brigade-size commands and the issue of Tatmadaw or Burman troops within their ranks.

In the meantime, ceasefire groups — whether agreeing to the BGF policy or not — generally continued their approval for the 2010 election. None sought to stand in their existing forms to contest the polls. But in a long-planned move, in September the KIO's Vice-Chairman Tu Ja resigned with five other officials to set up a new political party, the Kachin State Progressive Party, to canvas for pan-Kachin unity and stand in the election. Mon, Pao, Shan, and other nationality activists also considered the same strategy, working in conjunction with electoral and other ethnic-based movements. Their argument was that armed groups should be considered the military wing of ethnic movements in the post-independence era, but that new parties were needed for political progress in the twenty-first century.[27]

Many uncertainties remained. Although talks continued, tensions were high and front line forces often in a state of alert. In general, it appeared that the SPDC had made significant advances in undermining ceasefire and electoral opponents in advance of the 2010 polls. Despite considerable disquiet about the Kokang fighting and imprisonment of Shan leaders, opposition unity had been weak, with no other force coming to the MNDAA's aid and no consensus about the 2010 election.

At the same time, by the year's end, worries were declining among ceasefire groups that the SPDC would launch further offensives against non-BGF groups in the manner of Kokang. Instead, with Asian neighbours watching closely, opinion was growing that stability would be the SPDC's main priority during 2010 as the polls approached. For while smaller groups like the NDA-K and KNPLF could be co-opted into BGFs or local militia, larger forces such as the 6,000-strong KIO and 20,000-strong UWSA had well-organized troops that were likely to strongly resist any attempt to enforce a military solution.

As the year ticked down, there remained a long way to go. In his 2010 New Year address, describing 2009 as an extraordinary year of both opportunities and difficulties, the UWSA Chairman, Bao You Chang, reaffirmed commitment to solving differences through "negotiation"; but he also warned the people to be ready to combat "enemies" if attacked.[28] As continuing fighting in several borderlands warned, ethnic conflict in Myanmar was by no means at an end.

Non-ceasefire and Other Dissident Groups

The activities of insurgent groups were probably at their lowest ebb in any year since independence during 2009. A diversity of militant and non-ceasefire groups still exists around the Thailand, India, and Bangladesh borders.[29] Many are linked through such alliances as the Ethnic Nationalities Council (ENC), NDF, and NCUB, the last of which includes dissident groups such as the exile Members of Parliament Union. In recent years, however, most groups and their leaders are largely based on the periphery of (or outside) Myanmar's borders, and only four organizations — all of which are ethnic — have forces of any real military or operational size inside the country: the Karen National Union (KNU), Karenni National Progressive Party (KNPP), and Shan State Army (South) (SSA-S) on the Thai border, and Chin National Front on the India border.

Aside from the SSA-S, all lost further ground during 2009. Long the centre of militant activism on the Thai border, the KNU was again the main target of government counter-insurgency operations. The KNU has lost significant support and territory during the past fifteen years, and a joint offensive in June by the SPDC and the KNU's breakaway rival, the Democratic Karen Buddhist Army (DKBA), quickly captured remaining bases of the KNU's once-powerful seventh brigade in the borderlands north of Myawaddy. Over 3,500 refugees fled into Thailand and up to 200 combatants were killed or wounded during several weeks of sporadic fighting.[30]

KNU guerrillas remained active in other border areas, especially its fifth brigade area around Papun and sixth brigade area south of Myawaddy. In one ambush, the KNU reportedly killed a government Brigadier-General and several bodyguards near Bawgaligyi in May.[31] The KNU also linked up with its KNPP ally for operations that included the blowing up of power lines on the Lawpita-Taungoo electricity grid.[32] Landmines, especially, deployed by all sides, continued to inflict a high number of civilian casualties.[33] In an August press conference, Police Chief Brigadier-General Khin Yi also accused the KNU of lending support to underground groups, notably the Vigorous Burmese Student Warriors and All

Burma Students Democratic Front, whom he accused of plotting "terrorist acts", including some timed to coincide with the visit of UN Secretary-General Ban Ki-moon to the country.[34] KNU leaders, however, denied such allegations, including claims that it was responsible for an explosion that killed seven civilians at the Karen New Year festival in Papun in December.[35]

There were also reports of fighting by the SPDC with other ethnic non-ceasefire organizations during 2009. The KNPP, for example, claimed to have killed three government troops in an ambush in the Kayah state in March;[36] the SSA-S reportedly killed more than thirty government soldiers in the southern Shan state between May and July;[37] clashes occurred with Mon factions that rejected the NMSP ceasefire in the southern Mon state;[38] and the SPDC launched an attack in November on a base of the Khaplang faction of the National Socialist Council of Nagaland on the India border.[39]

During 2009, however, the military and political momentum generally remained with the SPDC. Militant and allied dissident groups held various meetings to discuss strategies. These included a seven-party alliance that pledged to "eliminate" the new constitution at a meeting on the Thai border in April.[40] A further grouping was announced at a conference in Jakarta in August, the Movement for Democracy and Rights for Ethnic Nationalities, which included the NCUB, ENC, and exile National Coalition Government Union of Burma (NCGUB) of MPs-elect and proposed a new "national reconciliation" programme.[41] Such alliances continued international lobbying with some effect, with activists regular voices at meetings in Europe, North America, and Australia.

Despite such rhetoric, militant groups were frequently preoccupied with internal problems of their own. After decades of borderland insurgency, regional trends have largely turned against opposition movements that include armed struggle. Part of the weakness of the borderland opposition in the SLORC-SPDC era was that, while agreeing on anti-military government objectives, they included both ethnic and politically-based movements, some of which (primarily ethnic) pursued armed struggle (e.g. the KNU) and some of which (primarily Burman) supported the NLD's non-violent goals (e.g. NCGUB). Since they were largely based in the conflict zones and non-Burman territories, there have always been organizational imbalances and different priorities which, for example, saw the ethnic ceasefire groups prefer to engage in dialogue with the military government as their pre-eminent need.

These inconsistencies were further amplified by difficulties in agreeing positions on the complex challenges that Myanmar politics frequently pose. A perennially contentious example arose in early 2009 during the latest exodus of Muslim refugees, often known as "Rohingya", from the Bangladesh border, this time by boat into Thai and other Southeast Asian waters.[42] For while most borderland opposition groups recognize the rights of Muslim communities in the northern Rakhine state, some do not accept "Rohingya" as a term of identity — a position also taken by the SLORC-SPDC.[43] The Muslim minority crisis on the Bangladesh frontier remains one of Myanmar's most serious.

However, undoubtedly the most challenging issue for borderland groups during 2009 was the prospect of the 2010 election. Most remained strongly opposed and wanted to support coordination through the new Movement for Democracy and Rights for Ethnic Nationalities that was agreed in August. But given that the NLD or other pro-democracy supporters might stand in the polls, some leaders wanted a more flexible position. This was reflected in September when the ENC, of which the KNU is a member, sent an unexpected letter to U.S. Senator Jim Webb after his Myanmar visit, rejecting armed struggle as a "solution" and stating that, because citizens have no choice but to vote, the ENC would "support eligible ethnic groups in running for office" to try and ensure an ethnic and democratic voice.[44]

In part, these differences reflected divergent opinions between hardliners and moderates over how insurgent or dissident groups in the borderlands should try to show leadership over the coming polls. But there was also recognition of the weakness (or non-presence) of many of these actors inside Myanmar and that, without pragmatic strategies that reached out to the people, they could face even greater marginalization in the years ahead. As long as they remained outside the political process, other parties and leaders were likely to emerge to claim to be the representatives of the people. The evidence was growing.

The KNU's difficulties were reflected in a frank interview by central executive committee member David Taw in the *Irrawaddy* magazine in March.[45] The failure to rejuvenate ageing leaderships and breakaways to the SPDC side had undermined the long-standing control of many veteran insurgent movements in the borderlands. In the KNU's case, six groups had defected since the mid-1990s, led by the DKBA which now rivalled in strength its mother party and was in frequent conflict with the KNU during the year.[46] Similar fragmentation had occurred among other armed nationality movements, including the Mon and Shan, and was reflected in periodic infighting that undermined ethnic unity.[47]

Compounding opposition difficulties were the changing attitudes of neighbouring governments. As business and political engagement in Myanmar increased, the days of laissez-faire tolerance of dissident groups along the borders appeared to be ending. Opposition weakness and infighting furthered these concerns. In

February the Thai authorities ordered the KNU not to organize activities from Thailand, and KNU and other opposition safe houses were raided several times during the year.[48] As pressures grew, in March Thailand's Foreign Minister Kasit Piromya made an offer to mediate in peace talks between the SPDC and KNU during a visit to Myanmar, subsequently meeting with KNU officials.[49] More unexpectedly, the SPDC was rumoured to have asked the Thai authorities to mediate with the SSA-S.[50]

Nothing developed from either of these discussions. But as these initiatives showed, after decades of conflict Asian neighbours were looking to achieve borderland stability in Myanmar's next political and economic era. Similar efforts to tighten security occurred on the China, Bangladesh, and India borders during 2009, with the Indian authorities especially concerned that insurgent groups from northeast India were using borderline sanctuaries to continue their struggles.[51]

This international squeeze and relative decline in fighting during recent years did not mean that there had been a halt to the ethnic conflicts inside Myanmar or that the humanitarian situation in front line areas had significantly improved. As the June offensive against the KNU or August fighting in Kokang showed, Myanmar remained a country where regular and guerrilla warfare continued between internal combatants in several regions. The Thailand Burma Border Consortium, for example, reported the relocation of another 120 ethnic minority communities in the eastern borderlands between August 2008 and July 2009, bringing the estimated number of internally displaced persons in these areas to 470,000.[52] Against this backdrop, Human Rights Watch reported that international calls increased during 2009 for an investigation into "war crimes and crimes against humanity" in the country.[53]

However, as insurgent defences weakened, this trend of persistent conflict and territorial retreat began to take its toll. For many years, a growing war-weariness and impoverishment has afflicted many communities in the borderlands and, with little prospect of resolution in sight, more refugees and opposition supporters continued to seek resettlement in third countries abroad. During 2009 the refugee feeding populations along the Thai border stood at around 130,000 (primarily Karen and Karenni). But with the number of those being resettled passing 50,000 since 2006 (mostly in the USA),[54] a major shift is clearly taking place in the border paradigms and culture.[55] Over two million migrants from Myanmar are also estimated to be living or working in Thailand, and this gradually appears to be becoming a more regulated part of the regional economy and human flow.[56] On a lesser scale, refugee and migrant communities continued to live on the Bangladesh (mainly Muslim) and India (mainly Chin) borders.

Insurgent groups and their allies are therefore likely to face a challenging time during 2010. After many difficult years, hopes remain among hardliners that controversy over the 2010 election or potential ceasefire breakdowns will change the internal landscape to their advantage. There were occasional warnings of discontent. Rumours continued of unhappiness within the DKBA over the SPDC's BGF plans and, despite the continuing infighting, KNU and DKBA leaders privately met in October.[57] Then in December two militant Pao factions that rejected the ceasefire of the PNO and Shan State Nationalities People's Liberation Organisation formed a new "Pao National Liberation Organisation" to oppose the polls.[58] But a major resumption in insurgent operations still appeared unlikely.

In its 2010 New Year statement, the KNU again called for a "united struggle against the common enemy, the SPDC military dictatorship".[59] Meanwhile the SSA-S resolved to step up the enlistment of troops at the tenth annual meeting of its political wing at Loi Taileng adjoining the Thai border.[60] But generally the political and military impetus remained with the SPDC. Opposition eyes were fixed on Senior-General Than Shwe and the SPDC to see when the military government would announce the 2010 election and make their next move.

International Dimensions

Asian engagement with Myanmar and its military government has gradually increased during the past two decades. In historic terms, 2009 could well turn out to be the most important year yet in setting the trends for long-term relations. This will have important implications for all of Myanmar's peoples, especially the ethnic nationalities who inhabit the borderlands.

Opposition groups feared that a harder-line of SPDC intent was predicted by the visit to Myanmar in June of Sri Lankan President Mahinda Rajapaska, fresh from his victory over the Liberation Tigers of Tamil Eelam, and Senior-General Than Shwe's reciprocal visit in November.[61] Rajapaska thanked Than Shwe for Myanmar's support,[62] and Deputy Minister for Defence Major-General Aye Myint made the parallels explicit at the eighth Shangri-La Dialogue meeting. While the world had "recently witnessed the successful end of a long-standing insurgency in Sri Lanka", he publicly asked why "people have forgotten about insurgency in Myanmar."[63]

Undoubtedly, however, the main influences in Myanmar were the three neighbouring states of China, India, and Thailand. Whatever the political and borderland difficulties (and they regularly occurred), diplomatic and economic exchanges continued, highlighted by the February visit to Myanmar of India's Vice-President Hamid Ansari and December visit of China's Vice President Xi Jinping. Thailand's army chief General Anupong Paochinda and Foreign Minister Kasit Piromya also visited the country. Engagement was not uncritical, with concerns expressed in different circles and meetings about the perennial challenges of political reform, border security, refugee outflow, illicit narcotics trafficking, and humanitarian needs. But in general, all Asian neighbours believed that the SPDC's political road map and the 2010 general election are the next steps to political reform and stability in Myanmar.[64] Among some authorities, sympathies do privately remain for the ethnic and opposition causes. But as the Thai raids on KNU safe houses or China's caution over the Kokang fighting showed (the Kokang are ethnic Chinese), it would need a far greater crisis in Myanmar for any Asian neighbour to change "constructive engagement" policies with the military government now.

Equally important, Asian investment and trade appears on the brink of an upsurge that could well transform the economy of Myanmar and its borderlands forever. Very belatedly, the isolationism, autarchic planning, and black market realities of Myanmar's post-colonial era could be coming to an end, with the country caught in the economic slipstream of its dynamic neighbours.

Recognition of these realities underpinned the review of U.S. policies during 2009, with Senator Jim Webb critical that "sanctions" by Western governments had allowed China to "dramatically increase its economic and political influence in Myanmar, furthering a dangerous strategic imbalance in the region".[65] During the November mission to Myanmar by U.S. Assistant Secretary of State, Kurt Campbell, his team met with ceasefire, UNA, and ethnic community leaders as well as the SPDC and NLD.[66] But other than expressing U.S. commitment to beginning "dialogue" with the SPDC, democratic opposition, and ethnic groups to support "national reconciliation", there was little concrete that the Obama administration had to offer the different ethnic peoples.[67]

In this vacuum, humanitarian aid remained a lead issue for most Western governments, a trend accelerated by international responses to the tragedy of Cyclone Nargis the previous year. Following the precedent of the Three Diseases Fund, it was announced during 2009 that the Global Fund to Fight AIDS, Tuberculosis and Malaria would return to Myanmar, and a new Livelihoods and Food Security Trust was established by a consortium of Western government donors. It is an agreed principle of these funds to extend humanitarian aid to the most vulnerable and needy in all regions of the country. At the same time, Western donors remained the principal funders of aid organizations, refugee relief, and political opposition groups around Myanmar's borders as well as campaigners in the West. In the United States and United Kingdom, especially, there was strong advocacy for the United National Security Council and other international bodies to take action because of the political and ethnic situation in Myanmar.[68] However, China, Russia, and other Asian countries rejected such calls.

In contrast, among neighbouring countries it was economic engagement that frequently attracted most attention. In geopolitical terms, potentially the most important development was confirmation that both oil and gas pipelines will be built along a 771-kilometre land route from the Rakhine state coast to China's Yunnan Province, with the Myanmar Government taking responsibility for security.[69] But this is only one element in many fields of infrastructure, trade, natural resource, and energy change involving China, India, and Thailand.[70] Gradually, many once off-limit or remote regions of Myanmar are being opened up by new business and infrastructure projects, such as the projected Trans-Asian Railway or the re-opening of the old Ledo Road between China, India, and Myanmar. India and Thailand are also involved in major cross-border projects, such as the Sittwe-Kaladan gateway project on the northwest frontier or the proposed Hat Gyi hydroelectric dam in the Karen state in the long-time heartland of the KNU insurgency.

How ethnic groups in Myanmar will respond to all these natural resource and development projects is not certain. But since most are based in or pass through the borderlands, ethnic reaction will be vital to their success. Discussions about these new projects accelerated among ethnic groups during 2009 alongside concerns about the 2010 election. Opinions were divided between those who see them as beneficial to progress for ethnic nationalities in the borderlands and those who contend that they are already providing grounds for a new generation of grievances. The precedents of the Yadana gas pipeline and over-logging in the frontier regions continued to bring criticism,[71] while the resumption of the Hat Gyi dam project, which had been halted after the KNU killed two Thai engineers, remained controversial.[72] But dissent also spread in ceasefire areas during 2009 over the start of the Myitsone Dam on the Irrawaddy confluence in the Kachin state and the new Shwe Gas project that will cross the Rakhine and Shan states on its way to China.[73]

The stage is thus delicately set. Many projects are only in early development. But with resource wars a common theme in conflict-torn states around the world, the perceptions of ethnic inclusion or exclusion could well determine political consequences in the years to come. A new chapter is opening; but by their timing, the economic initiatives by Asian neighbours appear inherently tied to the stability of the SPDC's political roadmap and will be followed with close scrutiny by all stakeholder groups during 2010.

Conclusion

Many predictions can be made about the future course of ethnic events in Myanmar. One way or another, the political landscape is scheduled to be reshaped through the 2010 general election and subsequent introduction of a new system of military-backed government that the SPDC describes as "discipline-flourishing democracy". All leading bodies and organizations — from the SPDC and mass Union Solidarity and Development Association to ethnic parties and the NLD — are faced with major challenges in political transformation. On the other hand, in a country with such a legacy of internal strife, history strongly suggests that national change is unlikely to be quick or dramatic but that surprises could yet be in store. Local volatility is always possible until inclusive peace and national reconciliation are truly established.

In general, however, 2009 provided many indications of the likely political trends if the SPDC roadmap endures. A new landscape of ethnic parties, some old and some new, will emerge to take part in the 2010 election, while other parties will retire or be marginalized in the non-legal wings. At the same time, militarization will not disappear in the ethnic border areas, where local militia, BGFs, and potentially the remaining ceasefire groups will continue to exercise some local control in conjunction with the Tatmadaw. The key issue for many ethnic groups will be how much representation and self-administration the nationality groups really exercise in the new system of government. In particular, many ethnic parties have already decided to put most effort into trying to win effective representation in the state or region legislatures rather than the two chambers of the national legislature in Nay Pyi Taw, where their individual (although not collective) presence will be small. They will also closely watch all administrative appointments and economic decisions made under the new presidential and executive system of government to analyze whether ethnic representation and rights are likely to be respected or ignored.

Against this, there will be other ethnic parties that will oppose the polls. Opposition has already been stated by the non-ceasefire groups; further peace talks are not expected. But the question remains how far such opposition will spread. If the NLD does not stand in the election, then it is likely that ethnic electoral and border or exile dissident groups will step up their opposition. Similarly, if a major ceasefire like that of the UWSA should break down, then ethnic conflict and insurgency could conflagrate again into more unpredictable directions and humanitarian sufferings consequently increase. But this, in itself, is not likely to change the long-standing paradigms in Myanmar politics of a united military-dominated government against diverse opposition. On this basis, any change in the Tatmadaw leadership or intentions in government could be the most significant differences affecting the SPDC road map in the year ahead.

Finally, perhaps the most critical judgement in history will be whether the election and new constitution prove processes by which sustainable reform and reconciliation can be achieved. It is the only national reform process in prospect. But at present, many aspects of the country's forthcoming transition are an unopened book. After decades of conflict and state failure, citizens want a process that can bring peace and democracy to the country. But many also worry that, depending upon how events in 2010 transpire, the landscape could be shaping for another generation of political contention and exclusion. If this should happen, the country's impasse would only continue. The warnings from history are clear.

Notes

[1] This was reiterated by Senior-General Than Shwe on Independence Day 2010: *New Light of Myanmar*, 4 January 2010.

[2] For an analysis by this author, see Martin Smith, *State of Strife: the Dynamics of Ethnic Conflict in Burma*. Policy Studies no. 36 (Washington, DC: East-West Center; and Singapore: Institute of Southeast Asian Studies, 2007).

[3] For a chart of ethnic parties and groupings, see Ibid., pp. 67–69.

[4] For an analysis of ethnic and civil society issues in conflict areas, see Ashley South, *Civil Society in Burma: The Development of Democracy amidst Conflict*. Policy Studies no. 51 (Washington, DC: East-West Center; and Singapore: Institute of Southeast Asian Studies, 2008).

[5] See note 3.

[6] Myo Myo and Kyaw Thu, "PNO Likely to Form Party", *Myanmar Times*, 12–18 October 2009.

[7] *Mizzima News*, "Shwe Ohn Invites Political Parties to Unite for Strong Opposition", 23 September 2009 <http://www.mizzima.com/news/inside-burma/2805-shwe-ohn-invites-political-parties-to-unite-for-strong-opposition.html>.

[8] See interview with Aye Thar Aung, secretary of the Arakan League for Democracy, "First the Constitution, Then the Election", *The Irrawaddy* 17, no. 8 (November 2009) <http://www.irrawaddy.org/article.php?art_id=17141>.

[9] Ba Kaung, "Ethnic Leaders Reject Election", *The Irrawaddy*, 14 January 2010 <http://www.irrawaddy.org/article.php?art_id=17581>.

[10] National League for Democracy, "The Shwegondaing Declaration", 29 April 2009.

[11]   S.H.A.N., "Shan Party Petitions Junta Chief for Meeting with Detained Leaders", 6 January 2010 <http://www.shanland.org/index.php?option=com_content&view=article &id=2876:shan-party-petitions-junta-chief-for-meeting-with-detained-leaders&catid=85: politics&Itemid=266>.

[12]   See, for example, National Council Union of Burma, Nationalities Youth Forum, Students and Youth Congress of Burma, Women's League of Burma, Forum for Democracy in Burma, "Joint Statement on 2010 Election Boycott", 10 October 2009.

[13]   See note 3.

[14]   Tom Kramer, *Burma: Neither War Nor Peace: The Future of the Cease-Fire Agreements in Burma* (Amsterdam: Transnational Institute, 2009).

[15]   For an analysis of the constitution, see International Crisis Group, *Myanmar: Towards the Elections*, Asia Report no. 174, 20 August 2009, pp. 6–12.

[16]   The observations in this section are made on the basis of interviews with ethnic representatives over several years, including ceasefire, electoral, and National Convention. A number requested anonymity.

[17]   See, for example, the speech of Vice–Senior General Maung Aye, *New Light of Myanmar*, 8 January 2010.

[18]   See note 16.

[19]   Most reported details about the BGFs are based on instructions given by Lieutenant-General Ye Myint to ceasefire leaders on 28 April. But there remained unanswered questions, including about territories and how many battalions each group would form.

[20]   See, for example, "The Relation between NMSP and SPDC on the 51st Anniversary of the Party Foundation; Interview with Secretary of New Mon State Party, Nai Hong Sar", *IMNA*, 24 July 2009 <http://www.monnews-imna.com/interviewsupdate. php?ID=11>.

[21]   Tom Kramer, "Burma's Cease-fires at Risk: Consequences of the Kokang Crisis for Peace and Democracy", Transnational Institute, Peace & Security Briefing no. 1, September 2009.

[22]   "Clarification of Brig-Gen. Phone Swe, Deputy Minister for Home Affairs Concerning with Kokang Incident", document circulated to foreign diplomats visiting the Kokang region, 7 September 2009.

[23]   For a ceasefire analysis, see Mary Callahan, *Political Authority in Burma's Ethnic Minority States: Devolution, Occupation and Coexistence*. Policy Studies no. 31 (East-West Center: Washington, DC; and Singapore: Institute of Southeast Asian Studies, 2007).

[24]   Besides the ceasefire groups and BGFs, there are other local militia in the borderlands supported by the government, such as Lahu militia in the Shan state.

[25]   "Ceremonies to Mark Formation of Frontier Forces Held", *New Light of Myanmar*, 11 November 2009.

26 Ryan Libre, "KIO Calls for Discussion of Panglong Agreement", *The Irrawaddy*, 2 November 2009 <http://www.irrawaddy.org/article.php?art_id=17112>.

27 For a recent interview with Tu Ja, see "Why Did Dr. Tuja Resign from KIO?" *Mizzima News*, 7 September 2009 <http://www.mizzima.com/edop/interview/2733-why-did-dr-tuja-resign-from-kio.html>.

28 Bao You Chang, "New Year Congratulatory Speech by Bao You Chang, General-Secretary of United Wa State Party, Chairman of Wa State, General Commander of United Wa State Army", 31 December 2009.

29 Armed opposition actors also continued to move in the China borderlands during 2009; but due to the ceasefires, no insurgent group was active in armed struggle.

30 For an analysis, see Brian McCartan, "Victory over KNU, New Order on Thai-Burma Border", *Mizzima*, 5 July 2009 <http://www.mizzima.com/news/inside-burma/2405-victory-over-knu-new-order-on-thai-burma-border.html>.

31 "Senior Burmese Commander Killed by KNLA Soldiers", *The Irrawaddy*, 13 May 2009 <http://www.irrawaddy.org/article.php?art_id=15630>.

32 *New Light of Myanmar*, 1 February 2009.

33 See, for example, Landmine Monitor, *Landmine Monitor Report 2009: Toward a Mine-Free World*, pp. 1029–40.

34 *New Light of Myanmar*, 8 August 2009.

35 "Junta Accuses KNU of Bomb Blast", *The Irrawaddy*, 18 December 2009 <http://www.irrawaddy.org/article.php?art_id=17422>.

36 "Burmese Troops Blame Villagers for Rebel Attack", *Kantarawaddy Times*, 23 March 2009 <http://www.bnionline.net/news/kantarawaddy/6021-burmese-troops-blame-villagers-for-rebel-attack.html>.

37 *S.H.A.N.*, "Patrols Recalled Following Clash", 21 July 2009 <http://www.shanland.org/index.php?option=com_content&view=article&id=2654:patrols-recalled-following-clash&catid=86:war&Itemid=284>.

38 For an analysis on local conditions, see The Mon Forum, "Living between Two Fires: Villager Opinions on Armed Insurgency", no. 1, January 2009.

39 Subir Bhaumik, "Burmese Army Targets India Rebels", *BBC News*, 6 November 2009 <http://news.bbc.co.uk/1/hi/8345885.stm>.

40 Ko Wild, "Burmese Oppositions Aligned to Form a 'United Front'", *Mizzima*, 7 April 2009. The groups were: ENC, NCUB, Women's League of Burma, Forum for Democracy in Burma, Students and Youths Congress of Burma, and the Nationalities Youth Forum <http://www.mizzima.com/archive/1946-burmese-oppositions-aligned-to-form-a-united-front.html>.

41 *UPI*, "Myanmar Democracy Group Offers Alternative", 14 August 2009 <http://www.upi.com/Top_News/2009/08/14/Myanmar-democracy-group-offers-alternative/UPI-10351250225078/>.

42 Human Rights Watch, *Perilous Plight: Burma's Rohingya Take to the Seas*, May 2009.

43 The non-ceasefire National United Party of Arakan, for example, is allied with the Arakan Rohingya National Organisation, but no group claiming Rohingya identity has membership of the twenty-eight-party NCUB.

44 Ethnic Nationalities Council letter to Senator Webb, 28 September 2009 <http://euro-burma.eu/doc/Letter_to_Senator_Webb_by_ENC-GS.pdf>.

45 "KNU in Serious Crisis", *The Irrawaddy*, 24 March 2009 <http://www.irrawaddy.org/article.php?art_id=15357>.

46 In March Captain Nay Soe Mya, son of the late KNU leader General Bo Mya, also crossed to the government side with over 150 followers: *New Light of Myanmar*, 10 April 2009. As intra-Karen fighting continued, in June the KNU reportedly killed a senior DKBA commander, Colonel San Pyone, who was believed to have been involved in the assassination of KNU General-Secretary Mahn Sha La Phan the previous year: see for example, McCartan, "Victory over KNU".

47 For example, in March a NMSP central committee member was assassinated by breakaway rivals; in May, the SSA-S reportedly killed in an ambush Moeng Zeun, commander of the SSA-S former 758th brigade, which had defected to the SPDC side to become a local militia.

48 Saw Yan Naing, "Burmese Dissidents Worry about Thai Crackdown", *The Irrawaddy*, 28 October 2009 <http://www.irrawaddy.org/article.php?art_id=17087>.

49 Saw Yan Naing, "KNU Says Ceasefire Agreements Essential for Peaceful Burma", *The Irrawaddy*, 8 April 2009 <http://www.irrawaddy.org/article.php?art_id=15454>.

50 *S.H.A.N.*, "Junta Holds Out Olive Branch to SSA South", 21 September 2009 <http://www.shanland.org/index.php?option=com_content&view=article&id=2736:junta-holds-out-olive-branch-to-ssa-south&catid=85:politics&Itemid=266>.

51 Vishwa Mohan, *Times of India*, "Myanmar Nod to Joint Ops against N-E Militants", 25 January 2010. Only the Naga armed struggle continues on both sides of the border in tandem, but the United Liberation Front of Asom and several other forces also cross the remote frontier.

52 Thailand Burma Border Consortium, *Protracted Displacement and Militarisation in Eastern Burma*, November 2009, p. 3.

53 Human Rights Watch, *World Report 2010: Events of 2009* (New York, 2010), pp. 270–78.

54 Thailand Burma Border Consortium, *Programme Report: January to June 2009*, pp. 7–10.

55 For a contemporary analysis, see Ashley South, "Governance and Legitimacy in Karen State", in *Ruling Myanmar in Transition*, edited by Monique Skidmore and Trevor Wilson (Canberra: Australian National University, forthcoming 2010).

56 Thailand Burma Border Consortium, *Programme Report: January to June 2009*, pp. 12–13.

57 Saw Yan Naing, "KNU, DKBA Hold Armistice Talks", *The Irrawaddy*, 30 October 2009 <http://www.irrawaddy.org/article.php?art_id=17101>.

58 *S.H.A.N.*, "Ethnic Merger Re-adopts Historic Name", 11 December 2009 <http://www.shanland.org/index.php?option=com_content&view=article&id=2848:ethnic-merger-re-adopts-historic-name-&catid=85:politics&Itemid=266>.

59 Office of the Supreme Headquarters, Karen National Union, "New Year Greetings & Call for National Unity by KNU", 1 January 2010.

60 *S.H.A.N.*, "Yawd Serk: Independence is Not Secession", 19 January 2010 <http://www.shanland.org/index.php?option=com_content&view=article&id=2884>.

61 See, for example, Arkar Moe, "Burma-Sri Lanka Connection: Religion and Terrorism", *The Irrawaddy*, 15 June 2009 <http://www.irrawaddy.org/highlight.php?art_id=16005>.

62 *Daily News*, "Strengthening Lanka-Myanmar Ties: President's Myanmar Visit Pays Dividends", 16 June 2009 <http://www.dailynews.lk/2009/06/16/news01.asp>.

63 *New Light of Myanmar*, 1 June 2009. Aye Myint, however, did qualify that the SPDC realized that "hard power alone is not fully effective in winning the counter-insurgency campaigns."

64 See, for example, *AFP*, "Myanmar Minister Pledges Free Election: ASEAN", 14 January 2010 <http://news.yahoo.com/s/afp/20100114/wl_asia_afp/aseanmyanmarpoliticsvote_20100114121046>.

    For a Chinese perspective, see Zhang Yunfei, *Xinhua*, "Sino-Myanmar Bilateral Ties, Co-op Deepening: Chinese Ambassador", 17 December 2009. See also Xiaolin Guo, "Peace, Conflict, and Development on the Sino-Burmese Border", Institute for Security and Development Policy, Policy Brief no. 13, 2 December 2009.

65 Jim Webb, "We Can't Afford to Ignore Myanmar", *New York Times*, 25 August 2009 <http://www.nytimes.com/2009/08/26/opinion/26webb.html>.

66 *New Light of Myanmar*, 5 November 2009.

67 Marwaan Macan-Markar, "US Mission's Meeting with Burmese Ethnics Signals Hope", *The Irrawaddy*, 5 November 2009 <http://www.irrawaddy.org/article.php?art_id=17162>.

68 The International Human Rights Clinic at Harvard Law School, *Crimes in Burma* (Cambridge, MA: 2009).

69 China National Petroleum Corporation, "Rights and Obligation Agreement Signed of Myanmar-China Crude Pipeline", 21 December 2009.

70 During Xi Jinping's visit, for example, fifteen other business agreements were also signed on hydroelectric power, finance, trade, economy, transport, technology and machinery. *People's Daily*, "Myanmar Official Media Hail Chinese Vice president's Visit", 22 December 2009 <http://english.peopledaily.com.cn/90001/90776/90883/6849022.html>.

71 See, for example, EarthRights International, *Total Impact: The Human Rights, Environmental, and Financial Impacts of Total and Chevron's Yadana Gas Project*

in Military-Ruled Burma (Myanmar). Washington, DC: September 2009; Global Witness, *A Disharmonious Trade: China and the Continued Destruction of Burma's Northern Frontier Forest* (London, 2009).

[72] Saw Yan Naing, "Survey Work Pressing Ahead at Hat Gyi Dam Site", *The Irrawaddy*, 19 August 2009 <http://www.irrawaddy.org/article.php?art_id=16600>.

[73] See, for example, Kachin Development Networking Group, *Resisting the Flood: Communities Taking a Stand against the Imminent Construction of Irrawaddy Dams*, October 2009 <www.burmariversnetwork.org>, and Shwe Gas Movement, *Corridor of Power: China's Trans-Burma Oil and Gas Pipelines* (Chiang Mai, 2009).

Philippines

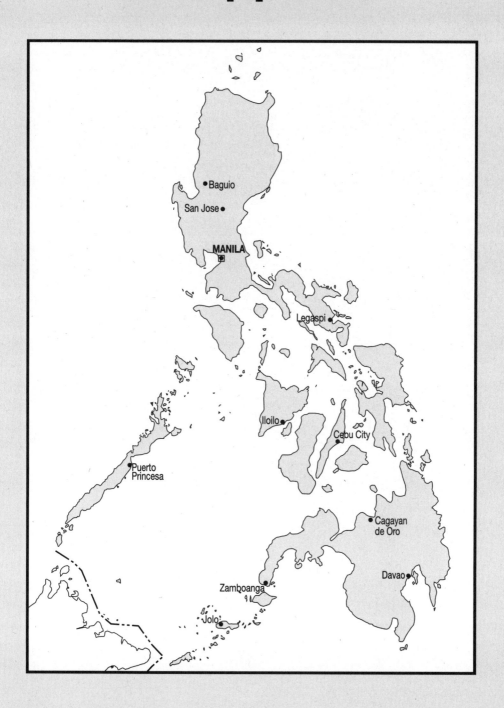

THE PHILIPPINES IN 2009
The Fourth-Quarter Collapse

Herman Joseph S. Kraft

The Year of the Fourth-Quarter Collapse

One of the most incongruous characteristics of Philippine society is the popularity of basketball among a people not noted for their height. The greater interest is in the professional game which is played in quarters rather than according to the amateur rule of dividing the game into two halves. To the Filipino fan, nothing evokes a greater thrill than the fourth-quarter rally, a situation where nothing that the favoured team does can go wrong and allows it to catch up with and surpass the score of the opposing team in the span of the last twelve minutes of the game. Moves are executed perfectly, a very high percentage of the shots go in, loose balls generally end up in or near the hands of their players, and close calls by the referee favour them. In other words, the hard work and skill of the players combined with good luck allow the favoured team to make up for what had generally been bad first three quarters to, as the cliché goes, snatch victory from the jaws of defeat. Conversely, the most dismaying development for the fan would be a situation where their favoured team has built a comfortable lead through three very competently played quarters but is suddenly unable to do anything right to protect the hard-earned lead in the last. The fourth-quarter collapse is a syndrome that has affected even the very best teams. Teams with the most disciplined and highly trained and skilled players can find themselves in situations where nothing works in the fourth quarter, and end up handing over to the opposing team what looked in the first part of the game like certain victory.

HERMAN JOSEPH S. KRAFT is the Executive Director, Institute for Strategic and Development Studies, Inc. and Assistant Professor, Department of Political Science, University of the Philippines at Diliman.

The analogy of the fourth-quarter collapse is a way of describing the Philippines in 2009. The end of 2008 did not give much room for confidence. There was concern about how the Philippines would cope with the long-term effects of the global financial crisis. There were projections of overseas Filipino workers being laid off and forced to come back to the country. Not only would the volume of remittances upon which the Philippine economy had become so reliant diminish, it would also intensify the expected effects of the financial crisis on the unemployment situation. As the country headed into the second half of 2009, these concerns were largely muted, if not completely silenced, and in fact gave way to some degree of optimism as government efforts at keeping the economy stable (including a stimulus package that promised to increase the country's total debt) took effect. It also helped that reforms in the financial system initiated in the aftermath of the Asian financial crisis and the fiscal policies enforced by Central Bank Governor Amando Tetangco enabled the Philippine financial system to weather the storm of the global crisis. And to a certain extent, the situation was also helped by the promise of change on the political horizon with scheduled presidential elections in 2010. As the country typically muddled through the first half of 2009, there was an increasing level of confidence that the country's prospects for the rest of the year would not hold any real unpleasant surprises. Even as there were still rumblings within the House of Representatives of possible moves for constitutional change, and dire warnings from the political opposition on the possibility of elections being discontinued because of the machinations of the administration in power, there was a sense that the country was moving slowly forward.

The extensive damage and hundreds of deaths caused by the onset of tropical storm Ketsana (locally referred to as Ondoy) towards the end of the third quarter, and the entry of Super Typhoon Parma (locally Pepeng) in the second week of October, however, changed the country's situation drastically. Their effects highlighted the vulnerabilities of a society whose government, across different administrations, had constantly taken politically-easy short-term action in the face of an inability to harness the political will to push needed infrastructure reform in support of development goals. Even as these twin disasters earned the country the sympathy of the international community, there were questions about whether it was just a matter of an unusual natural condition which the country was completely unprepared for, or an illustration of how the ignoring of plans to address the long-term effects of progress in favour of short-term moves have a way of getting back at you.

The international sympathy and goodwill that the country had accumulated from the Ketsana-Parma interlude very quickly dissipated when news of the murder of fifty-seven people in an election-related event emerged in late November. As more details were made public and evidence of the apparent culpability of a close political ally of the Arroyo administration emerged, the public outcry, both domestic and international, pushed President Gloria Macapagal-Arroyo into making a controversial decision to declare martial law in the province of Maguindanao. The decision was prompted by the realization that the political clan allegedly involved in the murders was supported by a private army that could have as many as 3,000 heavily armed men. Arresting those involved in the "Maguindanao Massacre" would require extraordinary legal powers, particularly the involvement of the Armed Forces of the Philippines (AFP). The situation in Maguindanao had hardly settled when reports came in of sixty-five people in Agusan del Sur province being kidnapped by heavily armed gunmen who were former members of the Citizen Armed Forces Geographical Unit (CAFGU), the armed auxiliary to the regular forces of the AFP. These two cases exposed a side of Philippine politics that had largely been unacknowledged by the government — the presence of armed groups that are supposed to be either part of the AFP or support the AFP in its operations but over which the control of the national government is nominal at best in many areas. In much the same way that the Ketsana-Parma case illustrated the lack of long-term foresight on the part of the political leadership of the Philippines across different administrations, the "Maguindanao Massacre" showed the effects of getting security on discount by sanctioning the existence of armed groups that claim either an explicitly legal status (because they are officially auxiliary forces of the AFP or the Philippine National Police, also referred to as the PNP) or at least the grudging tolerance of agents of the state because of the support that they give to the AFP or the PNP in counter-insurgency. The difficulty lies in the fact that regardless of their status, many of these groups owe their loyalty to private persons or companies rather than to the state. In instances where state interests diverge from that of the entities that hold the allegiance of these groups, the state has very little control over what these groups will or can do.

Whether natural or man-made, the disasters experienced by the Philippines in the last quarter of 2009 are partially explained by the long-standing practice of agents of the Philippine state, whether elected or appointed, to settle for measures that are politically expedient over the short-term. It just so happened that the consequences converged in the last quarter of 2009.

Well Executed Plays Despite Flawed Fundamentals: Riding Out the Economic Storm

The story at the end of 2008 was about the global financial crisis and its impact on the Philippine economy. There were very clear fears about the exposure of the Philippine financial system to external and domestic channels of risk.[1] Even more, there were concerns about how the financial crisis would affect the employment situation in the country. The depressed state of consumer spending in the United States and Europe was expected to force closures in manufacturing companies dependent on the export market. More importantly, the general contraction of the global economy was expected to lead to layoffs among overseas Filipino workers (OFW). Not only would they add to the expected rise in unemployment in the country, but the loss of their remittances (which already constituted around 10 per cent of the country's gross domestic product) would also have a telling effect on the Philippine Government's ability to finance its balance of payments.

By the first half of the year, the Philippine economy did better than expected, with the unemployment rate going down from 7.7 per cent at the start of 2009, to 7.5 by April, and to 7.1 in October.[2] This was in spite of the number of returning OFWs who had lost their jobs. The implementation by the Department of Labor and Employment as early as February of government programmes providing livelihood grants and training went far to ease the pressure on the labour market. The country's unemployment rate, however, was still the second highest in Southeast Asia, next only to Indonesia. Furthermore, the underemployment rate increased to 19.4 per cent in October from 18.4 in April and 18.2 in January — an indication of the nature of jobs generated by the government's job-creation programmes. Nonetheless, macroeconomic performance, while modest, was far from the worst case scenario feared.[3] Gross domestic product increased 1.8 per cent from a year earlier during the last quarter of 2009, an improvement over the revised 0.4 per cent gain in the three months through September.[4] Inflation was also expected to remain within target in 2010 despite the increase to 4.4 per cent in December due to the rising cost of food and oil.

Despite having avoided a plunge into a recession in 2009, the country's economy still displayed points of vulnerability. By the middle of the year, the budget deficit was already expected to balloon to 350 billion pesos because of the stimulus package and the expected decline in tax collection. The latter was due not only to the usual problems with capacity and corruption that taints agencies involved in revenue collection — especially the Bureau of Internal Revenue and the Bureau of Customs — it also reflected the impact of political obsequiousness on the part of politicians leading to popular if unwise policies such as the 5 per cent reduction of corporate income taxes and the increase in individual tax exemptions legislated by Congress in 2008.[5] These concerns could only be worsened by the effects of the damage caused by typhoons Ketsana and Parma. The infrastructure rebuilding that had to be undertaken would inevitably eat into the diminished coffers of the government. This would inevitably push the government's debt to around 4.8 to 4.9 *trillion* pesos (conservatively around US$104 billion).[6] Given the uncertainties of the global economy as the effects of the financial crisis lingered, the country's economic recovery going into 2010 remained in a wobbly state.

Offensive Fouls and Poor Defence: The Uncertain Drift towards Peace in Mindanao

The continuing fears about the economy notwithstanding, the downturn did not significantly contribute to any intensification of the communist insurgency being waged by the New People's Army (NPA), or of the secessionist movement of the Moro Islamic Liberation Front (MILF). At the same time, however, the planned resumption of peace talks with the CPP-NPA did not bear much fruit. On the other hand, talks between the Philippine Government and the MILF were once again under way more than a year after the Supreme Court had declared unconstitutional a preliminary agreement on an expanded autonomous region of Muslim Mindanao which led to the intensification of fighting in August 2008.

The Communist Party of the Philippines, which provides the political leadership for the NPA, had discontinued peace talks with the government when the Arroyo administration began to face a series of political crises in July 2005. Since then, the CPP leadership had argued that the instability of the current administration made negotiations unpredictable. Despite this stated policy, there was a tentative agreement reached between the government and the CPP to resume talks in Oslo on 28 August. This was initially postponed to September, and then indefinitely over a disagreement on the release of a number of CPP-NPA leaders in the custody of the government who would become members or consultants of the negotiating panel, and over the provision of immunity guarantees by the government to the members of the CPP panel. Both sides tried to pin the blame for the failure to hold talks on the other as they exchanged accusations over each other's lack of sincerity in wanting the talks to take place, much less succeed. Each side, however, actually showed no qualms in trying to undermine the other even when the talks to have peace talks were in their most sensitive stages.[7] Further complicating the situation was the continuing issue of extrajudicial killings which involved mostly known leftist activists and journalists. In his report submitted in April 2009, UN special rapporteur on extrajudicial, summary, or arbitrary executions, Phillip Alston, noted that even as the number of killings had decreased, there were still quite a number of cases being reported, especially in conjunction with the increased involvement of "death squads". More importantly, as in past cases, the government has made very little headway in establishing accountability for these new instances of killings and disappearances.[8]

In comparison, negotiations between the Philippine Government and the MILF over resuming peace discussions were successfully concluded and the peace talks opened in Kuala Lumpur on 8 December. The path to the negotiating table was nonetheless very bumpy. Between August 2008 and January 2009, clashes between the AFP and the MILF had left more than 150 soldiers, militiamen, and rebels dead.[9] On 26 December 2008, the MILF asked for clarification on a number of issues before they could agree to renewed peace talks. These included matters related to the previous agreement, the return of the international monitoring team (IMT), and the cessation of all military operations against the MILF, including against those field commanders that the Philippine Government accused of initiating the fighting in August 2008. It was made clear that these were not preconditions to talks but they were issues that had to be resolved.[10] The MILF was likewise not impressed when in January 2009, President Gloria Macapagal-Arroyo appointed a new presidential adviser for the peace process. They felt that this kind of political manoeuvre only further hindered the peace talks. Nonetheless, the process moved forward once the Malaysian Government agreed to act as facilitator. An International Contact Group (ICG) that is supposed to provide multifaceted support for the negotiations between the government and MILF panels was established on 16 November 2009 in Kuala Lumpur. Its membership is constituted by Japanese Ambassador to Malaysia Masahiko Horie, British High Commissioner to Malaysia Boyd McCleary, Turkish Chargé d'Affaires Yasin Temizkan, Steven Rood and Herizal Hazri of the Asia Foundation, Cynthia Petrigh and Kristian Herbolzheimer of Conciliation Resources, David Gorman of the Centre for Humanitarian Dialogue, and Din Syamsuddin and Sudibyo Markus of Muhammadiyah of Indonesia. It was agreed that the principal agenda of this round of talks would be the establishment of an IMT of ceasefire observers.[11] Both sides have already agreed to renew the terms of reference for the IMT and will invite Malaysia, Japan, Brunei, and Libya, along with non-government organizations (NGOs) such as the International Committee of the Red Cross (ICRC), the Mindanao People's Caucus (MPC), and the Non-Violent Peace Force (NVPF) to be members of the IMT.

Even as the government held out for the resumption of peace talks with both the CPP-NPA and the MILF, there have been continuing, if sporadic, engagements between the AFP (and the PNP) and armed insurgent groups. The MILF has also been implicated in bombings in Cotabato, Lanao del Norte, and Jolo in early January and in July.[12] It was, however, against the Abu Sayyaf Group (ASG) that extensive military resources were concentrated and operations sustained. On 15 January, the ASG took three representatives of the ICRC hostage. These included two Europeans, namely 62-year-old Italian national Eugenio Vagni and 38-year-old Swiss national Andreas Notter, and 44-year-old Filipino Mary Jean Lacaba. Thus began a six-month episode wherein the ASG utilized the hostages as bargaining chips to ease the military pressure on their main forces in Sulu.[13] The pursuit operations conducted had resulted in a number of clashes with the ASG, as well as forces of the Moro National Liberation Front (MNLF). All the hostages from the ICRC held by the ASG were released by July. Military operations were immediately intensified as the AFP concentrated over 3,500 battle-hardened troops against the ASG in Jolo.[14] The hostage situation illustrated that the situation in Mindanao was far from being resolved. Even as talks with the MILF were being negotiated, the conflict in the Southern Philippines would continue with the ASG. There are also continuing concerns over the involvement of the MNLF in some operations of the ASG, which also raised questions about the relationship between the MILF forces in the Jolo area and the ASG.[15] It should be noted that on 8 November, Asnawi Addan Salah, commander of the MILF 114th Base Command, was arrested at Zamboanga International Airport. He was wanted for his alleged involvement in the killing of fourteen Marines on 10 July 2007 who were involved in operations against the ASG.[16]

Looking for New Management: Presidential Elections in 2010

Despite the relief over the less than feared consequences of the financial crisis and the renewed expectations of talks with both the MILF and the CPP, the country looked forward to the initial arrangements for political change with the prospect of presidential elections in 2010. The Arroyo administration has been one of the most unpopular presidencies in the history of the country. Polls consistently showed negative net returns on public opinion of her administration. Political and corruption scandals had coloured the public's image of her presidency and obscured its economic accomplishments. It had to work through lingering questions about its legitimacy because of allegations of fraud surrounding the president's electoral victory in 2004, which have never been addressed to the satisfaction of the general public. Worsening the situation were the actions of President Arroyo's allies who sought, despite widespread popular opposition, to make amendments to the constitution to enable her to stay in power beyond the constitutionally mandated limit of a single six-year term as president — moves that were generally believed to have the blessings of the President herself.[17] The prospect of elections and a new administration would hopefully put an end to these issues and perhaps allow for the emergence of political space that would be unaffected by Arroyo's unpopularity.

The usual issues, however, initially coloured the prospective polls in 2010. There was speculation that the government was creating conditions for the discontinuation of elections in order to prolong the Arroyo presidency. Much of it revolved around the introduction of automated election mechanisms and rules.[18] Another speculation involved the possibility of Arroyo doing a Marcos and declaring martial law before the 2010 elections.[19] Yet another issue was who would be the administration's standard-bearer. There were strong indications that Vice President Noli De Castro would in fact be nominated as the ruling coalition's (Lakas-Kampi-CMD) presidential candidate. The obverse of this was whether or not the opposition would be able to unite under one banner and support one candidate. A related question to this was whether or not Joseph Estrada, the former President, would seek to run a second time and whether the constitutional ban on second terms would not be applied to his case.

The election calculus changed with the death of Cory Aquino at age 76 from cardiorespiratory arrest, the result of complications from colon cancer, on 1 August 2009. Corazon Cojuangco Aquino had become iconic not only as the woman who had opposed President Ferdinand Marcos, but even more so as the president who brought democracy back to the Philippines. Her support for and defence of the constitution set her against all of the presidents who came after her who sought to amend it for whatever reason. Her death also invited comparisons with President Arroyo, the second woman president of the Philippines.[20] Aquino's failings as a president did not detract from a general perception of her unquestionable personal integrity — a judgment against which Arroyo is unfavourably juxtaposed. In fact, her avid support for the principal witness against the government on the NBN-ZTE scandal, Rodolfo "Jun" Lozada, Jr., placed her directly at odds with President Arroyo who was at the centre of the controversy surrounding the case. The most significant immediate effect of her death, however, had nothing to do with her personally. Rather, her passing away raised expectations of the possibility of another Aquino presidency that would lead the country away from the scandal-and corruption-ridden politics of the Estrada and Arroyo administrations.

Senator Benigno "Noynoy" Aquino III gave in to public pressure to run for the presidency which galvanized after his mother passed away. He has since stood on the platform of change — more specifically change from the politics of the Arroyo administration. He was acclaimed as the standard-bearer of a resurgent Liberal Party when Senator Manuel "Mar" Roxas II, who had earlier indicated his desire to seek the party's nomination, gave way to Aquino in recognition of the strong popular wave of support for the latter's candidacy. Roxas instead agreed to become the running mate of Aquino as the vice-presidential candidate of the Liberal Party. The public's sympathy was immediately evident as opinion polls showed a majority of respondents swinging behind the Aquino bandwagon. As late as early December 2009, Aquino was still well ahead of his closest competitors for the presidency, at least of those who had signalled their intention to contest.[21]

Aquino's strong showing at the polls, however, made it unlikely for a united opposition slate to emerge. Other opposition politicians had earlier been the focus of discussions about a possible common line-up for offices of the president and the Vice President. Senator Francis "Chiz" Escudero was an early favourite for the position but more senior politicians were unwilling to give way. He eventually dropped out of the race leaving his party, the Nationalist People's Coalition (NPC), without a candidate. Former President Joseph Estrada signalled his intention to run when it became evident that even before Aquino became the Liberal Party's standard-bearer the opposition could not be expected to unite behind any single candidate. He was also confident that he would still be supported by the lower classes in Philippine society which had been his main support base in his successful bid during the 1998 presidential elections.[22] This premise, however, is being contested by former Senate President, Manuel "Manny" Villar, Jr. He has revitalized the Nacionalista Party and invested his not inconsiderable personal wealth in a very strong run for the presidency. Like Estrada, he has strong support from the poorer classes. Unlike Estrada, he also has some pull on the middle and upper classes. Senator Richard "Dick" Gordon has also put his hat in the ring with the former Chairman of the Metropolitan Manila Development Authority (MMDA), Bayani "BF" Fernando, as his running mate. Like Aquino, they are running on a platform of change, referring to their team as "The Transformers". Unlike Aquino (who has only served in the legislature), they are offering their past record as successful and highly respected local executives who had transformed their municipalities into progressive and well-administered cities.[23]

The inability of the opposition to put together a single slate should have been an advantage for the administration. The Lakas-Kampi-CMD coalition, however, was unable to settle on a candidate because of uncertainty about the willingness of Vice-President Noli De Castro to run. Eventually, the coalition chose the then Secretary of National Defence, Gilbert "Gibo" Teodoro, as their candidate for the presidency. He has since proven himself to have charisma and has been able to attract support from among university students and professionals. He is, however, burdened by the unpopularity of the Arroyo administration, of which he was a cabinet member, and the politics she and her allies represent. Polls indicate that he has a large gap to close, particularly in terms of his being able to reach out to the lower classes.

Beyond the question of the candidates, Philippine electoral politics this time around continues to follow old patterns. The first is the persistent weakness of party politics in the country. It is a truism to talk about the personality-based nature of Philippine politics. This makes it unnecessary for strong *party* machineries to ensure the strength of a candidate's bid. The revitalization of the Liberal Party and the Nacionalista Party, however, seemed to point to shifting development in this area. The platform of change that was emphasized by Aquino seemed to be ideologically opposed to Villar's closer adherence to traditional political formulas. The strong showing of both the Liberal and Nacionalista standard-bearers in polls, however, led to the migration of several noted politicians from the ruling coalition to the ranks of these parties. They included such luminaries as former Senator and Director General of the National Economic Development Authority (NEDA), Raphael "Ralph" Recto. He was accepted into the Liberal Party and expected to fill one of the senatorial candidate slots of the party.[24] This led to questions about the commitment to change on the part of the Liberal Party, and raised issues about how much difference there was between the "change" platform and the traditional politics that Villar seems to represent. This development has left the ruling coalition much weakened. Neither, however, does it guarantee that the Liberal and Nacionalista Parties will be able to sustain this momentum in favour of party-based politics, as a realignment of forces usually takes place after the elections.

A second development has been the participation of politicians identified with sectoral parties and who normally compete for membership in the House of Representatives as party list representatives in the senatorial race. Riza Hontiveros of Akbayan, a party identified with left-of-centre groups and highly critical of the Arroyo administration, is running as a Senate candidate with the Liberal Party.[25] Even more unusual is the Nacionalista slate, which includes detained marine Colonel, Ariel Querubin, who was charged with rebellion against the Arroyo administration, and Bayan Muna party list representative, Satur Ocampo, who is still identified with the National Democratic Front, the legal front of the CPP-NPA.[26] While this seems to indicate a mainstreaming of the party list agenda (which is normally sectoral in its scope), it could also show that both the Liberal and Nacionalista Parties are casting a wide net in their Senate slates to strengthen their parties to take advantage of what they perceive to be a strong presidential run by their respective standard-bearers. Arguably, however, the more important arena for party politics is the House of Representatives, where both the Liberal and the Nacionalista are still relatively weak in relation to the ruling coalition of the Lakas-Kampi-CMD, especially with President Arroyo deciding to run for Congress.

In December, President Arroyo filed her certificate of candidacy for representative of the second district of the province of Pampanga. This was met with immediate criticism from former Presidents Fidel V. Ramos and Joseph Estrada. The former contended that campaigning for the office even as she sat as the chief executive of the country created unfair election conditions. Reports indicated that as President, Arroyo had authorized 459 million pesos of projects for the second district of Pampanga — a claim that her office contested.[27] Nonetheless, Ramos called on Arroyo to resign first in order to "level the playing field".[28] Estrada, on the other hand, argued that in running for congress, Arroyo was demeaning the office of the presidency of the country. Others questioned how she would manage the campaign while at the same time dispensing her current office. Local political leaders in Pampanga, however, vowed to campaign for her, making it unnecessary for her to personally take time off from her duties as President in order to make appearances in the district she is running in. It was clear, however, that there were no constitutional impediments to her running for a lesser office than the one she holds at present. The situation, however, stretches the intention behind the constitutional term limits and does raise questions about its impact on the office of the presidency itself.

The Arroyo candidacy, however, is not the only issue that had to be settled regarding interpretations of the constitution and the term limits it imposes on the presidency. Estrada's bid to become President challenged the commonly held interpretation that anyone who had become President could not run for a second term. Arroyo's unprecedented nine years as President first came on the heels of the resignation of President Estrada (which Estrada contests) when she was Vice President, and then her successful run in 2004 on the grounds that she had never been elected as President and therefore could run then without having to change the constitution. Estrada's candidacy on the other hand does stretch the constitutional limits. His argument was that he did not complete his first term and so technically had not fulfilled the mandate given to him when he was elected in 1998. The Commission on Elections (COMELEC) allowed his candidacy to prosper based on the flimsy basis of letting the people decide on the matter. The decision, however, showed the fundamental weakness of Philippine electoral institutions, which have constantly been battered by members of the political elite seeking to stretch the legal limits of rules governing elections in the country.[29]

The Fourth-Quarter Collapse: Coping with Natural and Man-made Disasters

In late September the general sense of satisfaction with the country's state of affairs (despite all the complaints about specific issues, both economic and political) came crashing down with the onset of tropical storm Ketsana (Ondoy). This was followed less than a month later by Super Typhoon Parma (Pepeng). Around twenty tropical depressions, storms, and typhoons were identified as having entered the Philippine territory during 2009. A total of 1,124 fatalities were attributed to them, with damages estimated at up to US$903 million. Of these, 929 fatalities and US$803 million in damages were due to the combined effects of Ketsana and Parma.

On 26 September, Ketsana made its landfall at the border of Aurora and Quezon provinces shortly before noon with maximum winds of eight-five kilometres per hour near the centre. Within a few hours it approached Metro Manila and caused widespread flooding in the cities of Antipolo, Makati, Manila, Marikina, Malabon, Muntinlupa, Pasig, Quezon, San Juan, Taguig, and Valenzuela. Flooding also occurred in the nearby provinces of Bulacan, Rizal, Laguna and the other Southern Tagalog areas. Major roads in these areas (especially in Metro Manila) were rendered impassable because of huge flood currents and marooned cars. National Disaster Coordinating Council (NDCC) chair and National Defense secretary, Gilbert Teodoro, declared an overall state of calamity in Metro Manila and the other twenty-five provinces hit by the typhoon. This allowed officials to utilize emergency funds for relief and rescue. The economic region of Metro Manila and many adjoining provinces incurred damages to both infrastructure and agriculture.[30] Marikina City was arguably the most devastated region, where almost the entire city (less than 15 per cent of the city was not flooded) was submerged in water and mud. During the typhoon, the Marikina River broke its banks and transformed streets into rivers. Seventy-eight deaths were reported; the highest among Metro Manila cities. Outside of Luzon, several towns in the Cotabato and Sultan Kudarat areas were submerged. The national highway in Bulalo, Cotabato City was closed, isolating a number of towns for several days.

The Philippine Atmospheric, Geophysical and Astronomical Services Administration (PAGASA) documented a record-high amount of rainfall in twenty-four hours at 455 millimetres. The amount of rainfall recorded for six hours from mid-morning to mid-afternoon (341.3 millimetres) was comparable to what Metro Manila normally experiences in a month. The damage to property was estimated to be 6 billion pesos, including 4.1 billion pesos in damage to infrastructure, 1.9 billion pesos in damage to schools, and 882.525 million pesos in damage to agriculture. An estimated 126,721 hectares of rice farms were laid waste, affecting 3 per cent of the country's expected rice production. Ketsana also devastated some 1,374 hectares of corn plantations.[31]

Even as the country was reeling from the effects of Ketsana, Super Typhoon Parma was observed making its way into the Philippines. The NDCC advised local government officials in Luzon to evacuate all the people, if necessary, to secure their safety. Dams were opened and tons of water freed to avoid overflowing. In Isabela, the water released from Magat Dam was projected to pass through Cagayan River, for which reason people living near the river were evacuated. Angat Dam in Bulacan was also opened to let out tons of water, flooding the barrios of Calumpit and Hagonoy. The local officials took charge to evacuate people living in the area. Five *barangays* in Nueva Ecija were already flooded due to water released from Pantabangan Dam on 2 October. Parma made its landfall at north-eastern Cagayan that same day. By the time it had left the Philippines and weakened to a tropical depression less than a week later, more than 900,000 people had been affected and an already dire situation in Luzon had worsened. It would take more than a month for floodwaters to recede in some areas in Metro Manila, and even more in the towns around Laguna de Bae.

International sympathy for the Philippines immediately translated into massive assistance from various UN agencies and the governments of different countries. Even as government spokespersons emphasized the extraordinary nature of Ketsana's volume of rainfall, however, what became clear was the lack of preparedness of the government in handling this kind of situation. Ironically, the United States and the Philippines hosted a joint exercise for the ASEAN Regional Forum (ARF) in August 2009 on disaster relief operations. It was the first such exercise ever held under ARF auspices. Beyond the immediately obvious lack of capacity, the episode exposed an even deeper malaise in disaster planning and management. This was a case of a failure of the Philippine Government (across different administrations) to address an issue that had already been identified as a concern nearly forty years ago. Plans to address flooding in Metro Manila were completed and even partially implemented. Short-term planning horizons led to these plans not being completed or even just shelved.[32]

On 23 November 2009, fifty-seven people were killed by gunmen identified with Datu Unsay Mayor, Andal Ampatuan, Jr., son of the incumbent Maguindanao Governor, Andal Ampatuan, Sr. The murder victims included the wife of Esmael Mangudadatu, the Vice Mayor of the town of Buluan, his two sisters, an aunt, journalists, lawyers, aides accompanying them, and motorists who were unfortunate witnesses to the murder or were just mistakenly identified as part of the group. Mangudadatu was going to contest the younger Ampatuan for the office of Governor of Maguindanao, and his wife, Genalyn Tiamzon-Mangudadatu, was on her way to file his certificate of candidacy. Mangudadatu's sisters and aunt were accompanying her and the media was there to ensure that nothing untoward would happen as the Ampatuans had reportedly made threats should Mangudadatu go ahead with his election plans. In fact, to avoid the possibility of bloodshed, Mangudadatu had decided not to send any armed security with the group. The safety measures failed as the convoy with Mangudadatu's wife was flagged down near the town of Shariff Aguak by armed men. Reports that immediately emerged from an initial investigation by the soldiers from the 601st Brigade of the Philippine Army confirmed that those involved were police personnel and armed civilian volunteers identified with the Ampatuans.[33]

The Ampatuans are a political clan that has been in control of Maguindanao since 2001. Andal Ampatuan, Sr. was appointed by President Corazon Aquino as officer-in-charge of Maganoy (now Shariff Aguak) in 1986 right after the People Power Revolution. He was elected Governor of Maguindanao in 1998. It was, however, during the administration of Arroyo that the clan was able to expand its control over the Autonomous Region of Muslim Mindanao (ARMM). By aligning themselves with President Arroyo, and delivering the votes that ensured her election in 2004, the Ampatuans were able to impose their control over the region (particularly the province of Maguindanao) with a large degree of impunity. This partially explains the seeming cold-bloodedness of what has now been popularly dubbed as the "Maguindanao Massacre".

In the aftermath of the incident, the executive committee of the Lakas-Kampi-CMD political party unanimously voted to expel Maguindanao Governor Andal Ampatuan, Sr. and his two sons, Governor Zaldy Uy Ampatuan of the Autonomous Region in Muslim Mindanao (ARMM), and Mayor Andal Ampatuan, Jr. from the party. Andal Ampatuan, Jr., accused of being the primary instigator of the killings (he was the one who was being challenged by Mangudadatu for the governorship of Maguindanao), was surrendered by his brother Zaldy to the Presidential Adviser to the Peace Process, Jesus Dureza. This was supposed to indicate the willingness of the Ampatuans to be subjected to the judicial process. The younger Ampatuan denied the charges against him and claimed that he was at the provincial capitol in Shariff Aguak when the massacre took place. He pointed to the MILF, specifically Umbra Kato (one of the MILF commanders whose forces went on a rampage after the Supreme Court had declared unconstitutional the Memorandum of Agreement on Ancestral Domain that was supposed to be the basis for peace in Mindanao in 2008), as the culprits — a charge the MILF leadership dismissed.[34]

The international standing of the Philippines suffered with the incident. Meantime, outgoing U.S. Ambassador Kristie Kenney said that U.S. aid to Maguindanao has been suspended even though the U.S. Government's projects in various areas in Mindanao will continue.[35] It was predicted by critics that the Philippines could find itself on the next edition of the list of failed states annually reported by the Fund for Peace's Failed States Index, if it continued to have massacres, extrajudicial killings, and disappearances.[36] An even more important concern was the realization that disarming the supporters might lead to greater violence, especially when arrest orders were also issued for the elder Andal Ampatuan and his son Zaldy (to whom the younger Ampatuan had initially surrendered). On 4 December 2009, President Gloria Macapagal Arroyo issued Proclamation No. 1959 officially placing Maguindanao province under a state of martial law. The declaration also suspended the privilege of the writ of habeas corpus in the province. Executive Secretary Eduardo Ermita said the step was taken in order to avert the escalation of "lawless" violence in the province and pave the way for the swift arrest of the suspects in the massacre. The declaration, however, was heavily criticized even by erstwhile allies of the administration. Senator Miriam Defensor-Santiago warned that the martial law in Maguindanao could be used by interested groups to bring about a "bolder" martial law that would allow them to seize power and pre-empt national elections in 2010.[37] While the Senator did not include the President in her scenario, others were not so shy in directly criticizing her. Questions about the necessity of declaring martial law and its constitutionality were raised, and the possibility of expanding martial law to the rest of the Philippines and its implications for the elections were being speculated upon.[38] To forestall further political uncertainty arising from the issue of martial law in Maguindanao, it was lifted on 13 December 2009.

The whole episode, however, again showed the consequences of short-sighted government policy in allowing and even arming groups outside the AFP and the PNP to assist the latter two in maintaining peace and order in the country in the face of the threat of the NPA insurgency and the MILF and ASG secessionist movements. It must be noted that the phenomenon has been a long-standing part of the structure of the Philippine armed forces and is not something that the Arroyo administration should be held responsible for. The rise of the Ampatuans and their armed loyal following, however, is something that could be blamed on the Arroyo administration. Raids on several Ampatuan houses following the declaration of martial law yielded large numbers of firearms and ammunition.[39] There is evidence that some of these arms and ammunition in fact came from government arsenals.[40] A greater challenge, however, was disarming the heavily armed forces supporting the Ampatuans. These have been officially estimated to number around 2,000.[41]

The presence of armed groups outside of the AFP and the PNP but sanctioned by the Philippine state has been a historic phenomenon in Philippine politics. In many cases, these armed groups are supposed to be auxiliary forces under the operational control of regular military and police forces and are usually armed from government arsenals. These are the Citizen Armed Forces Geographical Units (CAFGUs) and the Civilian Volunteer Organizations (CVOs). There are, however, also various privately raised and organized groups that largely serve private and business interests but are tolerated by state authorities. It is not uncommon for these groups to be called upon to assist in operations involving state security. As in the case of the Ampatuans, however, many of the CAFGU and CVO personnel are loyal to local officials and, even if supposed to be part of the regular forces of the AFP or are auxiliary units to the PNP, actually constitute a private army. At present, these groups play a role in local security, especially in defending specific areas against NPA and MILF raiders in order to leave the regular forces free to conduct offensive operations. The second group, however, is more reflective of how stretched government resources are in counter-insurgency and other peace and order functions. Consequently, political and business groups raise their own private security forces as protection against increasingly aggressive and well-armed criminal organizations, the activities of insurgent groups, and, more often than not, against each other and other private entities to protect or advance their commercial or political interests. As indicated by the arms seized from the Ampatuans, this situation created a spiral of violence fed by the proliferation of firearms easy enough to procure in a country with weak gun-control laws and a permissive attitude towards gun ownership and use.[42]

Following the Maguindanao Massacre, an independent commission was established to oversee the dismantling of private armies in the country. This is a seasonal undertaking. Whenever there are elections, the AFP and the PNP are deputized by the Commission on Elections to dismantle private armies. Considering that it is a seasonal undertaking, the effort very obviously always falls short of success. Defense Secretary Norberto Gonzales noted that there are 132 private armed groups led by politicians in various parts of the country, with a combined strength of about 10,000 armed men.[43] Critics doubt that the commission can complete its task within a time period that would have an impact on the coming elections. Previous administrations that might have disbanded these armed groups have failed to do so — mainly because they have benefited from their existence. The commission, however, will "give more focus, emphasis and … put more teeth and impetus behind the campaign (of the PNP)."[44]

Conclusion

The disasters that overtook the Philippines during the fourth quarter of 2009 were in no small way attributable to flawed policies inherited from previous administrations and continued by President Arroyo. They were the consequence of a succession of political leaders guided not so much by public good considerations as being limited by varying and even conflicting demands on the government's limited resources by both public and private interests. In other words, these are the extreme effects of the inability of a system based on transactional and accommodative politics to recognize the need to adhere to policies with long-term horizons and consequences.

The effects of Ketsana on Metro Manila were certainly made worse by poorly maintained sewage systems and infrastructure for flood control that was never completed. This is the case despite the fact that Metro Manila regularly experiences floods whenever there are heavy rains — an often enough occurrence that should have impelled government officials to make and implement long-term plans for flood control. In the end, however, weak institutions (for which different administrations share responsibility for not seriously undertaking or enforcing reform policies) have made it very difficult to build the capacity for long-term policy undertakings. Flood control in Metro Manila is just one of these necessary but insufficiently addressed concerns.

The Maguindanao Massacre is another extreme case where administrations not committed to long-term institution-building have been unwilling to invest the necessary resources. CAFGU and CVOs are cheaper alternatives to building a capable security force made up of regular soldiers or police. The local nature of recruitment that goes into these groups, however, means that local officials have an influence on the process and a claim to the loyalty of those who have been recruited. In the case of the Ampatuans, the nexus of national and local politics (the reliance of President Arroyo on the Ampatuans to deliver Maguindanao during elections) with the imperatives of counter-insurgency (using the forces loyal to the Ampatuans to augment the AFP in their fight against the MILF) have created what one writer has described as "Frankenstein's monster" over whom the Arroyo administration really had very little direct control. The accusation that the Ampatuans for these past years have had impunity in their use of violence to enforce their rule over Maguindanao is but another way of saying that the Arroyo administration tolerated the behaviour of the Ampatuans because of political exigencies.

In the end, the 2009 fourth-quarter collapse experienced by the Philippines was a consequence of having a political class which over time has failed to provide the leadership needed to address the long-term needs of the country. Elections in the Philippines have always energized people with the prospect of change, and the 2010 polls are no different in this context. It is, however, very difficult to understand why this should be so, considering the kind of leadership electoral exercises have given the country. The wonder is really in the continuing faith that people show in a system that has been constantly falling short in producing inspired and effective national leaders.

Notes

[1] See International Monetary Fund, "The Philippines: Selected Issues", *IMF Country Report No. 09/63* (February 2009).

[2] See national statistics provided by the National Statistics Office of the Philippines <http://www.census.gov.ph>. See also Ronnel W. Domingo, "Ranks of Jobless Down to 7.5% in April", *Philippine Daily Inquirer*, 17 June 2009, p. B-1.

[3] See for instance Daxim Lucas, "Top Businessmen See Recession in 2009", *Philippine Daily Inquirer*, 12 November 2008, p. A-1.

[4] See statement of the Acting Director General of the National Economic Development Authority, Augusto Santos, on the national income accounts for the fourth quarter on 28 January 2010 <http://www.neda.gov.ph/ads/press_releases/pr.asp?ID=1143>. See also Karl Lester M. Yap and Max Estayo, "Philippines Raises Rediscounting Rate as Growth Accelerates", Bloomberg.com, 29 January 2010 <http://www.bloomberg.com/apps/news?pid=20601080&sid=a7R72Qw5bwHY>.

5   See Michelle V. Remo, "Budget Gap May be Higher than What Gov't Thinks", *Philippine Daily Inquirer*, 17 June 2009, p. B-1.

6   By March, the government's debt had already risen to 4.22 *trillion* pesos. See Iris C. Gonzales, "Gov't Debt Hits P4.22T in Mar", *Philippine Star*, 17 June 2009, p. B-4.

7   For example, see letter of Major Julio C. Osias IV in the *Philippine Daily Inquirer*, 13 January 2010, which accuses the CPP-NPA of being engaged in the drug trade. There have also been reports of a split in the ranks of the CPP over strategy as a number of politicians identified with the National Democratic Front have allied themselves with some of the more mainstream parties to run for seats in the Philippine senate. See Victor Reyes, "May Polls Spark Infighting within CPP-NPA", Malaya, 29 January 2010 <http://www.malaya.com.ph/01292010/metro1.html>.

8   See "Promotion and Protection of all Human Rights, Civil, Political, Economic, Social and Cultural Rights, Including the Right to Development", Report of the Special Rapporteur on Extrajudicial, Summary or Arbitrary Executions, Phillip Alston, on the Philippines during the Eleventh Session of the Human Rights Council of the United Nations (A/HRC/11/2/Add. 8), 29 April 2009.

9   International Crisis Group, "The Philippines: Running in Place in Mindanao", *ICG Asia Briefing No. 88*, 16 February 2009, p. 3.

10 Ibid.

11 See T.J. Burgonio and Cynthia Balana, "RP-MILF Peace Talks Resume in KL", *Philippine Daily Inquirer*, 9 December 2009, p. A-1.

12 See "About 2009 July Philippines Bomb Blasts", Andhranews.net <http://www.andhranews.net/Features/Events/2009-July-Philippines-bomb-blasts.asp>.

13 This was the principal demand apart from the ransom being asked for those taken hostage according to a letter sent by three of the leaders of the ASG to the military. See Maria Althea Teves and Purple Romero, "Timeline: Kidnapping of ICRC Hostages by the Abu Sayyaf Group", *ABS-CBN NEWS*, 31 March 2009 <http://www.abs-cbnnews.com/nation/03/31/09/timeline-kidnapping-icrc-hostages-abu-sayyaf-group>.

14 Alastair McIndoe, "Philippines Goes All Out against Abu Sayyaf", *Straits Times*, 18 July 2009, p. C6.

15 This does not mean that the MILF leadership itself condones the actions of their commanders in the field. Nonetheless, the relative autonomy of action that these commanders have from the political leadership does raise questions about what they will do in the event that the AFP's pursuit operations against the ASG or other rogue elements (including those from the MILF) intensify in their areas of jurisdiction. See Allan Nawal, "AFP Braces for Escalation of Hostilities vs. Maguindanao rebels", *Philippine Daily Inquirer*, 17 June 2009, p. A14.

16 Mike Frialde, "MILF Leader in Marines' Beheading Arrested", Philstar.com, 8 November 2009 <http://www.philstar.com/Article.aspx?articleId=521412>.

17 These included exploring different modalities of constitutional change which seemed to stretch the limits of constitutional provisions. See Gil C. Cabacungan, Jr.,

"4th Cha-cha Mode Bared", *Philippine Daily Inquirer*, 21 April 2009, p. A1. That the President was being consulted on these matters was clear in statements made by her political allies in the House of Representatives. See Edu Punay, "SC Junks Petitions vs. Con-ass", *Philippine Star*, 17 June 2009, p. 1.

[18]   See, for example, Christine Avendaño, "No Election Could Spark Revolution", Inquirer. net, 24 June 2009 <http://newsinfo.inquirer.net/inquirerheadlines/nation/view/20090624-212106/No-election-could-spark-revolution>.

[19]   See, for instance, Katherine Adraneda, "There is de Facto Martial Law in RP", Philstar.com, 22 September 2009 <http://www.philstar.com/Article.aspx?articleId=507565>. This is a charge that the administration has constantly denied. See Paolo Romero, "No Martial Law under GMA", Philstar.com, 21 September 2009 <http://www.philstar.com/Article.aspx?articleid=507232>.

[20]   See, for example, Benjie Oliveros, "Cory Aquino's Place in History", Bulatlat.com, 1 August 2009 <http://www.bulatlat.com/main/2009/08/01/cory-aquino%E2%80%99s-place-in-history/>.

[21]   "Aquino is Voters' Top Pick for President", *BusinessWorld Online*, 21 December 2009 <http://www.bworldonline.com/main/content.php?id=3543>.

[22]   See Ibid.

[23]   Gordon was the acclaimed Mayor of Subic when the U.S. naval base was still there. He was also responsible for the transformation of the town from one that was primarily dependent on the base for its economic survival to one that became an industrial and tourism hub. Fernando was the well-respected mayor of Marikina city; the city earned a reputation for orderliness, cleanliness, and good administration during his tenure as Mayor.

[24]   Lira Dalangin-Fernandez, "Liberal Party National Slate Out", Inquirer.net, 16 November 2009 <http://newsinfo.inquirer.net/breakingnews/nation/view/20091116-236597/Liberal-Party-national-slate-out>.

[25]   Ibid.

[26]   Michael Lim Ubac, "Strange Bedfellows in 2010 Senate Race", Inquirer.net, 16 November 2009 <http://newsinfo.inquirer.net/inquirerheadlines/nation/view/20091106-234524/Strange-bedfellows-in-2010-Senate-race>.

[27]   Joyce Pangco Pañares, "Arroyo Says No Favoured Treatment for Pampanga", manilastandardtoday.com, 8 January 2010 <http://www.manilastandardtoday.com/insideNews.htm?f=2010/january/8/news2.isx&d=2010/january/8>.

[28]   See Franco G. Regala, "Arroyo Battles Three 'Davids' in Pamapanga", MB.com.ph, 5 December 2009 <http://www.mb.com.ph/node/232650/arroyo-battle>.

[29]   Kimberley Jane Tan, "COMELEC Allows Erap to Run for President in May 2010 Polls", GMANews.TV, 20 January 2010 <http://www.gmanews.tv/story/182015/comelec-allows-erap-to-run-for-president-in-may-10-polls>.

[30]   See United Nations Office for the Coordination of Humanitarian Affairs, "The Philippines: Typhoon Ketsana and Parma", *Situation Report No. 11*, 20 October 2009.

31 Ibid.

32 See "Guingona Seeks Culture of Preparedness", Manilatimes.net, 3 October 2009 <http://www.manilatimes.net/index.php/component/content/article/86-special-reports/3272-guingona-seeks-culture-of-prepareness-developed>.

33 James Mananghaya, "Maguindanao Massacre", Philstar.com, 24 November 2009 <http://www.philstar.com/Article.aspx?articleId=526314&publicationSubCategoryId=63>.

34 John Unson and Edith Regalado, "MILF Denies Involvement in Maguindanao Massacre", Philstar.com, 28 November 2009 <http://www.philstar.com/Article.aspx?articleId=527510>.

35 Marvin Sy et al., "Commission Created to Oversee Dismantling of Private Armies", *Philippine Star*, 5 December 2009, p. 1

36 Vicente T. Villegas, "Why the Philippines is a failed state", BusinessWorld Online, 4 January 2010 <http://www.bworldonline.com/main/content.php?id=3951>. The Philippines ranked 53rd in the Failed State Index behind Indonesia (62) and Thailand (79), but ahead of Cambodia (49), East Timor (20), and Myanmar (13) among Southeast Asian states. See Fund for Peace, "Failed States Index Scores 2009" <http://www.fundforpeace.org/web/index.php?option=com_content&task=view&id=391&Itemid=549>.

37 Christine O. Avendaño, "'Bolder' Martial Law Seen", *Philippine Daily Inquirer*, 12 December 2009, p. A1.

38 Ibid., p. A8. See also Edson C. Tandoc, Jr. "Congress Set to Rule on Martial Law", *Philippine Daily Inquirer*, 12 December 2009, p. A2.

39 Katherine Evangelista, "Ampatuan Private Army Now Split into Three Groups", Inquirer.net, 8 December 2009 <http://newsinfo.inquirer.net/breakingnews/nation/view/20091208-240857/Ampatuan-private-army-now-split-into-3-groups>.

40 Marlon Ramos, "PNP: Ambush Not Staged: We're Risking Our Lives Doing Our Jobs", *Philippine Daily Inquirer*, 12 December 2009, p. A8.

41 Ibid.

42 See various chapters in Soliman M. Santos, Jr. et al., *Primed and Purposeful: Armed Groups and Human Security Efforts in the Philippines*. South-South Network (forthcoming)

43 Johanna Camille L. Sisante, "Private Armies, Coddlers to be Named, Charged by March", GMANews.TV, 8 January 2010 <http://www9.gmanews.tv/story/181093/private-armies-coddlers-to-be-named-charged-by-march>.

44 Marvin Sy et al., "Commission Created to Oversee Dismantling of Private Armies", *Philippine Star*, 5 December 2009, p. 1.

Singapore

SINGAPORE IN 2009
Braving a Grave New World

Azhar Ghani

For a proper perspective of what the year 2009 was like for Singapore, it would be useful to note what it was not. It was not like the years between 2004 and 2007. These were very good years for Singapore, with growth averaging almost 8 per cent. Neither was it quite like 2008, when the spillover optimism of the previous two years flowed through for about half the year. Indeed, 2008 had brimmed with promise. Singapore's global city credentials received a boost when it won the bid to host the first-ever Youth Olympics Games (YOG) in 2010. In September 2008, the dazzlingly lit Singapore skyline impressed the world as the inaugural Singapore leg of the Formula One Grand Prix race made its debut with the first night race in the series.

Yet, even as the champagne flowed at the glamour event, a global financial crisis was already brewing. With its strong external orientation, the Singapore economy has always been vulnerable to global economic shocks. And so the party that lasted almost five years had to end.

In the third quarter of 2008, Singapore fell into its first recession since 2002,[1] becoming the first Asian economy to do so. More bad news followed as the year turned. Singapore plunged deeper into recession in the fourth quarter of 2008 as gross domestic product (GDP) marked its biggest quarterly decline on record.[2] Growth for the year 2008 was an anaemic 1.1 per cent. Early government projections of a 1 to 2 per cent contraction in the Singapore economy for 2009 were quickly revised downwards to a contraction of 2 to 5 per cent.[3] This set the stage for a sobering 2009 as Singapore braced itself for the full impact of the stricken global economy. With the country in such a mood, it was not surprising that Singapore marked fifty years of self-government[4] quietly with little public celebration.[5]

Azhar Ghani is a Research Fellow at the Institute of Policy Studies, Lee Kuan Yew School of Public Policy, Singapore.

Economic distress brings social and political consequences as well. As it was, there were large demonstrations and strikes in Europe as people rallied against the economic fallout from the excesses of the global financial system. In Singapore, the socio-economic impact of the crisis was not lost on the government. Prime Minister Lee Hsien Loong identified three potential stress lines which might divide Singapore society as the economic pain deepens: between Singaporeans and foreigners; between the more successful and less successful; and between different races and religious communities.[6]

As the economic crisis played itself out around the world, it also became clear that fundamental shifts in the global economic and strategic balance were afoot. The United States' leadership in managing the global economy was questioned. Europe appeared in disarray. Japan was weakened by the sudden collapse of global consumer demand. And China and India were thrust into more prominent global roles either by default, at the urgings of the other players licking their economic wounds, or a combination of both. Along with this recalibration of economic power and responsibility came strategic adjustment. As a small state, the republic needed to understand and influence its environment in order to enlarge its external economic and strategic space.

In a way, the year 2009 was all about the economy. At the same time, it was not.

New Solutions: Dipping into Past Reserves

Singapore responded to the slump with a budget that Prime Minister Lee and Finance Minister Tharman Shanmugaratnam described as "not ordinary"[7] and "not normal"[8] respectively. Chalking up a record deficit of $8.7 billion, the $43.6 billion budget was loaded not just with decisive counter-cyclical measures and innovative relief measures, but also a whole lot of symbolism.

For one thing, instead of the customary February date, Budget Day was advanced to January, reflecting the urgency with which the government viewed the situation. Then, there were the many fiscal and policy precedents it set. Chief of these was the decision to dip into the country's past reserves. This was a first[9] for a government known for its financial prudence. The move — to the tune of $4.9 billion — was to fund the $4.5-billion Jobs Credit Scheme and the $5.8-billion Special Risk-Sharing Initiative (SRI). The decision to draw from past reserves was made despite Shanmugaratnam acknowledging that the government of the day had built up enough savings during its term to fund the two initiatives.[10]

Dipping into past reserves needed the assent of Singapore's elected President — the first time that such a request was made for the use of the so-called presidential "second key" to unlock the republic's past savings. Under the Singapore Constitution, the country's national reserves can be used only if both the government of the day and the elected president give consent.

The circumstances that led to the drawdown on the reserves also set another precedent. By dipping into the kitty at a time when Singapore faced a global economic meltdown, widely seen as the worst since the depression of the 1930s, the bar was set high for future governments. In Shanmugaratnam's own words, it was a move that "minimises the opportunity for future governments to call for unjustified uses for our past reserves."

While the decision to use past reserves was generally accepted, the process in which it was approved stirred a debate. When the budget was presented on 22 January, Shanmugaratnam announced that the President's in-principle approval was already in the bag.[11] This raised questions in some Singaporeans' minds as to how robust the protective "second key" was, given how the $4.9-billion presidential decision appeared so readily obtained by the government behind closed doors.

Several Members of Parliament (MPs) touched on the issue while debating the budget. Opposition MP Low Thia Khiang and Nominated MP Siew Kum Hong asked for more information on the process which led to the President's assent to the unprecedented move, especially since the government still had surpluses from its term in office; while several MPs from the ruling People's Action Party (PAP) wanted the government to provide clear ground rules for drawing on past reserves as a guide for future governments. Said Low, "The speed at which these two-key systems can unlock the past reserves is too fast for comfort."[12]

On 17 February, President S.R. Nathan called a press conference to explain his decision. He revealed that he gave his nod the day before Budget Day, taking just 11 days to decide after the government first sought his in-principle approval. The swiftness of the process, he said, stemmed from the urgency in giving the government the confidence to roll out measures to tackle the recession which could worsen if the government were slow in taking action:

> I recognised the importance of giving confidence to go ahead with the measures proposed in the Budget for the particular reference to past reserves bearing in mind [that] if the situation prolongs or worsens, negative consequences would have kicked in, making any measures too late to be of any effect... The urgency was quite evident, and I think 11 days was reasonable. If it had to be, it could have been shorter.[13]

The matter was considered closed after Nathan's explanation. With a recession billed as "the worst [Singapore was facing] since independence" looming, concerns over the process which led to the use of "second key" fell by the wayside. Whether Singaporeans were truly satisfied with the explanation is debatable. However, they very quickly moved on to other issues — as Singaporeans are wont to do when the authorities signal that any further debate could jeopardize the cohesiveness of the collective response to a national problem. Still, the public unease over the swift manner in which past reserves can be unlocked, with decisions made away from the public eye, had perhaps provided an indication of how Singaporeans would expect a more transparent approach for such future decisions.

Notwithstanding the questions over the process of approving the use of the reserves, the two initiatives funded by the move were enlightened solutions. Both schemes, which the government stressed would be temporary, were part of a $20.5 billion Resilience Package[14] designed to save jobs and help companies stay afloat during the recession.

Through the SRI, the government undertook to shoulder a considerable part of the potential losses to banks — up to $5.8 billion — if borrowers default. This risk-sharing measure was designed to encourage banks to lend money, allowing viable businesses, especially small- and medium-sized companies, to gain access to credit at a time when jittery banks made credit tight.

The Jobs Credit Scheme was particularly innovative. It was designed to offset part of employers' wage bills and involved the government allocating up to $4.5 billion to provide businesses with a cash grant of 12 per cent of the first $2,500 of the monthly wage for each employee who is either a Singapore citizen or permanent resident (PR). This was in effect a wage subsidy to employers, helping them reduce business costs and hopefully persuade them not to retrench workers.

While it would have been possible to save jobs by helping companies to cut costs in other ways, for instance corporate tax rebates, the Jobs Credit Scheme had its advantages. First, small- and medium-enterprises, which account for 60 per cent of jobs in Singapore and do not pay much corporate tax, would not have been sufficiently incentivized by corporate tax rebates to retain employees. Second, this reduction in the wage bill for businesses was effected without having to resort to a cut in the employers' mandatory contributions to the Central Provident Fund (CPF) of workers who are either Singaporeans or Singapore PRs. Although proven effective in helping companies reduce wage costs during previous recessions, a CPF cut comes with a price for affected workers. Given the CPF's role in meeting housing and healthcare needs in Singapore, a reduction in CPF contribution would affect more than their retirement needs.

Tying the scheme to employment of Singaporeans and Singapore PRs was an inspired move. It certainly made retaining these two groups of workers less expensive than before, making them more cost-competitive compared to foreign workers. This pro-resident effect was a political plus. The issue of foreigners in Singapore, who comprise about one in three of the workforce, has been a touchy subject for some time, with some Singaporeans wanting the government to do more to provide jobs for Singaporeans. The added advantage in the move lay in the fact that the subsidy came in the form of cash grants. This is a boon in a credit crunch, and an added incentive for businesses that want to improve their bottom line to favour retaining or hiring workers who are Singaporeans or Singapore PRs.

While there was no way of verifying the direct impact of the Jobs Credit Scheme, it was estimated to have saved some 30,000 jobs.[15] Its apparent efficacy was perhaps one of the reasons the scheme, meant to be for an initial one year, was extended for another six months, albeit with reduced quarterly payouts of 6 and 3 per cent of the first $2,500 of the monthly wages of affected workers. This extension, to last until June 2010, will cost the government an additional $675 million to be funded not from past reserves, but from the government's regular budget.[16]

Other more familiar economic stimuli included a 1 percentage point cut in corporate tax to 17 per cent, as well as several tax breaks to ease cash-flow. There was also the $4.4 billion spending on infrastructure projects. It might have been billed as the government's continued commitment — even in a downturn — to provide Singaporeans with a better home for the future, but there was no attempt to hide the fact that it was also a pump-priming effort to stimulate the economy. In all, there was a strong focus on helping businesses cope or even thrive. This was a clear articulation of the government's fundamental belief that the best way to help Singaporeans would be to help businesses succeed. In this perspective, successful companies would provide jobs for the people and contribute to Singapore's economy, fueling the creation of even more jobs.

New Strategy for the Economy?

For all the compliments the economic initiatives in the budget received, the severity and game-changing nature of the global economic crisis led to questions being raised over certain aspects of the government's long-term economic strategy.

Much has been said about the Great Singapore Bargain — of how Singaporeans have supposedly traded a large part of their individual and political freedoms for the material comforts made possible by the stability under the watch of the PAP.[17] In this scenario, the PAP's legitimacy to rule is tied to its ability to deliver the good life, and the economy makes or breaks the deal.

One of the most intriguing themes among alternative views advocated a sharper focus on growth for Singaporeans, not merely growth for the Singapore economy. Turning a long-held view of the government on its head, it challenged the notion that the good life will necessarily follow high growth.[18] This view eschewed a "growth for growth's sake" approach and suggested looking for paths — even growth moderated at a pace below maximum — that would make economic progress more beneficial to more Singaporeans in more and real ways other than an improvement in economic indicators such as an increase in per capita income.

As it is, Singapore's recent economic growth model appears to have achieved too little in delivering returns for Singaporeans, relative to foreign firms and foreigners. On average, only a 41 per cent share of Singapore's GDP goes to wages and salaries in the country, which is one of the lowest in the world for economies at a comparable stage of development. Indeed, Soon and Ong[19] showed that Singapore's remuneration share of GDP was somewhat lower than the other Asian newly industrialized economies (South Korea, Hong Kong, and Taiwan) and considerably lower than that of many developed economies (Japan, the United States, and the United Kingdom). The authors also concluded that Singapore has a First World per capita income, but a wage share which is more characteristic of Third World developing countries. At the same time, the foreign share of domestic production and income has increased to around 40 per cent. Indeed, in the boom years of 2004 to 2007, wages as a share of Singapore's GDP fell to about 42 per cent from a high of 47 per cent in 2001, suggesting there was some underpaying of wages even though profits had risen.[20]

In addition, the government policy of rolling out the red carpet for foreign investors also gave rise to the question of whether the opportunity costs — in terms of tax revenue foregone, or funds that could have been used to help local enterprises grow for instance — to Singaporeans have been too high.

Detractors of the "growth as an end" path also believe the approach has created a situation where Singapore has no choice but to import more and more foreign workers as the country's planners keep their eye firmly on growth targets.

The main argument against this was that such an approach relegates the impact of the numbers of foreigners on Singaporeans to almost an afterthought, with the main consideration being the need to achieve specific growth targets. Indeed, even with a levy and quota system introduced to control their numbers, foreign workers have grown in numbers rapidly over the years. In 2007, six in ten of the 235,000 jobs created went to foreigners; in 2008, they took seven in ten of the 222,000 jobs created.[21]

Currently, foreign workers number about one million, or 36 per cent of the workforce.[22] However, projections have indicated that there could be more than three million foreigners working in Singapore by 2030, forming half the workforce. This number will jump to almost ten million by 2050, making up 75 per cent of employees in the country.[23]

Issues related to the influx of foreign workers include: the depression of wages of low-skilled Singaporeans caused by the easy availability of cheaper foreign labour; the impact it has on productivity levels; the social problems caused by having large numbers of foreigners with different social norms and habits living among Singaporeans, especially if they were housed collectively in large numbers; and the increase in property prices caused by the influx of higher-skilled foreigners who rent or buy homes in Singapore.

New Bottle, Old Wine?

In a repeat of what happened in previous economic crises, the government convened a committee to look at how best Singapore can plan for the future, given the lessons from the challenges it had to overcome during the crisis, as well as the insights it gained on what the future might hold. On 25 June, the Ministry of Finance unveiled the members of the Economic Strategies Committee (ESC) and spelt out its mission to develop strategies to keep the economy growing — and spread the gains to Singaporeans.[24]

The twenty-five-strong committee, chaired by Finance Minister Shanmugaratnam, was drawn from the public and private sectors, as well as the labour movement. Its members included four other ministers: Manpower Minister Gan Kim Yong, Education Minister Ng Eng Hen, Second Finance and Transport Minister Lim Hwee Hua, and PMO (Prime Minister's Office) Minister Lim Swee Say, who is also the Secretary-General of the National Trade Union Congress (NTUC). Those from the private sector comprised representatives drawn from the manufacturing and services sectors, foreign and local enterprises, and academia.

Tasked with coming up with new and creative ways to grow the economy for the future of "at least ... the next ten years", the ESC would look into five broad areas: exploring new growth areas; anchoring global companies here and nurturing home-grown enterprises; attracting talent; creating high-value jobs for locals; and maximizing resources such as land and energy.

To facilitate this, the ESC has formed eight subcommittees to undertake in-depth reviews of the various issues. These subcommittees involve more representation from both the private and public sectors, widening the net for the ideas search. In addition, the ESC has also indicated that its work would involve extensive consultations with those beyond its main and subcommittees. All these efforts will culminate in key recommendations due in January 2010, and a full report by mid-2010. Led by a minister perceived as someone not averse to change, the ESC's recommendations and report should be something to look forward to.

Yet, the committee's parameters for providing new directions to the economy could have been restricted even before it started work, judging by what Prime Minister Lee said when he first announced that the ESC was to be set up. Speaking in Parliament on 27 May, he said that Singapore's approach to economic development and growth "remains valid". Instead, what needed to be reviewed were "our specific strategies to develop the different sectors of our economy", he added.[25]

New Politics? Giving a Bigger Voice to a Diversity of Views

The Great Singapore Bargain between Singaporeans and their government was sweetened a little in 2009 with the government announcing in May changes to the political system that aimed to provide more robust debates and greater diversity of views in the legislature.

Under the proposed changes, there will be at least nine lawmakers from opposition parties in Parliament, either elected outright or appointed to the House under the Non-constituency MP scheme for those who contest elections and lose; the presence of Nominated MPs in Parliament will also be permanent instead of having to be approved by each successive legislature, and their numbers increased from six to nine; and there will be fewer six-member Group Representative Constituencies (GRCs) and at least twelve single-member constituencies, up from the current nine, by the next election.[26]

Prime Minister Lee described the changes as a move to ensure that Parliament stays "in sync with the concerns and aspirations of Singaporeans and strengthen the role of Parliament as the key democratic institution where important national issues are deliberated and decided."[27]

A liberalization of sorts of the political system, the changes effectively ensured a higher number of opposition and non-partisan views. The changes also aimed to tweak the GRC system, effectively lowering — but not removing — the entry barriers for opposition participation in elections. This in turn will increase the likelihood of voters having the opportunity to exercise their rights to participate in the electoral process.

The perceived GRC hurdle has long been a complaint among resource- and talent-strapped opposition parties, which have always had difficulty finding enough candidates to stand for elections. With the majority of parliamentary seats allocated to GRCs, this shortcoming has limited their poll participation as it was not easy for them to field credible teams. In the past, this had resulted in elections in which the PAP was returned to power on Nomination Day when more than half of the parliamentary seats were not contested by the opposition. Voters in these walkover wards were thus unable to exercise their right to vote, depriving them of a direct participation in the process of picking their legislative representatives, and to some extent, the government. Indeed, Lee did say that, apart from "provid[ing] adequate voice for diverse views in Parliament, including non-partisan views and those who have voted for the opposition", the changes also "ensure that the government which is elected has a clear mandate to govern in the interest of Singapore".[28]

These changes in the real world followed some earlier changes in the reel and virtual worlds. In January 2009, the government accepted several recommendations from the Advisory Council on the Impact of New Media on Society (AIMS) to liberalize rules governing films and online material with political content.

Among the AIMS recommendations the government agreed to,[29] was to lift the blanket ban on the screening of party political films. It now allows the screening of "certain types of party political films" which have to be "factual and objective" without "dramatis[ing] or present[ing] a distorted picture". This change was effected in March 2009, when an amendment was made to the Films Act. The ban on political parties and their candidates from using films in online campaigns during election periods was also lifted. However, only films that pass the requirements of the amended Films Act are allowed.

In addition, the government also accepted AIMS's recommendation to extend the list of online political activities that are explicitly allowed by law during an election period. It now allows election candidates, their political parties and agents, and other members of the public to use podcasts, vodcasts, blogs, and other new media tools to "participate in Internet election advertising" during elections.

These changes should, however, not be seen as the PAP going politically soft or becoming kinder to those who aim to unseat it. They should instead be seen as carefully calibrated responses by the ruling party to help release any perceived pent-up desire within an increasingly politically-aware electorate for more alternative views via a bigger opposition voice in Parliament and greater political expression — even if it may be just on the Internet.

AIMS, for instance, was formed in April 2007, less than a year after the 6 May polling day for the 2006 general election. In that election, video clips of election rallies were posted online in defiance of strict rules that regulated the dissemination of polls-related information and opinion on the Internet. There was no record of action taken against those responsible for the postings, leading to a situation where the rules looked impotent.

That the changes came at a time when the Great Singapore Bargain could begin to look less like a good deal, with questions being raised about the government's long-term economic strategy and the benefits accrued to Singaporeans, was not lost on the more astute observers. However, it should be said that the PAP government is not known for knee-jerk solutions. AIMS was formed when the economy was booming and the Bargain looked sweet for most Singaporeans. No one could have planned for the release of the AIMS report in December 2008, and the government's response to the recommendations in January 2009, to happen at a time when the Singapore economy was sputtering. Likewise, the reforms to the political system should not be seen as just an exercise to sweeten the ground in bad times, but also as a bigger strategy in managing the long-term aspirations of the electorate.

New Lifts for Opposition Wards

In a shift from the PAP government's long-held stand, residents living in public Housing Development Board (HDB) flats in the two opposition-held wards of Potong Pasir and Hougang were told in July that they could expect to benefit from lift landings on every floor under the Lift Upgrading Programme (LUP) earlier than expected. After the 2006 general election, the government had said that the two wards would be placed at the end of the queue for the LUP.[30]

Started in 2001, the highly-subsidized LUP is popular with HDB residents, especially those living in older blocks. Older flats usually have one lift landing for every three or four floors. The government foots between 75 and 90 per cent of the bill, with the remainder shared between the town council and residents.

Upgrading has been completed on some 80 per cent of the eligible blocks, with work on the remaining 1,000 blocks due to be completed by 2014. Like other upgrading exercises for public housing,[31] the LUP has been a highly-politicized initiative dangled as a carrot for votes. During the 2006 election, a number of candidates promised to get residents onto the coveted project.

The government said the decision to move opposition wards from the end of the LUP queue was a matter of practicality — it wanted to take advantage of falling construction costs and the available capacity in the industry.[32] Yet, any notion that the PAP might be depoliticizing the publicly-subsidized LUP, by not discriminating against opposition wards anymore, was soon disputed by critics.

In October, when it was confirmed that these constituencies were getting the LUP, the announcement was not made by the wards' elected MPs, as has been the case with PAP-held wards. Instead, the task went to government-appointed advisers of the wards' grassroots organizations, maintaining the link between the popular programme and the PAP.[33]

The official reply from the Ministry of National Development (MND) to justify why opposition MPs should not manage the LUP was that the programme is a national scheme that ought to be managed by government representatives.

In a letter to the *Straits Times* Forum page, the National Development Minister's press secretary, Lim Yuin Chien, said in a reply to Workers' Party MP for Hougang, Low Thia Khiang:

> Mr Low is mistaken when he cites the "will of the people" expressed in general elections to justify why he should play a leading role in the LUP in Hougang. The will of the people expressed in general elections is to elect a government for the country as a whole; and not to elect separate local governments for each constituency.... Singapore has a one-level system of government. MPs, whether People's Action Party or opposition, do not constitute a local government in their constituency.[34]

Lim later wrote another letter, clarifying that the "roles of MP and adviser are distinct and separate, even though government MPs wearing their other hats of advisers are expected to perform both roles". According to Lim the government-appointed adviser's main role is to assist in implementing national programmes, such as government campaigns, and HDB's upgrading programmes, including the LUP.[35] Hence, opposition MPs cannot be appointed advisers "because they do not answer to the ruling party" even if they perform the role unsatisfactorily, and have "no constitutional or legal obligation to carry out national programmes on the Government's behalf". Lim also emphasized that the LUP is "not a town council programme" but a "national programme which receives most of its funding from the Government".[36]

These arguments appeared shaky to critics. For a start, even though opposition MPs would not be managing the LUP, their "local governments" — in the form of the town councils they manage — would still have to foot part, albeit a small part, of the bill. More significantly, notwithstanding the "distinct roles of MP and adviser", for some time now senior government leaders have also had a clear and public stand on empowering local governments and how the elections are linked to these entities. One might argue that this suggests a leading role for the elected local representative.

This stand on "local governments", which has not been either recanted, revised, or reviewed publicly to date, is best captured in a quote by then Prime Minister Goh Chok Tong before the 1997 general election:

> With town councils and community development councils, and my intention
> to give more power and responsibility to them (MPs), every election in
> a constituency is indeed a local government election.[37]

New Cabinet: Reshuffle 2009

On 26 March the government announced changes to the Cabinet, with Defence Minister Teo Chee Hean appointed a new deputy prime minister to replace S. Jayakumar.[38] Singapore has another Deputy Prime Minister, Home Affairs Minister Wong Kan Seng, who has held the post since 1 September 2005. Jayakumar, who moved into the PMO as a Senior Minister, however, retained his role as the Co-ordinating Minister for National Security. He also continued to oversee foreign policy matters which cut across ministries.

Significantly, Teo was also designated Acting Prime Minister in the official absence of Lee Hsien Loong, ahead of Wong. Teo, who has held portfolios in heavyweight ministries like Finance, Education and his current Defence appointment, had been widely tipped to become a Deputy Prime Minister for some years. The former chief of Singapore's navy has had a stellar political career, being appointed immediately to the frontbench after he was elected into Parliament during a by-election in 1992 on a PAP ticket. However, given the PAP's record of generational leadership transition, it looks unlikely for Teo to become the next Prime Minister as, at just three years younger than Prime Minister Lee, he is considered a political contemporary of the premier.

Indeed, Lee had described the new Cabinet line-up as a transition team with new ministers in position but with older ministers still around to "help out".[39]

He also indicated that the core of Singapore's fourth generation leadership had yet to be fully assembled. Nevertheless, the reshuffle ushered in a Cabinet that would be driven by a younger team. Of the twenty-one full or acting ministers in the new line-up, ten were elected in the last three general elections — in 1997, 2001, and 2006.[40]

In fact, apart from the Ministry of Home Affairs, which is headed by the sixty-two-year-old Wong and the Ministry of National Development led by sixty-one-year-old Mah Bow Tan, all other ministries are now helmed by those in their forties or fifties. With the exception of Wong and Mah, all other ministers above sixty years of age are now either holding special appointments, such as Senior Minister and Minister Mentor, or are in charge of portfolios dealing with specific issues that cut across ministries, such as national security or ageing.

Other than Teo's ascent to the deputy premiership, the other noteworthy appointment was Lim Hwee Hua's promotion to a full minister, making her the first woman to break the political glass ceiling. Lim, who was appointed Minister in PMO, also became Second Minister in Finance and Transport. She formerly held the lower rank of Senior Minister of State in the two ministries.

Two others were also promoted. Gan Kim Yong moved up to Manpower Minister, after one year as Acting Manpower Minister; while Lui Tuck Yew was appointed Acting Minister for Information, Communications and the Arts (MICA), after one year as its Senior Minister of State. Lui, who relinquished his portfolio as Senior Minister of State for Education in the reshuffle, was the fastest among the group of twenty-four who were voted into Parliament for the first time in 2006 to make it to the frontbench. He succeeded MICA Minister Lee Boon Yang, a twenty-five-year veteran politician who had asked to retire as a minister a few years ago.

Other changes included current office holders being given more portfolios, as well as the addition of a fresh office holder. S. Iswaran was given the job of Senior Minister of State for Education, in addition to his similar post at the Ministry of Trade and Industry (MTI). Lee Yi Shyan became Minister of State for Manpower, on top of his current job at the same level at MTI. Teo Ser Luck, who held the Senior Parliamentary Secretary post at the Ministries for Community Development, Youth and Sports, as well as Transport, was given an additional new role. He replaced another veteran, Zainul Abidin Rasheed — who continued as Senior Minister of State for Foreign Affairs — as Mayor of the North East Community Development Council. The fresh face was Sam Tan, who was appointed Parliamentary Secretary in MICA and MTI.

Prime Minister Lee indicated that the Cabinet changes "signal[led] that a younger team is in charge" and was "part of a continuing leadership renewal and testing out younger office holders for broader responsibilities". He said: "What we need to convey in this reshuffle is that we've reinforced and renewed the team, and we're moving ahead."[41]

The reshuffle was the second one since the 2006 general election. The first happened about a year before, on 26 March 2008.[42]

New Arrivals and New Citizens

As mentioned earlier in this chapter, one of the three stress lines identified as having the potential to divide Singapore was that between Singaporeans and foreigners. The issue is complex because Singapore has sizeable numbers of PRs and guest workers on permits relative to the citizen component. The population profile has a one-third foreigner content of 1.8 million, of which 1.25 million are transients and 533,000 PRs.[43]

Given such a mix, as well as the high-density living and finite resources available in Singapore, potential ruptures along this stress line are varied and many. They include friction in adjusting to alien cultures from East and West, foreigners displacing available Singaporeans in jobs, and the competition for living space, social services, and recreation.

Indeed, cracks along this line had already developed even before there were pressures from the economic slump. With mounting job losses in 2009, the fissures could potentially become more significant as private misgivings about the presence of foreigners became increasingly more public.[44] The fact that foreigners had taken a bigger share of the jobs created in 2007 (six in ten) and 2008 (seven in ten) did not help.

One silver lining for the government, however, was that Singaporeans appear to understand the government's rational case for foreign input to achieve higher GDP growth. According to a survey by the Institute of Policy Studies in late February 2009,[45] seven in ten Singapore residents felt that foreigners working in the country during the downturn have had no impact on their livelihood even though only 4 per cent believe they are better off with these foreigners around.

However, when asked to assess the impact of the presence of foreigners on the country, many more — 34 per cent — said Singapore is better off as a result. This indicated that while only a small section of those polled considered themselves to be better off with foreigners in Singapore, a larger number were able to see how the country can benefit from their presence.

The ability of native-born Singaporeans to look at the issue beyond their immediate self-interest could however be severely tested if tensions already caused by the growing numbers of foreigners — with concerns over their impact on demand for housing and schools, competition for jobs, and their ability to fit it — were to grow. Judging by the numerous times in 2009 that the subject was raised by Singaporeans, and addressed by government leaders, public sentiment on the issue could already be near a tipping point.

Anecdotal evidence suggests that even though many Singaporeans acknowledge the benefits of welcoming foreigners to the country, many among them also want the intake of foreigners, whether transient or permanent, to be made more gradual. There was even a suggestion that the government should manage the country's economic growth targets at levels that would moderate the influx of foreign workers and do more to keep native-born Singaporeans from leaving.

The government responded to this growing issue on several fronts. At the end of 2008, it set up a new Ministerial Steering Committee[46] to deal with issues arising from the presence of lower-skilled foreign workers in Singapore, whose penchant for gathering in large numbers in certain locations, as well as foreign ways, have caused unease among certain segments of Singaporeans. The committee aims to look into and provide for the needs of foreign workers in areas ranging from housing requirements to recreational activities, as well as ensure the harmonious coexistence between locals and these workers.

Next, a new council to bridge the local-foreign divide was formed. Aimed at "driv[ing] the integration agenda forward through a concerted effort", the National Integration Council (NIC) was set up in April and chaired by Community Development, Youth and Sports Minister Vivian Balakrishnan.[47] It comprises members from the public and private sectors, as well as from the community. The twenty-man council's work would largely revolve around the increasing number of foreigners who choose to stay in Singapore for the long haul. In 2008, for example about 20,500 foreigners took up citizenship in Singapore, while more than 79,000 became permanent residents. These figures were an increase of about 20 per cent over those in 2007.

Balakrishnan indicated that the main thrust of the measures the NIC would work on would be to promote mutual trust and foster a common sense of belonging between native-born Singaporeans and immigrants. The council has a special fund of $10 million which can be tapped by groups keen on social integration projects. The fund will pay for up to 80 per cent of such initiatives.

The government also started to tweak relevant policy measures. In June 2009, it imposed new restrictions on the flow of foreign workers into Singapore under the work permit scheme.[48] Under the old rules, an employer was allowed to hire one worker from "non-traditional" sources like China for every five locals he had on the payroll. Now, the ratio becomes more complex: he must have nine workers before he can hire one worker from China — at least five must be locals and the rest can be foreigners from "traditional sources" like Malaysia. Another change was the stricter requirements for workers from China to qualify as skilled workers. They must have at least a diploma verified by the Chinese authorities, when previously there was none.

Although described by the Manpower Ministry as "administrative" changes, the new rules have already caused some pain, especially in the services sector. The sector, which provides about two million jobs, employs about 508,000 foreigners. Some industry leaders had even predicted that the lack of foreign labour could be a significant problem for the sector, as too many jobs would be chasing too few candidates when the two integrated resorts (with casinos, hotels, and entertainment complexes) open in 2010 with new employment opportunities.[49]

In addition, the government has indicated that even though it already made "a clear distinction between citizens and PRs and others", it will make this differentiation "sharper over time to reflect the responsibilities and privileges of citizenship."[50] In December, the Education Ministry announced two upcoming measures in that direction: Raising school fees for PRs and foreigners starting from January 2011, and giving Singaporeans an edge when they ballot for places during Primary One school registration beginning July 2010.[51]

The actions outlined above will not be the end of the government's efforts to address a growing concern that could well be a key issue in the next general election — which has to be held by the beginning of February 2012. For one, the ESC mentioned previously in this chapter is also looking at the issue. Its key recommendations are expected in January 2010, and a full report will follow in June that same year — giving the government a narrow window to come up with answers that would satisfy a majority of the electorate.

New World: Riding on a Transformed Global Order

The fundamental shifts in the global economic and strategic balance caused by the financial crisis unfolded as the year progressed. By the time the storm clears, the world would have changed, and Singapore will have to adjust or risk losing relevance.

Singapore's small size and external trade-dependency are factors that have made it particularly vulnerable to economic and strategic externalities. The republic has, however, shown a certain nimbleness in navigating through the major strategic plays of the big countries and carving a viable external space of its own. Its diplomatic moves in 2009 reflected this ability, as it very quickly came to terms with new realities brought about by the financial crisis.

As the markets in the United States and Europe looked unlikely to return to their former vigour anytime soon, Singapore began to focus more of its attention on emerging Asian powers and potential new markets in the Middle East. China, for one, received a fair bit of high-level attention, with the three most senior members of the Cabinet — Prime Minister Lee Hsien Loong, Senior Minister Goh Chok Tong, and Minister Mentor Lee Kuan Yew — making separate visits to Chinese cities. Membership in the Association of Southeast Asian Nations (ASEAN) was a key diplomatic asset despite the imperfections of the regional organization. ASEAN's economic integration plans would provide more opportunities and space for Singapore, and ASEAN's central role in the regional architecture of East Asia would contribute to the peace and security of the region. As such, Singapore was active in promoting the interests of ASEAN and the body's linkages with the rest of the world.

In 2009, Singapore hosted the Asia-Pacific Economic Co-operation (APEC) forum. APEC's twenty-one member economies account for 40.5 per cent of the world's population, 54.2 per cent of its gross domestic product, and 43.7 per cent of global trade. Its members include global economic and strategic powerhouses the United States, China, and Russia. The forum has worked to reduce tariffs and other trade barriers across the region — an objective very much aligned to Singapore's national interests.

The APEC meeting in November 2009 thus presented the republic with a unique opportunity to better influence the shaping of its external space. By the time it ended, Singapore had every reason to smile, as trade-friendly pledges were made. First, APEC members collectively reaffirmed their commitment to keep markets free and open, and even identified specific steps to promote the goal. Second, a potential Asia-Pacific-wide free trade area was given a boost with the United States committing to engage the four economies, including Singapore, already on board. Last but not least, APEC members also pledged to "maintain our economic stimulus policies until a durable economic recovery is secured", providing some assurance that the recovering economy would not suffer a relapse.[52]

Conclusion

The year 2009 was certainly fraught with searching questions for Singapore. It would have been as likely a time as any for the government to lose its bearings, as it tried to cope with the fallout from the global financial crisis. Yet, to its credit, the Singapore Government retained its clarity of vision. It did not panic, and did what was necessary for the country to navigate circumstances that its leaders accepted as being beyond their immediate influence. Changes that had to have been planned for some time, such as the freshening of the leadership as well as the moves to open up the country's politics, went ahead. Despite the unusual challenges in 2009, in some fundamental ways, it was reassuringly business-as-usual for Singapore.

Yet, the year also showed that it would not be business as usual for the Singapore leadership as it prepares the country for the future. When things went well for Singapore, alternative voices on how the country's economic affairs could be improved were often drowned out by the sounds of the republic's successes. Grievances such as the emerging one against foreigners were more readily put aside by Singaporeans as the rewards of the country's success trickled down to them.

In 2009, however, even the most basic premises of how the global financial system operates were questioned. As old assumptions were placed in doubt and new realities developed, it was as good a time as any for alternative voices to be heard.

The responses of the Singapore Government to the financial crisis were bold, and signalled both ability and resolve. Still, questions remained. Did they really address the issues at a strategic level or were they just long-term tactics in an unchanged strategy? Given the nexus between the economy and politics in the Singapore context, other issues that surfaced during the downturn might continue to generate debate even after things improve.

Notes

[1] On an annualized quarter-on-quarter basis, growth in the third quarter of 2008 declined by 6.8 per cent — a successive quarterly contraction after the fall of 5.3 per cent in the second quarter.

[2] Singapore's economy contracted at a seasonally adjusted, annualized quarter-on-quarter pace of 16.4 per cent in the fourth quarter of 2008, accelerating the decline from a 6.8 per cent decline in the third quarter, according to the Ministry of Trade and Industry. It was the biggest contraction since the government began publishing seasonally adjusted data in 1976.

3   On 21 November 2008, the government first projected growth for 2009 to be from −1 to 2 per cent. This was later revised downwards to −2 to 1 per cent on 2 January 2009, before being quickly revised downwards again to −5 to −2 per cent within the same month, on 21 January 2009.

4   After 140 years of British rule, Singapore elected its first local government, installed on 5 June 1959, with Lee Kuan Yew as prime minister.

5   Events to commemorate fifty years of self-government largely revolved around annual activities like the National Day Parade on 9 August and other National Day celebrations. In contrast, when Singapore marked twenty-five years of self-government in 1984, the government organized a myriad of specific activities to celebrate the nation's achievements thus far, culminating in an $18-million multimedia National Exhibition that ran from 15 November to 30 December 1984.

6   Goh Chin Lian, "3 Potential Areas of Divide to be Tackled", *Straits Times*, 2 May 2009.

7   In his speech at the Singapore-MIT Alliance Tenth Anniversary Dinner at the Ritz-Carlton Millenia Singapore on 2 January 2009, Lee said the budget would not be ordinary "either in its contents or its overall fiscal stance", and would focus on keeping companies afloat, so that they can provide jobs for Singaporeans.

8   Shanmugaratnam also described the budget as "not even a normal counter-cyclical Budget", highlighting the $20.5-billion Resilience Package as the largest the Singapore government has undertaken in response to an economic downturn.

9   The Singapore Government had actually earlier in October 2008 sought the President's approval for the use of the reserves, when it moved to guarantee all bank deposits in Singapore. The guarantee, to be in place until 31 December 2010, is backed by $150 billion of past reserves. The move was made in response to similar moves already made by several countries in the region, including Hong Kong, Australia, New Zealand, Indonesia and later, Malaysia. In a joint press statement issued on 16 October 2008, the Ministry of Finance and the Monetary Authority of Singapore noted that financial institutions in Singapore could be disadvantaged compared to their regional competitors if the Singapore Government guarantee was not put in place. However, the $150-billion sum was only a potential draw, not an actual one. To date no government payout has been made, and the probability of one happening before the December 2010 deadline remains low.

10   Tharman Shanmugaratnam, Budget Speech 2009 delivered in the Singapore Parliament, 22 January 2009. In his speech, Shanmugaratnam said: "The Government has sufficient savings built up during this term of government to fund the measures we are taking and the resulting budget deficit. Nevertheless, we have decided instead to fund the two extraordinary measures within the Resilience Package from our past reserves." Later, in the Budget Debate round-up speech on 5 February, he reiterated that "the Government does have sufficient accumulated savings within the current term to fund the FY2008 and FY2009 deficits without drawing on past reserves".

11 Ibid.

12 Aaron Low, "Call to Explain President's Decision, Set Guidelines", *Straits Times*, 4 February 2009.

13 Sue-Ann Chia, "Why I Said Yes", *Straits Times*, 18 February 2009.

14 Tharman Shanmugaratnam, Budget Speech 2009 delivered in the Singapore Parliament, 22 January 2009.

15 Tilak Abeysinghe and Gu Jiaying, "Measuring its Effectiveness", *Straits Times*, 16 February 2009. In this commentary piece contributed by the National University of Singapore's (NUS) Abeysinghe and Gu, the authors wrote that a simulation based on a macro-econometric model of the Singapore economy maintained by the NUS Department of Economics indicated that the impact of the Jobs Credit Scheme will extend beyond a year even if the scheme were to end after four quarters. While the simulation indicated that only about 30,000 jobs would be saved in 2009, more than 120,000 jobs are likely to be saved over three years because of the scheme.

16 Ministry of Finance Press Release, "Jobs Credit Scheme to be Extended for Six Months with Two Reduced Payouts", 13 October 2009.

17 In his book *Freedom for Sale* (London: Simon and Schuster, 2009), John Kampfner went as far as to say that Singapore is the model for this system of trade-off between state and citizens. He wrote: "I am constantly struck by the number of well-educated and well-travelled people there I know who are keen to defend a system that requires an almost complete abrogation of freedom of expression in return for a good material life. This is the pact. In each country it varies; citizens hand over different freedoms in accordance with their own customs and priorities."

18 For example, in an article for the *Edge Singapore*, "Reassessing Singapore's Economic Future: The Post-crisis World Economy — A New Model of Growth?" Manu Bhaskaran detailed the downsides of high GDP growth. He noted that pushing the economy to grow at such a high rate may hurt Singaporeans, citing the recent experience of the 7.8 per cent growth from 2005 to 2007. To achieve that high growth, Singapore allowed in a lot of foreigners, resulting in several unintended negative effects. The inflow of unskilled foreign workers depressed the wages of lower-skilled Singaporeans, especially the older and more vulnerable members of society; the overall large inflow of people over a short space of time resulted in higher housing costs, higher inflation, and worsening congestion. In addition, much of the growth was concentrated in the foreign-dominated sectors of high-end manufacturing and high finance, which meant that foreigners received most of the benefits. Data also shows that while Singapore enjoys one of the highest per capita incomes in the world, at US$37,597 in 2008, profits take about 46 per cent of GDP, which is extremely high in comparison with most developed economies. Almost half of this extraordinarily high profit share went to foreign-owned companies, leaving an unusually low share of the GDP for the average Singapore citizen, whether he is an employee or a businessman.

19 Soon Teck Wong and Ong Lai Heng, "First World Per Capita Income but Third World Income Structure? *Statistics Singapore Newsletter* (2001) (the newsletter of the Economics Accounts Division, Singapore Department of Statistics).

20 These figures were detailed in the written reply by Minister of Trade and Industry Lim Hng Kiang to Question No. 106 submitted by Nominated MP Siew Kum Hong in Parliamentary Notice Paper No. 30 of 2008. Part of the question asked about the percentage of wages as a component of GDP in Singapore for the last fifteen years up to 2007. The percentages, as supplied by the Department of Statistics were as follows:

Year	'93	'94	'95	'96	'97	'98	'99	'00	'01	'02	'03	'04	'05	'06	'07
Percentage of GDP (%)	43	42	42	42	42	45	44	43	47	46	45	42	42	42	41

21 According to the Ministry of Manpower's "Labour Market 2008" report, local employment grew by 64,700 in 2008 compared to a 156,900 growth in employment of foreigners. In 2007, the figures were 90,400 for locals and 144,500 for foreigners.

22 Figures from the Ministry of Manpower's "Labour Market 2008" report.

23 Projections for foreign labour up to 2034 were detailed in Hui and Hashmi (2007). Projection for foreign labour in 2050 attributed to Hui in the *Straits Times* article on 13 November 2009. The article also mentioned a projection for the year 2030.

24 See the Economic Strategies Committee website <http://www.esc.gov.sg/>.

25 Sue-Ann Chia, "Panel to Prepare for Long-term Growth", *Straits Times*, 28 May 2009.

26 Lee Hsien Loong, Speech in Parliament, 27 May 2009 <http://www.pmo.gov.sg/News/Speeches/Prime+Minister/Transcript+PM+Lee+speech+in+Parliament.htm>.

27 Ibid.

28 Ibid.

29 Ministry of Information, Communications and the Arts Press Release, "Remarks by Dr Lee Boon Yang, Minister for Information, Communications and the Arts, at the media conference on the Government's response to the recommendations made by the Advisory Council on the Impact of New Media on Society (AIMS)", 9 January 2009 <http://app.mica.gov.sg/Default.aspx?tabid=79&ctl=Details&mid=540&ItemID=934>.

30 Lydia Lim, "Upgrading for All Wards, But PAP Ones First", *Straits Times*, 11 June 2006. "Mah Bow Tan on Upgrading", *Straits Times*, 11 June 2006. In these reports, National Development Minister Mah Bow Tan reiterated the PAP policy of giving lift upgrading priority to PAP wards, calling upgrading a "major election platform of the PAP". Indeed, from the 1997 general elections on, PAP leaders have been invoking the "local government" argument in a bid to undermine the opposition's "by-election" strategy (this involves returning the PAP to power on nomination day) by making

Singaporeans vote for not only the national government but also the MP who will best represent interests at the constituency level. Mah said that "there is no change, that policy still remains." Describing the policy as something that the PAP believed to be "something we have to do", Mah argued that "it is not unreasonable for these residents to be in front of the queue for upgrading, if they have supported the PAP candidates."

[31] Ibid.

[32] Kor Kian Beng and Cai Haoxiang, "Potong Pasir, Hougang to Get Lift Upgrading", *Straits Times*, 14 July 2009.

[33] Sue-Ann Chia and Cai Haoxiang, "Non-PAP Wards Get Lift Revamp", *Straits Times*, 3 October 2009.

[34] Letter from Lim Yuin Chien, Press Secretary to the Minister of National Development to the Forum, *Straits Times*, 13 October 2009.

[35] Letter from Lim Yuin Chien, Press Secretary to the Minister of National Development to the Forum, *Straits Times*, 27 October 2009.

[36] Ibid.

[37] Quote from Goh Chok Tong's speech at the People's Action Party's Twenty-fourth Ordinary Party Conference, *Straits Times*, 19 November 1996.

[38] Prime Minister's Office, "Press Statement from the Prime Minister on Changes to Cabinet and Other Appointments", 26 March 2009 <http://www.pmo.gov.sg/News/ PressReleases/Press+Statement+from+the+PM+on+Changes+to+Cabinet+and+Other+ Appointments.htm>.

[39] Edited transcript of Prime Minister Lee Hsien Loong's Press Conference on Cabinet reshuffle on 30 March 2009 at the Istana <http://www.pmo.gov.sg/News/Speeches/ Prime+Minister/Transcript+of+Press+Conference+on+Cabinet+Reshuffle.htm>.

[40] The full list of ministers and acting ministers with their portfolio and the year they were elected in parentheses: Lee Hsien Loong (Prime Minister/1984), Goh Chok Tong (Senior Minister/1976), Lee Kuan Yew (Minister Mentor/1955), S. Jayakumar (Senior Minister and Co-ordinating Minister for National Security/1980), Wong Kan Seng (Deputy Prime Minister and Minister for Home Affairs/1984), Teo Chee Hean (Deputy Prime Minister and Minister for Defence/1992), George Yeo (Minister for Foreign Affairs/1988), Mah Bow Tan (Minister for National Development/1988), Lim Boon Heng (Minister, Prime Minister's Office/1980), Lim Hng Kiang (Minister for Trade and Industry/1991), Lim Swee Say (Minister, Prime Minister's Office/1997), Yaacob Ibrahim (Minister for Environment and Water Resources/1997), Khaw Boon Wan (Minister for Health/2001), Tharman Shanmugaratnam (Minister for Finance/2001), Ng Eng Hen (Minister for Education and Second Minister for Defence/2001), Vivian Balakrishnan (Minister for Community Development, Youth and Sports/2001), Raymond Lim (Minister for Transport and Second Minister for Foreign Affairs/2001), K. Shanmugam (Minister for Law and Second Minister for Home Affairs/1988), Gan Kim Yong (Minister for Manpower/2001), Lim Hwee Hua

(Minister, Prime Minister's Office; Second Minister for Finance; Second Minister for Transport/1997), Lui Tuck Yew (Acting Minister for Communications, Information and the Arts/2006).

[41] Edited transcript of Prime Minister Lee Hsien Loong's Press Conference on Cabinet reshuffle on 30 March 2009 at the Istana <http://www.pmo.gov.sg/News/Speeches/Prime+Minister/Transcript+of+Press+Conference+on+Cabinet+Reshuffle.htm>.

[42] Prime Minister's Office, "Press Statement from the Prime Minister on Changes to Cabinet and Other Appointments", 29 March 2008 <http://www.pmo.gov.sg/NR/rdonlyres/B69818A2-150E-4455-9D4D-1AB211185D84/0/29Mar08Cabinetappt.pdf>.

[43] Department of Statistics, "Population (Mid Year Estimates) and Land Area 2009 <http://www.singstat.gov.sg/stats/keyind.html>.

[44] The issue came up in several dialogues ministers had during visits to various constituencies, as well as several parliamentary debates. In fact, there were many online comments questioning why it was not a highlight of Prime Minister Lee Hsien Loong's 2009 National Day Rally Speech — a state-of-the-nation address considered the most important in Singapore's political calendar. Many actually wondered if there was an attempt to downplay an issue which was becoming increasingly emotive. Indeed, underscoring just how important the issue has become was the fact that Minister Mentor Lee Kuan Yew chose to address the topic in his speech during his annual appearance at the National Day dinner of his Tanjong Pagar constituency on 13 August 2009. Like the National Day Rally speech, Lee Kuan Yew's annual Tanjong Pagar GRC National Day dinner speech is keenly followed by political observers and analysts for insights and indications of possible policy directions. Lee Kuan Yew's influence in the government is such that his speech at this humble grassroots event, understandably a key event in Singapore's political calendar when he was Prime Minister, has remained so even after he stepped down as the head of Singapore's Government on 28 November 1990.

[45] "IPS Perception of Policy in Singapore Survey (1): Resilience in the Economic Crisis, February 2009", Institute of Policy Studies, July 2009 <http://www.spp.nus.edu.sg/ips/docs/events/pops/POPS_Feb%2009_Full%20Report%20for%20Website.pdf>.

[46] A report in the *Straits Times* by Sue-Ann Chia, "New Govt Panel Overseeing Foreign Worker Issues", dated 1 April 2009, said that the Ministerial Steering Committee was formed in January 2009. However, in his speech at the opening of Avery Lodge, a dormitory for foreign workers, Manpower Minister Gan Kim Yong said the committee was formed "late last year". It was interesting to see that no official announcement was made when the committee was formed, given how concerns over foreign workers were mounting.

[47] Ministry of Community Development, Youth and Sports, "MCYS Media Release No. 15/2009: National Integration Council to foster social integration", 26 April 2009 <http://www.mcys.gov.sg/MCDSFiles/Press/Articles/15-2009.pdf>.

[48] See the Ministry of Manpower's website for the "Administrative Changes to the Work Pass System" <http://www.mom.gov.sg/publish/momportal/en/communities/work_pass/work_permit/e-services_and_forms/administrative_changes.html>.

[49] Goh Chin Lian, "Services Sector Feels Pinch of Foreign Workers Controls", *Straits Times*, 28 August 2009. Goh Chin Lian, "Foreign Workers: How to Strike that Fine Balance?" *Straits Times*, 12 September 2009.

[50] Prime Minister's Office Press Release, "Transcript of Prime Minister Lee Hsien Loong's Speech at the NTU Students' Union Ministerial Forum on 15 September 2009", 15 September 2009 <http://www.pmo.gov.sg/News/Speeches/Prime+Minister/PM+Lee+s+speech+at+the+NTU+Students+Union+Ministerial+Forum.htm>.

[51] Jeremy Au Yong, "School Fee Changes for Non-Singaporeans", *Straits Times*, 21 December 2009.

[52] APEC Leader' Declaration at the Seventeenth APEC Economic Leaders' Meeting, 14–15 November, Singapore, "Sustaining Growth, Connecting the Region" <http://www.apec.org/apec/leaders__declarations/2009.html>.

ROOTING FOR THE FUTURE
Views for the Heritage Sector in Singapore

Michael Koh

Throughout history, great philosophers, leaders, and scholars have espoused culture and the arts as a vital ingredient in shaping a moral, well-rounded, and forward-looking people that can build and sustain a society beyond the immediate future. Indeed, the greatest cities and societies were not just centres of political or economic power; they were also the gathering grounds for cultural advancement. During the golden age of every civilization, these cities were hubs for intellectual and artistic creation that attracted the best minds from near and far.

Today, the myriad surveys conducted by influential magazines such as *Forbes* and *Monocle* have continued to espouse the positive impact of arts and culture on city rankings. In the face of intense competition among cities to attract talent, it is indisputable that culture and the arts are crucial to the making of a vibrant, distinctive global city, and that one's experience of the culture and heritage of a city can be the tipping point for deciding what constitutes that elusive "quality of life" that makes a particular city a good place to work and live in.

Over the past few decades in Asia, it can be said that, in the imperative for survival and the pursuit of the economic dream, some societies may have overlooked the timeless importance of heritage and culture. No blame should be cast for this, because providing for the basic needs of one's people is the most important requirement of good governance. The good news is that for the young cities and societies that have previously pursued economic priorities and succeeded, the time has come for the pursuit of a "golden age" of creative and cultural revival.

MICHAEL KOH is the Chief Executive Officer of the National Heritage Board, and the National Art Gallery, Singapore.

A City and its Foundation

In any construct of a successful, liveable city, culture plays a significant role. This role can be understood through the analogy of a building and its foundation. A building is perceived as aesthetically pleasing, an icon to be celebrated, to be lived in, to be experienced, to be a work place; which we can marvel and wonder at. We are prepared to spend heavily on the material finishes so that it can be a highly sought after and tradeable commodity. What often goes unnoticed is the foundation on which these buildings are built on. Most of us forget about the pilings that go deep into the ground and how they are made, the way it anchors itself on solid ground to provide the core strength and stability to keep the creation above standing. More often than not, we look for the most cost and time efficient way to construct the foundations because they cannot be seen, whilst we spare no expenses for expensive finishes for the building above.

Similarly, the anchors of a country lie in its pillars of foundation, rooted in the solid ground of good governance that ensures the effective functioning of society. Just like a building, a society that lacks a strong foundation of values, traditions, and heritage, will be easily swayed in times of stress. In particular, for a multicultural society like Singapore, its past and heritage form the bridge to the cultural understanding of its people. The pillars of this cultural understanding are tolerance and acceptance of diversity. Like a building's foundation, it is the shared heritage and culture that sustains a society as it grows, evolves, and navigates new challenges.

However, in the ideals of modern societies — which are often premised on the concept of financial returns and shareholder dividends — one will find that promoting and preserving one's heritage to build the pillars of cultural understanding is an intangible and immeasurable goal. Indeed, one cannot measure the "performance and returns" of cultural understanding, or put into numbers how much a society loves and treasures its heritage. Therein lies the tension for policymakers that have been entrusted with the mission of promoting culture. To the cultural sector, the intrinsic value of the arts is beyond measure. To the economists, the arts and cultural sector is typically perceived as a "bottomless pit", with no tangible or immediate returns on investment. This perception sometimes influences decision makers who hold the knife to the financial pie — how do they then decide who gets the largest portion and what justifies the cuts?

The essential foundation of any civilized modern day society requires monetary investment and the commitment of resources to heritage and culture.

The distribution of funds towards this area needs to be recognized amid the gamut of priorities that every country and city has. It is in this process of national level prioritization that we in the heritage industry have to reiterate the invaluable contributions that heritage makes to the long term growth and survivability of any society.

In the case of Singapore, it is recognized that arts and culture contribute to the positioning of Singapore as a vibrant global city, as an arts and lifestyle hub that is buzzing with activity, making it a great place to live, work, and play in, and a quality avenue for tourism expenditure and extended stay. Looking into the future of the unwritten pages of our history, our work in rooting Singaporeans in our heritage leaves us with a great legacy and responsibility for future generations. This in itself, is value beyond measure.

A Heritage Revival

In recent years, the heritage sector in Singapore has strengthened by leaps and bounds. There is renewed interest in heritage and culture among the general public. Heritage activities span a wider range of educational and lifestyle interests, and Singapore's heritage and cultural products are reaching out to new segments of the population.

Numbers of visitors to museums and heritage outreach activities have reached record highs. The number of visitors to the National Heritage Board's (NHB) museums has risen from 1.34 million in FY (financial year) 2006 to 2.62 million in FY 2008;[1] and attendance at our outreach events like the Singapore HeritageFest has risen dramatically from 2.93 million in FY 2006 to 6.31 million in FY 08.[2]

Around a million tourists[3] traverse the halls of our national museums each year. The economic implications are clear; that the ability of the heritage sector to attract tourism translates to economic dividends of extended tourist stay and spending. Significantly, these numbers also show the increased global interest in cultural understanding and learning beyond one's own national borders.

Partly contributing to this trend is the evolution of museums to become more attractive and lifestyle oriented. Our museums are no longer regarded as dusty repositories of forgotten artefacts, and have transformed themselves into exciting destinations for visitors of all ages. The exhibitions and programmes of our institutions are more engaging and relevant, attracting children, students, young adults, and others. At the same time, the NHB museums continually strive for critical praise among the international museum community. Our exhibits and curated shows are travelling overseas to top-tier cultural cities like Paris, proving that Singapore has a cultural heritage that can stand alongside the treasures of great and ancient civilizations.

This heritage revival is increasingly recognized by the media that acknowledge the accelerating interest and growth in the heritage and cultural sector. The extensive media reports on the NHB and our museums, both global and local, accrued to an approximate value of S$45.3 million in FY 2008.[4] International press such as the *International Herald Tribune, New York Times, Newsweek, TIME,* and *South China Morning Post* have featured our museums and exhibitions in the past few years.

All this has contributed positively towards raising the awareness of and interest in heritage in Singapore, and towards positioning Singapore as a vibrant global city ready to face the future. More importantly, as heritage infuses the population with a sense of their personal histories and the history of their community and nation, the foundations of our cultural understanding grow, and Singapore as a society gains a stronger sense of identity in the process.

Surveys conducted in 2008 and 2009[5] have shown that increasingly, more and more Singaporeans are interested in their heritage. More than ninety per cent of those surveyed are proud of their heritage and feel that it is important to be aware of the heritage, traditions, and roots of oneself and others. The biennial *Heritage Awareness Survey (HAS) 2008*[6] reflected that more and more Singaporeans are participating in heritage activities, and that Singaporeans strongly laud the government's efforts in heritage conservation and promotion. The Heritage Awareness Index (HAI)[7] — reflecting heritage knowledge, appreciation and involvement among Singaporeans — reached an all-time high of 6.34 points (out of 10) in 2008, up from 5.24 in 2002.

As Singapore evolves with the shifting tides of globalization and rises to meet the economic challenges of the twenty-first century, culture and heritage continue to contribute towards anchoring our society — with its unseen pillars that make up the foundation of our country.

But more can be done if a true cultural flourishing is to be achieved. Not only will heritage need to capture the hearts of Singaporeans, our cultural offerings will also need to stand tall and engage with global citizens. Regardless of their globalized or outward looking nature, the heritage and cultural offerings of Singapore must first of all be for Singaporeans and by Singaporeans.

Highlighted in the paragraphs below are ten strategies that we at the NHB hope will bring Singapore to the next level of heritage awareness and engagement.

Strategy 1: Develop Singapore's Very Own Museum and Arts Quarter

The unique characteristics of Singapore's historic Bras Basah and Padang precinct[8] together with existing cultural infrastructure, have great potential to create a comprehensive, congruent arts and heritage district. Imagine London's museum district right next to New York's SoHo — this is the potential of Singapore's cultural hive in the Civic District.

Existing museums that create a critical mass in this precinct include the National Museum of Singapore, Asian Civilisations Museum, Singapore Art Museum, Peranakan Museum, Singapore Philatelic Museum, and the upcoming National Art Gallery, Singapore (which will open in 2014). They are within walking distance of one another, and visitors can easily spend an entire day exploring our museums without the need to travel all over the island. Lending variation to the museum landscape, a wide array of arts institutions such as Sculpture Square, Nanyang Academy of Fine Arts, and LASALLE College of the Arts add to the richness of the precinct's cultural presentations. This core is further layered with other enriching institutions such as the National Library, The Arts House, The Substation, and upcoming private museums in the area.

We can reinforce, update and grow our existing facilities to further strengthen this critical mass. Investments in infrastructure and capabilities, such as by developing the Asian Civilisations Museum, the Esplanade – Theatres on the Bay, which has been touted as the region's best centre for performing arts, and the National Art Gallery, are all necessary for attaining the precinct's arts and cultural potential. Strategic support and development can enhance these institutions into more robust entities to entrench their positions further as world class arts and heritage venues. Pedestrian accessibility and increased connectivity to and within these clusters are vital for visitors to have an optimal urban experience. Land use policies need to be reviewed and incentive schemes developed to facilitate artists' street markets and the setting up of art galleries, studios, and other dynamic enterprises that constitute an "energized" museum and arts quarter.

A whole government approach to market and brand the entire precinct is also required to put our Civic District up there with the likes of Vienna's Museum Quarter, Berlin's Museum Island, London's Museum Mile, and Washington DC's Smithsonian Mall.

Strategy 2: Endear Our Historic Buildings to Our People

We often read in the foreign press about famous historic monuments, castles and homes, such as Chatsworth and Burghley House in the United Kingdom. Great western classics have been written about them and important historical events have occurred there. Many of these buildings are open to the public for viewing, and even for holiday visits. Through these buildings, a piece of history comes alive, giving society a physical place to anchor its memories and past achievements.

In Singapore, we too have our share of historic buildings and homes. However modest they may be, compared to the great castles and palaces of Europe, they still reflect the culture of our forefathers. Through the Preservation of Monument Board's (PMB) efforts, sixty-one buildings have been gazetted as national monuments. The Urban Redevelopment Authority (URA) has also conserved some 7,000 heritage buildings and structures, many of which are the humble shophouses where our forefathers grew up and forged new lives.

Regrettably, some historic homes have made way for development, such as Lim Nee Soon's home, the house of Lim Bo Seng, and Eu Villa. But for those that survived the onslaught of redevelopment, their current destinies are a far cry from their past glory. Fabled houses such as Matilda House and Alkaff Mansion exist in stages of disrepair. Changi Cottage, where significant events in history occurred, is intact but seldom visited. Of the former Admiralty House and Command House, which were the homes of key military personnel of the British armed forces during the colonial period, the former still exists and is currently a tenanted state property and the latter has been partly converted into a UBS training centre.

Public access is often restricted for historic buildings that have been converted for a new modern use. The URA has saved a historic colonial house located in a prime area of Singapore, which has since been upgraded to become an exclusive clubhouse for the well-heeled in a new residential condominium.[9] The beautiful officers' barracks at Sentosa is now the exclusive six-star Capella Hotel. There is nothing wrong with the conversion of heritage houses in this manner, as it leverages on the private sector to spare the funds to save these buildings and keep them "alive" for the future. However, by building fences around these historically rich buildings, we are keeping our children away from a valuable and fun lesson about our country's past. Our students, locals, and tourists may never get to see this part of our history, to view a past way of life, to experience an actual building or a room where a significant moment of history took place. The lesson is not just about history; it is about our national identity as well.

We would like to propose the formation of a National Trust or National Register of all the historic buildings or homes, with four preliminary ideas: (1) The Trust will protect buildings of heritage significance, which are either at risk of being demolished to make way for urban development, or have not been conserved in a manner that enables the public to fully appreciate their historical value; (2) For State-owned historic buildings, we suggest funds be set aside for the restoration of these buildings and educational events around these buildings; (3) For private homes, we propose to incentivize the owners through tax benefits to allow visitors to make private tours, perhaps on weekends; (4) We can develop a volunteer guides programme that educates visitors about the historic houses.

Strategy 3: Instil Historical Pride in Local Areas

Over the years, NHB has been marking significant historic sites to serve as physical and psychological reminders of our shared history. To date, there are eighty-six marked historic sites around Singapore. Supported by other government agencies, schools, and the community, NHB has also been developing heritage community trails which incorporate national monuments and heritage sites, as well as putting up heritage markers and storyboards containing nuggets of information about the history of the places. Such efforts have extended past the Civic District and Singapore River area to suburban Queenstown, Jalan Besar, Balestier, and Bukit Timah. To date, there are six trails documenting this community history.

Reaching out further to engage the community in their local areas, we have published heritage trail guides, and trained adults and students to be physical guides on trails. These initiatives have been popular among residents and students as they provide a sense of ownership and belonging to the area.

We believe more can be done to build on our initiatives. For instance, the different community trails can be linked to the island-wide Park Connector Network, to develop an urban-natural trail with interesting pockets of heritage, nature, and arts areas. Working with the community, we can retain our memories of the past even if the physical structures have been lost, through commemorative markers, pictures, or small heritage galleries. We can commemorate key events or structures in our history, even going back to a more ancient past where history's tale has yet to be told — the Singapore Stone (believed to date back to the thirteenth century or earlier) which was once sited at the mouth of the Singapore River, can be remembered with a marker that associates the river with its colourful and enigmatic past.

Strategy 4: Strengthening Community Bonds

Using heritage to bring people together, to forge bonds within communities, has been a hallmark of NHB's mission. Drawing from our past and the relatively humble roots that our country sprang from, we can find common touchpoints that Singaporeans of different demographic groups can identify with and relate to. To spread this message, NHB uses fun and engaging platforms that include the efforts of the Ministry of Community Development, Youth and Sports' (MCYS) programmes and NHB's Singapore HeritageFest, as well as the popular bus adventure tours, Expedition "H". These platforms create more awareness of our shared heritage and allow participants to catch a glimpse of the different communities that coexist in Singapore.

We are also developing the capability to reach out to Singaporeans of different demographics, to bring our heritage offerings to more people — beyond the walls of the museums — by bringing travelling exhibitions to the heartlands, in shopping centres, schools and libraries, right where people live. We engaged popular local comedian Mark Lee as our ambassador for one of our programmes. His message was simple, that if he could visit museums after not having been since his student days, and appreciate the exhibitions and content, then so could everyone. Some intellectuals reacted with dismay saying that we were dumbing down, but the resulting wave of grassroots and public support was overwhelming. To the public at large, it showed that we were actively reaching out to Singaporeans from all walks of life and actively making our museums accessible for all.

NHB publications, such as *10 Stories: Queenstown through the Years*, target children as well as adults. Such publications are a result of the systematic collection of oral history accounts from the community, and are deeply meaningful. However, more can be done to document our many other communities as we collect their memories for the future.

The challenge lies in getting a fast-paced, results-oriented breed of Singaporeans to take time to get to know one another, to make this process fun and informative, and to encourage Singaporeans to join NHB in this mission. Over the years, NHB's pool of volunteers has expanded to about 1,000, comprising students, retirees, and expatriates. Many of the volunteers are trained to conduct guided tours in our museums, in English, Mandarin, and Japanese. We are especially grateful for the dedicated volunteerism of the Friends of the Museums and Museum Volunteers. We also hope to offer Malay and Tamil tours in future so as to extend our outreach even more.

Through such community platforms, more members of the public will hopefully discover their shared commonalities and develop even closer bonds with their community.

Strategy 5: Embracing the New Media Age

In reaching out to the community, NHB has been actively leveraging on the new media and Web 2.0 revolution that is changing the way communications, collaboration, and engagement are conducted in the twenty-first century. With more youths and adults actively engaging one another online and forming new communities on the World Wide Web, outreach efforts have to enter this space and grasp the emerging opportunities that are unfolding for the heritage sector. Access to NHB websites, blog sites such as Yesterday.sg and Facebook groups has been proliferating, and much of the content is generated not by NHB but by our online visitors and users.

We are actively extending museum and heritage space online, by showcasing collections of artworks and artefacts in SgCool.sg and archival materials in digital format online on www.a2o.com.sg, using innovative information technology applications and new media platforms to make these heritage resources both informative and interactive. We also made our first foray into heritage gaming, working with students on *Mission Darkstar*.

We must now further consolidate our archival resources of old documents and oral history recordings online, and bring a fuller suite of museum services to an online audience, such as transferring exhibitions to the Internet, and enabling online shopping for publications.

Strategy 6: Developing the Heritage Talent

As a city state with people as the most important resource, it is vital to have a steady flow of talent in and out of Singapore — experts, specialists, and professionals who can provide insights in museum management. The arts and cultural sectors are still lagging behind other financially lucrative sectors in terms of manpower and talent. Nonetheless, NHB has built up professional expertise in areas such as artefact conservation, archiving, and curation of and research into the material culture of the region. Its expertise is associated with excellence by Association of Southeast Asian Nations (ASEAN) countries, and we have through ASEAN-COCI (Committee on Culture and Information) cooperation programmes conducted training for some of them.

Looking forward, Singapore can strive to be a centre of excellence for ASEAN in the cultural and heritage sector, and offer courses and consultancy services for Singaporeans and ASEAN talent. The Heritage Conservation Centre can become such a centre of excellence in the aspect of conservation, and the National Archives of Singapore in archiving national records and governmental memories.

We can help in the development of the ASEAN cultural sector through exchanges and conferences, connecting the region with other global networks. The biannual ASEAN Museum Directors' Symposium has been a successful platform to discuss and share valuable lessons across the ASEAN family of museums. Such efforts can raise professionalism and attract more talent to join the heritage and cultural sector, which is crucial for its long term sustainability.

Strategy 7: Building Research and Scholarship Cornerstones

Research and scholarship are the key foundation upon which museums hone their curatorial and collections expertise. NHB's extensive network with global counterparts and its specialized domain knowledge on Asian cultures and museology allow it to offer unique, fresh perspectives from both the East and West. Singapore is therefore well-placed to become a hub for scholars and museum experts to pursue scholarship in the areas of Asian culture and the arts.

To attract international talent, scholars and partners, NHB can facilitate education programmes for the skills required in the fields of museology and heritage. Singapore is already beginning to attract talent in research and scholarship through its investment in research and development. It can further expand its cultural think tanks by linking up with academic cultural and arts institutions that want to establish themselves in Singapore, or work with overseas universities to conduct more sponsored programmes to explore more case studies, co-curate exhibitions of mutual interest, and even set up a joint research centre with a world renowned museum.

In this way, we can strive to stay competitive against other more affluent or resource rich countries, which are buying over franchise museum brand names to enhance their cultural tourism status.

Strategy 8: Building on Cultural Philanthropy

Philanthropy forms an important support for museum development worldwide. To sustain the vibrancy of the heritage landscape, we require the support of like-minded advocates who want to see heritage and culture flourish.

Our heritage supporters have helped us build state-of-the-art heritage institutions, acquire important pieces to fill the gap in our collections, organize crowd-pulling and memorable programmes, as well as showcase world-class exhibitions. They have also allowed us to launch inspiring publications, provide for scholarships to train talent, sharpen our programming and operational strategies, and strengthen our outreach.

Singapore has benefited immensely from the donation of world renowned Chinese artist Wu Guanzhong. The artist presented 113 pieces of his artworks to the Singapore Art Museum (SAM) as a way of spurring the development of the local art scene. Through his generous donation, SAM is now home to the world's largest collection of his art in a public institution and tasked to keep this for the future. Wu's donation is also an example of the synergy between the museum and the public domain. It shows the mark of confidence that people have in our museums as guardians of the nation's heritage.

NHB aims to encourage sustainable philanthropy through different channels. At the foundational level, it continually maintains connection with the people it serves and the people and corporations that support it. It shows its appreciation through the annual *Patron of Heritage Awards*, as well as other platforms to honour their donations. At the operational level, NHB takes the utmost care to uphold professional standards, to assure the donors that their collections will be well cared for, and to guarantee that their funds will be used properly and wisely.

Looking ahead, we want to further cooperate with our benefactors to work out platforms and incentives to spur greater private sector participation in the heritage ecosystem. These channels are relevant for the donors beyond Singapore's shores, which NHB will continue to try to attract by strengthening its standing in the international museum arena.

Strategy 9: Cultivating the Heritage Ecosystem

For heritage to truly engage with a population, it needs an active private sector that champions and sustains the arts and heritage sector with creative initiatives and enterprises. Beyond the community engagement initiatives and collaborative projects that NHB drives, NHB also recognizes the need to catalyze the larger heritage ecosystem, whose health is key to the longer-term sustainability and vibrancy of the larger sector. NHB's Museum Roundtable provides support for fifty-three private museums and galleries in Singapore. We actively promote entrepreneurship that leverages on heritage to develop creative products. Empowered by schemes such as NHB's Heritage Industry Incentive Programme (Hi^{2}P), we are seeing bold displays of creative ideas, vigour, and determination — along with business acumen — to embrace heritage as a platform. Heritage-themed children's books, private museums, Internet/television featuring heritage topics, and even T-shirts with heritage-inspired themes, are some of the positive market responses.

Recognizing that finding affordable, useful spaces in land-scarce Singapore can be a problem for emerging enterprises, NHB has recently collaborated with the Singapore Land Authority (SLA) and the private sector to adapt two prime-area state properties into unique integrated arts and museum lifestyle venues that promise to deliver a diverse and enjoyable museum experience for the public.

Such private endeavours add new dimensions and perspectives to our social and cultural fabric, adding to the vibrancy of the arts and culture landscape. In time, through catalytic initiatives and creative collaborations with public and private sector players, NHB hopes to see more independent museums and galleries, more creative businesses that leverage on our heritage and culture, as well as new talent and capabilities in the arts and heritage sector.

Strategy 10: Engaging the Region and Beyond

Culture can be a powerful tool that transcends boundaries and builds connections among societies and nations, and NHB has actively championed cultural appreciation and understanding to reach out to Singapore's closest neighbours. Most recently, to celebrate warm diplomatic relations with our neighbours, NHB organized country-themed festivals, with Vietnam Festival in 2008 and Philippines Fiesta in 2009. Through such festivals, Singapore's population gains a deeper appreciation of the history, culture, and arts of those other countries.

We are also actively exporting our collections, to enable others to appreciate our heritage and understand Singapore better. Our Peranakan collection will be displayed in the Musée du Quai Branly in Paris later this year, allowing a slice of this fascinating and uniquely Southeast Asian community to be understood and appreciated by Western audiences.

The arts and culture also have a strong attractive potential to anchor a city as a hub for interaction and exchange. After Venice's decline as a major power, it rejuvenated itself by attracting visitors from around the world through art. The Venice Biennale — one of the world's most prestigious art festivals — is its greatest achievement, drawing Europe and the world to Venice with country pavilions in the Giardini and Arsenale areas of the city since 1895. Together with the National Arts Council (NAC), NHB hopes to build the Singapore Biennale to an event of prestige and renown. This strategy of establishing a cultural hub with multiple international linkages dovetails with the larger framework of Singapore's engagement of the world.

Becoming a Smithsonian of the East

With "Asia Rising" and the centre of global gravity shifting to the East, Asia's evolving creative and cultural network is brimming with promise and opportunity. The brilliant minds, artists, and creatives who will rise to prominence as the Asian countries develop further will bring to our region iridescent ideas and artistic breakthroughs that will shape the twenty-first century of culture.

Situated in the heart of the Southeast Asian region, our inclusive culture, diverse ethnic composition, and regional interconnectedness place Singapore in a good position to play a key role in this Asian cultural renaissance. As an established hub for Asia, Singapore can position itself as a key node in this cultural network, as a place where exciting exchanges occur, dynamic artists collaborate, and where intellectuals and scholars develop greater understanding into the vast landscape of Asian art and culture.

With a family of museums and a growing knowledge centre with strong professional expertise, NHB has the potential to become the anchor for this centre of cultural discovery and flowering — the Smithsonian of the East. We can leverage on our hub positioning to develop talent, attract scholars, and enhance our community heritage and cultural offerings so that they reach out to both international and domestic audiences, to anchor Singapore as an arts gateway of the future.

There is no prescribed path to becoming the Smithsonian of the East. Setting in place a master plan featuring the strategies discussed above can provide a roadmap to help Singapore achieve its goal of bringing heritage to all, and making it enriching and accessible to Singaporeans and overseas visitors from all walks of life. With a foundation firmly rooted in a common heritage, Singaporeans can stand strong as a people with a shared dream for Singapore's future.

Notes

As CEO of the National Heritage Board since 1 September 2006, Michael Koh has been rebranding the museums and heritage sector in Singapore. He has injected a fresh perspective into the heritage experience by transforming Singapore's museums into contemporary lifestyle destinations.

1 In FY 2008, NHB museums had a record breaking year with 2.62 million visitors, up 41.1 per cent from the previous financial year. This figure is based on visitor numbers to seven NHB museums and interpretative centres: the Asian Civilisations Museum, Memories at Old Ford Factory, National Museum of Singapore, Peranakan Museum, Reflections at Bukit Chandu, Singapore Art Museum, and Singapore Philatelic Museum.

2 In FY 2008, NHB's outreach efforts continued to scale new heights with a record 6.31 million Singaporeans and tourists participating in various heritage activities conducted outside NHB museums and heritage institutions — an encouraging increase of 44.9 per cent from FY 2007's 4.36 million participants. These outreach activities serve a public educational role and are held in locations heavily frequented by the public such as schools, shopping centres, libraries, and other heartland hangouts. Some examples include the Singapore HeritageFest and other travelling exhibitions.

3 This finding was derived from the inaugural survey conducted by the Singapore Tourism Board and the National Heritage Board in 2008, on visitor demographics and perceptions of selected institutions under the Museum Roundtable — a grouping of over fifty museums in Singapore.

4 Using the publicity metric based on calculating the advertising value equivalent of the total media coverage and reports related to NHB and its museums and institutions, NHB assigns a monetary value to the amount of media coverage it has received over the period of its financial year. It serves to provide a rough indication of the value of NHB's media exposure.

5 Every year since its inaugural festival in 2004, NHB commissions a survey to evaluate whether the objectives of Singapore HeritageFest (SHF) are met. In 2009, the surveys were conducted over the festival duration from 16 to 26 July 2009 with visitors at the main festival hub at Suntec City and six satellite hubs in heartland malls, as well as participants who signed up for various festival events such as Fun On Foot Treasure Hunt and heritage bus tours. The key findings for *SHF 2009* were derived from a questionnaire survey of 1,400 Singaporeans, using face-to-face interviews.

6 The key findings for HAS 2008 were derived from a questionnaire survey of 1,000 Singaporeans, using face-to-face interviews conducted from August to September 2008. A study commissioned by NHB and carried out by the National University of Singapore's Department of Geography, HAS 2008 follows two previous surveys conducted in 2002 and 2006.

7 The figures from the HAS serve as heritage indicators used for the derivation of the Heritage Awareness Index (HAI). The HAI reflects how Singaporeans view their level of personal involvement with heritage activities, how much they value the role of local heritage, their confidence in imparting heritage knowledge, and their personal

interest in cultural traditions and customs. The higher the index, the greater the overall levels of heritage awareness among Singaporeans.

8   The Bras Basah district and Padang area are culturally vibrant areas in Singapore's central business district, and house several historically significant landmarks. Rich in architectural and cultural heritage, these areas contain a unique complementary blend of the new and the old. In particular, the Bras Basah–Bugis district is hailed as an enclave for the arts, culture, learning, and entertainment.

9   One of the largest clubhouses in any condominium project in Singapore, the two-storey, 16,000 square feet colonial house is at the heart of the prestigious Orchard Road condominium, Draycott 8.

Thailand

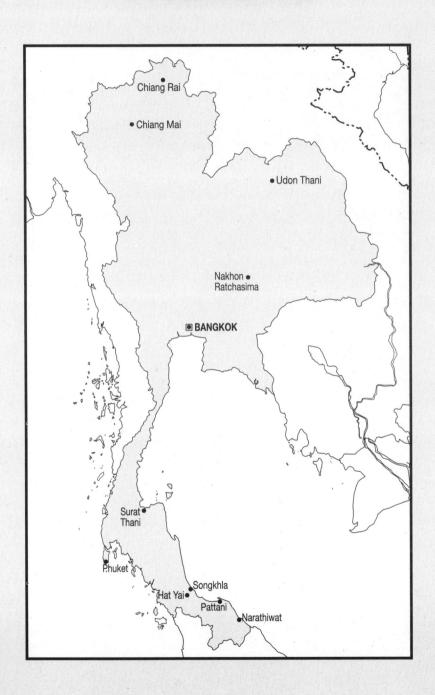

THAILAND IN 2009
Unusual Politics Becomes Usual

Chairat Charoensin-o-larn

On 17 December 2008, a young Democrat Party leader, Abhisit Vejjajiva, was sworn in as Thailand's twenty-seventh Prime Minister and the third Prime Minister within the same year. He inherited a weak economy and a society divided for three years due to the country's unusual political situation.[1] In his speech following the swearing-in ceremony, Abhisit pledged to be "Prime Minister for everybody" and to defend the monarchy as a revered institution.[2] Abhisit won parliamentary support to become Prime Minister by persuading key factions of the now-defunct People's Power Party (PPP) and its minor former coalition parties to switch sides to vote for him. This is alleged to have been made possible through the lobbying of the head of the army, General Anupong Paochinda.[3] Abhisit's swearing, in a way, signaled the end of the era of political domination in Thai politics by Thaksin Shinawatra that had lasted for almost eight years (2001–8).

However, the manner in which Prime Minister Abhisit assumed power also signaled a return to the old *nam nao* (polluted) type of dirty/money politics typical of Thai politics in general and of the Thaksin regime in particular. Did this mean that Thai politics would return to the same old-fashioned jockeying for position and self-interested bargaining? How could the costly, devastating protests and demonstrations of the People's Alliance for Democracy (PAD) culminate in a return to exactly the same kind of politics against which they had fought with such determination? The rise to power of Abhisit has once again shattered the myth of political activists and moralist crusaders that Thai politics can be easily cleaned up by simply blaming and removing one controversial person from the political scene — the most notable recent example being, of course, the fugitive

CHAIRAT CHAROENSIN-O-LARN is Associate Professor, Faculty of Political Science, Thammasat University, Bangkok, Thailand.

former Prime Minister Thaksin. A new government was installed, yet the same old regime remained intact.

Prime Minister Abhisit came with an abundant supply of political goodwill, notably hope. Hope to return the country to normalcy, hope to restore the economy, hope to uphold the monarchy, and hope to reunite the nation — the same old hopes that the coup of 19 September 2006 had stirred with little fulfilment. A *Bangkok Post* columnist described the drama of Thai politics of the recent past with these words: "It is like burning the whole house down just to get rid of a few dirty rats."[4] In any case, those who supported the idea of having a government led by the Democrat Party reasoned that it was necessary to have "a functioning government",[5] which Thailand had not had for almost a year. However, this optimistic view must be put to the test because there is no guarantee that Thailand will have a functioning government in the midst of the existing deep divide. Besides, Newin Chidchob, the leading faction that made possible the formation of the Abhisit government, is notorious for its practice of vote buying, which was one of the main reasons used to discredit the previous Thaksin administration and his proxy governments. The hypocrisy of Thai politics is much evident here.

As a reward for those who helped make the new government possible, it gave the important portfolios of the Transport and Interior Ministries to the Newin faction of the Bhumjaithai Party while the Defence Ministry went to a retired general who has a close relationship with the army chief. In recognition of the support of the PAD, which had helped bring down the Thaksin regime, the post of Foreign Minister went to an active spokesperson of the PAD who had once called Cambodian Prime Minister Hun Sen a "scoundrel" and who supported the closure of the two major airports.

Obviously, Thai politics has reached a point of no return. The past few years have seen the rise of both a political consciousness and high expectations among the Thai people, in particular the rural masses, due mainly to the politicization of the rural Thai voters through the enactment of the 1997 constitution and the populist politics initiated by former Prime Minister Thaksin. Thaksin's populist politics, no matter how problematic they might have been, did bring about a nationwide rise in political consciousness among rural voters. The now-abolished constitution of 1997 nurtured an "ideology of democracy" among the people of Thailand.

The current political divide in Thailand did not derive from economic disparity between urban and rural people. In other words, this has not been a class-based conflict, as some academics have argued recently. Rather, it stems from different views on the fundamental constitution of Thai democracy and politics. These different views have manifested themselves in two versions of democracy: (1) an elite-led democracy, as reflected in the PAD protests and the posture of the Democrat Party and the urban elites under the label of democratic government with the king as head of state; and (2) a mass-based, populist form of democracy such as the one ushered in by Thaksin and his Thai Rak Thai (TRT) Party.

Furthermore, contempt for rural voters as ignorant and uninformed among educated urban elites such as those of the PAD has until now not posed any problem for an authoritarian regime and a bureaucratic polity. However, under Thaksin's populist politics, the election process shifted the balance of power in favour of the rural masses. This new balance of power has become a political threat to the Thai elites. Thus, the current political conflict initiated by the Thaksin regime is by and large about the cleavage between traditional elites and the rural masses, who have begun to develop a different view of what constitutes democracy. As the rural masses have come to dominate and dictate the election process, a significant resistance against popular democracy has developed among Thai elites leading to what Rancière has called a "hatred of democracy",[6] resulting in a feeling of contempt for both democratic elections and the rural electorate that has been expressed in such pejorative terms as "populism", the "Thaksin regime", and the "grassroots". The partial election of members of the senate under the 2007 constitution and the PAD's proposed "New Politics" in which seventy per cent of the Members of Parliament will be appointed reflect this contempt. The recent transformation of the electoral system under the now-abolished 1997 constitution, particularly the institution of the party-list ballot, brought about fundamental changes in Thai politics.[7] These changes have astonished the traditional Thai elites. It was their bewilderment that led to the 19 September 2006 coup, the activism of the PAD, the rewriting of the constitution, and a return to the normalcy of elite-led democracy under the Abhisit government.

Momentous Events

In 2009 Thailand experienced yet another year of important events deserving of the epithet "The Society of the Spectacle".[8] To begin with, the Abhisit government had to read its statement of policy, as required by the constitution, at the Foreign Ministry instead of Parliament, because the red-shirted protesters blocked the entrance to Parliament. The opposition Puea Thai Party (PTP) boycotted the reading and sought from the Constitution Court a ruling on the legitimacy of the Abhisit government. While it criticized the PPP's populist policies, the Abhisit government nevertheless extended water, bus, rail, and electricity subsidies for another six months to help low-income households struggling with the sudden downturn in the economy.

The Australian writer, Henry Nicolaides, was sentenced by a Thai court to three years in jail for defaming the Crown Prince. He pleaded guilty and later was pardoned by the King.[9] Nicolaides' case was one of many pending in the Thai court on *lèse-majesté* charges following the 19 September coup. Suvicha Thakhor, a former oil engineer, was sentenced to ten years in jail for posting web materials deemed insulting to the royal family,[10] while Daranee Charnchoengsilpakul, better known as "Da Torpedo", one of the key anti-government speakers for the United Front for Democracy against Dictatorship (UDD), was sentenced to eighteen years in prison for her speeches at a rally in 2008 that were deemed offensive to the monarchy.[11] Suvicha was the first to receive a *lèse-majesté* ruling based on the controversial Computer Crime Act. Many websites were closed down by the invocation of this act.[12] The rise in *lèse-majesté* charges prompted fifty prominent international scholars and public figures in March to call on the Abhisit government to stop using these charges as devices to suppress freedom of expression and to manipulate power.[13]

Thailand celebrated its traditional New Year or Songkarn Days in April with a riot by the red shirts, whose aim was to bring down the Abhisit government but who were met with bloody suppression. A few days after the riot, a failed attempt to assassinate the PAD's leader, Sondhi Limthongkul, took place in the heart of Bangkok. Amazingly, Sondhi escaped the rain of gunfire with a minor cut on his head. Rumour had it that the military wanted to get rid of him after having successfully crushed the red shirts. In mid-August, there was a huge rally to coincide with the submission by the red shirts of their petition of 3.5 million signatures to the King to seek royal pardon for their beloved leader, the fugitive former Prime Minister Thaksin Shinawatra.[14] The petition put tremendous pressure on the Abhisit government.

One of the most notable events of 2009 took place on 21 September when the Supreme Court's Criminal Division for Political Office Holders acquitted Newin Chidchob and a large number of other defendants in the rubber sapling case.[15] In the widely anticipated "trial verdict of the year", the judges decided that all forty-four defendants were not guilty on charges of corruption and malfeasance. The verdict was controversial in several senses. Above all, the purpose of the 19 September 2006 coup was to demonstrate to the Thai people that several Thaksin administration cabinet ministers, high-ranking civil servants, and some business people at the Charoen Pokphand conglomerate had been involved in large-scale corruption amounting to 1.44 billion baht in the procurement of ninety million rubber saplings to help poor farmers set up a new rubber plantation. Second, it was the very first corruption case in which the coup-appointed Assets Scrutiny Committee (ASC) alleged malfeasance on the part of the Thaksin administration. Since corruption was one of the main reasons for the military to stage the coup, therefore, the court's acquittal raised serious doubts concerning the corruption charges against the Thaksin regime.

Third, the case was controversial in the sense that the Office of the Attorney General (OAG) had recommended that the ASC further substantiate its evidence prior to bringing the case to a court of law. However, the ASC did not comply. Instead, it chose to pursue the case itself through the National Anti-Corruption Commission.[16] The OAG pointed out that the ASC's insistence on going ahead with the case without sufficient evidence had ruined the reputation of the state. Fourth, one of the five politicians who was freed from the case was the infamous Newin Chidchob, the former Deputy Agricultural and Cooperatives Minister under the Thaksin regime and the power broker who had made possible the formation of the Abhisit government. The court acquittal substantially helped to clear his name. After learning of the verdict, Newin was seen with tears in his eyes, pledging irrelevantly to "protect the monarchy until my last breath". Ironically, the case was initiated when Newin was on Thaksin's side but was concluded when he was with the ruling coalition government. Therefore, the acquittal did not come as a big surprise. For former Prime Minister Thaksin Shinawatra, the verdict proved the military wrong and allegations of corruption concerning his regime to be obviously false.

Finally, rumour had it that the verdict was leaked to the defendants before it was made known in the courtroom.[17] The government and the Supreme Court judges denied this rumour as groundless. The denial was a direct response to the petition of the Law Review of Thailand, an advocacy group which cited as evidence the prediction of the PAD's leader Sondhi Limthongkul that there would be an eight-to-one decision for an acquittal. Moreover, the Law Review of Thailand also filed a complaint with the National Anti-Corruption Commission demanding a graft investigation to check into the assets of the nine judges and all forty-four defendants in the rubber sapling affair. It seemed that Newin and his Bhumjaithai Party might have known about the verdict in advance, as a party was held to celebrate one day ahead of the verdict.

The fifteenth ASEAN Summit was held in October 2009 with little fanfare, with Thailand playing host. The ASEAN leaders had to go through a number of changes in date and venue. Initially, the summit was scheduled to be held in Bangkok under the Samak government, then moved to Chiang Mai by the

Somchai government, and finally to Pattaya by the Abhisit government. The Pattaya ASEAN Summit was abruptly ended when the red-shirt demonstrators stormed the venue. The ASEAN leaders were hurriedly evacuated, thus destroying the government's credibility. The summit was finally held in Hua Hin in late October. Unfortunately, it ended with a war of words between Abhisit and Cambodian Prime Minister Hun Sen over the latter's proposed appointment of Thailand's ex-premier Thaksin Shinawatra as his economic advisor. The relocation of the summit underlined the impact of domestic turbulence on an international event. Then, in late October, a rail strike occurred in the south that fast became another potential threat to the stability of the coalition government.

In October, there were ill-timed rumours concerning the King's failing health and the appointment of a viceroy, causing the stock market to falter. The Stock Exchange of Thailand (SET) index dropped 7.2 per cent during the 14 and 15 October trading sessions as the rumours spread. From 19 September the King had been treated at Siriraj Hospital for a lung inflammation. The rumours were so widespread that the Palace and the Princess had to deny them publicly. The King's unannounced public appearance in an electric wheelchair to pay homage to the statue of King Rama V on the latter's memorial day in the hospital compound on 23 October helped stop the rumours. It is obvious that they had been designed to create panic and an opportunity for economic and political gain.[18] The bottom line of the panic was the focus on the unspoken issue of succession. Most Thai and foreign investors would feel insecure if the present monarch were not around.[19]

Needless to say, violence in the restive south has remained unrelenting since January 2004 and has become part of the people's daily lives. The average number of violent attacks reported was 86 per month in 2009 compared with 60 per month during 2007 and 2008. Most attacks were drive-by killings and bomb explosions. According to the Deep South Watch, in the period between January 2004 and August 2009, 3,611 people were killed and 6,073 injured.[20] Worse still, in May the Songkhla Provincial Court cleared security officials of misconduct in connection with the Tak Bai incident, in which 85 demonstrators were killed by suffocation in October 2004 while being transported to a military camp. The court ruled that members of the military were just carrying out their duty and could not be blamed for what had happened. Besides, they were acting under an emergency law which protected them from civil, criminal, or other liabilities while performing their duties.[21] No feasible solutions are in sight to give hope for a return to normalcy in the south. This is simply because the successive Thai governments have been fighting with faceless enemies who appear to be able to pick and choose their targets at will. It is sobering to hear Deputy Interior Minister Thaworn Senneam, who is in charge of the south, tell a newspaper reporter that it would take "at least twenty years" to bring the situation in the deep south back to normal.[22]

In early November, former Prime Minister General Chavalit Yongchaiyudh, now chairman of the PTP, Thaksin's new party after the dissolution of the PPP in late 2008, floated the idea of giving autonomy to the three southernmost provinces of Yala, Pattani, and Narathiwat in the form of a special administrative zone such as the Pattani City Administration.[23] His idea was met with strong criticism from the Abhisit government. If the suppression of the red-shirt protesters during the Songkarn riots exposed the structure of inequality in Thai society wherein the red and yellow shirts were treated differently, then this idea for solving the problem of violence in the south revealed what constitutes the unthinkable and unspeakable in Thai society. Autonomy for the south is a forbidden notion in the vocabulary of Thai politics.

From 20 September to 4 December an organized patriotic campaign was held, initiated by the Office Minister of the Prime Minister's Office, Satit Wongnongtoey, of the Democrat Party, who is in charge of the government's public relations.[24] The campaign, which took place in all seventy-six provinces of the country, had people taking turns singing the national anthem, and this was broadcast live on state-run television at six o'clock in the evening, the hour when the flag lowering ceremony is held nationwide. The broadcasts took place every day, with the provinces appearing in Thai alphabetical order. The campaign was to end in Bangkok on the eve of the celebration of the king's birthday, which is on 5 December. The project was an unexpected success, probably because the Thai people were fed up with all the political and social divisiveness framed by the main opposition groups and decided to express their frustration by doing something different.

Patriotic sentiment in Thai society has been strong since the 19 September coup. Immediately after the coup, there was talk of nationalizing the telecommunication industry because ousted prime minister Thaksin had sold his telecommunication enterprises to investors in Singapore, thus raising security concerns among the Thai elites. There was a report in a local newspaper in early October that two policemen had been punished for missing one of the daily flag raising ceremonies at the Metropolitan Police headquarters in Bangkok.[25] Attending the daily flag raising and lowering ceremonies along with singing the national anthem has become one of the policies of the Abhisit government aimed at promoting national unity. It is worth mentioning that there was a recent attempt to issue a law that would require all vehicles on the public streets to stop when the national anthem is sung in conjunction with the flag raising and lowering ceremonies. Fortunately, this has not been realized.

Environmental conservation and business investment interests clashed in early March when the Rayong Administrative Court designated the Map Ta Phut industrial estate area as a pollution-control zone. Furthermore, the Chiang Mai Administrative Court ordered the Electricity Generating Authority of Thailand (EGAT) to pay compensation worth three billion baht to villagers affected by the pollution from its lignite power plant in the Mae Mo district of Lampang. An order from the Administrative Court on 29 September to suspend seventy-six industrial projects in the Map Ta Phut area sent a shock wave through the business community in Thailand. The suspension came after villagers and environmental groups accused the industry of malpractice for allowing projects without soliciting the opinions of locals and independent environmental organizations as required under Article 67 of the 2007 constitution and under a resolution of the National Environment Board (NEB).[26] Chemical and cancer-causing substances had been found to be high in the affected areas, putting the lives of villagers at risk. The court ruling was interpreted by the business community as an obstacle to investment in Thailand as it would jeopardize new investment in other sectors such as tourism and agriculture.

The overall picture of the economy in 2009 was quite bleak.[27] The global financial crisis hit Thailand hard early in the year. The global recession that started in the United States had a bearing on the fall in Thai exports, which are the main engine of growth, accounting for 70 per cent of the country's gross domestic product (GDP). A fall in exports could mean a recession. The Ministry of Commerce estimated that the whole-year exports for 2009 would shrink by 13 to 15 per cent from the previous year.[28] In the first ten months, exports dropped by 15.6 per cent to 4.25 trillion baht. Exports for all product sectors fell. The strength of the baht during the last ten months ranged roughly from 36.2 per U.S. dollar to 33.1, and it has continued to rise, putting more pressure on exports. The Thai-Cambodian conflict further contributed to the fall in exports. The overall inflation rate was estimated at −0.9 per cent. Tourism, another engine of growth, was also in decline. For the first nine months, foreign arrivals totalled 9.89 million, dropping 12.1 per cent from the same period in 2008. This drop was due mainly to the reduced travel demand because of the global recession and concerns over security in Thailand.[29] Unemployment hit one million early in the year but dropped to 440,000 at the end of the year. The normal level of unemployment in Thailand is 350,000. The improvement was due to the government stimulus programmes and the recovery of exports, according to the Finance Minister.[30] Nonetheless, at the end of the year, another wave of financial turmoil seemed to threaten when the massively debt-laden Dubai World was reported to be in a state of crisis.[31] However, the Finance Minister insisted that the crisis would not affect the Thai economy, which was gradually recovering.[32]

Prime Minister Abhisit has been greeted by red shirts wherever he goes, confronted by the trademark red plastic foot-shaped clappers made in China, accompanied by the noisy shouts of "Abhisit get out" — reminiscent of the PAD's "Thaksin get out" not long before. Such greetings ensure tight and costly security arrangements for the Prime Minister, whose aspiration to be Prime Minister "for everyone" has yet to be realized. During his trip to Lop Buri Province, for example, his motorcade was pelted with plastic water bottles, slippers, and human faeces.[33] Abhisit's recent trip to deliver a compensation cheque to Grandma Hai in Ubon Ratchathani Province — after her thirty-two-year struggle to recover her land lost to a government dam construction project[34] — was made possible only through a helicopter-borne military operation and the presence of 5,000 security personnel to prevent the red shirts from getting close to him. In late November, it was reported that an announcer for a community radio station in Chiang Mai threatened to kill the Prime Minister during his planned visit to the province, which happens to be the stronghold of the pro-Thaksin red shirts.[35] Abhisit later cancelled this trip.

If in the early part of the year Thailand was criticized for mistreating the Muslim Rohingya boat people from Myanmar by forcing them back into the Andaman Sea with little food and water, then at the end of the year Thailand faced further "international" condemnation over its forced repatriation of 4,000 ethnic Hmong from the refugee camp in Phetchabun to Laos.[36] The Hmong, an ethnic minority in the mountainous northern region of Laos, were recruited as guerrilla fighters by the U.S. military in its "secret war" against the communist forces in Laos during the Cold War era. Despite international concern, no other country had expressed any interest in accepting the Hmong for resettlement. Meanwhile, Thailand has never recognized the Hmong in Phetchabun as refugees but instead classified them as illegal migrants. Thailand was criticized for not allowing the UN High Commissioner for Refugees (UNHCR) access to the Hmong to determine the eligibility for their refugee status. Citing the peaceful situation along the Thai-Lao border, the Hmongs' status as illegal migrants, and its agreement with the Lao government, the Abhisit government implemented its deportation plan successfully.

On 28 December, the chiefs of the three armed forces, together with senior military officers and prominent figures, visited Privy Council President General Prem Tinsulanonda at his Si Sao Thewes residence to wish him a happy new year. The event was politically significant in at least two ways. First, it clearly demonstrated the unity among the armed forces in support of General Prem. Since the September coup, Prem has become the main target for relentless attacks by the red shirts, who regard him as Thailand's leading anti-democratic force. The attacks on Prem, whose position is Chief Royal Advisor, have increasingly sown the seed of doubt about the red shirts' loyalty to the monarchy. Second, dressed in army uniform, Prem strongly urged his well-wishers to read a newspaper article written by one of the core members and leading spokesperson of the yellow-shirted PAD. The main thrust of the article was that the nation was in the early stage of a civil war because the red-shirt UDD had planned massive rallies at various locations in early January 2010 to topple the Abhisit government at all cost.[37] According to the article, one of the locations the red shirts planned to organize their massive rallies scheduled for 11 January 2010 would be the residence of former Prime Minister and Privy Councillor Surayud Chulanont at Khao Yai Thiang forest in Nakhon Ratchasima's Sikhiu district. The red shirts accused Surayud of building his house in the national forest reserve. The article ended by citing the Chinese proverb that if one wanted to capture the general, one must kill his horse first. The general in this context is certainly ex-premier Thaksin Shinawatra and the horse is of course a reference to the red shirts. It would be quite worrisome if the Thai elites take this Chinese saying seriously. The last time Prem put on his army uniform was in August 2006, shortly before the 19 September coup, in which he gave a series of lectures to call on the armed forces to be loyal to the King, not the Thaksin government. Being aware of the political implication, Prem played down his military attire by stating that the uniform made him feel "healthy and strong".[38] It remains to be seen whether history will repeat itself. Meanwhile, General Anupong Paochinda, the army chief has assured the Thai public that the army would act as a stabilizer to prevent both bloodshed and a coup in the nation.[39]

On 23 December about 300 red shirts demonstrated outside the headquarters of the office of the Election Commission (EC) in protest against the latter's failure to decide on the party dissolution case against the Democrat Party.[40] The Democrat Party was accused of having unlawfully obtained a 258-million-baht donation from TPI Polene. Instead of making a decision on the case, the EC chose to have its Chairman, Apichart Sukhagganond, who was concurrently the Political Party Registrar, decide whether to dissolve the Democrat Party. Ironically, Apichart had made his stance known earlier that he would drop the party dissolution charge against the Democrat Party.[41] The delay in the case was undoubtedly seen by the red shirts and the opposition Puea Thai Party (PTP) as further evidence of "double standards" or unequal treatment between the Democrat Party and the now-defunct TRT and PPP. In the cases involving the TRT and PPP, the EC could reach its decision expeditiously.

The Abhisit government planned to report on its first year performance on the afternoon of 23 December. However, in the morning of that day, Puea Thai MP and one of the core leaders of the red-shirt UDD, Jatuporn Promphan, released the second part of a classified document said to be prepared by the Foreign Ministry. The document outlined guidelines for action against Cambodia as well as plans to "get rid of" fugitive ex-premier Thaksin Shinawatra.[42] The first part of the document was released a week earlier. The idea was to steal the limelight from the government's planned performance report. According to Jatuporn's interpretation, the term "get rid of" in the document was a code phrase for "killing" because Thaksin was perceived in the document as a "key factor" in destabilizing the Abhisit government and thus must be eliminated. Citing the document, Jatuporn accused the Abhisit government of hatching a secret plan to kill Thaksin and to wage war with Cambodia.[43] However, Abhisit denied both allegations.[44] A few days before this drama, Sivarak Chutipong, who was arrested in Cambodia for obtaining Thaksin's flight schedule when the latter visited Cambodia in early November, had received a pardon from the Cambodian King after being sentenced to seven years in jail on a spying charge. Upon returning to Thailand, Sivarak said that he felt like a victim of a political game conducted by both governments. He credited his release to ex-premier Thaksin and the opposition Puea Thai Party.[45]

On the surface, the Thai political landscape in 2009 was more tranquil than in the previous year, which had been marked by turmoil and an absurd brand of street politics carried out by the yellow-shirt members of the PAD.[46] However, Thailand in 2009 was still plagued by many problems resulting from the profound political division following the 19 September coup.[47] It seemed that in 2009 the same old-style politics of co-optation by politicians and the Thai power elite had overtaken the street politics of the previous year. However, this belied some fundamental changes in Thai society and politics. The most remarkable was the rise of new political actors — mainly the red shirts — who were equipped with a new political consciousness and rising expectations. Therefore, it is argued here that the Thai political landscape in 2009 was not quite the same "politics as usual" that the Thai elites might have hoped for when they successfully installed the

Abhisit-led government. The political divide remained real and intense in 2009. Many parts of the country became a virtual restricted zone for members of the Abhisit government. Perhaps, when the Prime Minister spoke at the forum of the Foreign Correspondents Club of Thailand in mid-January 2009, it was premature for him to state that "we are back in business". At the same forum Abhisit went on to say that his government would carry out its duty with transparency and good governance and that his cabinet would work "without corruption and without violation of human rights".[48]

Allegations of Corruption

The Abhisit government has been mired in a series of corruption allegations since its inception. Most of these corruption scandals were associated with the implementation of the government economic stimulus package "Thailand Strength" (*Thai Kem Kaeng*), which had a budget of about 1,496 billion baht, derived mainly from external loans.[49] Above all, it was alleged that those in control of the funds in a multitude of schemes asked for an overly high corruption cut of 20 to 25 per cent — the going rate was generally 5 to 10 per cent. Literally almost daily there would appear new corruption scams associated with the Thailand Strength project. They ranged from the school milk programme, in which the milk was spoiled, to the purchase of new flagpoles at inflated prices of 49,500 baht each under the nationwide patriotic campaign to sing the national anthem, the procurement at extremely high prices of medical equipment that was unsuitable for use in community hospitals,[50] and corruption in the twenty-six billion baht community sufficiency project, which involved the purchase of drinking water machines that communities did not need and the extortion of money in exchange for placing these products in the community sufficiency stores.

Most of these corruption allegations involved ministers and politicians from the ruling Democrat Party. The first cabinet member from the Democrat Party to resign was Social Development and Human Security Minister Witoon Nambutr. Witoon quit under pressure from the opposition PTP to take responsibility for the distribution of rotten canned fish to flood victims in the south.[51] In February, a supply of school milk was found substandard due to price collusion.[52] Irregularities in the school milk project's bidding saw spoiled milk given to students nationwide. The Rural Doctors Society in October exposed the wrongdoings involving the procurement of medical equipment under the Public Health Ministry, which is under the control of the Democrat Party.[53]

Corruption in the coalition parties, particularly the Bhumjaithai, was also widespread. The most controversial case was a project involving the leasing by the Transport Minister of 4,000 NGV (Natural Gas Vehicle) public buses worth over sixty billion baht. The bus-leasing project was crucial in at least two senses. First, it revealed the infighting between the ruling Democrat and Bhumjaithai parties. Second, it also demonstrated the old-style politics of bargaining for trade-offs. The bus-leasing project was the brainchild of the Samak government, but it failed to get through due to public opposition. It needs to be mentioned that Abhisit strongly opposed the project when he was the opposition leader. The project was repackaged and enlarged into a mega-project by the Newin faction of the Bhumjaithai Party. Abhisit sought to delay the project by asking the National Economic and Social Development Boards to study and find the best option for the country between buying and leasing the buses. However, in late September the Cabinet approved the project after a deal was struck between the Democrat and Bhumjaithai parties. Thanong Khanthong, a newspaper columnist for the *Nation*, posted in his blog on 3 June that one Member of Parliament informed him that the bus-leasing commission amounted to twenty billion baht and the Democrat Party could have earned five billion baht if they went along and voted for the project, which became known as the "mother of all political deals".[54] Moreover, there was speculation that the deal was made in exchange for the Bhumjaithai Party's support in the referendum on the constitutional amendment proposed by the Democrat Party.

Thai society in general is confounded by all these allegations of widespread corruption. The leaders of the 19 September coup used corruption as the main reason for ousting the Thaksin administration. Now corruption is back with the military-backed Abhisit government. Ironically, the mainstream Thai media tend to pay little attention to corruption scandals associated with the Abhisit government; in other words, the only corruption that gets attention is that which is linked to Thaksin and his proxy governments.

The main thrust of the Thailand Strength project is not raising productivity and expanding domestic markets, but rather the strengthening of the two main parties in the present coalition. Moreover, the ideas behind the project are by and large a carbon copy of the populist programmes of the Thaksin administration. Unsurprisingly, leading businessmen gave the government a poor average score of 5.3 out of 10 in a survey on its performance in tackling the country's economic problems.[55] A day before the survey result was released, the Chamber of Commerce announced that it would propose its own version of the national strategy for business sectors because the government lacked consistency in its policy in this area.[56]

Prime Minister Abhisit's image of "Mr Clean" and the credibility of his government were eroding fast. PAD leader Sondhi Limthongkul was quoted as saying that corruption under the Abhisit government was "worse than Thaksin". According to one poll, 50 per cent of the respondents believed that the Thailand Strength project lacked transparency.[57] In addition to corruption scandals, the practice of "double standards" was a source of conflict between the two sides of the political divide and helped fuel the discontent of the red shirts.

Coalition Rifts

Conflict within the coalition has been mainly between the ruling Democrat Party and its major coalition partner, the Bhumjaithai Party. Basically, the source of discord stems from conflicting interests and power struggles in the reshuffling of high-ranking bureaucrats in the fight to gain advantage in the general election, which was anticipated to take place in early 2010. Knowing full well that the Democrats are dependent on them for the coalition's survival and therefore cannot afford to put the stability of the government at risk, the Bhumjaithai leaders did not hesitate to ask for what they wanted in order to prepare for the next general election. The very first sign of a rift between the two parties broke out within a month after the formation of the coalition when Transport and Communications Minister Sopon Zarum of the Bhumjaithai Party proposed a single-airport policy by shutting down the Don Mueang Airport.[58] The idea was to make Suvarnabhumi the country's only airport as well as to promote Thailand as an aviation centre and tourism hub for Southeast Asia. This policy was a reversal of that of the previous government. Don Mueang had been reopened on 25 March 2007 to relieve the congestion that occurred after all flights had been moved to Suvarnabhumi on 28 September 2006. Abhisit and his Democrat Party opposed the idea, but backed down for fear of causing instability in the coalition. Later the Bhumjaithai Party proposed its controversial project of leasing 4,000 public buses instead of purchasing them. As mentioned earlier, Abhisit and his party sought help from the National Economic and Social Development Board by asking it to study the project. The Bhumjaithai Party interpreted this move as a delaying tactic on the part of the Democrats. They retaliated by objecting to the Democrat Party's plan to offer state land to poor farmers at a very low rent (10 baht per *rai* per year).

The most notorious example of conflict between the two parties involved the appointment of the new National Police Chief. It was reported that Abhisit supported Police General Prateep Tanprasert, an Inspector-General. Meanwhile Abhisit's Secretary, Niphon Prompan, Democrat Deputy Prime Minister and Party Secretary General Suthep Thuagsuban, and the Bhumjaithai Party's leaders favoured Police General Chumpol Manmai, a Deputy Police Chief who was a classmate and former supporter of ex-premier Thaksin Shinawatra. The appointment encountered a complication when a rumour appeared in the media that there had been a "special signal" to pick Police General Chumpol to become the new Police Chief. News of the "special signal" was so widespread that the entire kingdom knew about it. Curiously, Abhisit acted as if he did not know anything about the affair and chose to oppose this "special signal" by sticking to his choice. Possibly there was another "special signal" for which Abhisit was waiting. Or, it could be that he wanted to be his own man by not listening to both his Secretary and party's Secretary General and Deputy Prime Minister. The Police Chief saga continues at the time of this writing. The only option open to Abhisit under the circumstances was to appoint his nominee as Acting Police Chief.

Conflict over the appointment of the new police chief had not only earned Abhisit the resignation of his secretary,[59] it also widened a rift within the Democrat Party.[60] The seriousness of the "special signal" affair was such that it resulted in Abhisit's failure to win endorsement for his favourite candidate as the new police chief despite calling for a meeting of the Royal Thai Police Office Board several times and despite himself being chairman of the board. It was unthinkable for Abhisit to see his candidate being rejected by a commission comprised primarily of the "prime minister's men".[61] As a result, Abhisit's image as a capable national administrator and the credibility of his government were severely tarnished.[62]

Furthermore, Abhisit was seen as interfering in police affairs[63] by first removing the then police chief, Police General Patcharawat Wongsuwan , a brother of the Defence Minister, retired General Prawit Wongsuwan of the Bhumjaithai Party, and then by appointing Police General Wichean Potephosree as acting police chief. Patcharawat was demoted because he failed to provide proper security for Abhisit during the red-shirt protest in April. Besides, Police General Patcharawat was seen as loyal to ex-premier Thaksin. He used force to disperse the yellow-shirt PAD protesters on 7 October 2008, when two people were killed and scores injured. A month before his mandatory retirement, the National Anti-Corruption Commission found Patcharawat guilty of malfeasance in the crackdown on the PAD protesters. Patcharawat resigned but Abhisit threatened to block his resignation and fire him instead.[64] However, this did not happen. Patcharawat retired as scheduled while the Abhisit government resolved to have him removed retroactively. This was understandable because during the conflict rumour had it that Defence Minister General Prawit would step down, causing concern about the stability of the coalition government.[65] This, too, did not happen.

In addition to the police-chief appointment, there were conflicts between the Democrat and Bhumjaithai parties over the annual reshuffle of provincial governors and permanent secretaries of several ministries.[66] Provincial governors play a strategic role in serving the interests of political parties in the general election. The Bhumjaithai Party has successfully consolidated its power through reshuffling in the Interior, Commerce, and Transport Ministries. At the Interior Ministry, for example, the party has its men as Permanent Secretary and Director General of all of the most powerful departments in the ministry. However, the party failed to control the appointment of high-ranking police officials, which was more under the control of the Democrat Party.[67]

Conflict over the appointment of bureaucrats came to light in the appointment of the new Permanent Secretary for Commerce. The Bhumjaithai Party, which is in charge of the Commerce Ministry, preferred that Yanyong Puangrach, Director General of the Internal Trade Department, become the new Permanent Secretary. However, Abhisit opposed this, reportedly as a direct response to the Bhumjaithai Party's blocking of his choice for the new police chief.[68] It took Commerce Minister Porntiva Nakasai a great deal of effort to get Yanyong appointed. It was reported that another reason Abhisit was reluctant to appoint Yanyong was simply because the latter once spoke to him in a disrespectful manner at a Cabinet meeting, causing Abhisit such embarrassment that Yanyong had to be asked to leave the meeting. Yanyong's show of insolence thus caused him a delay in his appointment.[69] A dispute within the Ministry of Commerce over the reshuffle and other internal management matters between the Bhumjaithai minister and the Democrat Deputy Minister Alongkorn Polabutr was also reported. Discord between the Democrat Deputy Prime Minister in Charge of Economic Affairs, Korbsak Sabhavasu, and the Bhumjaithai Commerce Minister over a crop mortgage scheme was another source of conflict between the two coalition parties. In early November it was reported that Korbsak did not approve the sale of 200,000 tons of tapioca flour to China because the sale did not first get approval from the cabinet. This made Bhumjaithai Party officials furious.

Another good example of the infighting between the two main coalition parties was over the rail strike in the south. The State Railway of Thailand (SRT) labour union called for a train stoppage in mid-October after an engineer was dismissed.[70] In early October a train derailed in Prachaup Khiri Khan at Khao Tao station, resulting in seven deaths and eighty-eight injuries. The driver of the ill-fated train passed out at the controls and the automatic brake failed to function. The strike was aimed at protesting against the failure of management to protect a worker from risk. The union argued that sending out trains that were not in good condition could put the lives of both passengers and workers in danger. The union demanded that the SRT Governor resign for his incompetent management, that the workers who joined the strike not be punished, and that the locomotives in the deep south must be maintained in good working condition. The suspension of rail services left thousands of passengers stranded at several stations in the southern provinces.[71]

The Bhumjaithai Transport Minister together with the SRT management fired several workers, including the union leaders. In addition, the SRT management recruited qualified drivers of the locomotives to replace those on strike and took over the trains from the strikers with the help of the police and the military. Pressured by the general public, who believed that the SRT labour union was holding the Thai people hostage by suspending services, the Democrats, whose strongest constituency is in the south, mediated the solution to the problem. Democrat Deputy Interior Minister Thaworn Senneam reached an agreement in talks with the union leaders. But the Bhumjaithai Party leaders stated in public that they would not abide by the agreement, insisting instead that the workers and the union leaders must be sacked after instigating the stoppage.[72] Transport Minister Sopon Zarum openly called for Abhisit to take full responsibility if the sacked union workers were reinstated.[73] The strike thus created a rift within the coalition government because the ruling Democrat Party cut a deal with the labour union without consulting Sopon, who, as Transport Minister, should have been responsible for dealing with the matter.

The southern SRT union workers have a close connection with the PAD, and union leader Sawit Kaeowan is one of the second-generation leaders of the PAD, holding a position in the PAD's newly founded New Politics party (NPP). After the Transport Minister fired the union workers and the Abhisit government seemed to do nothing, Suriyasai Katasila, Secretary General of the PAD and of the NPP, came out to challenge the Democrat Party for yielding easily to the pressure of the Bhumjaithai Party. Suriyasai openly asked whether the Democrats still wanted to be friends with or foes of the PAD and the NPP. In another development, the Transport Minister turned the crisis into a golden opportunity by proposing a new plan to reform the debt-ridden SRT.[74] Actually, before the October stoppage, the railway union called for a strike in June in protest against the Abhisit government's plan to restructure the SRT.[75] The union ended its strike after the government accepted its demand for a delay in its privatization plan.

The rift between the two major coalition parties could be seen in other areas as well. For example, Bhumjaithai House Speaker Chai Chidchob, father of Newin Chidchob, the de facto leader of the party, showed his dissatisfaction with Abhisit by abruptly cancelling a parliamentary session in late August in order to block the moving of the 2010 budget bill. This was in response to the cutting of his 700 million baht special budget for the House of Representatives that supported seminars and trips abroad by MPs.[76] Moreover, the Bhumjaithai Party went ahead and submitted its own version of a political amnesty bill to Parliament without consulting the ruling Democrats, who opposed the move. This was done through the Bhumjaithai House Speaker putting the draft bill on the House agenda. However, the bill met with little enthusiasm from all sides concerned.

After all these rifts, what has held the two parties together? The simple answer is Thaksin Shinawatra. If the House of Representatives is dissolved and an election is held today, Thaksin would more than likely take over the helm. Therefore, both parties need time to strengthen their position. The paradox of Thai politics at this juncture is this: if an election were to be held today and Thaksin's PTP wins, there would likely be more violence and turmoil in the country. But if Thaksin has to be kept at bay, as has been the case since the coup, then the government in power cannot run its usual business, as the Abhisit government demonstrated throughout 2009.

The Spectre of Thaksin

Fugitive ex-premier Thaksin Shinawatra, a nomad in a Deleuzian sense,[77] has become a thorn in the side of Thai politics since his ouster in the 19 September 2006 coup. Despite leading a nomadic life, Thaksin's movements outside the territory of the Thai state have had an enormous impact on the political landscape of the country.[78] Unarguably, Thaksin was and still is a divisive force in Thai society and politics. A single day does not pass in which his activities are not covered, by either the Thai or the international media. Thaksin has thus become a spectre haunting the Thai establishment and his political opponents alike ever since he was forced to leave the country.[79] Thaksin adroitly exploits all means of modern communication technology available in a globalized world to gain access to his supporters inside Thailand. These range from a video-linked phone-in during the rallies of his political arm, the UDD, better known as the red shirts, to the launching of his own websites www.thaksinlives.com and www.thaksinlives.com/radio, to Twitter on thaksinlives and thaksinbiz, and to Facebook, SMS, personal interviews, articles for the international press, and direct calls to his supporters in

Thailand.[80] A "Thaksin Beef Noodle" restaurant was recently opened in Singapore and others will probably be popping up elsewhere.[81]

Dressed in a red shirt, Thaksin celebrated his sixtieth birthday on 26 July 2009, telecasting from Dubai to greet his well-wishers at different locations throughout Thailand. In his birthday speech, Thaksin announced the setting up of a "global TV network" to promote Thai OTOP (One Tambon One Product) products, to broadcast reality shows about Thai poverty and possible solutions, and to provide educational programmes for Thai students.[82] Thaksin was said to be making direct calls to talk to taxi drivers and to people in the countryside. These kinds of borderless communication technologies enable Thaksin to conduct his political campaign in an unfettered and nomadic manner. In short, these technologies have helped keep Thaksin vividly in the consciousness of his supporters and opponents. The profound impact of Thaksin's telephone calls could clearly be seen when such calls helped a PTP candidate in Sakon Nakhon win by a landslide a by-election over a candidate from the arch-rival Bhumjaithai Party in June 2009. Thaksin made his calls to *kamnans* and village headmen for the support of the PTP candidate.[83] Moreover, Thailand's first Internet-based television station was officially launched on 23 November. This twenty-four-hour service, "Voice TV", is owned by two of Thaksin's offspring and is aimed at younger-generation viewers. The service is also made available to all 500,000 DTV satellite subscribers, who are mainly red shirts.[84] Thaksin's media moves forced the Abhisit government to order all state agencies to launch their own Facebook and Twitter accounts to keep the public informed around the clock concerning government activities.[85]

Thaksin's latest move in early November to have Cambodian Prime Minister Hun Sen appoint him the Cambodian Government's economic advisor has strained fragile Thai-Cambodian relations. The Abhisit government perceived the appointment as interference in Thailand's internal politics because Thaksin was a convict and should be extradited to serve his term rather than being appointed state advisor. It also showed the Cambodian Government's disrespect for the Thai judicial system. Premier Hun Sen openly announced that he considered Thaksin a political victim and would never send him back to the Thai authorities. Hun Sen further fuelled the anger of the Abhisit government by stating that he would provide asylum to former Prime Minister Thaksin if he so wished. What causes great concern to the Abhisit government is the possibility that Thaksin would use nearby Cambodia as his political base to attack the government.

Meanwhile the Abhisit government saw the incident as a golden opportunity to elevate its political ratings, which had reached their lowest point, by choosing to play the dangerous ultra-patriotic card in the same fashion as its political ally outside the Parliament, namely, the PAD.[86] If Thaksin has at his disposal the PTP to fight his causes in Parliament and the red-shirt UDD in the street, then the Abhisit government also has its Democrat and other coalition parties to support it in Parliament and the PAD in the street. Each side of the conflict has its own television station to produce and circulate its own propaganda: ASTV for the yellow-shirt PAD, P Station for the red-shirt UDD, and the state-run NBT (formerly channel 11) for the Abhisit government.

The Abhisit government recalled its Ambassador to Cambodia, arguing that the appointment was both harmful to the Thai judicial system and that it adversely affected Thai public sentiment.[87] Amid its own ultra-patriotic hype, the Abhisit government threatened to revoke unilaterally all memorandums of understanding with Cambodia.[88] The Cambodian Government retaliated by recalling its Ambassador to Thailand and threatening to close the border between the two countries. The tension has put Thai-Cambodian trade, worth trillions of baht, in disarray.

The worsening relations between the two neighbouring countries, that are critical to the stability of the ASEAN community, has prompted deep concern among other ASEAN leaders. Surin Pitsuwan, a Democrat Party member and Secretary General of ASEAN, suggested that the Abhisit government accept Indonesia's offer to mediate the dispute. But Abhisit declined, citing the matter as an internal affair that would not hinder the work of ASEAN. Abhisit has viewed the whole situation through the lens of ultra-patriotism, seeing Thaksin, a convict and now a traitor, and not the socio-political structure of the country, as the only cause of Thailand's problems and seeing Prime Minister Hun Sen as being malignly influenced by Thaksin.

In addition to Thaksin and his allies, a variety of political moves on the part of the Abhisit government have also helped evoke the spectre of Thaksin in the imagination of the Thai public. News of the revoking of Thaksin's police rank and royal decorations, for example, have further driven a wedge between those already divided by their support for or opposition to Thaksin,[89] as had the earlier revoking of Thaksin's Thai passport. The characterization of anyone who criticizes the government as Thaksin's "proxy," a traitor, or someone who is disloyal to the Thai monarchy has further intensified the divide. The hatred of Thaksin among the Thai establishment and the Abhisit government has helped to create the spectre of Thaksin to such a level that it has become a frame of reference and a guideline for the Abhisit government to administer the country. In short, the elites' hatred of Thaksin has created the justification for the actions against him.

In October 2009, Thaksin called upon his PTP to abandon the agreement on the amendments to the 2007 constitution and seek instead to reinstate the 1997 Constitution, which had been abolished by the September 2006 coup. Faced with this predicament, Prime Minister Abhisit threatened to stop the amendment process. Actually, the Democrat Party was never enthusiastic about supporting these amendments. It did so after being strongly urged to do so by its coalition partners. The amendment process was part of the deal the Democrat Party made with its coalition partners while forming the coalition. Abhisit slowed the process by first setting up a national reconciliation committee to study how to amend the Constitution before proposing to call for a referendum on the amendment bill.[90] Indeed, a termination of the amendment process would be an advantage to the Democrat Party — and the Party could absolve itself of breaking the deal with its coalition partners. So far, the Democrat Party is the only party which has not been affected by Article 237 of the 2007 Constitution. This article, which is one of the six articles the coalition partners wanted to amend, concerns political parties and the punishment of party executives. If electoral fraud is found involving one or more of the executives, the entire party has to be disbanded and its executives barred from politics for five years. Several coalition parties in the Abhisit government were affected by this article.[91]

During the red shirts' rallies that ultimately led to the bloody Songkarn riot, Thaksin video-linked phone-in calls to the rally every night to incite the protesters. On the night of 27 March Thaksin openly named General Prem Tinsulanonda as an architect of the 19 September 2006 coup and revealed that Prem was the man he once labeled "a charismatic extra-constitutional figure" who, despite being a Privy Council President, always meddled in Thai politics.[92] On another night during the same rally, Thaksin urged red-shirt protesters throughout the country to come out in force for a mass protest to fight for "major change in the country".[93] When Thaksin successfully persuaded General Chavalit to become Chairman of his PTP, it caused a big stir in Thai establishment circles because General Chavalit's diplomatic clout and military connections could strengthen the party. General Prem, who rarely talks to the media, came out in public to warn General Chavalit to "think carefully", otherwise his move would risk being treated as "an act of betrayal against the country".[94] Not deterred by General Prem's admonition, a group of retired but still influential military and police officers who were Thaksin's former classmates at the Armed Forces Academies Preparatory School flocked to join the PTP.[95] Finally, when his red-shirt supporters called for a mass demonstration to take place on 28 November, Thaksin called it off, reasoning that the timing would not be appropriate as it was close to the King's birthday. Red-shirt leaders then postponed the rally "indefinitely".[96] Thaksin's political clout thus remains omnipresent. However, it was speculated in the media that the postponement was a Thaksin gesture to make a deal with the government: if he is allowed to return to Thailand without a jail term, then he would keep the red shirts from agitating against the government. There was no response from the government.[97]

Role of the Military

There has been a critical shift in the role played by the Thai army in its relations with the Thai public. In the past, the people of Thailand dared not come out to demonstrate in force for fear of being used as a pretext for the army to stage a coup. But now, Thai people are adopting protest and demonstration as a means to create situations where the army can intervene in politics to get rid of their enemies. The PAD's rallies against Thaksin and his proxy governments served this purpose well. Second, the armed forces have been the greatest beneficiary of Thailand's recent political turmoil. Their annual budget has increased substantially since the coup in 2006. Prior to the coup, the military worked with a limited budget of 86 billion baht. It rose dramatically to 115 billion baht in 2007, 143 billion baht in 2008, and 167 billion baht in 2009 — an almost 100 per cent increase within three years. It was reported in late September that the armed forces received another 10 billion baht while Abhisit attended the G-8 meeting in New York.[98] Allegedly, this was in exchange for the army's promise not to launch a coup while he was away. An increase in the budget is thus inseparable from an increase in power.

Third, the pattern of military dominance in Thai politics has changed from that of the "white knight" who appears in times of crisis to rescue the nation by shaking things up and then setting the new rules of the political game, to that of the critical referee. Action or inaction on the part of the armed forces in a critical political situation means the survival of the sitting civilian government. The military refused to follow the orders of two civilian governments of the PPP to stop the PAD's siege of Government House and the airports in 2008 but suggested instead that the government either resign or dissolve the Parliament. However, it was more than ready to disperse the red-shirt protesters during the bloody Songkarn riot. Both incidents made a great difference to the governments concerned. Therefore, a sitting civilian government now has to rely heavily upon the support of the armed forces to stabilize its regime. Under these circumstances, the armed forces are not one part of the state machinery but acting as a state within the state.

Thus, previous attempts to depoliticize the military and make it subordinate to civilian authority, as in all mature democracies, have completely failed. The army has recently insisted that to be professional it needs to be "independent" from politics. The army chief once argued that a political problem must be resolved by political means. The army does not belong to the government. Rather, it belongs to the country and the Thai people. And its primary role is to protect the throne. This is quite interesting because the army now is not playing the role of power holder but acting as the decisive factor in the political arena. The military now can control Thai politics from behind the scenes. The Thai military has successfully transformed itself from the guardian of democracy to the self-proclaimed protector of the country and the monarchy. Both goals seem to be beyond the capability of the civilian government and politicians, ultimately leaving the task to the armed forces. In this regard, the Abhisit government, which the armed forces helped install, is experiencing a delusion of grandeur. The real power maker is the military.

Fourth, the resurgence of the military in politics was made possible by the imposition of the Internal Security Act. This act gave a new lease on life to the Internal Security Operations Command (ISOC), which plays an important role in internal security. The Prime Minister assumes the titular leadership of ISOC while the army chief is the real power holder. When a state of emergency is declared or the Internal Security Act is invoked, it allows the army chief to mobilize troops to maintain peace and order. The Abhisit government has invoked the Internal Security Act several times to control the red-shirt rallies. The military has full authority under the security act to do whatever it deems necessary. In addition to the security act, the armed forces also have the Defence Ministry Act, which prohibits the Prime Minister from meddling with the reshuffle of the military.

Finally, the armed forces have shown that they are masters of the political game during the recent Thai-Cambodian row. While the Abhisit government shallowly assumed the ultra-patriotic mode at the expense of the national interest,[99] the military, on the contrary, chose to befriend their Cambodian counterparts. The military argued that the conflict had been between the two governments but not the armed forces of the two countries. They even staged a friendly two-day meeting of the General Border Committee (GBC) in Pattaya to settle border disputes through peaceful means. The Thai and Cambodian armed forces agreed to cooperate at all levels to ensure the safety and peace of the people of the two countries.[100] It is evident here that the Thai armed forces do not act as a security arm of the government. Rather, they have become their own boss. This is not a good sign for democratic government. Taken together, the armed forces are now more powerful than at any time over the past two decades.

Conclusion

Thailand's political landscape by the end of 2009 was still plagued with problems emanating from the disruption of the democratic form of government by the most recent coup.[101] In medical terms the body politic of Thailand has been really sick since the coup. All social and political institutions are facing a crisis of credibility and hence legitimacy. After three years of political turbulence, Thai politics has come to resemble greatly the Japanese Bunraku puppet theatre, as aptly described by the French literary critic Roland Barthes[102] in the sense that all political forces have come out into the open. Nobody is hiding behind any cover and nobody is spared from the political mess, including the Privy Council president. However, in the midst of the crisis, the military has emerged as the "biggest winner".[103]

The political awakening of the Thai rural masses and the ascendancy of the military in Thai politics would be the two main contending forces that will shape Thai politics in 2010.

Notes

I would like to thank John Benson, Carlo Bonura, Geoff Husic, Coreen Phuengkasem, and Thanasak Saijampa for their kind support.

[1]   The two Prime Ministers before him were Samak Sundaravej and Somchai Wongsawat, both from the People's Power Party (PPP), the reincarnation of ousted Prime Ministers Thaksin Shinawatra's Thai Rak Thai (TRT) Party, which was dissolved by the junta-appointed Constitutional Tribunal in May 2007. Samak died of liver cancer in late November.

[2]   "PM Abhisit Vows to be 'Prime Minister for Everybody'", *The Nation* (online), 18 December 2008.

[3]   Both General Anupong Paochinda and Newin Chidchob, a leader of the defectors' faction, became "persons of the year" of *The Nation* newspaper. See "Persons of the Year, Masters of the Game", *The Nation* (online), 29 December 2008.

[4]   Sanitsuda Ekachai, "Some Taking Matters into Own Hands", *Bangkok Post* (online), 18 December 2008.

[5]   Veera Prateepchaikul, "Into the Unknown with Newin", *Bangkok Post* (online), 22 December 2008.

[6]   Jacques Rancière, *Hatred of Democracy*, trans. Steven Corcoran (London: Verso, 2006).

7   See, for example, Erik M. Kuhonta, "The Paradox of Thailand's 'People's Constitution'", *Asian Survey* 48, no. 3 (2008): 373–92, and Allen Hicken, "The 2007 Thai Constitution: A Return to Politics Past", *Crossroads* 19, no. 1 (2007): 128–60.

8   Guy Debord, *The Society of the Spectacle,* trans. Donald Nicholson-Smith (New York: Zone Books, 1995/2002). In Thailand this means a society in which images replace substances, rhetoric takes over speech, and sensation and distorted information overshadow accurate information.

9   *Bangkok Post*, 22 February 2009, p. 1.

10 Surasak Glahan, "Man Gets 10 Years For Insulting Monarchy", *Bangkok Post*, 4 August 2009, p. 1.

11 "Royal Slur Gets Da Torpedo 18 Years Jail", *Bangkok Post*, 29 August 2009, p. 1.

12 "Prachatai's Webmaster Held by CSD", *Bangkok Post*, 7 March 2009, p. 3.

13 "International Scholars Call for Reform of Thailand's Lèse Majesté Law", Press Release, 4 March 2009. In May 2008, a former Prime Minister's Office Minister, Jakrapob Penkair was forced to resign after being accused of *lèse-majesté* in a talk to the Foreign Correspondents Club of Thailand (FCCT) in Bangkok on 29 August 2007. Jakrapob now lives in exile.

14 Thaksin was sentenced in October 2008 by the Supreme Court's Criminal Division for Political Office Holders to two years in jail for abuse of power in helping his then-wife Khunying Potjaman Damapong buy a prime piece of land in Bangkok from the state at much less than the market price in 2003, while serving as prime minister.

15 "Rubber Sapling Scandal: Teary Newin Gets a New Lease on Life, Leaving Many Worried", *The Nation* (online), 22 September 2009.

16 "OAG Furious Over Sapling Case Fiasco", *Bangkok Post* (online), 23 September 2009, and "Graft Acquital: Prosecutors Blame AEC for Failed Case", *The Nation* (online), 23 September 2009.

17 "Rubber Sapling Verdict: Leaking of Verdict Groundless: Suthep", *The Nation* (online), 24 September 2009.

18 "Rumours on HM's Health are Deplorable", *The Nation* (online), 16 October 2009, and "Princess Says King 'Doing Well'", *Bangkok Post*, 17 October 2009, p. 1.

19 For an analysis of the Thai monarchy, see James Ockey, "Monarch, Monarchy, Succession and Stability in Thailand", *Asia Pacific Viewpoint* 46, no. 2 (2005): 115–27.

20 Assawin Pakkawan, "Changes Urged to Reporting Casualty Numbers in the South", *Bangkok Post*, 27 September 2009, p. 4, and <http://www.deepsouthwatch.org/nod/343>.

21 "Court Clears Military in Tak Bai Case", *Bangkok Post*, 30 May 2009, p. 3.

22 "Fixing South 'Will Take 20 Years'", *Bangkok Post*, 8 August 2009, p. 3.

23 "Chavalit Pushing Special Zone for South", *The Nation* (online), 2 November 2009.

24 "About Politics: Sing Your Lungs Out", *Bangkok Post*, 31 October 2009, p. 12.

25 "Flagged Down", *The Nation* (online), 9 October 2009.

26 Apinya Wipatayotin and Mongkol Bangprapa, "PM Moves to Free Rayong Projects from Suspension", *Bangkok Post*, 31 October 2009, p. 4.

27 Bhanupong Nidhiprabha, "The Hard Road Ahead for Thailand's Economic Recovery", *Asian Economic Papers* 8, no. 3 (2009): 113–37.

28 Phusadee Arunmas, "Export Slowdown Eases With 3% Slide in October", *Bangkok Post*, 21 November 2009, p. B1.

29 Chatrudee Theparat, "Chumpol: 14m Arrivals Still Possible", *Bangkok Post*, 21 November 2009, p. B10.

30 "Korn Sees Employment Returning to Normal", *Bangkok Post*, 28 November 2009, p. B1.

31 "Dubai Debt Crisis Rocks Markets", *Bangkok Post*, 28 November 2009, p. 1.

32 "Ministers Set to Discuss Dubai, Dong", *Bangkok Post*, 29 November 2009, p. 1.

33 "Losing Our Sense of Identity", *The Nation* (online), 15 September 2009.

34 "The Poor Understand the Word 'Use' and 'Abuse'", *The Nation* (online), 25 September 2009.

35 "Abhisit Gets Radio Death Threats", *Bangkok Post*, 21 November 2009, p. 1.

36 "Repatriation of Hmong", *The Nation* (online), 28 December 2009, "General Insists Hmong Head Home Voluntarily", *Bangkok Post* (online), 29 December 2009; "Govt Boots out Hmong to World Fury", *Bangkok Post* 27 December 2009, p. 1.

37 "Rogue Generals on Thaksin's Payroll Cry for Final Showdown", *The Nation* (online), 29 December 2009.

38 "Read All About It—It's a 'Civil War'", *Bangkok Post* (online), 29 December 2009; "Prem Plays Down His Wearing of Military Attire", *The Nation* (online), 30 December 2009. The recommended article is Chirmsak Pinthong, "Rao kamlang you nai yuk songkram klangmueang" (We are in the era of civil war), *Naew Na* daily, 28 December 2009: 3.

39 "Army Determined to Prevent Bloodshed and a Coup", *The Nation* (online), 29 December 2009.

40 "Daeng puen krung klang khom kor kor tor kheu tam phaeo ban" (Red stirs the city, angry at EC, threatens to burn house), *Thai Post*, 24 December 2009: 1–2.

41 "Apichart to Decide Democrat Party Case after New Year", *The Nation* (online), 23 December 2009.

42 "Jatuporn Reveals More Papers", *Bangkok Post* (online), 23 December 2009.

43 "Jatuporn Insists Govt Plan to Kill Thaksin", *The Nation* (online), 23 December 2009.

44 "No Plan for War with Cambodia, Says Abhisit", *Bangkok Post*, 26 December 2009, p. 1.

45 "Thaksin Supporters Flock to Cambodia", *Bangkok Post*, 20 December 2009.

46 James Ockey, "Thailand in 2008: Democracy and Street Politics", in *Southeast Asian Affairs 2009*, edited by Daljit Singh (Singapore: Institute of Southeast Asian Studies, 2009) pp. 315–33.

47   John Funston, ed. *Divided Over Thaksin: Thailand's Coup and Problematic Transition* (Singapore: Institute of Southeast Asian studies, 2009).

48   *Bangkok Post*, 15 January 2009, p. 1.

49   *Matachon Daily*, 14 October 2009, p. 1.

50   Apiradee Treerutkuarkul, "Health Procurement Projects Put on Hold", *Bangkok Post*, 3 October 2009, p. 2.

51   *Bangkok Post*, 28 January 2009, p. 2, and 4 February 2009, p. 1.

52   *Bangkok Post*, 21 February 2009, p. 1.

53   "Health Officials Linked to Equipment Scam", *Bangkok Post* (online), 14 October 2009.

54   <http://blog.nationmultimedia.com/thanong/2009/06/03/entry-1>.

55   Phusadee Arunmas, "Govt Scores Poorly on Economy", *Bangkok Post*, 30 November 2009, p. 1.

56   Phusadee Arunmas, "Business to Give Its View on Economy", *Bangkok Post*, 29 November 2009, p. 3.

57   "Poll Faults *Kem Kaeng* Scheme", *Bangkok Post*, 4 October 2009, p. 3.

58   *Bangkok Post*, 9 January 2009, p. 1.

59   *The Nation* (online), 5 October 2009.

60   "Where Did Mr. Nice Get So Slippery?" *Bangkok Post*, 12 September 2009, p. 12.

61   Tulsathit Taptim, "Are All the PM's Men Revolting", *The Nation* (online), 21 August 2009.

62   "Abhisit says He's Still in Driving Seat", *Bangkok Post*, 22 August 2009, p. 1.

63   "Poll: Police Chief Delay Due to PM's Interference", *Bangkok Post*, 18 October 2009, p. 3.

64   "The Big Issue: Police Chief Blues", *Bangkok Post*, 13 September 2009, p. 2.

65   "Prawit Vows to Stay on in Defence", *Bangkok Post*, 12 September 2009, p. 3.

66   "Coalition Discord Set to Heat Up", *Bangkok Post*, 2 September 2009, p. 1.

67   *Thai Rath* (online), 24 November 2009; Piyanart Srivalo, "Ruling Coalition is Slowly Drifting Apart", *The Nation,* 2 December 2009, p. 16A.

68   Piyanart Srivalo, "Top Appointments Renew Coalition Tension", *The Nation* (online), 2 September 2009.

69   "Sorry About My Choice of Words", *Bangkok Post*, 19 September 2009, p. 12.

70   *Bangkok Post*, 17 October 2009, p. 1.

71   "Southern PAD Chapter Back Railway Union", *Bangkok Post* (online), 23 October 2009. Within a week, the stoppage cost the SRT 43 million baht in damages: 25 million baht in lost passengers and 18 million baht in lost freight charges.

72   "Not Another Coalition Scrap", *Bangkok Post*, 7 November 2009, p. 12.

73   "More SRT Rallies Mean No Resolution: PM", *The Nation* (online), 4 November 2009; "Sophon Would Never Hold Me Responsible: PM", *The Nation* (online), 5 November 2009.

74   Piyaporn Wongruang, "Getting the Rail Network Back on Track", *Bangkok Post*, 8 November 2009, p. 4.

75 "Please Sir, Stop the Strike", *Bangkok Post*, 27 June 2009, p. 12.

76 "Has Abhisit Begun to Regret that Embrace? *The Nation* (online), 27 August 2009.

77 Gilles Deleuze and Felix Guattari, *A Thousand Plateaus: Capitalism and Schizophrenia*, trans. Brian Mussumi (Minneapolis: University of Minnesota Press, 1987), pp. 351–427.

78 Martin Petty, "Thaksin Raises Stakes with New Offensive", *Bangkok Post*, 7 November 2009, p. 9.

79 The idea of spectre is borrowed from Jacques Derrida, *The Specters of Marx*, trans. Peggy Kamuf (New York: Routledge, 1994), and Jean Baudrillard, *The Mirror of Production*, trans. Mark Poster (St. Louis: Telos Press, 1975).

80 "Depending on Tactics?" [*Panhar you thi luk kheaw?*] *Thai Rath* (online), 2 November 2009.

81 Pavin Chachavalpongpun, "Where's the Beef? In a Name, Plenty", *Bangkok Post*, 5 December 2009, p. 11.

82 Details of the event are provided by Tulsathit Taptim, "Follow it with the Electors: Now, the Real 'Big Surprise'", *The Nation* (online), 27 July 2009.

83 Aekasach Sattaburuth, "Puea Thai Wins by a Landslide", *Bangkok Post*, (online), 22 June 2009.

84 "Thaksin Television?" *The Nation* (online), 24 November 2009.

85 *The Nation* (International Edition), 16 November 2009.

86 "Support for Govt Rockets after Protest", *Bangkok Post*, 7 November 2009, p. 3.

87 Achara Ashayagachat, "Recalling Ambassador Seen as 'Over-Reaction' in Dispute", *Bangkok Post*, 7 November 2009, p. 3.

88 Wassana Nanuam, "Navy Chief Warns Govt on MoU", *Bangkok Post*, 21 November 2009, p. 3.

89 "Stripping Thaksin Medals Could Re-ignite Social Conflict", *Bangkok Post*, 1 November 2009, p. 3.

90 Kamol Hengkietisak, "Constitution Amendment Faces Hurdles", *Bangkok Post*, 17 October 2009, p. 10.

91 Other items to be amended include Article 190, which requires the government to seek approval from Parliament on all international agreements, and Article 265, which prohibits Cabinet members, Members of Parliament, their spouses, children, or people acting for Cabinet members, or Members of Parliament to hold any positions in government agencies or state enterprises.

92 "Prem, Surayud 'Behind Coup'", *Bangkok Post,* 28 March 2009, p. 1.

93 "Thaksin: No Negotiation", *Bangkok Post*, 4 April 2009, p. 1.

94 "Puea Thai Slams Prem over Warning to Chavalit", *Bangkok Post*, 18 October 2009, p. 3.

95 "Chavalit's Intrigues only Add Fuel to Fire", *Bangkok Post*, 24 October 2009, p. 2.

96 "Red Shirted Protest Postponed Indefinitely: Veera", *The Nation* (online), 25 November 2009.

[97]   "The Big Issue: Wheeler Dealer", *Bangkok Post*, 29 November 2009, p. 2.

[98]   "The Public Purse", *Bangkok Post*, 27 September 2009, p. 2.

[99]   Supalak Ganjanakhundee, "Road to Nowhere", *The Nation*, 2 December 2009, p. 16A.

[100] Wassana Nanuam, "Border Rows to be Fixed 'Amicably'", *Bangkok Post*, 28 November 2009, p. 2.

[101] A detailed account of this period is provided by Chairat Charoensin-o-larn, "Military Coup and Democracy in Thailand", in *Divided over Thaksin: Thailand's Coup and Problematic Transition*, edited by John Funston (Singapore: Institute of Southeast Asian Studies, 2009), pp. 49–79.

[102] Roland Barthes, "Lesson in Writing", in *Image Music Text*, trans. Stephen Heath (London: Fontana, 1977), pp. 170–78.

[103] Chang Noi (pseud.), "Military Biggest Winner in Political Conflict", *The Nation* (online), 2 February 2009.

"UNITY" AS A DISCOURSE IN THAILAND'S POLARIZED POLITICS

Pavin Chachavalpongpun

On the night of 19 September 2006, the military rolled its tanks onto the streets of Bangkok; it was Thailand's seventeenth military coup since the country abolished the absolute monarchy and adopted democracy in 1932. General Sonthi Boonyaratglin, leader of the coup, rationalized the military intervention by stressing, "Thai society has become polarised as never before, with mass confrontations between supporters and opponents of the former prime minister (Thaksin Shinawatra) threatening to turn violent."[1] Sonthi was referring to the months-long protestations staged by the People's Alliance for Democracy (PAD) which began in late May 2006 against Thaksin. The PAD, similarly, claimed that the Thaksin government tended to seek benefits for itself in an illegal way which led to social disunity.[2]

Three years on, in a move to resolve the protracted political deadlock, Prime Minister Abhisit Vejjajiva called on his Cabinet members and all Thais to do their duty to help return Thailand to a society in harmony. Abhisit said, "Everyone should think of what we can do to enjoy normality again."[3] In reality, the gap between the two opposing political camps, one that supposedly supports Thaksin and the other that protects the interests of the Bangkok elite, has remained wide and is indeed threatening the much-celebrated Thai discourse of "unity". This is taking place in the country which has never been officially colonized and is proud of its independence thanks to, as claimed by Thai leaders, the national trait of unity.[4] Recent developments within the realm of Thai politics where the Bangkok elites and red shirts have competed fiercely in the safeguarding of their own interests seem to suggest that the underlying premises of the notion of unity might now be obsolete.

PAVIN CHACHAVALPONGPUN is Fellow and Lead Researcher for Political and Strategic Affairs, ASEAN Studies Centre at the Institute of Southeast Asian Studies.

This short essay argues that the discourse of unity has always been in the jealous possession of the Thai traditional elite. Unity is indeed a top-down concept, defined and driven by the leaders. They urge their citizens to uphold unity particularly in times of crisis. There are obvious advantages of unity. It is important to recognize that unity had served the country well in the past and allowed political leaders to rally support from the public against internal and external threats. However, equally important is the fact that the discourse of unity also has an unseen usefulness for the leaders. It has been employed to strengthen the power of the ruling elite and at the same time to curb views and ideas that could jeopardize their political position. Unity in the political sense signals the quality of oneness, sameness, and agreement. It is often defined as the state of being undivided or unbroken completeness or totality with nothing wanting. Unity can denote a combining of all the parts, elements, and individuals into an effective whole.[5] Hence, unity can be antithetical to diversity, dissension, and pluralism. It can serve to maintain the political status quo, to alienate all other alternatives in politics, and even to delay any development toward democracy since the latter promotes respect for diversity and dissimilarity. From this perspective, the elite's call on the Thais to practice unity is not necessarily contributory to the solution of the crisis; they instead choose to close their eyes to the different political beliefs that already prevail. With this in mind, the state-endorsed reconciliation policy needs a serious reinterpretation.

The fundamental question is: For what and whom is the unity? In the current struggle for power among various political players, it is clear that the Bangkok elite have used the discourse of unity as their weapon to isolate Thaksin and his followers while accusing them of breaking up the completeness of the Thai nation with their dissenting political viewpoints. Moreover, there has also been an attempt among the ruling elite to merge the discourse of unity with the concept of Thainess. Those who create disunity might not be "Thai", as they care little about what constitutes and consolidates the nation. In this view, a nation, without unity, may exist, but it is in danger of social and political instability. This justification becomes a vital ingredient for the traditional elite to maintain its hegemonic position in the Thai state.[6] However, today, the red-shirts are challenging the elitist concept of unity. In fact, one of their leaders, Jakrapob Penkair, forewarned, "Little time is left for reconciliation."[7] They have pressurized the Bangkok elite to come to terms with the seismic shift in the people's political thoughts, forcing them to broaden the political domain and compromise with diverse opinions as witnessed in other normal democratic societies.

Unity as a Political Device

Unity in the Thai consciousness is a malleable and manipulative notion. It is normally translated into Thai as *khwam samakki*, but this translation is not cast in iron. It is sometimes referred to *khwam pen an nung an diew kan*, or oneness, and can be interchangeable with *ekkachan*, or consensus. During the height of colonialism, the Siamese monarchs incessantly called for unity among their subordinates in order to survive the threat of the Europeans. Matthew Copeland, however, argued that this exercise was not only about the struggle between Siam and the West, but also between a succession of Siamese rulers and their recalcitrant subjects.[8] King Chulalongkorn (1868–1910) opposed the Western concept of democracy because he claimed that it could bring disunity among the Siamese.[9] Likewise, King Vajiravudh (1910–25), son of Chulalongkorn, banned the first text on economics in Thai because it was not suitable for Thai society. He argued that, apart from the Thai monarch, Thai people were all equal under him. Thus, economics might cause disunity or disruption because it was concerned with social strata of rich and poor.[10] During his reign, the Chinese were also made outcasts in Siamese society, and seen as a menace to his unified kingdom. He wrote the tract, *The Jews of the East*, criticizing the ethnic Chinese, particularly the immigrant traders, who allegedly sought to deepen the social division, in part because of their economic affluence in Siam. Thus, the discourse of unity is so elastic that it has been used not only to contest different ideologies but also different races who could pose a potential threat to royal power.

The elite's need to inculcate a sense of national unity in order to lock the people inside the cage of conformity continued intermittently throughout the Cold War period. In the 1970s as Thailand was ruled by a series of despotic regimes, the military elite made use of their radio stations to broadcast two programmes daily at 6:45 a.m. and 6:00 p.m. to call for order and unity and to stimulate nationalism and the awareness of national security amid communist threats from within and without.[11] The military depicted Thailand as being surrounded by all kinds of danger; only unity and strong leaders would be able to navigate the country out of such a precarious environment. This echoed the earlier statement made famous by wartime Prime Minister Field Marshal Phibun Songkhram (1938–44 and 1946–57) who reiterated, "When the country is undergoing crisis and is devoid of anything to cling to, just follow the leaders."[12] In this context, while unity was surely necessary in order to safeguard the nation, it was also used to nurture obedient citizens, and as a tool for regime consolidation. State media and education played an important role in ingraining unity in the people.

"Unity is Power" has become a famous national slogan endorsed by the Thai state which urged the Thais to unite and not to divide.[13] Nationalist songs were composed to remind the Thais that any ideology different from that of the state was intolerable. *Ru Rak Samakki* (Love Unity) and *Rak Kan Wai Thued* (Love Each Other), for example, tell the Thais to avoid disharmony, to love each other despite their different backgrounds, and to defend the monarch from internal and external challenges.[14] The obedient society, encapsulated within the discourse of unity, had governed Thai life at least until the advent of Thaksin in 2001.

The massacre of student demonstrators at Thammasat University in 1976 revealed how the state was willing to use force to restore the so-called national unity and to castigate non-conformists. Pro-democracy students protested against the return to Thailand of Field Marshal Thanom Kittikachon, a dictator who had been forced from power three years earlier but had then entered the country as a Buddhist monk. This movement began to take form after long years of dissatisfaction among intellectuals and university students who abhorred successive dictatorships and refused to constrain their unconventional political views within the state-constructed discourse of unity. The impulse of the ruling elite to prescribe unity and to set guidelines for members of society to obey for the ultimate maintenance of their political status, has been a deep-seated one throughout the modern history of Thailand. But during the six years of his rule, Thaksin gave the poor a relatively better life and stimulated their political thought, especially in a defiant manner, against the traditional elite. As the power of the rural dwellers grew and expanded thanks to Thaksin, the established trinity of institutions that had long called the shots in Thailand — the military, the monarchy, and the bureaucracy — encountered an emerging political culture different from their own. Consequently, they have undertaken efforts, more strenuously than ever, to advocate national unity and chastise those who allegedly instigate the opposite. They punished Thaksin with a military coup for rupturing consensus in Thai politics, a two-year jail term for his conflict of interest,[15] and seized parts of his assets on the ground that he abused his power while serving as Prime Minister. The struggle over the discourse of unity among Thais can at times be violent and oppressive. Charges of treason, rebellion, and *lèse-majesté* are nowadays common.

The Safeguarding of a United Society

Thailand is becoming an increasingly polarized nation. Ironically, while proudly presenting their country as truly democratic and even calling it the "Land of the Free", the traditional elite have refused to acknowledge the rising pluralism and free political thought in society. With the backing of factions in the military and the palace, the yellow-shirted PAD has proclaimed itself as the custodian of the political consensus where the power traditionally lies in the hands of the Bangkok elite. In this process, eliminating the elected Thaksin seemed legitimate because he challenged that political consensus and threatened national unity. This explained why the PAD's illegal activities, such as the occupation of Government House and the seizure of Bangkok's two airports, were blatantly tolerated since they were part of the battle against Thaksin and his proxies. Enraged by social injustice, the red shirts have railed against the traditional elite's double standards.[16] Today, the yellow and red shirts represent two different political stances, thus making any political reconciliation an uphill task. The PAD wants to further solidify the power of the traditional elite with its idea of "new politics" in which thirty per cent of a future parliament would consist of elected members while seventy per cent would be appointed.[17] On the other hand, the red shirts have campaigned for a more open political space and broad-based political participation, even when their political ideology has remained somewhat ill-defined. The red-shirted supporters in far-flung regions have thoroughly detested the Bangkok-centric politics.[18] What they really want is a sense of political inclusion, not unity nor political consensus. Jakrapob declared, "This is the last chance for the old powers and the aristocracy to stand with the people."[19]

As Thailand's power struggle became more intense, the traditional elite seemed to return to their usual stance of calling for unity in order to invalidate other emerging political ideas. Anand Panyarachun, former Prime Minister (March 1991 to March 1992 and June to September 1992) and known for his close relationship with the Palace, implicitly reproached Thaksin for bringing crisis to the country and warned that Thailand could become a failed state unless there was a concerted effort to end division.[20] Meanwhile, General Prem Tinsulanonda, former Prime Minister (1980–88) and now President of the Privy Council, said in his interview with the *Far Eastern Economic Review* on 18 September 2006, one day before the military coup:

> In this country, we consider that we belong to the King. The armed forces [belong to the king]. That is what we take oath [on] and have to profess — that we have to belong to the King. So that makes it easier to understand.... Do you know horse racing? In horse racing they have the stable and the owner of the stable owns the horse. The jockey comes and rides the horse during the race, but the jockey does not own the horse. It is very easy [to comprehend]. A good government can make a

> good jockey [with] ethics and moral standards.... My country is about
> 800 years old, and we run the country as a kingdom. We will never be
> a republic or be without the King. So that is the trick — the only thing
> that induces the people together. So, as long as we have the King, "this
> very, very good King" we have right now, we will go ahead either slowly
> or rapidly, but we will be united.[21]

Prem's reference of the King conveys a strong political message. This is because
King Bhumibol is the only monarch most Thais can remember and has been
seen by many Thais as the symbol of national unity.[22] As head of state, the King
has the responsibility to ensure that his kingdom is peaceful and unified. Kanok
Wongtrangan suggests that the King's thought on good citizens revolves around,
among others, the concept of unity. To the King, "the people must have unity
so that the country can progress and prosper, as well as remain secure. Unity
leads to the survival of the nation, pride, and dignity. Unity is the strongest
force in the land and when it is achieved it will inspire the people in the nation
to be unanimous in attempting to ... create progress and security."[23] Unity
has thus been a main subject in many of the King's speeches. For example,
in his birthday speech of December 2007, the King said, "Whether soldiers
or civilians, we must be united, like our legs must be united — which means
one goes forward and one pushes back before moving forward. Without unity,
the country will face disaster."[24] Similarly, in his speech to an audience at his
seaside palace in August 2009, the King warned that the country could collapse
if its feuding political factions did not unite. He said, "Recently, I feel that our
country could fail, because nobody is working in harmony. They are competing
with each other and no one understands what the other is doing."[25] Promoting
national unity has become a fundamental lifelong project of the King. Kevin
Hewison argued that King Bhumibol's legacy has been to define a conservative
monarchy, supporting stability and order, authority and tradition, unity and
solidarity, and national chauvinism.[26] Michael Connors noted that the King's
political interventions were intended to restore order and calm, and that he
was considered as a mediating power between hostile social forces.[27] This role
reaffirmed the King's emphasis on unity and discipline. However, it is clear
that the royally-endorsed concept of unity has been politically exploited by
some of the traditional elite. They have occasionally used the King's speeches
to gain political advantages against their political rivals. As Thaksin moved to
shift the political equilibrium toward benefiting his own emerging cliques and
his voters in the poor regions, the traditional elite interpreted his intention as
a malicious attempt to weaken the foundation of the royal institution which

celebrated unity and solidarity, thus placing him in serious conflict with the monarchy.

The Obsolete, Detrimental Discourse?

Thailand has gone through a series of turbulent times in the past fifty years, from encountering the communist threats inside and outside its border, the massacre at Thammasat University in 1976, the Black May of 1992,[28] to the financial crisis in 1997. But none caused such seismic shifts in the Thai political landscape as the present crisis that is drawing deep divisions between the two camps of power. On the surface, this crisis could be construed simply as elements competing for power. At a deeper level, it has had a tremendous impact on political culture, the way the Thais define themselves and their fellow countrymen, as well as the meaning of the Thai nation in the age of greater political consciousness among the grassroots. It is over three years since Thaksin was removed from power; and the split between his supporters and the pro-establishment faction is growing ever stronger. The stereotypes on both sides are as crude as they are entrenched: while Thaksin and the red shirts supposedly strive for a democratic change, the traditional elite are seemingly conservative and resist the shift in status quo. But these stereotypes are also troublesome and slippery. There has been no indication that the democratic commitment of Thaksin and the red shirts is genuine. Likewise, there has been no proof of whether the yellow shirts and the Bangkok elite are more democratic than Thaksin and his followers.

So far, the parties concerned have not found a mutually acceptable solution to the profound polarization without having to sacrifice their own political standing. The traditional elite, in particular, keep on proposing that all must work toward assuring national unity, seeing it as the key to healing the divisions, yet refusing to let go of their domination of power. In the meantime, the red shirts seem to be determined to transform Thailand's political entity from the one long governed by the aristocrats, or in the words of Jakrapob, the *khun nang*, to the one that serves the interests of the rural working class, or the *phrai*.[29] With the lack of compromise, this process of political transition occasionally sets off violence and therefore negatively affects the national economy. Signs of compromise are missing. Thai historian Charnvit Kasetsiri, in an interview, argued that the old concept of unity was out of sync with the reality of today. He observed, "The kind of very obedient submissive population is gone. No more will the general public accept what people at the top say."[30] Thongchai Winichakul, another Thai historian, added to this argument:

> An insistence on unity leaves little room for dissent. Every political culture deals with the tension between unity and harmony versus diversity and dissent. But the difference is in how they understand and deal with this tension and how they reduce or solve the tension. The ultimate articulations of unity and harmony in Thailand consist of "loyalty to the monarchy and the rigid notion of a single territorial state". Whatever the notion of unity, the "show" or the public display of unity and reconciliation is as important as its essence.[31]

The traditional elite insist on upholding a sense of national unity and building an orderly society where the three pillars shaping the national identity — nation, Buddhism, and the King — must not be violated. Meanwhile, the "fourth pillar" as a new definition and essence of Thai national identity has been emerging. This fourth pillar represents the democratic and liberal society which is increasingly powerful and influential. Thaksin and his red-shirted movement have quickly taken advantage of the emerging liberal environment to reinvent their own image as pro-democracy. The unending political stalemate in Thailand derives from the fact that the connection between the traditional three pillars and the emerging democratic society has not been made. Indeed, the traditional elite have perceived the emerging democratic and liberal society as a threat to their power interests. Accordingly, they are willing to go to any length to protect these interests even if this would result in brutal conflicts.

In this new environment, the discourse of unity itself is fast losing its spell. It fails to operate effectively in the face of Thailand's growing pluralism. Panitan Wattanayagorn asserted, "Core values are being reorganised, and sometimes there are conflicting values. That is quite normal. When a less democratic society is going through a traditional period to a more democratic one, from a closed to a more open one, from a traditional to a modern one, then you have conflicting views."[32] How to stop the political conflict in a peaceful manner is vital to the success of the Thai political transition. In this regard, exercising unity does not necessarily guarantee the peaceful end of the turmoil. Indeed, it could be detrimental if the traditional elite keep on abusing the concept of unity to control the dissidents. The new actors want a rearrangement of the political equilibrium so that it is even-handed and non-discriminatory.

Conclusion

Thailand has changed drastically over the years. New factors have emerged, and new players have entered the political scene. They have begun to exert their influence in the political process and refused to remain passive. During much of Thailand's economic boom over the past two decades, these new players, mostly residing in the poor provinces, watched wealth pass them by and go to the hands of the Bangkok urbanites. What they craved for was political inclusion and a fair share of the country's economic prosperity. But what they got were soap operas and official messages that stressed unity and conformity.

One of the root causes of the persistent conflict originates in the unbending mentality of the traditional elite who continue to forbid dissenting voices. They have instead further sanctified the traditional notion of unity while seeking to rebuke those outside of their network through a variety of methods. These people were forced to comply with the orders of the ruling elite and sacrifice their political conviction for the sake of peace and order. Yet, a peaceful and orderly Thailand does not benefit them politically. It, on the contrary, strengthens the already firm grip on power of the ruling elite. This grip on power is likely to be tightened further as Thailand approaches the final phase of the Bhumibol reign. Hence, appeals for national unity are growing louder. At the same time, the punishment against those who cause disunity is getting more severe. Room for compromise is apparently shrinking.

Rightly, Thitinan Pongsudhirak has suggested that a new consensus is imperative if Thailand is to regain its footing. That consensus would have to be based on mutual respect and accommodation.[33] The reinterpretation of the discourse of unity is indeed imperative. It is especially imperative at this critical time when the conflict between two opposing camps has shown no sign of ending and when those outside the elite's network are attempting to create a hegemony of the emerging notion of respect for diversity and political differences.

Notes

[1]   Ministry of Foreign Affairs of Thailand. *Handbook on Thailand's Political Situation*, Thailand: News Division, Department of Information, Ministry of Foreign Affairs of Thailand, 2007.

[2]   This is the statement of Samart Mangsang, one of the PAD's core leaders, translated and summarized from ASTV *Manager Daily*, in "Why Thaksin Gets Stronger?" 2Bangkok.com, 10 April 2009 <http://newsgroups.derkeiler.com/Archive/Soc/soc. culture.thai/2009-04/msg00305.html> (accessed 7 November 2009).

[3]   "Parties Promise to Honour Royal Call for Unity", *Bangkok Post*, 7 December 2009.

[4]   The Thai national anthem celebrates the notion of unity as the embodiment of the Thai nation. In its first line, it says, "Thailand is the unity of Thai blood and body".

Elsewhere in the song it emphasizes, "All Thais intend to unite together. Thais love peace but do not fear to fight. They will never let anyone threaten their independence." The anthem's lyrics were composed by Luang Saranupraphan.

[5] *Merriam-Webster's Dictionary of Synonyms: A Dictionary of Discriminated Synonyms with Antonyms and Analogous and Contrasted Words* (Massachusetts: Merriam-Webster, 1984), p. 844.

[6] See, Pavin Chachavalpongpun, *A Plastic Nation: The Curse of Thainess in Thai-Burmese Relations* (Lanham: University Press of America, 2005), p. 10.

[7] Nirmal Ghosh, "Little Time Left for Reconciliation", *Straits Times*, 21 April 2009.

[8] Matthew Phillip Copeland, "Contested Nationalism and the 1932 Overthrow of the Absolute Monarchy in Siam". (Ph.D. dissertation, Australian National University, 1993), p. 9.

[9] King Chulalongkorn stated in 1885, "Bringing a parliamentary form of government to Siam is similar to applying the book on how to grow wheat in Europe to the planting of rice in Siam, which will not lead to bountiful harvest." Quoted in Pisanu Sunthraraks, "Luang Wichit Watakan: Hegemony and Literature" (Ph.D. dissertation, University of Wisconsin-Madison, 1986), pp. 45–46.

[10] Thongchai Winichakul, *Siam Mapped: A History of The Geo-Body of A Nation* (Honolulu: University of Hawai'i Press, 1994), p. 4.

[11] Ibid., p. 9.

[12] See, Toemsuk Numnonda, "Mueang Thai Yuk Chuea Phunam" [When Thailand followed the leader], in *Thammasat University Journal* 7, no. 1 (July–September 1977).

[13] See <http://learners.in.th/blog/berrylove/321226> (accessed 19 January 2010).

[14] The two songs were composed by Nakorn Thanomsap who, in 2000, received the nation's distinguished artist award in the cultural field by the Office of the National Cultural Commission of Thailand.

[15] Thaksin has been sentenced in absentia to two-year's imprisonment for conflict of interest. Some doubt if Thaksin's conflict of interest is the real issue here. Mike Billington seems to suggest that the fact that Thaksin is "more popular" than the King could have been the reason behind the overthrow of his government and his jail term. See, Mike Billington, "Blow Dealt to British Subversion in Asia", *Executive Intelligence Review* 36, no. 43 (30 October 2009).

[16] Thitinan Pongsudhirak, "New Consensus is Needed for Thailand", *Straits Times*, 4 November 2009.

[17] The PAD believes that with this new political model, future politicians would be able to exercise their powers responsibly with clear limits — an obvious anti-Thaksin measure. See Pavin Chachavalpongpun, "In Thailand with the PAD: 'New Politics' or New Communists?" *Opinion Asia*, 29 September 2008 <http://opinionasia.com/InThailandwiththePAD> (accessed 8 November 2009).

18 Peter Vail, "Red Shirts Not Just a Proxy of Thaksin", *Straits Times*, 16 April 2009, p. A22.

19 Nirmal Ghosh, "Red Shirts' Plan Massive Protest", *Straits Times*, 4 April 2009, p. C4.

20 Surasak Glahan, "Thailand at Risk of Becoming a Failed State", *Bangkok Post*, 31 August 2006. Anand gave this statement during his speech at Bangkok's Ambassador Hotel organized by the Thai Journalists Association on 30 August 2006.

21 Prem's interview with Colum Murphy, 18 September 2006. In "General Prem Tinsulanonda", *Far East Economic Review*, 19 September 2006 <http://www.feer. com/interviews_premium/2006/september/general-prem-tinsulanonda> (accessed 25 September 2009).

22 Office of His Majesty's Principal Private Secretary (OPPS), *A Memoire of His Majesty King Bhumibol Adulyadej* (Bangkok: Office of His Majesty's Principal Private Secretary, 1987), p. 11.

23 Cited in Kanok Wongtrangan, *Naeo Phrarachadamri Dan Kanmeuang Khong Prabatsomdet Phrachaoyuhua* [Royal edicts on politics and government of the King, (Bangkok: Sathaban Thai Suksa, Chulalongkorn University, 1988), pp. 190–91. Quoted in Michael Kelly Connors, *Democracy and National Identity in Thailand* (Copenhagen, Nordic Institute of Asian Studies, 2003), pp. 132–33.

24 Ambika Ahuja, "Thai King Calls for Unity Ahead of Vote", Associated Press, 5 December 2007 <http://hicomrade.wordpress.com/2007/12/05/afp-awestruck-crowds-greet-thai-king-on-his-80th-birthday/> (accessed 8 November 2009).

25 "Unite, Thai King Tells Rival Factions", *Sunday Times*, 23 August 2009, p. 2.

26 Kevin Hewison, "The Monarchy and Democratisation", in *Political Change in Thailand: Democracy and Participation*, edited by Kevin Hewison (London: Routledge, 1997), p. 63.

27 Connors, *Democracy and National Identity in Thailand*, p. 131.

28 Black May 1992 is a common name for the 17–20 May 1992 popular protest in Bangkok against the government of General Suchinda Kraprayoon (April–May 1992) and the bloody military crackdown on the pro-democracy movement led by Major-General Chamlong Srimuang that followed.

29 Interview with Jakrapob Penkair, Bangkok, 26 June 2008.

30 Quoted in Nirmal Ghosh, "Seismic Shifts Challenge Thai Elites to Compromise", *Straits Times*, 4 September 2009, p. A2. Charnvit is Professor of History at Thailand's Thammasat University.

31 Ibid. Thongchai teaches at the University of Wisconsin-Madison.

32 Ibid. Panitan is a political scientist currently on leave from Chulalongkorn University to serve as Prime Minister Abhisit's spokesman.

33 Thitinan, "New Consensus is Needed for Thailand".

Timor-Leste

TIMOR-LESTE IN 2009
Marking Ten Years of Independence or Dependence on International "Assistance"?

Selver B. Sahin

The progress on tackling the residual problems of the 2006 political and security crisis helped Timor-Leste enjoy relative stability in 2009. This is evidenced by the generally calm security environment with almost no instances of violence, closure of all the camps for internally displaced persons (IDPs), and the availability of critical commodities such as fuel and rice at affordable prices subsidized by the government. The improvement in the security environment is also mirrored in positive public perceptions reported in a country-wide opinion survey, in which over four-fifths (87 per cent) of 1,120 respondents indicated in December 2008 that they felt safer in their communities compared to 2006.[1]

Little progress, however, was made towards addressing the structural problems that triggered the 2006 crisis. These include the reforming of the security institutions, strengthening the rule of law, and alleviating poverty. The already-flawed security sector reform, focusing on the handover of policing responsibilities from UNPOL (United Nations Police) to PNTL (National Police of Timor-Leste), was complicated by increasingly strained relations between the AMP (Parliamentary Majority Alliance) government and UNMIT (United Nations Integrated Mission in Timor-Leste) in 2009. The release of an ex-militia member on 30 August, the day that marks the tenth anniversary of the UN-sponsored vote for independence, once more highlighted the continuing challenge of estab-lishing an independent justice system with the capacity to sustain the rule of law within society.

Selver B. Sahin is a Research Fellow within the School of Global Studies, Social Sciences and Planning of RMIT University, Melbourne, Australia.

According to International Monetary Fund (IMF) estimates, the country achieved a 12.8 per cent growth rate in the non-oil gross domestic product (GDP) in 2008, which has proudly been cited by the country's leadership to illustrate the economy's improving health. But this growth was largely driven by increased domestic consumption, fuelled by the government's injection of more oil money into the economy in the form of public transfers, subsidies, and infrastructure spending rather than an improvement in the production capacity of the economy. Furthermore, most of the recovery and development initiatives have so far been concentrated in the capital Dili, while there has been almost no substantial improvement in the infrastructure and living conditions for the majority of the population residing in dispersed rural areas, something which I also personally witnessed during my short visit to the country three and a half years after my first visit in February 2006.

Reforming the East Timorese Security Sector

The undertaking of the security sector reform towards professional, effective, and accountable development of the East Timorese armed forces and the police, which were part of the security problem in 2006, has been a messy process from the outset. Many actors are involved in the security sector reform but it is not clear who is doing what. Who is leading the process? What kind of strategic approach and action plan, if any, has been adopted to manage the challenges to the safety and well-being of society and the state? And, perhaps most importantly, who will be held responsible in case something goes wrong in the future? UNMIT tends to stress the "assistance" rather than "executive" character of their mandate. The government wants to take the lead but does not seem to have an inter-institutionally agreed, comprehensive implementation plan, while being dependent on a few key individuals and relations between them.

The military, where the 2006 crisis originated, was excluded from the UN-"assisted" security sector reform because neither the UN nor the Timorese government was willing to engage with the army. It was left to its own dynamics and the reform process has been carried out on a bilateral basis. No vetting process has been initiated and the key military figures identified in the report of the UN's Commission of Inquiry (CoI) as having responsibility for the 2006 crisis and violent events have enjoyed immunity from prosecution. Brigadier-General Taur Matan Ruak, Chief of Staff of the F-FDTL (Falintil — Defence Forces of Timor-Leste) retained his position, becoming an increasingly popular public figure. Roque Rodrigues, Minister of Defence of the time, was appointed by

President Ramos-Horta as his adviser on security sector reform. Portugal and Australia are the two biggest donors and provide training and advisers. China, Japan, Malaysia, Indonesia, New Zealand, Brazil, India, and the United States are also involved in the capacity-development of the army to varying degrees.

The focus of the security sector reform has rather been on the police. The transfer of policing responsibilities from the UN police to the national police dominated the course of the restructuring of the PNTL in 2009. Although it was frequently emphasized by UNMIT that the handover of executive policing authority was not guided by a "fixed timeline" but a phased-approach, it was largely driven by the growing dissatisfaction of the Timorese police with the vetting and mentoring processes and the government's increasing pressure for the transfer of executive policing authority to the national police.[2] Speaking to the Parliament in mid-March 2009, President Ramos-Horta, for instance, announced that a new "formal mechanism" would be established by the government to coordinate efforts in major issues of national interest, including the reform of the security system. The president, on the other hand, made no reference to the UN and its "assistance" role in the conduct of a comprehensive review of the future roles and needs of the police and the military, which was endorsed by the Security Council in 2006. It has in fact become a kind of mystery whether the review will be completed at all. According to a senior security expert from UNMIT's security sector support unit, who suggested that they have been doing the review "behind the scenes, without antagonizing" the government, the best case scenario for its completion and publication as a report is likely to be August 2010.[3] This, however, would not help much to reform the security system through addressing institutional and regulatory gaps and overlaps, given that the Timorese Government has already drafted a national security legislation, which foresees the integration rather than separation of the security institutions.

UNMIT's pursuit of a country-wide screening process for the PNTL rather than focusing on the Dili police only, which largely disintegrated during the 2006 crisis, already fostered discontent among the Timorese police officers, who continued to work during the violent events. The provision of less than successful mentoring and training by UNPOL members coming from more than forty countries with differing policing approaches and training skills exacerbated the already-strained relations. The Timorese Government's lack of political will to dismiss the police officers involved in serious crimes during the 2006 violence also affected the process, undermining UNMIT's efforts to curb political interference in the police service. The Timorese-led Evaluation Panel, established by the government in August 2006 to make recommendations to the Secretary of State for Security on the suitability of PNTL members for service, failed to convene between January and September 2009. By September, UNMIT completed the final certification of 92 per cent of approximately 3,200 Timorese police officers, while some 250 officers were facing pending criminal and disciplinary charges. In addition to this, 71 PNTL members facing human rights and integrity issues were still unregistered and 63 of them were still on the payroll.[4] This represents the continuing challenge of depoliticizing the national police, which was one of the factors that sparked the 2006 crisis, as emphasized in the UN's CoI report.

Rivalries between the security forces also continue to be a serious concern. The Joint Command structure, which subordinated the police to the military command following the assassination attempts in February 2008, is generally considered a success in attaining its objectives — preventing the relapse of violence and apprehending the rebels without shooting a bullet. The joint security operations, on the other hand, led to an increase in the allegations of human rights violations and ill treatment received by UNMIT.[5] No member of the security forces has yet to be held accountable.[6] The Timorese political leadership was of the view that the joint security operations also helped the military and the police reconcile their differences and restore public confidence with the two institutions, which were involved in deadly clashes on Dili's streets in May 2006. However, whether the conduct of joint operations denotes the healing of the deep-rooted rifts between the two organizations or a public display of unity motivated by pragmatic and institutional concerns is debateable. The operations served to bring the two rival institutions against the rebels and provided a significant test case to show their administrative and operational capacity to the government and society as well as to their *malae* (Tetum word for foreigner) supervisors and "capacity builders".

The military's refusal to surrender four F-FDTL soldiers, sentenced by the Dili District Court to imprisonment of between ten and twelve years for the killing of eight unarmed PNTL officers on 25 May 2006 is illustrative of continuing institutional rivalries. While one of the soldiers was later pardoned by President Ramos-Horta in late-December, the other three F-FDTL members have remained in a military facility in the army's headquarters in Dili without civilian oversight, and reportedly continued to receive their salaries.[7] They have also yet to pay the compensation to the victims' families, who are seeking legal advice as to how to enforce the civilian court ruling.[8] Indicating the persisting lack of political will to enforce the rule of law, this particular issue can also be read as the military's message to the police and, by extension, to the civilian authorities that "it is they who are in charge!"[9]

Another major issue of concern is the controversial "easterners-westerners" divide, which once again came on the agenda towards the end of 2008. Following the dismissal of approximately 600 "westerner" soldiers in early-2006, which precipitated the violent incidents in Dili three years ago, the army has come to be increasingly associated with Lorosa'e, denoting the eastern districts of Baucau, Viqueque, and Lautem. In an anonymous flyer circulated in Dili in October 2008, a group of PNTL members demanded that the new head of the police service be from the western part of the country.[10] The country's Prosecutor-General, Longuinhos Monteiro, born in Maliana of the western district of Bobonaro, was appointed the new PNTL commander in March 2009. His appointment, however, raised criticisms from the opposition Fretilin and civil society organizations. They argued that the government's choice of a person from outside the institution was politically motivated and ran the risk of creating command and loyalty problems within the police. Monteiro is known for sending summons in October 2008 to senior army officers to provide their individual statements concerning the violent events in 2006 and his blaming of President Ramos-Horta for the delays in trials, recommended by the UN's Commission of Inquiry.[11] As an interesting point of note, in response to the criticisms regarding his appointment, Monteiro stressed his military background as qualifying him for the position, which can be read as his effort to appease the army as well as his intention to institutionalize the police service along military lines: "I have some background from Indonesia where I was a soldier. I have experience in the Indonesian army, I have experience in the [pro-independence] Falintil guerrillas and I have experience in leading one full battalion of the army."[12] This became more apparent when the PNTL commander participated in a weapons familiarization and shooting competition hosted by the ISF (International Stabilization Force) in Dili in May. Later the images of a group of PNTL officers, in charge of border security, conducting a paramilitary style exercise in uniforms with heavy weapons in central Dili, appeared in the media in August.[13]

In addition to these problems, the national and international security forces, particularly the Portuguese National Republican Guards (GNR), were increasingly involved in a power struggle, which, according to an UNPOL officer, represents a "who wants to be the big guy game".[14] In an incident in the Maliana market in early-June 2009, the military intervened to break-up a fight between two martial arts groups, although the UNMIT police and PNTL were already on the scene and engaged in controlling the situation. F-FDTL members reportedly pointed their weapons at the UNMIT police.[15] The Timorese Government gathered a national team to investigate the events and concluded that "there was no indication of

F-FDTL members having 'pointed weapons at the chests of UNPOL members'".[16] According to the Timorese Secretary of State for Defence, Julio Tomas Pinto, UNPOL presented an "inaccurate" record of the Maliana events that can only serve to "discredit" the military.[17] The incident was referred to the UN Secretary-General's October 2009 report with no mention of the controversial gunpoint issue.

On another occasion in June, an off-duty Timorese policeman, alleged to have been assaulted by several GNR officers at a restaurant in Dili, discharged a firearm at the vehicle of the GNR members. The incident once again fuelled sovereignty sensitivities within the political and military leadership, already frustrated with the international security presence, which has come to be seen as an "occupying force".[18] One government official was quoted in the media, stating that "Timor-Leste was a sovereign country and was not reined in by Portugal, which was why the GNR police should respect the existing human rights convention in the country."[19] In August, General Ruak, who once more raised Falintil's heroic role during the resistance in an interview with the media, said that foreign forces "should have left Timor-Leste by now".[20] As an interesting point to note, the F-FDTL commander also commented that the East Timorese leadership felt difficulty in fulfilling the expectations of the people but despite the "scare of 2006, the country is on track" and it is "not a failed state",[21] indicating the military's increasing interest in politics and national development.

Against this background of increasingly tense relations between the national and international security forces, the assessments on the professional integrity of Timorese police officers, and the administrative, operational, and logistical readiness of the individual districts and units were carried out by joint assessment field teams, consisting of civilian and police representatives from the Timorese Government and UNMIT. The teams assessed the degree to which a set of mutually agreed criteria[22] were met through interviewing and surveying police officers over a range of issues, from their knowledge of "fundamental" policing responsibilities and institutional principles to their compliance with human rights standards when carrying out their duties. They scored the responses they received along a ten-point scale, with five being set as the "minimum standard for readiness".[23] The results were then analyzed by the Timorese-UNMIT Joint Technical Team to decide on the next stage. As of late-October 2009, assessments were completed in all but two (Dili and Bobonaro) districts. By December, the national police resumed policing responsibilities in four relatively less-problematic districts, Lautem, Oecussi, Manatuto, and Viqueque, while UNPOL will continue to monitor the performance of the national policemen and provide advice and operational support when required. Dili, where the 2006 crisis originated and the hostilities between the police and defence forces led to the institutional and organizational collapse of the PNTL, will be handled at the final stage. There is however a shared belief among UNPOL staff that the Timorese police, relying on UNMIT's resources such as transport, mobile phone cards, office equipment, and case filing systems, lack the necessary logistics, which is one of the criteria set for the handover of policing responsibilities. They also avoid providing a clear answer to the question of whether PNTL have the institutional and operational capacity to effectively and appropriately respond to a security situation similar to the one in 2006, once the UN police have withdrawn.[24] However, given the limited progress that has so far been made, it is unlikely to expect that the longer the UNPOL stays, the more it will contribute to strengthening the organizational and operational capacity of the PNTL.[25]

The weakness of the police has, on the other hand, facilitated the military's ambition to position itself in internal security. This is reflected in the newly drafted national security legislation,[26] which is based on the disbanded joint military-police command. The draft law on national security, described as being informed by an "integrated national security" framework, approaches security from a "crisis management" perspective rather than identifying and regulating actual and potential threats and risks to the safety and well-being of individuals, communities, society, and the state. This is despite the importance of delineating inter-institutional responsibilities to avoid future conflict being stressed in the government's five-year development programme adopted in 2007.[27] Beyond a vague reference to the "subsidiary and complementary nature" of the joint employment of the security institutions, there is no clarity on the crucial issue of who would be in command in "crisis" situations involving "public calamity, natural catastrophes or disasters and serious disturbances of law and order". The joint deployment of the security agents in these vaguely defined terms is framed as a solution to producing "preventive measures in the realm of internal security", conditioned by the perceived disappearance of the "traditional separation between Defence (External Security) and Security" as well as by the 2006 crisis and the February 2008 attacks. Somewhat ironically, this internal security framework, however, is reminiscent of certain elements of the organization of the Indonesian security institutions of the past, under which the East Timorese people suffered greatly. The Indonesian system was based on an order and security first approach, subordination of the police and intelligence services to the military, and the military's exercise of an extensive control over the population.[28] This is mirrored in the language of the text emphasizing the maintenance of order rather than law enforcement[29] and the envisioned employment of the military "additionally, in other missions in support of civilian authorities" as well as its development of "civilian-military cooperation capabilities, with a special focus on the traditional social-cultural structure of the country".

The Weak Execution of the Rule of Law

The release of a former militia leader in August 2009 highlights the continuing challenge of political interference in the justice system, which is already suffering from a number of institutional constraints in implementing the rule of law. These limitations include the lack of qualified legal staff, insufficient court facilities, an increasing backlog of cases, and its limited outreach capacity to the population, most of whom rely on traditional forms of justice. Maternus Bere, a Timor-Leste-born Indonesian citizen, indicted by the UN's serious crimes unit in 2003 for crimes against humanity, was arrested by the national police on 8 August following his entry into the country for a family gathering. The district court of Suai ordered him to be held in the Becora prison in Dili, pending his trial for his alleged involvement in murder, rape, kidnap, and torture following the announcement of the UN-sponsored independence referendum in 1999. On 30 August, he was however handed over to Indonesian authorities as, reportedly, Indonesian Foreign Minister Hassan Wirajuda refused to attend the anniversary celebrations until Bere was transferred to the Indonesian embassy.[30] While the Minister of Justice, Lucia Lobato, described his release as a political decision that had to be made, Prime Minister Gusmao accepted entire responsibility for this act. In response to these developments, the President of the Court of Appeal, Judge Claudio Ximenes, issued a public warning against the legal consequences of the violation of the new penal code and launched an investigation into the freeing of Bere without a court order.

The opposition Fretilin (Revolutionary Front for an Independent Timor-Leste) and Kota (Association of Timorese Heroes) parties, which argued that the pro-Indonesian militia leader's release was a "clear assault" on the Constitution and the country's laws, lodged a no-confidence motion. The government survived the vote held on 12 October by a margin of 39 to 25 against the motion. The debates in Parliament, among other things, highlighted the persistence of personal rather than legal and constitutional interpretations of the state's core concepts and the still unresolved rivalries within the Timorese elite, dating back to decades earlier. According to the Prime Minister, since Bere is not even a Timorese citizen, his release was irrelevant to Timor-Leste's national interest, which he urged should be defined from a "broader understanding" that takes into account the volume of trade relations, the presence of 8,000 Timorese students in Indonesia, and the neighbour's diplomatic support for joining international forums.[31] The debates in Parliament also indicated once more that the Timorese leaders are far from resolving their decades-old differences, while promoting the idea of reconciliation with Indonesia. The Prime Minister, who disassociated himself and the parties in the coalition from the tragic events that occurred before and during Indonesian occupation, claimed that it would be in Fretilin's interest to present an amnesty proposal to escape from accountability for the past human rights crimes:

> What gains or benefits might this Government, which was formed only by Parties not directly involved in the killings of 1974 and 1975, derive from the presentation of a draft Amnesty Law?... No AMP Party, therefore, included in the Government that I lead, is accountable for the violence and killings that took place from April 1974 to August 1975!... No AMP Party is accountable for the imprisonment and inhuman torture of Francisco Xavier do Amaral, and for the execution of dozens of innocent people, which took place in 1977!... No AMP Party is accountable for the deaths of so many civilian and military resistance fighters during the Support Bases!

Balancing reconciliation with justice, which is essentially a challenging task in post-conflict settings, has become even more complicated in Timor-Leste, where most of the population was victimized and seriously traumatized by their long-exposure to violence. It is a small, poverty-stricken country completely dependent on its powerful neighbour from imports such as fuel and instant noodles to its bid for ASEAN (Association of Southeast Asian Nations) membership. It is therefore beyond Timor-Leste's capacity to push Indonesia to establish accountability for the past. In addition to this, the lack of international will to set up a tribunal recommended by the UN's specialized human rights agencies in 2000 and 2005[32] has also shaped the Timorese leadership's "pragmatic" position. However, what is neglected here, as one analyst from La'o Hamutuk, a respected local civil society organization, rightly points out, is that legal and political processes reinforce each other.[33] That is, bringing to trial people like Maternus Bere and other alleged perpetrators of serious crimes, some of whom are still serving in the Indonesian military and involved in human rights violations in West Papua, is an important case in point not only for promoting a culture of rule-based society in Timor-Leste but also for consolidating democratic practices and human rights in Indonesia. Therefore, the Timorese leaders' "leaving the past behind" approach tends to "sabotage" the democratization process in Indonesia[34] as well as the work done by civil society organizations towards raising awareness about what happened in the past in an attempt to prevent its recurrence in the future.

The logic that shapes the Timorese leadership's "move on" approach is that it is impossible to deliver perfect justice because this requires the trial of thousands of people, including the East Timorese themselves, involved in human rights violations. During his speech on the tenth anniversary of the UN-sponsored referendum, Jose Ramos-Horta rejected Amnesty International's recent call to establish an international tribunal to try those responsible for the past human rights violations. Later, in an interview with Al Jazeera in October 2009, the president once again dismissed the claims that the East Timorese people are still waiting for justice to be done:[35]

> If the issue of justice was so important, justice about the past, for the common people in the case of an ex-militia, who was conditionally handed over to the Indonesian embassy, you would have had thousands of people demonstrating in the streets in Dili. Not one!

The political leadership's claim that the East Timorese people are not interested in justice, however, does not exactly reflect the views of society, evidenced in the Asia Foundation's 2008 opinion survey. The survey found that over 90 per cent of respondents thought that individuals who have committed murder should not be able to "avoid punishment".[36] Therefore, the granting of presidential amnesties in the name of promoting reconciliation in May 2008 to ninety-four prisoners, including those sentenced for the militia violence during 1999 and former Minister of Interior Rogerio Lobato, convicted for illegal weapons distribution in 2006, sends a dangerous message to society that justice does not apply equally to everyone, especially to the elites.[37] This in turn fosters a sense of division in society, which the Timorese political leadership tends to ignore. This division is between the beneficiaries and non-beneficiaries of independence. That is, those who have found their place on the winners' side in the post-independence period and those who are still disadvantaged and feeling that their sacrifice and loss during the resistance went unacknowledged. The following testimony of an East Timorese woman to the Commission of Truth and Reconciliation (CAVR) years ago in this respect illustrates the basics of this intra-societal division:

> I lost my husband because of this struggle. Two of my children also died during the Indonesian occupation. When we fought back then we never considered our fate, we just fought and sacrificed everything we owned. Now I am alone and must support myself by gardening although I am no longer strong since I am already old … I will not … hold office like

> these important men who once fought together with us. All I ask for is
> my right to a decent life as the family member of a fighter. I got this
> way because my husband and children disappeared. The important men
> are not permitted to forget us [just because they] now have a strong
> chair stuck on the ground. In the past, when their positions were not yet
> certain, we fought together.[38]

This issue constitutes the essence of the problems surrounding the delivery of
justice which involves a social and economic dimension. It is therefore not in their
personal capacity that Xanana Gusmao or Ramos-Horta should make the critical
decision on whether there should be an international tribunal. After all, despite
all the sacrifices they made in the past, for most of the people, they represent a
small group of "winners" today.

Socio-Economic Development

The slogan of "goodbye conflict, welcome development" was the theme of the
second Timor-Leste and Development Partners meeting held in early-April 2009.
The donors congratulated the AMP government for its performance towards meeting
the national priority areas, including security and strengthening the justice sector,
and declared that the country has now entered into the stage of consolidating
peace and development.[39] This positive atmosphere was complemented by the
statistical data provided by the IMF, according to which the country's total income
measured by gross national income (GNI) per capita, which includes oil and
gas revenues, increased to US$1,650 in 2007, while the non-oil GDP achieved a
12.8 per cent growth in 2008.[40]

However, this growth was stimulated by increasing government spending
(Table 1), financed through large transfers from the nation's Petroleum Fund,
rather than a substantial improvement in the production capacity of the economy.
This is evidenced in the country's growing import dependency in 2008.
While the non-oil exports, mostly coffee, amounted to only US$13 million,
merchandise imports reached US$258 million in 2008.[41] According to a World
Bank report released in November 2008, poverty increased approximately
14 per cent in the period between 2001 and 2007, with almost half of the
population living on less than US$1 per day. Youth unemployment, estimated
to be 40 per cent, remains very high. Children, who constitute about 43 per
cent of the country's population of 1 million, form 49 per cent of the poor.
Growing at an annual rate of 4 per cent, the population is likely to double within
two decades. The country ranks 162nd out of 182 nations in the UNDP's 2009

TABLE 1
Whole of State Budget Expenditure between 2006 and 2009
(in US$ million)

Expenditure Category	2006	2007	2008	2009
Salaries and Wages	29.0	35.5	50.3	93.1
Goods and Services	63.5	135.2	235.7	248.0
Minor Capital	3.6	9.6	50.8	38.1
Capital Development	2.4	11.2	127.3	205.3
Public Transfers	2.5	17.7	89.0	96.4
Public Debt Interest	0.0	0.0	0.0	0
Total Expenditure	101	209.2	553.1	680.9

Source: Adapted from General Budget of the State and State Plan for 2010, 1 January to 31 December 2010, 15 October 2009.

Human Development Index, representing a drop of 12 places compared with 2007/8.

According to former Special Representative of the UN Secretary-General Atul Khare, these figures indicating a low human development level are "absolutely incorrect" and cannot be relied on to measure the progress the country has made since its near total destruction ten years ago and assess its socio-economic development, which "has largely been … a success".[42] The AMP government, which took office in August 2007, on the other hand, tends to blame Fretilin for the increasing poverty during the period covered in the said World Bank report.[43] The government's increasing reliance on the Petroleum Fund, which was established in 2005 for the effective use of the country's oil and gas revenues for current and future generations, however, has become a major concern not only to the opposition and civil society organizations but to the World Bank and IMF as well. In a confidential memo leaked to the media in July 2008, the two international financial institutions stressed inadequate budget planning and execution systems and poor implementation capacity both in the government and the private sector as the reason for the chronic expenditure shortfalls.[44] While this is accepted behind closed doors, the government's accelerated execution of the budget has often been presented as a sign of good economic performance to the public.[45]

In January 2009, Parliament approved the 2009 state budget with expenditures of approximately US$681 million, of which US$589 million was to be funded from the Petroleum Fund. This was well above the estimated sustainable income, defined by law in terms of 3 per cent of the nation's "petroleum wealth", corresponding to US$408 million. While no transfer was made during the first quarter of 2009, US$200 million was withdrawn during the second quarter. By October, the petroleum revenue reached US$5.3 billion, with plans to withdraw US$207 million during the third and fourth quarters. In early-November, however, the government requested the transfer of US$312 million from the Petroleum Fund, increasing the total amount of transfers to US$512 million in 2009.[46]

The government's concern with subsidizing the economy and addressing potentially destabilizing challenges through public transfers to the "petitioners", veterans, internally displaced persons, civil servants, and vulnerable groups makes sense. These short-term gains however need to be accompanied by long-term, specifically-targeted solutions such as investing in agriculture, infrastructure, tourism, and human capital, especially in rural areas, where approximately three-quarters of the population live. The effective and transparent use of oil revenues constitutes the most important aspect of this development strategy. The AMP government prioritized rural development in its 2009 national recovery and development programme but most of the efforts have so far focused on the capital. The state's penetration into communities in remote areas has remained very limited. This is manifested in their continuing reliance on traditional forms of justice provided by village (suco) chiefs and their limited knowledge about the state institutions and their roles. The results of an opinion survey conducted by the International Republican Institute (IRI) in late-2008 for example indicate that over half of the respondents (52 per cent) had not heard about the Petroleum Fund, which the AMP coalition has increasingly relied on to finance public expenditures. Of those who knew about it, only 25 per cent rated the government's use of the fund money as "very good or good".[47]

Lack of transparency tends to fuel corruption allegations. The country, which fell from 123rd place to 145th in 2008, dropped again to 146th out of 180 nations in 2009 in the Transparency International's corruption index. The government has recently established an anti-corruption commission likely to be headed by former Fretilin MP Aderito de Jesus Soares, who is completing his Ph.D. at Australian National University. The country's Ombudsman, Sebastiao Ximenes, is, however, highly critical about the government's will to fight corruption. In an interview with *Tempo Semanal* in December, Ximenes complained about the lack of progress in the twenty-eight cases of allegations of corruption he submitted to the Office of the Prosecutor-General for further investigation and taking to trial.[48]

The government's awarding of contracts for rice imports to sixteen companies through a closed tender process in 2008 once again came on the agenda in 2009. In a programme aired by the Australian Broadcasting Corporation (ABC) in June, Prime Minister Gusmao was alleged to have signed off on a US$3.5 million rice contract to a company in which his daughter, Zenilda Gusmao, was also a stakeholder. It was later argued that Zenilda Gusmao resigned from the company before the contract was signed. President Ramos-Horta asked the Ombudsman's Office to investigate the allegations concerning government contracts worth US$56 million. The Ombudsman initiated an investigation process which has yet to be completed.

Gender-based violence also continues to be a serious impediment to social development. According to the crimes statistics provided by UNMIT, instances of assault and domestic violence constitute 40 per cent of the crimes reported. The Asia Foundation's opinion poll in this respect suggests that people's attitudes towards domestic violence and women's status have slid back over time, despite the growing engagement of civil society in raising public awareness and encouraging women's participation in the nation-building process. The proportion of Timorese who think that a man hitting his wife is categorically wrong has dropped from 75 per cent in 2004 to 34 per cent in 2008, while the ratio of approval of women speaking on their behalf in local justice processes fell from 69 per cent to 39 per cent over the same period.[49] The results of another study on sexual and gender-based violence, announced in August, revealed that patriarchal beliefs about women's roles in society, religion, and preconceived notions of sexuality make the talk of sexual violence in the community taboo. It was conducted in the border districts of Covalima and Bobonaro between May and October 2007 as part of UNIFEM's (United Nations Development Fund for Women) global programme for encouraging women's participation in peace-building. A head of a village in Bobonaro was quoted in the study as saying, "why should we raise the issue, we should only discuss these amongst each other".[50]

Last but not least, two summary reports published in 2009, once more indicated the weakness of the current foreign aid framework, known as the "boomerang effect". According to the data compiled by La'o Hamutuk, the international community has allocated a total of US$5.2 billion to spend on programmes related to the country's reconstruction and development since 1999.[51] When this is added to some US$3 billion which the Governments of Australia and New Zealand provided for military expenditures, it increases to US$8.8 billion.[52] However, only about 10 per cent of this money actually ended up in Timor-Leste's economy, while most of the rest went into covering the expenses of security forces, administration, and salaries of consultants.[53]

Foreign Relations

The year 2009 also witnessed China, which was the first country to establish diplomatic relations with Timor-Leste when it became formally independent in May 2002, expanding its economic interest in the country. This is manifested in the provision of training programmes for Timorese civil servants and university scholarships for the country's youth as well as in the financing of the construction of government buildings in Dili, such as the new Presidential Palace, the Ministry of Foreign Affairs, the Ministry of Defence, and headquarters for the defence forces. The Timorese Government, which awarded the Chinese Nuclear Industry 22nd Construction Company a US$390 million contract in October 2008 to build three power plants using heavy oil, has bought two long-range coastal patrol boats from Beijing for US$30 million. The lack of transparency during the conclusion of the deal and unsuitability of the boats for the tropical and rough conditions in the Timor Sea, however, has led to criticisms in the country.[54]

China's engagement with Timor-Leste, which is guided by a long-term strategic approach, is shaped by Beijing's desire to balance the U.S. influence in the Southeast Asian region, the prospect for Timorese entry into ASEAN, and to gain access to the country's rich oil and gas resources.[55] In this respect, China provides significant alternative options to the Timorese leadership. The government's interest in boosting bilateral cooperation with Beijing, in other words, is not only shaped by meeting the country's socio-economic development needs but also by its interest in strengthening its position in its dealings with Jakarta and Canberra. For instance, in October, Timorese Minister of Foreign Affairs Zacarias da Costa, who visited Beijing in June to strengthen bilateral cooperation and secure China's support for Timor-Leste's entry into ASEAN, stated that his country was negotiating a loan from China to fund new infrastructure projects. This includes the construction of a pipeline from the offshore Greater Sunrise oil field to Timor-Leste.[56] The Greater Sunrise is estimated to contain around 300 million barrels of condensate and 8.3 trillion cubic feet of natural gas. According to the maritime boundary agreement Timor-Leste and Australia concluded in January 2006, the two countries would receive an equal share of royalties from the Greater Sunrise reserves. This, however, requires the conclusion of a consensus on where this oil and gas would be processed. The Timorese Government, quite understandably, favours the construction of a pipeline on its southern shores rather than the establishment of a processing centre in Darwin, Australia — linking offshore oil revenues with the economy and creating jobs. To this end, the government contracted Malaysia's state-owned energy company Petronas to carry out a feasibility study, which found the pipeline project technically viable.[57]

China's growing influence in the country, on the other hand, is becoming a concern to Australian policymakers. Canberra is already critical of Beijing's expansion of military capabilities and its rising political profile in Southeast Asia and the Pacific, as identified in the Rudd government's defence white paper released in May. The Timorese Government's recently announced plans to develop a naval base were, for example, reported in the media as an indication of China's rising "military influence in a region traditionally regarded by Canberra as its own".[58]

Conclusion

Compared with the previous period between 2006 and 2008, Timor-Leste enjoyed relative stability and security in 2009, defined in terms of the absence of rioting or gang violence. The underlying factors which caused the 2006 violence, however, still remain as a potential challenge to the prospect of the country's political development and social cohesion. These include the reform of the security sector, strengthening the rule of law, and reducing poverty. The security sector reform, which focused on the handover of policing responsibilities from the UN Police to the national police, has been constrained by increasingly strained relations between the national and international authorities. The Timorese police resumed policing responsibilities in four districts but it is questionable whether the UNMIT police created a professional, effective, and accountable police service. The military, which was excluded from the UN-endorsed security sector reform, on the other hand, has positioned itself in internal security, which was formalized in the newly drafted national security legislation. The release of Maternus Bere on the day that the Timorese people voted for independence ten years ago once more indicated the structural problems with implementing the rule of law and ending a rising culture of impunity, which, according to President Ramos-Horta, is one of those "academic jargons" that "someone coin[s] and everybody repeat[s]".[59] The society, on the other hand, is still challenged by poverty, unemployment, and limited access to basic services, especially in rural areas, while the IMF-estimated double digit growth rate has frequently been cited in the media and policy circles to indicate the health of the country's economy. In the meantime, the international community, involved in the country's political and social reconstruction since 1999, continues to "assist" with the national recovery, sustainable development, and peace-building process.

Notes

1   Silas Everett, *Law and Justice in Timor-Leste: A Survey of Citizen Awareness and Attitudes Regarding Law and Justice 2008* (Dili: The Asia Foundation, 2009).

2   International Crisis Group, "Timor-Leste: No Time for Complacency", *Update Briefing: Asia Briefing no. 87*, 9 February 2009.

3   Interview with the author, UNMIT, Dili, 2 November 2009.

4   United Nations, "Report of the Secretary-General on the United Nations Integrated Mission in Timor-Leste", Security Council Document S/2009/504, 2 October 2009, para. 19.

5   UNMIT received allegations of fifty-eight incidents of ill treatment by F-FDTL and PNTL members between 11 February and 22 May 2008, when the state of siege was lifted in the western district of Ermera, where the rebels were based. UNMIT, "Report on Human Rights Developments in Timor-Leste: 1 September 2007–30 June 2008. The Security Sector and Access to Justice" <http://www.ohchr.org/Documents/Countries/UNMIT200808.pdf>.

6   UNMIT, "Report on Human Rights Developments: 1 July 2008 to 30 June 2009. Rejecting Impunity: Accountability for Human Rights Violations Past and Present".

7   Ibid.

8   Ibid.

9   Interview with the author, UNMIT, Dili, 2 November 2009.

10   "Escalating Tensions among East Timor Police" ABC Radio Australia <http://www.radioaustralia.net.au/programguide/stories/200810/s2378758.htm> (accessed 10 November 2008).

11   "East Timor Prosecutor Blames President over Trial Delay" ABC Radio Australia, 10 October 2008 <http://www.radioaustralia.net.au/programguide/stories/200810/s2388203.htm> (accessed 18 October 2009).

12   Quoted in Matt Crook, "East Timor: 'Political' Appointment of Police Chief Resented", Inter Press Service (IPS), 23 March 2009 <http://www.etan.org/et2009/03march/22/23polit.htm> (accessed 12 May 2009).

13   See for example <http://thediliinsider.blogspot.com/2009/08/goodbye-conflict-hello-development-hk33.html> (accessed 5 September 2009).

14   Author's discussions with UNPOL officers, Dili, 25 October 2009.

15   UNMIT, "Report on Human Rights Developments: 1 July 2008"; Simon Roughneen, "East Timor: Security Sector Relapse?" *World Politics Review*, 31 July 2009.

16   Julio Tomas Pinto, "Reforming the Security Sector: Facing Challenges, Achieving Progress in Timor-Leste", Tempo Semanal blog, 18 August 2009 <http://temposemanaltimor.blogspot.com/2009/08/ssr-in-timor-leste.html> (accessed 2 September 2009).

17   Ibid.

18   UNMIT, "Report on Human Rights Developments: 1 July 2008".

19   Quoted in Silas Everett, "United Nations Police Withdrawal from Timor-Leste: A Graceful Exit?" *The Asia Foundation*, 25 March 2009.

20   "East Timor Defence Chief: Foreign Troops Should Have Left by Now", *Lusa*, 27 August 2009.

21   Ibid.

22   The handover process was conditioned on the achievement of the four-point criteria agreed between UNMIT and the Timorese Government: (a) the capacity of PNTL to appropriately and effectively respond to the security situation in a given district; (b) final certification of at least 80 per cent of police officers in a given district or unit to be handed over; (c) availability of operational and logistical means; and (d) institutional stability which involves the capacity to enjoy command and control and community acceptance.

23   Author's discussions with UNPOL officers from Canada, Australia, Turkey, Romania, Jordan, and Malaysia, Dili, 29–31 October 2009.

24   Ibid.

25   International Crisis Group, "Handing Back Responsibility to Timor-Leste's Police", *Asia Report*, no. 180, 3 December 2009.

26   The national security legislative package contains three draft laws, on national security, internal security, and national defence.

27   Democratic Republic of East-Timor Presidency of the Ministers' Office, *IV Constitutional Government Program 2007–2012* <http://www.laohamutuk.org/misc/AMPGovt/Govt ProgramEng.pdf> (accessed 26 March 2009).

28   For a good discussion of the organization of the Indonesian armed forces in the past and present, see Joseph L. Derdzinski, *Internal Security Services in Liberalizing States: Transitions, Turmoil, and (In)Security* (Farnham, England: Ashgate, 2009) chapter 3.

29   Interview with the author, La'o Hamutuk, 5 November 2009.

30   La'o Hamutuk, "Maternus Bere Indicted for Crimes against Humanity in Suai Church Massacre and Other Laksaur Militia Activities", 13 November 2009 <http://www. laohamutuk.org/Justice/99/bere/09MaternusBere.htm> (accessed 17 November 2009).

31   Intervention — Response by His Excellency the Prime Minister Kay Rala Xanana Gusmão on the Occasion of the Motion of No Confidence (Plenary Session of the National Parliament, 12 October 2009).

32   United Nations, "Situation of Human Rights in East Timor", Report on the Joint Mission to East Timor Undertaken by the Special Rapporteur of the Commission on Human Rights on Extrajudicial, Summary or Arbitrary Executions, the Special Rapporteur of the Commission on the Question of Torture, and the Special Rapporteur of the Commission on Violence Against Women, its Causes and Consequences, A/54/660 (10 December 1999); United Nations Office of the High Commissioner for Human Rights, "Report of the International Commission of Inquiry on East Timor to the Secretary-General", A/54/726, S/2000/59 (31 January 2000); "Report to the Secretary-

General of the Commission of Experts to Review the Prosecution of Serious Violations of Human Rights in Timor-Leste (the then East Timor) in 1999", 26 May 2005.

33 Interview with the author, La'o Hamutuk, Dili, 5 November 2009.

34 Ibid.

35 "101 East-East Timor: Waiting for Justice", Al Jazeera English, 21 October 2009.

36 Everett, "Law and Justice in Timor-Leste".

37 International Crisis Group, "Timor-Leste: No Time".

38 Quoted in Galuh Wandita et al., "Learning to Engender Reparations in Timor-Leste: Reaching Out to Female Victims", in *What Happened to the Women? Gender and Reparations for Human Rights Violations*, edited by Ruth Rubio-Marin (New York: Social Science Research Council, 2006), p. 319.

39 "2009 Timor-Leste Development Partners Meeting: Summary Notes from Rapporteur Team" <www.mof.gov.tl/en/ae/TLDPM2009/summary-compilationoftldpmrapporteurn otes.pdf> (accessed 27 September 2009).

40 IMF, "Timor-Leste and Development Partners' Meeting", *IMF Statement*, 2–4 April 2009.

41 La'o Hamutuk, "Submission to Committee C, RDTL National Parliament from La'o Hamutuk Regarding the Proposed General State Budget for 2010" <http://www.laohamutuk.org/econ/OGE10/sub/LHSubPNComCOGE10En.pdf> (accessed 6 November 2009).

42 Anthony Deutsch, "E. Timor Aid — Where Did Billions Go? *Associated Press*, 7 September 2009.

43 "East Timor's AMP Government Combats Poverty Legacy of Previous Fretilin Govern-ment", *East Timor Law and Justice Bulletin*, 27 November 2008; "UN Development Rankings a Symptom of the Past", *Dili Weekly*, 23–29 October 2009.

44 World Bank and IMF, "Timor-Leste Petroleum Fund: A Case for Caution, Note Prepared by the World Bank and IMF", May 2008 <http://wikileaks.org/wiki/Worldbank_memo_on_withdrawls_from_Timor_Petroleum_Fund_2008> (accessed 3 February 2009).

45 See, for example, World Bank <http://siteresources.worldbank.org/INTTIMORLESTE/Resources/EAPUpdateTimorLeste.pdf>.

46 La'o Hamutuk, "Timor-Leste Petroleum Fund: September 2005 and November 2009" <http://www.laohamutuk.org/Oil/PetFund/05PFIndex.htm> (accessed 15 November 2009).

47 International Republican Institute, Timor-Leste National Survey Results, 10 November–16 December 2008 <http://www.iri.org/asia/easttimor.asp> (accessed 20 May 2009).

48 Tempo Semanal, "Internet Exclusive: A New Budget for Timor-Leste. But Questions About Corruption Persist", 2 December 2009.

49 It must be noted that in the 2008 survey 44 per cent of respondents reported that "depends on" the case. This statement was not offered as an option in 2004, which may have had an impact on the results. Irrespective of this, however, the current

proportion of those who disapprove of such practice without exception (34 per cent) remains very low. Interestingly, more women (24 per cent) than men (18 per cent) continue to believe a man has a right to hit his wife if she misbehaves. Everett, "United Nations Police Withdrawal", pp. 44–45.

[50] "Baseline Study on Sexual and Gender-Based Violence in Covalima and Bobonaro Districts Released", UNMIT Press Release, 13 August 2009.

[51] La'o Hamutuk, "How Much Money Have International Donors Spent on and in Timor-Leste? A briefing paper from La'o Hamutuk, September 2009" <http://www.laohamutuk.org/reports/09bgnd/HowMuchAidEn.pdf> (accessed 20 October 2009).

[52] Deutsch, "East Timor Aid".

[53] Ibid; La'o Hamutuk, "How Much Money".

[54] Ian Storey, "China's Inroads into East Timor", China Brief 9, no. 6, 19 March 2009.

[55] Loro Horta, "Timor-Leste: The Dragon's Newest Friend", Research Institute on Contemporary Southeast Asia (IRASEC), Irasec Discussion Papers, no. 4, May 2009.

[56] "East Timor to Negotiate Loan from China for Infrastructures", Macau Hub, 15 October 2009.

[57] Storey, "China's Inroads".

[58] Mark Dodd, "Chinese Base Plan Causes Headache", The Australian, 23 November 2009.

[59] "101 East — East Timor", Al Jazeera English.

Vietnam

Southeast Asian Affairs 2010

VIETNAM
A Tale of Four Players

Alexander L. Vuving

Who are the key players of Vietnamese politics? What characterizes its dynamics? What is to be expected of it in the next few years? This essay is an attempt to address the above questions. It suggests that the politics of Vietnam can be imagined as a game between four key players. If the government is defined as the central authoritative locus of politics in a country, then the Vietnamese Government is caught primarily between regime conservatives, modernizers, rent-seekers, and China. Each of these players is a bloc of diverse actors that share an ultimate strategic goal or inclination.

The distinction of the three Vietnamese blocs deserves further explanation. The criterion for sorting someone to a bloc is the person's priority or inclination when it comes to fundamental issues such as ideology (whether the country should be open or closed to liberal ideas from the West) and the Communist Party's relation to the nation (whether the party is superior or inferior to the nation). The conservative is one who is more likely to opt for a "closed door" and "party first" policy, the modernizer for openness and the whole-nation's perspective, and the rent-seeker for whatever that brings him or her most money.

In their discourse, leaders often use the vocabulary of the day but their emphasis will reveal where they stand. A regime conservative, such as former General Secretary of the Vietnam Communist Party (VCP) Le Kha Phieu, may embrace the ideas of "intra-party democracy", "socialist-oriented market economy", and Vietnam as a "modern nation" and a "friend and reliable partner to other countries", but his emphasis is on the class nature, as opposed to a whole-nation nature, of the party's core interests, preserving the country's "socialist" identity, and contrasting it with the "capitalist and imperialist" West. Modernization, reform, democracy, and international integration, if adopted, are only means to a

---

ALEXANDER L. VUVING is Associate Professor at the Asia-Pacific Center for Security Studies.

higher end, and if necessary, can be sacrificed. That higher end is the continuation of the communist regime.[1]

A modernizer, such as the late Prime Minister Vo Van Kiet, may vow to maintain "the leadership role of the party" and build "socialism", but his visions of the party and socialism are completely different from those of the conservatives. Kiet and other modernizers within the VCP want a party that regards the interests of the entire nation as its own and define socialism as "a rich people, a strong nation, and a just, democratic, and civilized society". Patriotism, not Marxism-Leninism, is the bonding and guiding idea of the modernizers. Whereas conservatives such as the VCP chiefs Do Muoi, Le Kha Phieu, and Nong Duc Manh emphatically asserted that "national independence and socialism" (meaning insulation from Western and liberal influence plus communist rule and identity) are the fundamentals of Vietnamese policy, Kiet proposed in a classified letter to the VCP Politburo in August 1995 to replace them with "nation and democracy".[2] Although advocating multiparty democracy is impossible for mainstream elite modernizers because it is taboo, modernizers support more and deeper political reform to broaden democracy and enhance effectiveness.

Rent-seekers are opportunists who seek to maximize benefits, usually gained from government-granted privileges, regardless of the national interest as defined by either the conservatives or the modernizers. As will be seen in the next section, Vietnam's rent-seekers is a special group of profit-seekers that is more powerful than the latter because it has a monopolistic power in its back.

All the three key blocs — regime conservatives, modernizers, and rent-seekers — are present both in and outside the ruling party and the government and represented at every echelon of policymaking. Their fault lines cut across generations, regions, and institutions. Most Vietnamese leaders stand more or less consistently within a bloc but some have changed blocs over time and others are more agnostic. Prominent conservatives include VCP General Secretaries Do Muoi (1991–97), Le Kha Phieu (1997–2001), Nong Duc Manh (2001–present), and former State President Le Duc Anh (1992–97). The modernizers were represented in the top leadership more energetically by the late Foreign Minister Nguyen Co Thach (1982–91), the late Prime Minister Vo Van Kiet (1991–97) and former National Assembly Chairman Nguyen Van An (2001–6), and less markedly by former State President Vo Chi Cong (1987–92) and former Prime Minister Phan Van Khai (1997–2006). Former State President Tran Duc Luong (1997–2006) can be seen as a rent–seeker. The late VCP General Secretary Nguyen Van Linh (1986–91) changed from a modernizer to a conservative during 1989. And State President Nguyen Minh Triet (2006–present) is an agnostic.

The politics of Vietnam is played out on four major planes — the economy, core domestic politics, state-society relations, and foreign relations. Its dynamics in each of these areas shows a distinct feature. The one on the economic front is the crisis of Vietnam's growth model. At the core of domestic politics, there is the confluence of money, power, and world views, or to put it more elegantly, profit, power, and perspectives. The emergence of civil society, especially mainstream elite civil society, is increasingly setting the trend in state-society relations. In the geopolitical arena, a central focus of Vietnam's politics lies in efforts to self-help in China's backyard.

The year 2009 offered telling snapshots of Vietnam's politics with regard to its key players and the features of its dynamics. The discussion below will outline some contours of Vietnamese politics through an examination of its four players and four features, illustrated by events and developments throughout 2009.

The Confluence of Profit, Power, and Perspectives

Since the launch of *doi moi* (renovation) in 1986, Vietnam has been experimenting with a mixture of communism and capitalism. This experiment is a conflict-ridden cohabitation of two grand strategies pursued by two camps that can be called the "regime conservatives" and the "modernizers". I call them so because the central objective of the former is to preserve the communist regime whereas that of the latter is to modernize the country by introducing elements of capitalism and liberalism.[3] Despite the fact that these two camps represent the co-ruling grand strategies, they are not the only key players of Vietnamese politics. The cohabitation has created a third bloc that takes advantage of the mixture and is highly adaptive to that "brackish water" environment. The third bloc tries its best to maintain the communist-capitalist mixture that supports its way of life. As capitalism offers opportunities to make profit, while communism offers a monopoly of power, a mixture of the two creates conducive conditions for both using money to buy power and using power to make money. The third bloc, which can be called the "rent-seekers", uses money to manipulate politics, and once having access to Communist Party power, uses the political monopoly to reap hyper-profits.[4] Unlike the conservatives and the modernizers, the rent-seekers are not guided by vision; they are guided by profit motive.

As Vietnamese politics is characterized by a coexistence of communism and capitalism, it is intuitive to think that most political conflict in Vietnam can be seen along the conservative-versus-modernizer line. Yet this model is not accurate. It is not accurate because it either ignores the rent-seekers, which in many cases are key players, or regards them as just profit-seekers, who, as conventional wisdom suggests, prefer capitalism over communism. In this model, then, the rent-seekers will tend to side with the modernizers against the conservatives. In actuality, however, Vietnam's rent-seekers tend to side with the conservatives when it comes to the continuation of Communist Party monopoly and with the modernizers when it comes to allowing party members to own large properties and operate capitalist businesses. The rent-seekers are a species specialized to live in the "brackish water" of commercialism under communist rule. With the power monopoly of the Communist Party in their back, they are markedly more powerful than other profit-seekers. Given the existence of that third bloc, the politics of Vietnam is, at one level, the contestation between regime conservatives and modernizers, but at another level, the confluence of money, power, and world views.[5]

The year 2009 revealed the confluence of profit, power, and perspectives through several affairs, two of which are arguably most prominent. On 19 November, the Can Tho City Appeals Court upheld a lower court verdict reached in August against Tran Ngoc Suong, popularly known as Mrs Ba Suong, on a charge of running an off-the-books welfare fund. A former Director of the state-owned Song Hau Collective Farm who was awarded the title of a Labour Hero by the government, Suong was sentenced to eight years in jail and ordered to repay some 4.3 billion dong (US$240,500). The verdicts caused a public outrage in which several high-ranking officials and prominent public personalities spoke out in support of Suong. Former vice-president Nguyen Thi Binh, a conservative, said that Suong's sentencing was "unfair" as she had "devoted her whole life to improving the lives of thousands of farmers" and "maintained the fund not for her personal benefit", a portrayal that was echoed by the reform-minded press and validated by the journalist Huy Duc, who had reported on the Song Hau Farm and Mrs Suong for years. The news media also reported that the Song Hau Farm was awarded two Labour Medals by the government and regarded as a showcase of socialism where the state retained land-use rights but provided relatively good welfare services.

While the public outrage was mainly motivated by the moral aspect of the case, it was expected that the socialist state would intervene to support a hero of its cause. But it did not. In fact, Suong was represented at the court by reform-minded lawyers and the public support for her mobilized by reform-minded media. With regard to the state's action, the court received instructions from the Can Tho City party leadership, and after a few weeks of intensive reporting, the media was ordered to stop talking about the case of Mrs Suong. Behind the scenes the Can Tho City Government had decided to allocate the lands of the Song Hau Farm to an industrial park and urban project. The Deputy Secretary of the Can Tho City Party Committee, Pham Thanh Van, was recorded as telling Suong: "You will retire and land safely in good name if you return the lands of the farm [to the city]".[6]

The second case involves Jetstar Pacific Airline (JPA), a joint venture of the State Capital Investment Corporation (SCIC) with the Australian airline Qantas in which the Vietnamese state-owned enterprise (SOE) owns the majority stake of 70 per cent. In late 2009, a controversy was sparked after a State Audit Agency probe of SCIC figured out that while JPA's chief executives caused a loss of US$31 million in a fuel hedging business, they earned more than the executives of comparable SOEs. The controversy also involved questions about unusually high salaries for SCIC executives. In early December, Luong Hoai Nam, former JPA chief executive and a high-ranking official of SCIC, was detained by police for his involvement in the fuel hedge, while two Australian JPA executives were prevented from leaving Vietnam.

JPA's predecessor was Pacific Airlines (PA), a domestic joint venture with the state flag carrier Vietnam Airlines (VNA) as the majority stakeholder. Established in 1990, PA represented an effort by modernizers to introduce a degree of competition in Vietnam's aviation industry. However, the maintenance of this element of competition proved difficult. After ten years in operation, PA posted a cumulative loss of more than US$10 million.[7] Although an offspring of VNA, PA was reportedly not welcome by its mother company.

The monopolistic position of the state flag carrier became a harder reality for PA's successor. The confluence of money, power, and world views can be discerned in a report by *Herald Sun*:

> [In mid-2009], Prime Minister Nguyen Tan Dung was forced to intervene when supplies of jet kerosene were cut off when Vietnam Airlines stopped its tankers refuelling Jetstar Pacific's fleet. Jetstar Pacific's latest run of problems started last July when it reported its first profitable month after 18 years of flying, initially as Pacific Airlines. At that time the Transportation Ministry ordered Qantas to strip the Jetstar name and distinctive orange branding off the six-jet Jetstar Pacific fleet, claiming it 'too Australian'.[8]

As veteran Vietnam watcher Carlyle Thayer argues,

> the issue was caused by Jetstar Pacific's success after mid-2009 when it turned a profit after cutting costs and increasing market share (18 per

cent to 25 per cent) at the expense of Vietnam Airlines. Jetstar Pacific's aggressive promotion of cheap fares rankled. I see a parallel with the 2006 ANB-AMBRO case when a state bank lost money in currency conversions, in Jetstar Pacific's case the State Capital Investment Corporation lost due to fuel hedging. In both cases Vietnamese security/police have criminalized business management and poor decisions. The Dutch paid several million to get off the hook and I suspect Qantas/Jetstar will have to pay a fine or compensation so SCIC, a state-owned enterprise, will not be out of pocket.... There is obviously a state-enterprise interest group at work. It is about getting money out of Qantas when their in-country staff hedged and lost on fuel prices. This affected the State Capital Investment Corporation which is a major shareholder in Jetstar.[9]

A Growth Model in Crisis

Over the last two decades, the confluence of money, power, and world views in reform-era Vietnam has resulted in an economic path that most benefits rent-seekers. In its early stages, this capital-driven path was paralleled by a labour-driven path and showed remarkable growth patterns. Impressed by the country's growth records in the previous decade, in 2005 Goldman Sachs identified Vietnam as one of the "Next Eleven" countries that "could potentially have a BRIC-like impact in rivalling the G7."[10] Goldman Sachs studies projected that in 2025 Vietnam could be the world's seventeenth largest economy and in 2050 it could become the fifteenth. The projections were premised on the condition that "these economies can stay on their current paths".[11] But soon after the release of these reports, Vietnam's growth model showed signs of serious problems. During 2008, the inflation rates surged to higher than 20 per cent, forcing the government to put the brakes on its growth-first policy and switch gears to an anti-inflationary programme. Much in line with our prediction on these pages, the bubbles blew up when the investment fever following Vietnam's accession to the World Trade Organization (WTO) met with bottlenecks in the country's administration, institutions, infrastructure, and education system.[12] On top of that came the global financial crisis that started the same year.

An economy with foreign trade surpassing gross domestic product by roughly one and a half times, Vietnam was hit hard by the global crisis. It dramatically reduced the amount of foreign investments and shrunk the size of foreign markets for Vietnamese products. The volume of foreign direct investments (FDI) approved in 2009 was US$21.5 billion, or 70 per cent less than the previous year. The amount of FDI that were disbursed in 2009 is estimated at US$10 billion, falling by 13 per cent from that of 2008. Vietnam's exports in 2009 are estimated to have shrunk by 9.7 per cent to US$56.6 billion, while imports decreased by 14.7 per cent to US$68.8 billion. A significant part of the reduction of Vietnam's exports in 2009 resulted from lower prices of the country's main export commodities such as oil, rice, coffee, and coal. Vietnam's crude oil export value, which accounts for 11 per cent of the nation's total exports, is estimated to have plunged by 40 per cent though the export volume decreased only 2.4 per cent. In 2009, Vietnam registered a record volume of rice export and a year-to-year increase by 25.4 per cent in volume, but its value, which accounts for 4.8 per cent of the total exports, fell 8 per cent. Likewise, the coffee export, which accounts for 3 per cent of the total exports, rose by 10.2 per cent in volume but shrunk by 19 per cent in value, and the coal export, which accounts for 2.3 per cent, fell by 4.5 per cent in value despite an increase of 29.9 per cent in volume.[13]

The economic crisis triggered a new round of debates on the fundamental directions of Vietnam's policies. For regime conservatives, the current crisis is clear proof that the supervising and controlling role of the state is crucial to the functioning of the economy. Conservatives also praise the superiority of the one-party system in weathering crises. They argue that it helps maximize mobilization and create consensus at a time when these are most desirable but usually hard to attain. These views were aired, for example, in the remarks by To Huy Rua, who is Head of the Propaganda Department of the VCP, at the fifth Sino-Vietnamese ideology conference in December 2009. But the VCP chief propagandist, who was elected to the Politburo at the Ninth Plenum of the Party's Central Committee in January 2009, did not represent the views of the conservatives only. Echoing the modernizers, Rua acknowledged that the crisis provides an opportunity to restructure the economy and contended that the restructuring must be oriented towards a new growth model that is based on "dynamic comparative advantages" and incorporates the concept of "sustainable development". This new thinking on development is aimed at reconciling the three goals of economic growth, social fairness, and environment-friendliness.[14]

Apparently avoiding highly controversial issues, Rua's speech remains silent on the role of the state-owned enterprises, which is a key point of contention between the conservatives and the modernizers. Regime conservatives want to retain the dominant role (*vai tro chu dao*) of the state sector in the economy. In their vision, the national economy rests on the SOEs as its pillars, the biggest of which will serve as the nation's "iron fists" — strong competitors in the international market and a powerful tool of governance, both economic and political. Unlike private entities, SOEs are to obey the party and the government and fulfil political tasks set by the party-state. In return, they have privileged access to policymaking, credit, land, and other resources owned by the state. The intertwinement of the state and its own companies is reflected in the fact that the board presidents of the largest state-owned conglomerates are members of the VCP Central Committee, which by statute is the most powerful policymaking body in the country during the time between the party congresses.[15]

Modernizers, however, see the state-owned conglomerates as "dinosaurs in a juvenile economy".[16] They point out that these enterprises have failed to become the nation's iron fists — neither have they emerged strongly in international competition, nor have they accomplished well the political tasks. Rather, they try to capitalize on and perpetuate their state-sanctioned privileges and monopolistic position — for their own profit. As a result, they become producers of inefficiency and corruption.[17] Restructuring of the SOEs is thus a central point in the modernizers' agenda. Particularly, modernizers urge to change the ownership structure of the SOEs towards more privatization. Assessing the present situation, modernizers argue that Vietnam's growth model has reached its apex and restructuring is the key to both overcoming crises and avoiding the middle-income trap. Most modernizers agree that this should be a comprehensive restructuring that includes transforming the ownership structure of the SOEs, overhauling the economic institutions and regulations, and restructuring the domestic markets and enterprises.[18]

The government tries to combine the views of both the regime conservatives and the modernizers. Nevertheless, its focus is on fixing short-term problems which threaten its authority. When the global crisis arose, it quickly switched gears from anti-inflation to anti-slowdown (December 2008). Its central response was a stimulus package that cost up to US$8 billion. When the economy showed signs of recovery and the spectre of inflation threatened to come back, the government devalued the dong by roughly 5 per cent against the U.S. dollar, increased the central bank's benchmark interest rate to 8 per cent, and ended the stimulus programme earlier than expected (late November, early December 2009).[19] With a 5.32 per cent growth rate, Vietnam stood out, alongside China, Indonesia and Cambodia, as one of only a few economies in East Asia that expanded more than 2 per cent in 2009.

However, Vietnam has paid a high price for this short-term success. Vietnam is one of only a few countries with both a fiscal budget deficit and a current-account deficit.[20] On top of that, the country has run a huge foreign trade deficit for more than a decade. At the same time, as the Governor of Vietnam's central bank acknowledged, the country's foreign debt had risen dramatically in 2009 compared with recent years. The International Monetary Fund places Vietnam's external debt at one-third of the country's gross domestic product (GDP), and the National Assembly's Committee for Budget and Finance puts the total government debt at 44.6 per cent of the GDP.[21] The combination of these factors causes a large dilemma for the government. The three-way deficits put an enormous pressure on the dong to weaken. A drastic depreciation of the dong may boost the exports and reduce the import surplus but may also cause negative psychological effects and enlarge the foreign debts. But maintaining an artificially high value of the dong for too long would exhaust the already thin foreign reserves. Analysts estimated that dollar sales aimed at stabilizing the dong during 2009 have shrunk Vietnam's foreign-exchange reserves to US$16.5 billion, which is enough for less than three months of imports. Outside in the region, Vietnam's neighbours such as China, South Korea, and Thailand all have added substantially to their reserves.[22]

Vietnam's relatively high growth rate conceals dismal inefficiencies. In 2009 the incremental capital-output ratio (ICOR), which measures the inefficiency of investment spending, soared to 8.05 from 6.92 in 2008 and 4.76 in 2007.[23] These are markedly higher compared to other high-growth countries in their pre-peak investment stages. For example, Japan's ICOR in the 1960s and South Korea's ICOR in the 1980s were just above 3. More recently, China's ICOR increased from about 3 for the 1990s to nearly 4 in average for the period from 2001–8 and is estimated at about 6.7 for 2009.[24] Vietnam's extremely high ICOR also indicates that the country's economic growth is driven primarily by capital enlargement, not productivity enhancement. If Vietnam stays on the current path, the economy is not likely to take off, as the Goldman Sachs projections suggest, and a crash is possible.

The Rise of Civil Society

A characteristic of the Leninist regime is the Communist Party's monopoly of all social spheres. When the regime allows some elements of capitalism and liberalism, as in Vietnam and China today, the party's control of the public sphere loosens, making some space for civil society. The glimmerings of civil society in Vietnam have two major causes. First, the introduction of limited economic liberalization has created a social sphere populated by private entities and economically independent individuals. Second, there is an ongoing conflict within the ruling elite between the regime conservatives and the modernizers. As the state ideology favours the former, the latter are in a weaker position, with those in the government playing rather the role of a minor coalition partner. Given these circumstances, the modernizers have a need to use and enlarge the part of the public sphere that is not under state control, so they can raise their voice when it does not align with the state ideology and official party line.

Vietnam has been loosening its totalitarian regime for a quarter of century, but throughout the first fifteen years or so, civil society could hardly enter the launching pad, not to speak of having taken off. A major barrier for Vietnam's civil society is the Communist Party's paranoid suspicion that civil society will act against it. More exactly, it is because the conservatives are still strong. Vowing to modernize the country, the party has agreed that society should be ruled by law and private associations should be allowed. As early as 1992, the government began drafting legislation on civil society organizations to govern the rapidly expanding private associational activity. But after almost two decades with eleven drafts, the bill has yet to be passed.[25]

In the last five years, however, Vietnam's civil society seemed to be rolling onto a launching pad. Some remarkable indications of this development can be observed. The first is the return of independent policy-discussing organizations. Starting in 2005, hundreds of citizens began to form new political parties and organizations that challenge Communist Party rule.[26] In September 2007, after Prime Minister Nguyen Tan Dung disbanded the Advisory Group to the Prime Minister that he inherited from his predecessors, several prominent intellectuals, including leading members of the former Advisory Group, established the first ever independent policy think tank in socialist Vietnam, the Institute of Development Studies (IDS). Members of the think tank included such personalities as the economists Le Dang Doanh, Tran Duc Nguyen, and Tran Viet Phuong, who had served generations of party and government chiefs as major advisers; former Ambassador Nguyen Trung, who was an adviser with a ministerial rank to former Prime Minister Vo Van Kiet; former Vice President of the Vietnam Chamber of Commerce and Industry Pham Chi Lan; leading scholars such as the mathematician Hoang Tuy and the historian Phan Huy Le; and prominent thinkers such as Nguyen Quang A, Tuong Lai, and Nguyen Ngoc.

During the last decade the space for public discussion has widened exponentially due to the application of Internet-based communication tools ranging from emails to online forums, and, more recently, blogs and Facebook. The state-owned press has also gained significant autonomy vis-à-vis the state. An eminent case is VietNamNet, an online news outlet with popular websites such as vietnamnet.vn and tuanvietnam.net. Founded in 1997 by Nguyen Anh Tuan, a reform-minded computer engineer, it moved within only a few years to the forefront of Vietnamese journalism and became a major venue for independent and pro-reform views of public issues. Seen as a recalcitrant web portal, in 2007 it was put under the direct supervision of the Ministry of Information and Communication with the conservative Le Doan Hop at the top. Nevertheless, VietNamNet emerged after that even stronger as an advocate of greater reform.[27] Dense online communications both empower and "spill over" into offline activities. A case in point and an indication of Vietnam's nascent civil society is the December 2007 street protests organized by Internet-based groups against China's plans to set up an administrative unit to govern two archipelagos that Vietnam claims in the South China Sea.

Three factors have arguably driven the rise of civil society in Vietnam. The first is the country's deeper international integration, marked by its accession to the WTO in 2006/7. The event signified not simply Vietnam's participation in a global trade agreement but the completion of its travel from one world to another — from a socialist community to a non-socialist one. The second factor behind the emergence of Vietnam's civil society is the spread of new communication tools that help ordinary citizens to increase their communications and connections and make monitoring by the authorities much more difficult. The third factor is the perception of a Chinese threat. This provides a moral high ground and a reason acceptable to the government for civil society activities that, though not initiated by the authorities, appear to defend the national interest.

The year 2009 witnessed a dramatic development of civil society in Vietnam. On 5 January, the day that Prime Minister Dung convened a meeting with his cabinet to discuss a mega-project on bauxite mining in South Central Vietnam and the VCP Central Committee started its ninth plenum, General Vo Nguyen Giap, the only living founding father of the socialist republic, wrote a letter to the prime minister calling for a suspension of the bauxite plans. The letter remained at first unpublicized but on 10 January a copy of it was leaked to the public on the popular website viet-studies.info. On the 14 January, one day after the party meeting closed and upon the news that the government decided to go ahead with the project, the online newspaper VietNamNet decided to publicize the General's letter on its website, making the dissenting view heard to a wider domestic public. In his letter, Giap pointed to concerns of scientists and activists about "the serious risk to the natural and social environment posed by bauxite exploitation projects". He wrote that in the early 1980s he had overseen a study on whether to mine for bauxite in the region, and that Soviet experts had advised against the project because of "the risk of long-term, very serious and insurmountable ecological damage posed not only to the local population but also the population and the plains of South Central Vietnam".[28]

Although at Giap's time the government had decided against bauxite mining, during the "industrialization era" a decade later it reversed the decision. In the December 2001 Vietnam-China joint statement, VCP Secretary General Nong Duc Manh pledged to cooperate with China on exploiting bauxite in South Central Vietnam.[29] This looked like Manh's gift on the occasion of his inaugural visit to China after becoming the VCP chief, but it also could have been done at the Chinese request, as Vietnam had invited U.S. and Australian firms to study the projects during the 1990s. However, Chinese involvement in such a major project at a strategically important area was apparently not approved by the modernizers in the government, including then Prime Minister Phan Van Khai.[30] On the one hand, modernizers tried to delay the project with China. On the other, they tried to multinationalize it by drawing in Thais, Russians, Americans, and Australians. However, the project was accelerated after Nguyen Tan Dung replaced Phan Van Khai as Prime Minister in 2006. In June 2008 at the VCP chief Nong Duc Manh's visit to China, the two sides issued a joint statement that reiterated China's interest in cooperating in developing Vietnam's bauxite industry. After Dung's visit to Beijing in late October hundreds of Chinese came to work in various sites in two provinces.

Dung's determination to implement the pledge made by Manh is puzzling. But a look at the circumstances may reveal some interesting insights. In the previous months a financial crisis was coupled with Japan's suspension of its US$1 billion aid package. The Japanese decision was prompted by a graft scandal involving Ho Chi Minh City party boss Le Thanh Hai, a close ally of Dung. At the eighth plenum of the VCP Central Committee (2–4 October), Dung was heavily criticized for the poor economic performance of his Cabinet.[31] Manh reportedly asked Dung to step down as Prime Minister. Later, Chinese sources reported that Dung received substantial Chinese economic assistance during his late October visit.

Although critics of the bauxite project had appeared in the pro-reform news media as early as 2007 when the Prime Minister approved it, the project only became a hot issue when it started to be implemented in late 2008. After General Giap's January 2009 letter, it quickly became the topic of a great national debate. It was a divisive issue even within the top VCP leadership. In late April, the VCP Politburo issued a "conclusion" that took a compromising stance that vowed to continue the project but to pay more attention to its social, ecological, and national security effects. President Nguyen Minh Triet, Vice Prime Minister Truong Vinh Trong, and Party Standing Secretary Truong Tan Sang, the number two in the VCP apparatus, were reportedly among those who disagreed with the bauxite deal, though publicly they had to support the government position and thus throw their weight behind the project.

While the bauxite deal was dividing the party, it was a unifying factor in the society outside. It helped to forge a coalition of nationalists and environmentalists. In this coalition, concerns of national security merged with concerns of human security and were focused on one target — China. The year 2009 witnessed a wave of debates on various aspects of the Chinese threat, ranging from illegal Chinese workers who are entering the country in the thousands, to hazardous Chinese products flooding the domestic markets, Chinese attacks on Vietnamese fishermen, and China's perceived violation of Vietnam's sovereignty in the South China Sea.

The combined security and human security concerns underlying the anti-China protests have placed them on a moral high ground. This situation both encouraged the protesters and made repression by the authorities more difficult. In June, the jurist Cu Huy Ha Vu filed an unprecedented lawsuit against the Prime Minister for breaking national laws in an attempt to fast-track the bauxite mining project. Four days after the Politburo convened (26 April) to review policy on bauxite mining an anti-bauxite petition signed by 135 scholars and intellectuals was delivered to the National Assembly. The petition stated that "China has been notorious in the modern world as a country causing the greatest pollution and other problems".[32] The leading petitioners — Professors Nguyen Hue Chi and Nguyen The Hung and the writer Pham Toan — went on to set up a website titled "Bauxite Vietnam", which within months hit a record number of visits. As Carlyle Thayer has noted, "By May 2009, the anti-bauxite network of 2008 had grown into a national coalition including environmentalists, local residents, scientists, economists, retired military officers and veterans, retired state officials, social scientists, other academics and intellectuals, elements of the media, and National Assembly deputies. These critics were all mainstream elite".[33] Whereas public opposition to bauxite mining did extend to religious leaders and political dissidents, what is new and significant about the activities of civil society in 2009 is the rise of mainstream elite dissent motivated by intertwined national and human security concerns. This chapter focuses on the rise of mainstream elite civil society that, because of the proximity to state power and because of many parallels with what happened in the late 1980s in Eastern Europe, may be consequential.[34]

The authorities responded to the political dissent that was widening by clamping down on critics. From late May to early July 2009, several pro-democracy activists, including Tran Huynh Duy Thuc, an Internet entrepreneur, Le Cong Dinh, a high-profile lawyer, and Nguyen Tien Trung, a renowned activist, were arrested for "spreading propaganda against the state", a charge that in December would be amended to include violation of Article 79 which carries a maximum death penalty for "carrying out activities aimed at overthrowing the people's administration".[35] On 24 July the Prime Minister signed a decree known as Decision No. 97 limiting scientific and technological research. Under this decree, critical feedback (*phan bien*) on policy issues, a recently allowed tool to rationalize governance, is no longer allowed to be publicized but only sent to the relevant authorities. On 14 September, the day before the decree took effect, Vietnam's only independent think tank, IDS, decided to disband in protest. On 28 August the Ministry of Public Security issued instructions proscribing political commentary and limiting blogs to personal matters. About the same time, three prominent bloggers were detained and a renowned journalist fired from his job.

Journalist Huy Duc, who blogged under the name "Osin" (Housemaid), was dismissed from the newspaper *Saigon Tiep Thi* after writing a blog entry that praises the fall of the Berlin Wall and accuses the former Soviet Union of imposing on Eastern Europe "a regime which deprived men of fundamental rights".[36] Duc was far from being a dissident; he had had a close relationship with the late Prime Minister Vo Van Kiet and was his biographer. The three bloggers arrested included Bui Thanh Hieu and Pham Doan Trang in Hanoi and Nguyen Ngoc Nhu Quynh in Nha Trang. Hieu, who blogged under the name "Nguoi Buon Gio" (Wind Trader), was famous for his "Dai Ve chi di" series, which mimics the style of ancient Chinese literature and tells a fictitious story of the states Ve and Te that exposes the unpatriotic objectives of Ve's leaders and the country's subservient posture vis-à-vis Te as a result of those objectives. Ve and Te are two ancient Chinese states, but the initials of their names and the activities of their leaders as described by the author allude to Vietnam and China (*Trung Quoc* in Vietnamese). However, as Hieu told the BBC Vietnamese service later in an interview, he was detained for his involvement in printing and distributing T-shirts with slogans against the bauxite deal and in support of Vietnam's claims to the Spratly and Paracel Islands.[37] These were also the activities for which Quynh, who blogged under the name "Me Nam" (Mother Mushroom), was questioned by police.[38] The third blogger, Doan Trang, was editor of the online magazine TuanVietNam, an offshoot of VietNamNet, and had written several articles in these and other websites criticizing China's role in the partition of Vietnam in 1954, its role as a hegemonic power, and its territorial claims in the South China Sea. She was arrested probably not for those writings, as the international press presumed, but for reporting an intervention of a Chinese Embassy counsellor with the Vietnamese Ministry of Information and Communication in which the Chinese noted that the opinions voiced by some Vietnamese newspapers were "unfriendly" to China and the Vietnamese media should be placed under control.

Fearing a movement that is inspired by patriotism and anti-regime sentiments, regime conservatives launched a campaign against what they called "the strategy of peaceful evolution". On 25 June, the VCP Propaganda Department issued a "propaganda concept paper" on "strengthening the struggle against plots and activities of 'peaceful evolution' in the ideological and cultural area". The concept paper notes that it follows up on the 24 April 2009 decree by the Party Central Secretariat. The paper describes the background of the propaganda campaign as the surge since the Tenth Party congress (2006) of the strategy of "peaceful evolution" and "cultural invasion" by hostile forces in order to "eliminate the socialist regime and the Vietnamese cultural identity". Other features of the situation are the trends of "self-evolution", "self-transformation", and "deviation from the socialist path" among party members and government officials. The paper identifies the West and the United States as the main hostile forces. It regards the U.S. Peace Corps as an organization specialized in propaganda and subversion activities, and the U.S. programme of education cooperation with Vietnam a means to transform Vietnam into a Western country. The paper asserts that influenced by liberal ideas from the West, some Vietnamese leaders and journalists have recently placed too much emphasis on the role of critical feedback (*phan bien*) and misused "social power" (civil society forces) to attack the leadership role of the party and the socialist state.[39] This is a clear reference to the modernizers. As close ties with the West, critical feedback, and strengthening civil society are major policies supported by the modernizers, the propaganda campaign represents a unilateral move by conservatives in their political battle against the modernizers.

Immediately after the release of the Propaganda Department concept paper, the Ho Chi Minh City Party Committee's newspaper *Saigon Giai Phong* published a series titled "Marxist-Leninist Theory and Socialism: A Trend or a Necessary Law?" (29 to 5 July and 6 to 10 October), which from 3 November would become a joint programme with the Ho Chi Minh City Television channel HTV9 under the title "A Necessary Law". This programme was scheduled to be continued until the eightieth anniversary of the VCP, 3 February 2010. It would address issues such as the collapse of communism in Eastern Europe and the return of socialism in Latin America, and attempt to uncover the nature of capitalism through analyses of the global financial crisis.[40] In late August, the People's Army newspaper (*Quan Doi Nhan Dan*) launched a long-term series entitled "Defeating the Strategy of 'Peaceful Evolution'", which two weeks later would be joined by a weekly rubric titled "Preventing and Fighting Peaceful Evolution". However, most of the other major media outlets did not respond positively to the call of the Propaganda Department. The pro-reform news website VietNamNet with its flagship TuanVietNam even stepped up its crusade for what, if judged from the spirit of the concept paper, would be regarded as "peaceful evolution" and "self-evolution" and "deviation from the socialist path".

The authorities' clamping down on the nationalists and modernizers did not seem to create the necessary fear. After their releases, Nguoi Buon Gio continued his "Dai Ve chi di" series, Doan Trang emerged even stronger as an advocate of patriotism and good governance, and Me Nam's memoirs of her detention were publicized in several blogs despite police request that she stop blogging. Towards the year's end, TuanVietNam launched a series of articles on "Vietnam and the Development Model in the New Decade", all of which adopt nationalist standpoints and regard the rise of China as both a central parameter of the present and future world and a potential threat.[41] In one of these articles, former Ambassador Nguyen Trung calls for "building a political regime that is identical with the Fatherland", an allusion to a change of the regime from the current one that is identical with the Communist Party. He claims that "the most salient achievement of the 25 years of *doi moi* is democracy" and notes that democracy is still considered a threat of peaceful evolution, and that that is why reform continues to be obstructed.[42]

The fact that Trung's article has not been removed since reveals that a regime change from a Leninist to a democratic national state has gained substantial support among Vietnam's ruling elite. This is also an indication that even if the modernizers still cannot fully redress the imbalance of power between them and the conservatives, the limits to their actions have been dramatically widened.

Self-help in China's Backyard

The emergence of Vietnam's two-headed grand strategy dates back to the second half of the 1980s. When communism collapsed in Eastern Europe during 1989, the ruling VCP was faced with a strategic choice between keeping the regime or changing it. Regime conservatives, based on the view that world politics is driven by the antagonism between socialism and capitalism, which has become imperialism in the present stage of history, and ultimately on the self-perception of Vietnam as an "anti-imperialist" (read: anti-Western) champion, preferred regime preservation and advocated "political stability". Modernizers, based on the view that world politics is driven by national interests and globalization ("internationalization" was their term in the late 1980s), and ultimately on the self-perception of Vietnam as a "backward" country, urged to conduct more reform.

The foreign policy linchpin of the modernizers is international integration. Modernizers envisage a change in Vietnam's international role from a socialist state to a democratic national state that is fully integrated into the world community. More specifically, they place a strong emphasis on cooperation with regional neighbours, in Southeast Asia as well as the larger Asia-Pacific region, and developing close ties with the advanced industrial countries. On the contrary, the central foreign policy orientation of the regime conservatives is "anti-imperialism", which includes combating the West and their perceived strategy of "peaceful evolution" against the communist regime. In the post-1989 era, regime conservatives see a key means to achieve their objectives in building a strategic alliance on an ideological basis with China.[43]

Beginning with Nguyen Van Linh in 1990 and continued by his successors Le Kha Phieu and Nong Duc Manh, these VCP General Secretaries all sought a strategic alliance with China. Although a formal "comprehensive strategic cooperative partnership" was only declared in 2008, Vietnam had informally titled China its "strategic ally" already since the 1990s.[44] The prevalence of anti-imperialism over integration in Vietnam's grand strategy after 1989 ensured that none of the country's ties with strategically important foreign states other than China (with the exception of Laos) was strong enough. For example, conservatives blocked — successfully at first — Vietnam's joining of ASEAN, its bilateral trade agreement with the United States, and its accession to the WTO.[45] This has driven Vietnam into a semi-dependent position vis-à-vis China.

Beginning in mid-2003, the modernizers have stood on a more or less equal footing with the conservatives. The turn was due primarily to the awing and perceived threatening effects of the U.S. invasion of Iraq. It occurred when the conservatives realized that they were living not in a multipolar world but a unipolar one with the United States at the top.[46] The new balance of power between the conservatives and the modernizers meant that although Vietnam still remained in China's backyard, the chance that it would jump out of it was substantial.

At the same time, during the last five years, China was becoming both more powerful and more assertive. The rapid and steady rise of China, coupled with the U.S. quagmire in Iraq and Afghanistan, and the financial crisis since 2008, has put Beijing in a much stronger position than ever before.

China is both rapidly building up its military and more willing to assert itself in the South China Sea, where it has major territorial disputes with Vietnam. In 2008 commercial satellite imagery confirmed that China was constructing a major naval base at Sanya on Hainan Island. At the same time, China has extended an airfield on Woody Island in the Paracels and consolidated its facilities at Fiery Cross Reef in the Spratlys. In early March 2009, Chinese vessels harassed the U.S. naval ship *Impeccable* at a site seventy-five miles south of Hainan and about the same distance off the Vietnamese coast. The standoff was followed by the collision of a Chinese submarine with a towed sonar array by the *USS John McCain* on 11 June. In May, China announced a unilateral fishing ban in the South China Sea above the twelfth parallel from 16 May to 1 August. This was the height of the Vietnamese fishing season. Eight modern Chinese vessels were dispatched to enforce the ban. Throughout the year, the Vietnamese news media reported several cases in which Chinese vessels seized and detained Vietnamese fishing boats. In one instance a Chinese fishery vessel rammed and sank a Vietnamese boat. In August, when two Vietnamese fishing boats sought to avoid a tropical storm by seeking safe haven in the Paracel Islands, they were detained by Chinese authorities. In an unprecedented reaction, Vietnam not only demanded the boat's release, but also upped the ante by threatening to cancel a meeting that had been scheduled to discuss maritime affairs. In May, after Vietnam submitted a joint proposal with Malaysia and a separate claim extending their continental shelf beyond the 200 nautical mile limit set by the UN Convention on the Law of the Sea, China quickly lodged a protest but did not make a formal submission. However, China documented its maritime claims by attaching a map containing its traditional "nine dash lines" which form a U-shaped area embracing virtually the entire South China Sea. It would appear to be the first time that the People's Republic of China has officially presented its claim in this matter.[47]

Over the western borders of Vietnam, China stepped up its investments and involvements in Laos, Vietnam's closest ally. Within a few years, China surpassed Thailand as the largest foreign investor. As a result of Chinese migrants, money, and influence, the north of Laos is taking on a Chinese character.[48] Chinese activities over the last few years and especially events in 2009 have left the Vietnamese little doubt that China's intentions include control of the South China

Sea, which Vietnam sees as its front door, and influence in mainland Indochina, which Vietnam regards as its backyard.

Vietnam's responses to the Chinese challenges are, again, a mixture of different foreign policy pathways. In line with the modernizers' views, Vietnam has accelerated its force modernization programme, decided to internationalize the South China Sea issues, and boosted its own influence in Laos and Cambodia. On 26–27 November 2009, the Diplomatic Academy of Vietnam and the Vietnam Lawyers' Association conducted an international workshop on South China Sea Security, the first of its kind to have taken place in Vietnam, with the participation of a large number of leading scholars on the topic from several countries.

In early December, Defence Minister Phung Quang Thanh paid a visit to the United States, which also led him to the headquarters of the U.S. Pacific Command. In Hawaii he boarded a submarine, and in Washington Thanh asked for the lifting of an arms embargo that was in effect since the end of the Vietnam War.[49] When visiting France right after his U.S. trip, Thanh asked France to help Vietnam train army medical personnel and sell helicopters, transport aircraft, and other modern military equipment to Vietnam.[50] At the same time, Prime Minister Nguyen Tan Dung visited Russia to sign contracts for the purchase of six Kilo-class submarines (for a price tag of about US$1.8 billion), a dozen Sukhoi Su-30MK2 fighter jets (US$600 million), and other military equipment. The deals had been negotiated years ago, but the conclusion at the time of a financial crisis signalled Vietnam's determination in modernizing its military forces. In exchange for Russia's acceptance of barter and incremental payment, Dung offered Moscow to cooperate in building Vietnam's first nuclear power plant.[51]

When the Prime Minister went to Russia and the Defence Minister to the United States and France, Vice Defence Minister Nguyen Huy Hieu was in South Korea to discuss military cooperation and arms trade, and VCP chief Nong Duc Manh paid a visit to Cambodia during which the two countries signed a treaty to free up cross-border navigation in the Mekong River.[52] Less than two weeks later, an investment promotion meeting jointly organized by the Vietnamese and Cambodian Governments took place in Ho Chi Minh City with the presence of both countries' Prime Ministers. At the meeting Vietnamese enterprises pledged to invest up to US$6 billion in the coming years.[53] If this goes ahead, Vietnam would become Cambodia's second largest foreign investor, only after China. Four months earlier, on 31 August, a similar meeting to promote Vietnamese investments in Laos was held in Ho Chi Minh City. According to a Lao official who attended the meeting, Vietnam was topping the 46 foreign countries investing in Laos with a total investment volume of US$2.08 billion.[54]

In line with the regime conservatives' views, Vietnam continued to maintain dense exchanges with China and tried to tighten the bonds with the latter on the basis of a common enemy (the United States) and a shared ideology (communism). As General Le Van Dung, head of the Political General Directorate of the Vietnam People's Army, who was in China on a week-long visit in late October, said in an interview given to *Tuoi Tre* newspaper on 22 December, "As concerns our issue with China in the South China Sea, we are trying our best to solve it, and in the near future we [Vietnam] will discuss, negotiate, and demarcate the maritime borders with our friend [China]. So the situation would be gradually stabilized and we keep strengthening our relations with China in order to fight plots of the common enemy".[55]

Conclusion

The politics of post–Cold War Vietnam is a game of four key players. The modernizers emerged from the crisis of socialism and the rise of globalization in the 1980s. But the weight and proximity of China has been a major factor supporting Vietnam's regime conservatives. The coexistence of communism and capitalism has provided a favourable environment for the rent-seekers. Over the past two decades, rent-seekers have conquered most of the commanding heights of the Vietnamese economy. In domestic politics, a tacit alliance of regime conservatives and rent-seekers are keeping reform at bay, only to meet with more vigorous opposition from the modernizers. In foreign affairs, China's assertiveness has reduced the effectiveness of Vietnam's deference, a foreign policy pathway preferred by the conservatives. Vietnam responds by boosting internal and external balancing, a pathway advocated by the modernizers.

In 2010 Vietnam's political system will be focused on stabilizing the economy, keeping the ASEAN events safe, and preparing for the Eleventh Party Congress that is scheduled to be held in January 2011. Under these circumstances and barring a major crash, the restructuring that the modernizers are urging is unlikely to happen. Vietnam will likely continue its capital-driven development path until the bubbles burst again. But a major change in Vietnamese politics may only be triggered by such a crash. Vietnam's economic, domestic, and foreign policy each will continue to be a mixture of elements advocated by conservatives, rent-seekers, and modernizers but the three areas are likely to evolve along different paths. The economic policy will include some minor restructuring efforts but is likely to be dominated by rent-seekers. In domestic politics, the regime is likely to tighten its grip amid louder calls for radical change from the mainstream elites. Vietnam's international behavior will be less submissive toward China but efforts to establish a strategic partnership with the United States are likely to be thwarted by disagreements over the government's approach to human rights.

Notes

The author wishes to thank Ben Kerkvliet, Steven Kim, Daljit Singh, and Carlyle Thayer for their valuable comments and Kylee Kim for her effective assistance. The views expressed here are the author's own.

[1] Le Kha Phieu, "Dang Cong san Viet Nam tam muoi Xuan" [The Vietnam Communist Party at eighty], *Nhan Dan*, 3 February 2010 <http://www.nhandan.com.vn/tinbai/?top=37&sub=130&article=167420>.

[2] Vo Van Kiet, "Thu gui Bo Chinh tri" [Letter to the Politburo], 9 August 1995, *Dien Dan*, no. 48 (January 1996): 16–25. For Phieu's insistence on "national independence and socialism", see Phieu, ibid.

[3] In my earlier work I called the two Vietnamese grand strategies "anti-imperialism" and "integration". These names refer to the central foreign policy orientation of the two grand strategies. I called them so because my earlier work mainly addressed Vietnam's foreign policy.

[4] Rent-seeking is a special profit-seeking behavior that makes a benefit primarily from monopoly privileges and influencing government regulations.

[5] For a different discussion of the intertwinement of profit and power in communist Vietnam, see Bill Hayton, "Vietnam's New Money", *Foreign Policy*, 21 January 2010 <http://www.foreignpolicy.com/articles/2010/01/21/vietnams_new_money>.

[6] For background information, see "As Clamor against Suong Verdict Grows, Officials Vow to Dig for Truth", VietNamNet Bridge, 27 November 2009 <http://english.vietnamnet.vn/reports/200911/As-clamor-against-Suong-verdict-grows-officials-vow-to-dig-for-truth-881145/>; "NA Committee May Intervene in Labour Hero Case, Security Minister Orders Report", VietNamNet Bridge, 24 November 2009 <http://english.vietnamnet.vn/reports/200911/NA-Committee-may-intervene-in-labour-hero-case-Security-minister-orders-report-880585/>; Huy Duc, "Sau ba Ba Suong la cac 'nong truong vien'" [Behind Mrs Ba Suong there are the farmers], Blog Osin, 1 December 2009 <http://www.blogosin.org/?p=1074>.

[7] Dinh Thang, "Pacific Airlines thanh Jetstar Pacific: Nhieu lan dan" [From Pacific Airlines to Jetstar Pacific: A life of hardship], *Tien Phong*, 11 January 2010 <http://www.tienphong.vn/Tianyon/Index.aspx?ArticleID=183030&ChannelID=2>.

8   Geoff Easdown, "Power Struggle Strands Execs", *Herald Sun* (Australia), 11 January 2010 <http://www.heraldsun.com.au/business/power-struggle-strands-execs/story-e6frfh4f-1225818205174>.

9   Personal communication, 16 January 2010.

10   Goldman Sachs Global Economic Group, *BRICs and Beyond* (Goldman Sachs, 2007), p. 131. BRIC is an acronym invented by Goldman Sachs to refer to a group of rising great economies including Brazil, Russia, India, and China.

11   Ibid., pp. 139, 140.

12   Alexander L. Vuving, "Vietnam: Arriving in the World — and at a Crossroads," in *Southeast Asian Affairs 2008*, edited by Daljit Singh and Tin Maung Maung Than (Singapore: Institute of Southeast Asian Studies, 2008), pp. 375–77.

13   Vietnam General Statistics Office, "Socio-Economic Situation in 2009," December 2009 <http://www.gso.gov.vn/default.aspx?tabid=413&thangtk=12/2009>.

14   To Huy Rua, "Cuoc khung hoang tai chinh toan cau va nhung van de dat ra doi voi Viet Nam" [The global financial crisis and the issues it raises for Vietnam], *Nhan Dan*, 14 December 2009.

15   For a discussion of the role of SOEs, see Vu Quang Viet, "Vietnam Economic Crisis: Policy Follies and the Role of State-Owned Conglomerates", in *Southeast Asian Affairs 2009*, edited by Daljit Singh (Singapore: Institute of Southeast Asian Studies, 2009), pp. 389–417.

16   Phan The Hai, "Dan khung long cua nen kinh te vi thanh nien" [The dinosaurs of a juvenile economy], TuanVietNam, 12 November 2009 <http://tuanvietnam.net/2009-11-10-dan-khung-long-cua-nen-kinh-te-vi-thanh-nien>.

17   Pham Minh Tri, "Muon chu dao phai tu than" [If you want to be dominant, you must be independent], TuanVietNam, 9 November 2009 <http://tuanvietnam.net/2009-11-06-muon-chu-dao-phai-tu-than>; Huy Duc, "Van chua het nhung tro ngai cu" [Old obstacles still exist], Interview with former Trade Minister Le Van Triet, *Sai Gon Tiep Thi*, 25 May 2009 <http://www.sgtt.com.vn/detail23.aspx?newsid=51921&fld=HTMG/2009/0524/51921>.

18   Hoang Phuong, "Khong tai cau truc quan ly, moi no luc khac la vo nghia" [Without restructuring economic governance, any other efforts remain meaningless], TuanVietNam, 19 May 2009 <http://tuanvietnam.net/khong-tai-cau-truc-quan-ly-moi-no-luc-khac-la-vo-nghia>.

19   Vu Trong Khanh and Patrick Barta, "Hanoi Tightens Reins on Credit", *Wall Street Journal*, 3 December 2009, p. A13.

20   James Hookway and Alex Frangos, "Vietnam Devalues Its Currency", *Wall Street Journal*, 26 November 2009, p. 23.

21   "Vietnam Acknowledges Growing Foreign Debt", Deutsche Presse-Agentur, 17 November 2009.

22   Hookway and Frangos, "Vietnam Devalues".

23 Author's calculation based on data from the Vietnam General Statistics Office.

24 Pivot Capital Management, "China's Investment Boom: The Great Leap into the Unknown", report dated 21 August 2009, p. 2.

25 For more discussion, see Carlyle A. Thayer, "Vietnam and the Challenge of Political Civil Society", *Contemporary Southeast Asia* 31, no. 1 (2009): 1–27.

26 For detailed discussions, see ibid. and Carlyle A. Thayer, "Political Legitimacy of Vietnam's One-Party State: Challenges and Responses", *Journal of Current Southeast Asian Affairs*, no. 4 (2009): 47–70.

27 For a story of VietNamNet by Nguyen Anh Tuan, see his "From VietNet to VietNamNet: Ten Years of Internet Media in Vietnam", Discussion Paper #43, Shorenstein Center on the Press, Politics, and Public Policy, Harvard University, 2007 <http://www.hks.harvard.edu/presspol/publications/papers/discussion_papers/d43_nguyen.pdf>.

28 "Dai tuong Vo Nguyen Giap gop y ve du an bo xit Tay Nguyen" [General Vo Nguyen Giap offers advice on the Central Highlands Bauxite Project], VietNamNet, 14 January 2009 <http://www.tuanvietnam.net/2009-01-14-dai-tuong-vo-nguyen-giap-gop-y-ve-du-an-bo-xit-tay-nguyen>; "Vietnam's War Hero Giap Urges to Halt Bauxite Mining Plans", Agence France Presse, 15 January 2009. For the photocopy of Giap's letter at Tran Huu Dung's website: <http://www.viet-studies.info/kinhte/Thu_VNGiap_NTDung.pdf>.

29 "Vietnam-China Joint Statement" (2 December 2001), Vietnam News Agency, 4 December 2001.

30 The sites of the bauxite projects are in the provinces Dak Nong and Lam Dong in the Central Highlands region, which military strategists called the "roof of Indochina" and whose strategic importance is reflected in the saying "who controls the Central Highlands will control South Vietnam". The Dong Nai and Be Rivers that run through Vietnam's largest industrial and metropolitan areas stem from those two provinces.

31 Quoc Phuong, "Hoi nghi Trung uong 8 'mang tinh tinh the'" [The eighth party plenum is reactive to short-term situation], *BBC Vietnamese*, 2 October 2008.

32 Seth Mydans, "War Hero in Vietnam Forces Government to Listen", *New York Times*, 29 June 2009, p. A6.

33 Thayer, "Political Legitimacy of Vietnam's One-Party State", p. 51. See the same work for more details on the bauxite controversy and other protests in 2009.

34 For discussions of broader civil society activities, see Thayer, "Vietnam and the Challenge of Political Civil Society", and Thayer, "Political Legitimacy of Vietnam's One-Party State".

35 "Vietnam Activists Could Face Death Penalty", Deutsche Presse-Agentur, 11 December 2009.

36 "Berlin Wall Post Costs Vietnam Blogger Job", Agence France Presse, 27 August 2009.

37 "'Nguoi Buon Gio' ke chuyen" ["Wind Trade" tells his story], BBC Vietnamese, 9 September 2009 <http://www.bbc.co.uk/vietnamese/av/2009/09/090909_blogger_ iv.shtml>.

38 "Vietnam Police Release Another Detained Blogger", Reuters, 12 September 2009. Quynh's memoirs of her detention were later publicized on the blog Ban cua Me Nam (Mother Mushroom's Friends) at <http://menamtg.multiply.com/>.

39 The concept paper was released on the Internet at the Web Portal of Quang Ninh Province but later removed. A photocopy of the paper can be found at <http://www. viet-studies.info/kinhte/DeCuongTuyenTruyen.pdf>.

40 Mai Huong, "Ra mat chuong trinh 'Quy luat tat yeu'" [Programme "A necessary law" is launched], *Saigon Giai Phong*, 4 November 2009 <http://www.sggp.org. vn/chinhtri/hocthuyetmaclenin/2009/11/207493/>.

41 "Loat bai: Viet Nam va mo hinh phat trien trong thap ky moi" [Series: Vietnam and the development model in the new decade], TuanVietNam, 11 January 2010 <http:// www.tuanvietnam.net/2009-12-31-loat-bai-viet-nam-va-mo-hinh-phat-trien-trong-thap- ki-moi>.

42 Nguyen Trung, "Xay dung che do chinh tri dong nghia voi To quoc" [Building a political regime identical with the fatherland], TuanVietNam, 31 December 2009 <http://www.tuanvietnam.net/2009-12-27-xay-che-do-chinh-tri-dong-nghia-voi-to- quoc->.

43 Alexander L. Vuving, "Grand Strategic Fit and Power Shift: Explaining Turning Points in China-Vietnam Relations", in *Living with China: Regional States and China through Crises and Turning Points*, edited by Shiping Tang, Mingjiang Li, and Amitav Acharya (New York: Palgrave Macmillan, 2009), pp. 229–45.

44 Alexander L. Vuving, "Strategy and Evolution of Vietnam's China Policy: A Changing Mixture of Pathways", *Asian Survey* 46, no. 6 (November 2006): 812, 816–17.

45 Nguyen Trung, "Nguoi tai bi do ky va khong duoc trong dung" [Talents are begrudged and underused], VietNamNet, 9 February 2006 <http://www.vietnamnet.vn/ chinhtri/doinoi/2006/02/539842/>; "Vao WTO: Viet Nam bo lo mot nuoc co" [Joining WTO: Vietnam lost an opportunity] (interview with former Prime Minister Vo Van Kiet), VietNamNet, 4 January 2006 <http://www.vietnamnet.vn/chinhtri/doingoai/ 2006/01/528944/>.

46 Vuving, "Strategy and Evolution of Vietnam's China Policy", pp. 817–18.

47 This paragraph is adapted from Carlyle A. Thayer, "Recent Developments in the South China Sea: Implications for Peace, Stability and Cooperation in the Region", paper presented at the workshop on "The South China Sea: Cooperation for Regional Security and Development", Hanoi, 27–28 November 2009, pp. 5–11.

48 Denis Gray, "Laos Fears China's Footprint", Associated Press, 6 April 2008; Martin Stuart-Fox, "Laos: The Chinese Connection", in *Southeast Asian Affairs 2009*,

edited by Daljit Singh (Singapore: Institute of Southeast Asian Studies, 2009), pp. 141–69.

49 "Hop tac quoc phong Viet-My phat trien tich cuc" [Vietnam-U.S. defence cooperation develops positively] (interview with Defence Minister Phung Quang Thanh), Vietnam News Agency, 17 December 2009.

50 "Vietnam Seeks Military Deals with France: State Media", Agence France-Presse, 18 December 2009.

51 "Viet Nam ky hop dong mua tau ngam cua Nga" [Vietnam signs deals to purchase Russian submarines], BBC Vietnamese, 16 December 2009; Huynh Phan, "Dien hat nhan va ODA trong quan he doi tac chien luoc" [Nuclear power and ODA in strategic partnerships], *Sai Gon Tiep Thi*, 5 March 2010 <http://www.sgtt.com.vn/Detail3.aspx?ColumnId=3&newsid=63735&fld=HTMG/2010/0304/63735>.

52 "Viet Nam-Han Quoc mo rong hop tac quoc phong" [Vietnam and Republic of Korea broaden defence cooperation], Vietnam News Agency, 17 December 2009.

53 "Viet Nam, Campuchia ky thoa thuan toi 6 ty USD" [Vietnam and Cambodia sign agreements worth up to US$6 billion], Vietnam News Agency, 26 December 2009.

54 Trung Hieu, "Nhieu co hoi dau tu vao Lao" [Many investment opportunities in Laos], *Phap Luat Thanh Pho Ho Chi Minh*, 31 August 2009.

55 "Tim moi cach giai quyet van de Bien Dong" [Making every effort to solve the South China Sea issues] (interview with General Le Van Dung), *Tuoi Tre*, 22 December 2009 <http://www.tuoitre.com.vn/Tianyon/Index.aspx?ArticleID=354571&ChannelID=3>.

VIETNAM AND RISING CHINA
The Structural Dynamics of Mature Asymmetry

Carlyle A. Thayer

Ever since the Vietnamese nation-state emerged as an independent entity in the first millennium it has had to contend with "the tyranny of geography". Vietnam shares a common border with China its giant neighbour to the north. Even today, with a population of eighty-eight million, Vietnam ranks as a middle sized Chinese province. As a major study by Brantly Womack notes, the bilateral relationship has been embedded in a structure of persistent asymmetry throughout recorded history.[1]

This chapter focuses on how Vietnam's leaders manage relations with a rising China. Womack's theory of asymmetry provides a useful framework for analyzing this relationship. Womack argues "disparities in capacities create systemic differences in interests and perspectives between stronger and weaker sides".[2] The larger power always looms more importantly to the weaker than the reverse. This structural factor results in over attention to the bilateral relationship on the part of the weaker state because more is at risk. The result, Womack concludes, is that weaker states are "prone to paranoia".[3] Conversely, the stronger power is less attentive to the details of the bilateral relationship with a weaker state. These contrasting views often lead to misperception.

Womack argues that Sino-Vietnamese hostility over Cambodia in the 1980s (which he terms "hostile asymmetry") led to a stalemate when both sides realized that they could not prevail. This led to a period of negotiated normalization (1990–99) in which both parties came to recognize and accept the interests of the

CARLYLE A. THAYER is Professor of Politics, School of Humanities and Social Sciences, University College, The University of New South Wales at the Australian Defence Force Academy.

other. Normalcy, according to Womack, does not alter the asymmetric nature of relations; but it ushers in a new phase that he terms normal or mature asymmetry. According to Womack, "[n]ormalcy might be called 'mature asymmetry' because it is grounded in a learning experience and it has the capacity to be long term and stable."[4] In other words, both parties adopt mutual expectations of the other's behaviour. The stronger expects deference, while the weaker expects that its autonomy will be acknowledged.

Mature asymmetric relations are kept peaceful by careful management by both parties. Womack identifies a number of methods to manage bilateral relations.[5] One method is to rely on past precedent to shape common expectations of how the bilateral relationship should proceed. Another method is through "diplomatic ritual" or the exchange of high-level delegations, through which each party reassures the other. For example, Vietnam can be expected to offer assurances to China that its power will be respected and not challenged; in return Vietnam can expect assurance from China that its autonomy will not be violated.

A third method for managing bilateral relations is to remove contentious issues from the political front burner. This can be done by reformulating the issues in dispute in order to stress common interests. For example, territorial disputes can be reformulated as a border control issue designed to promote trade. Or contentious issues can be relegated to the purview of specialist working groups for resolution. Both parties can also buffer their relations through common membership in multilateral associations and adherence to international agreements. The weaker party also has the option of joining other smaller states in a regional organization or allying with a third party.

This chapter will review the structural dynamics of Sino-Vietnamese relations in the current period of mature asymmetry. It will examine the key bilateral and multilateral mechanisms that assist in managing Sino-Vietnamese relations and the challenges posed by territorial disputes to the stability of mature asymmetric relations.

Bilateral and Multilateral Mechanisms

The People's Republic of China was the first state to recognize communist Vietnam, in January 1950. Initially bilateral relations were as "close as lips and teeth" but the bonds of socialist solidarity frayed during the Vietnam War. In the late 1970s bilateral relations turned acrimonious over a number of issues — border security, Vietnam's treatment of ethnic Chinese, Hanoi's alignment with Moscow, and the "Kampuchea problem". Relations turned hostile when Vietnam invaded

Cambodia in late 1978 and China retaliated by attacking Vietnam's northern border in early 1979.

Vietnam and China remained in a state of hostilities for a decade. By the mid to late 1980s both sides recognized that the military situation in Cambodia had reached a stalemate and the conflict could only be ended through political negotiations. In September 1989 Vietnam unilaterally withdrew its military forces from Cambodia. This set the stage for both parties to initiate the process of normalization of their relations at a secret summit of party leaders in Chengdu in southern China in September 1990.

Formal normalization did not occur until November 1991, pointedly only after Vietnam had agreed to China's demand for a comprehensive political settlement in Cambodia. Both sides then exchanged high-level party and state delegations. Major areas of agreement and expectations for the future were set out in joint communiqués issued in 1992, 1994, and 1995 following these discussions. Contentious border issues were assigned to specialist groups for negotiation. Military-to-military contact was resumed. The period from 1990 to 1999 may be viewed as a transition period from "hostile asymmetry" to "normal asymmetry".[6]

Party-to-Party Relations

Vietnam and China are both socialist one-party states. Unlike China, where the same individual holds the posts of Party General Secretary and State President, in Vietnam these posts are separated. Nevertheless, relations between the Vietnam Communist Party (VCP) and the Chinese Communist Party (CCP) provide a very important mechanism for managing their bilateral relations.

Bilateral political relations between Vietnam and China were formally codified by party leaders who met in Beijing from 25 February to 3 March 1999. At this summit General Secretary Le Kha Phieu and Secretary General Jiang Zemin adopted a fourteen character guideline calling for "long-term, stable, future-orientated, good-neighbourly and all-round cooperative relations".[7] Notably the summit was held on the twentieth anniversary of the Sino-Vietnamese border war (17 February to 16 March 1979).

Regular summit meetings between party leaders provide the opportunity for wide-ranging discussions and an impetus for the resolution of various outstanding issues. For example, during the visit of Secretary General Do Muoi to Beijing in July 1997, he and General Secretary Jiang Zemin agreed to settle land border issues by the end of 2000 and also reach an agreement on the delimitation of the Gulf of Tonkin. Secretary General Nong Duc Manh visited China following national party congresses in 2001 and 2006. During Manh's 2006 visit, for example, it was announced that after talks with his counterpart Hu Jintao, the two leaders agreed to boost trade, set up joint projects in energy development, speed up border demarcation, and enhance security cooperation.[8]

Bilateral relations were further cemented by the exchange of party delegations from Central Committee Departments, administrative units, and specialists on socialist ideology. In March 2009, for example, Pham Quang Nghi, a member of the VCP Politburo and chief of Hanoi Party Committee, visited Beijing to meet with his counterpart, Liu Qi, a member of the CCP Politburo and chief of the Beijing party municipal committee. In June, a delegation of the CCP Central Committee's Organisation Department visited Hanoi for discussions with its Vietnamese counterpart. In August, a secretary of the VCP Central Committee made a reciprocal visit. Also in August, He Yong, member of the CCP Central Committee Secretariat and Deputy Secretary of the Central Commission for Discipline Inspection visited Hanoi for talks with Nguyen Van Chi, head of the Central Committee's Inspection Commission. The two sides discussed "theory and experiences regarding inspection, discipline and strengthening the party and corruption control". He Yong was received by General Secretary Nong Duc Manh.

In late September–early October, Hoang Binh Quan, head of the VCP External Relations Commission, visited Beijing for talks with Wang Jiarui, Director of the CCP's International Liaison Department, on specific measures to be taken to implement high-level agreements on border and economic issues. Quan was received by General Secretary and State President Hu Jintao. Also in October, Lu Hao, First Secretary of the Secretariat of the CCP Central Committee, visited Hanoi to meet with Ngo Van Du, a member of the Party Secretariat and Director of the General Office of the VCP Central Committee.

In December, the CCP and VCP held their fifth seminar on ideology in Xiamen, Fujian province, attended by 200 people. The CCP was represented by Liu Yunshan, head of the Publicity Department of the CCP Central Committee; Vietnam was represented by To Huy Rua, head of VCP Commission of Information and Education and head of the party's Central Theoretical Council. At the end of the month Rua received Zhang Xiaolin, editor-in-chief of the CCP journal *Quishi*. Rua told his guest that the two party journals "should share experience" in order to reach the common goals of both parties, including the construction of socialism. In sum, party-to-party ties have been used to identify common ground between former antagonists.

State-to-State Relations

In December 2000, Vietnam and China codified state-to-state relations at a summit meeting in Beijing. Presidents Tran Duc Luong and Hu Jintao, signed a "Joint Statement for Comprehensive Cooperation in the New Century".[9] According to this document, "[b]oth sides will refrain from taking any action that might complicate and escalate disputes, resorting to force or making threats with force".[10] The 2000 Joint Statement set out the long-term framework for cooperative bilateral state-to-state relations with a provision for the regular exchange of high-level delegations led by their respective State Presidents, Prime Ministers, other ministers, national legislatures, and other political organizations.

In 2006, Vietnam and China set up a joint Steering Committee on Bilateral Cooperation at the deputy prime ministerial level to coordinate all aspects of their relationship. The Steering Committee was to meet on an annual basis alternating between capital cities. The first meeting was held in November 2006, the second in January 2008, and the third in March 2009. At the third meeting it was agreed to set up a hotline to deal with urgent issues.[11]

In June 2008, following a summit of party leaders in Beijing, Vietnam and China declared that they would raise their bilateral relations to that of strategic partners.[12] By October the following year bilateral relations had matured sufficiently for Vietnam and China to announce plans to draw up a "strategic cooperative partnership".[13] By the end of the year Vietnam and China exchanged 267 delegations of which 108 were at deputy minister level or higher.[14]

In 2009, Prime Minister Nguyen Tan Dung made two official visits to China. In April he attended the Boao Forum on Hainan island where he discussed economic cooperation, trade, and contentious South China Sea issues with Premier Wen Jiabao. He returned in October to attend the Tenth Western Chinese International Trade Fair in Chengdu, Sichuan province. Prime Minister Dung addressed the Second West China International Cooperation Forum whose aim was to strengthen cooperation in economics, investment, tourism, and science and technology between China and foreign partners. While in Chengdu Dung met with Wen Jiabao and they agreed to resolve maritime issues through negotiations (see below). Four other high-level state visits worthy of note took place in 2009. In April, Vietnam's Minister of Education, Nguyen Thien Nhan, held discussions in Beijing with his counterpart on student exchanges. In August, Vietnam's Minister of Internal Affairs, Tran Van Tuan, visited Beijing for discussions with the Minister of Human Resources and Social Security, Yin Weimin. Their discussions focused on the management of state cadres and the structure of the state apparatus at central and local level. The following month, a delegation from the Chinese People's Political Consultative Council National Committee, led by its Chairman, visited Hanoi and attended the seventh national congress of the Vietnam Fatherland Front. Finally, in October, Vu Huy Hoang, Minister of Industry and Trade, paid a working visit to Beijing for discussions with his counterpart Chen Deming, Minister of Commerce. The two Ministers discussed measures to raise two-way trade to US$25 billion by 2010. These discussions followed up on agreements signed in Hanoi in September at the first meeting of the Vietnam-China Trade Cooperation Working Group under the Economic-Trade Cooperation Committee.

Military-to-Military Relations

The first defence contacts between Vietnam and China since their 1979 border war were initiated in 1992 with the exchange of delegations from the External Relations Departments of the Vietnamese and Chinese Defence Ministries in February and May, respectively. Following normalization of relations both sides agreed to demine the border and dispose of unexploded ordnance. More broad-based defence relations evolved slowly.

The 2000 Sino-Vietnamese Joint Statement provided for multi-level military exchanges. In November 2001, the People's Liberation Army Navy (PLAN) guided missile frigate *Jiangwei II* made a port call to Ho Chi Minh City, marking the first visit of a Chinese naval vessel to a Vietnamese port since reunification. Subsequently, Chinese naval vessels visited Vietnam in November 2008 and August 2009. Two Vietnamese ships made a port visit to China in June.

Defence relations up to 2005 appear to have been almost entirely focused on border security and ideological matters. In the period between 2002 and 2005, Vietnam's Minister of National Defence visited China four times without reciprocation. There were more balanced exchanges by Chiefs of the General Staff, heads of the general political departments, and other high-level delegations.

Bilateral defence relations entered a new phase in April 2005 with the initiation of annual defence security consultations along the line of similar meetings between China and Thailand and the Philippines. In October 2005, the Chinese and Vietnamese Defence Ministers tentatively discussed cooperation between their national defence industries.

Between 2005 and mid-2009, Vietnam sent eleven high-level military delegations to China (including two visits by the Minister of National Defence) and hosted nine high-level delegations in return (including one visit by the defence minister).[15] In a major new development, in April 2006, Hanoi received Defence

Minister Cao Gangchuan, who came to promote China's military technology and professional training as well as to complete arrangements for joint naval patrols.[16] Cao was also briefed on the tenth party congress. On 27 April, the Chinese and Vietnamese navies conducted their first joint patrol in the Gulf of Tonkin with the aim of providing security for fishermen and oil exploration. This was a first for the Chinese navy.

In August 2006, Vietnam's new Defence Minister, Phung Quang Thanh, visited Beijing to discuss cooperation between national defence industries and reciprocal training of high-level military officers.[17] That same month party leaders Nong Duc Manh and Hu Jintao met in Beijing and issued a joint communiqué that noted "both sides spoke positively of ... the joint patrol conducted by the navies of the two countries in the Tonkin Gulf".[18] By the end of 2009, a total of four joint patrols had been conducted.[19]

In October 2006, Lieutenant General Le Van Dung, head of the Vietnam People's Army General Political Department, journeyed to China to discuss professional military training exchanges.[20] The following year his Chinese counterpart made a reciprocal visit to Vietnam; and both sides exchanged visits by regional military commanders. In 2008, Vietnam's Deputy Minister of National Defence held discussions in Beijing with China's Commission for Science, Technology and Industry on cooperation in personnel training, frontier and coastal defence, and "other fields".[21] The issue of professional military training was raised in March 2009 during a visit to Hanoi by Chen Bingde, PLA Chief of the General Staff. After discussions with his counterpart, General Nguyen Khac Nghien, the two agreed to continue joint naval patrols and to conduct search and rescue operations. In October 2009, Lieutenant General Le Van Dung returned to Beijing to further ties between the two General Political Departments.

Multilateral Institutions

Vietnam's relations with China are also structured on a multilateral basis through membership in ASEAN, the ASEAN Regional Forum, and other multilateral bodies (ASEAN Plus Three and the East Asia Summit). When Vietnam joined ASEAN in 1995 it agreed to adhere to all multilateral arrangements already entered into between ASEAN and China. In 1997, ASEAN and China formalized their cooperation by establishing the ASEAN-China Joint Cooperation Committee as "the coordinator for all the ASEAN-China mechanisms at the working level".[22] When China became an ASEAN dialogue partner, it regularly participated in the annual ASEAN Post-Ministerial Conference consultation process.

In November 2002, ASEAN and China signed three major documents: Framework Agreement on Comprehensive Economic Cooperation between ASEAN Nations and the People's Republic of China (the foundation for the China-ASEAN Free Trade Area), Joint Declaration between China and ASEAN on Cooperation in Non-Traditional Security Fields, and Declaration on the Conduct of Parties in the South China Sea (DOC). The DOC was a non-binding document that enjoined its signatories to resolve their disputes by peaceful means and "to exercise self-restraint in the conduct of activities that would complicate or escalate disputes".

In early 2004, ASEAN and China set up a joint working group to implement the agreement. The most promising development, an agreement on joint seismic testing between the national oil companies of China, the Philippines, and Vietnam, signed in March 2005, however, lapsed when it expired.

In October 2003, China acceded to the ASEAN Treaty of Amity and Cooperation, and China and ASEAN issued a joint declaration establishing a strategic partnership. A Five-year Plan of Action (2005–10) was drawn up in late 2004. This plan included, inter alia, a joint commitment to increase regular high-level bilateral visits, cooperation in the field of non-traditional security, security dialogue, and military exchanges and cooperation.[23]

In sum, Vietnam has been able to buffer its relations with China through membership in ASEAN and other multilateral organizations. But multilateralism has proven to be a weak reed with respect to South China Sea issues. No progress has been made to upgrade the DOC into a Code of Conduct, and when tensions arose in 2007–8 Vietnam was essentially left on its own to deal with China (see below).

Challenges to Mature Asymmetry

Border Disputes

Immediately after the normalization of relations in 1991, Vietnam and China inaugurated discussions at the expert level to work out a settlement of their disputes involving the land border and Gulf of Tonkin. The first expert-level discussions on dispute management were held in October 1992. A year later, government-level talks led to a landmark agreement on the principles for the settlement of territorial disputes.

The land border and Gulf of Tonkin disputes were separated and each assigned to a specialist joint working group. The joint working group on land issues first met in February 1994 and concluded in December 1999 after sixteen meetings. The joint working group was kept under pressure to conclude an agreement as a result of the intervention of high-level leaders. For example, in October 1998, during the visit to Beijing by Prime Minister Phan Van Khai, China and Vietnam announced their determination to settle boundary issues — land border and the Gulf of Tonkin — by 2000. Two months later Vice President Hun Jintao visited Hanoi and in discussions with his counterpart agreed to settle land boundary issues before 2000 and the Tonkin Gulf not later than 2000. On 30 December 1999 China and Vietnam signed a land border agreement during the visit to Hanoi by Premier Zhu Rongji. Both sides ratified the treaty in 2000 and the process of placing stone markers along the border was completed at the end of 2008.

In August 2009, the Deputy Foreign Ministers of Vietnam and China, Ho Xuan Son and Wu Dawei, met in Hanoi to hammer out a series of agreements related to border control and management. At the follow on discussions held in Beijing in November, the two sides signed three agreements — a protocol on demarcation of the land boundary and marker planting, an agreement on land boundary management, and agreement on land port/border gates and their management. A number of issues were left unresolved (developing tourism at the Ban Gioc waterfall and free passage of ships at the Bac Luan river mouth) and the two vice ministers agreed to hold discussions and settle these issues during 2010.

The joint working group on the Gulf of Tonkin first met in March 1994 and held seventeen meetings before concluding. As noted above, high-level leadership discussions provided the impetus to reach agreement. In December 2000, Vietnam and China signed the Agreement on the Demarcation of Waters, Exclusive Economic Zones and Continental Shelves in the Gulf of Tonkin and the Agreement on Fishing Cooperation in the Gulf of Tonkin.

The settlement of land border and Gulf of Tonkin issues set the stage for the adoption of the Vietnam-China Joint Statement for Comprehensive Cooperation in the New Century (discussed above).[24] Vietnam and China then commenced working group discussions on delineating the waters in the mouth of the Gulf of Tonkin. The fifth meeting of the working group was held in Hanoi in January 2009. In November, the Chinese and Vietnamese Deputy Foreign Ministers agreed to accelerate these discussions and to include consideration of cooperation in protecting the marine environment and search and rescue operations at sea.

In contrast to the land border and the Gulf of Tonkin issues, Vietnam and China have not been able to resolve their sovereignty disputes over the South China Sea. It was excluded from the agenda of working-level discussions held in the early 1990s. It was only in November 1994, during the visit of President Jiang Zemin, that the two sides agreed to discuss the South China Sea. Expert-level discussions on maritime issues commenced in November 1995 and quickly bogged down over disagreement over the agenda. Ten rounds of talks were held over the next decade without result.

In November 2009, following commitments by Premier Wen Jiabao and Prime Minister Dung in Beijing the previous month, the Deputy Foreign Ministers of China and Vietnam agreed to initiate expert-level consultations to formulate guidelines for the long-term resolution of South China Sea issues. This approach appears to parallel discussions on the land border that resulted in the 1993 agreement on the principles to settle the dispute.

South China Sea

Without question Sino-Vietnamese territorial differences in the South China Sea have emerged as the most serious challenge to the stability of "mature asymmetry" despite attempts by Hanoi to manage this issue through high-level exchanges and joint working groups. In January 2007, China and Vietnam held the thirteenth round of discussions on border and territorial issues in Nanning. According to the Vietnam News Agency, "both sides discussed in depth measures to maintain peace and stability in the East Sea (South China Sea), without any action to complicate or widen disputes. They agreed to continue the negotiation mechanism in order to seek a basic and long-term solution that is acceptable to both sides".[25]

While the Nanning talks were in session, the VCP Central Committee convened its fourth plenum from 15–24 January. This meeting directed that a national "Maritime Strategy Towards the Year 2020" be drawn up to integrate economic development of coastal areas with the exploitation of marine resources in the East Sea. Vietnamese economists estimated that by 2020, the marine economy would contribute up to 55 per cent of GDP and between 55–60 per cent of exports. Vietnam's maritime development strategy was completed during 2007 but was not released publicly.

Chinese officials reportedly acquired a copy of this classified document.[26] China then began to apply pressure on foreign firms that were likely to be involved in developing Vietnam's maritime sector, warning that their commercial operations in China would suffer if they developed areas claimed by China. In June, British Petroleum (BP) temporarily suspended plans to launch a new US$2 billion project to develop energy resources in the Nam Con Son basin after the Chinese Foreign Ministry declared BP's plans "illegal and invalid" and an encroachment upon Chinese territorial sovereignty.[27] ExxonMobile officials revealed that they too had been warned not to proceed with an agreement they had signed with

Vietnam to explore for energy resources off Vietnam's coast.[28] China's foreign ministry confirmed that it had made clear its position to the "relevant side" (i.e. ExxonMobil).[29] Vietnam publicly put on a brave face and attempted to brush off China's diplomatic pressure.[30]

In April 2007, Wu Bangguo, Chairman of the National People's Congress, told his visiting Vietnamese counterpart, Nguyen Phu Trong, that the two countries should tackle boundary issues appropriately in an effort to maintain stability in the South China Sea.[31] On the same day, President Hu Jintao told Trong, "China is ready to work with Vietnam to appropriately deal with the issue of land and maritime borders to jointly maintain peace in the border area".[32] Nevertheless, it was clear to Vietnam that despite Beijing's assurances its long-term plans to develop its maritime area were now hostage to China's opposition.

China's behind-the-scenes actions were accompanied by greater Chinese diplomatic and military assertiveness.[33] In 2007, a number of incidents in the South China Sea cumulatively built up friction between Hanoi and Beijing. Early in the year Vietnam protested when China placed boundary markers on the Paracel Islands.[34] In April, Chinese naval vessels detained four Vietnamese fishing boats near the Spratly islands sparking a diplomatic protest from Hanoi. On 9 July, a Chinese vessel that was harassing Vietnamese fishing boats in waters near the Paracel Islands collided with and sank one boat that resulted in the death of a Vietnamese fisherman. In mid-November, PLAN exercises near the Paracels elicited another Vietnamese diplomatic protest. But no action was more inflammatory than the decision of China's National People's Congress (NPC) to create the Sansha county level town in Hainan province with administrative responsibility over three archipelagoes in the South China Sea, including the Paracel and Spratly islands. No doubt the head of the NPC, Wu Bangguo, was disingenuous when, seven months earlier, he urged Vietnam to enhance mutual trust.

News of the NPC's actions provoked unprecedented anti-China student demonstrations in Hanoi and Ho Chi Minh City on 9 and 16 December 2007. China immediately lodged a protest. Vietnam's Ministry of Foreign Affairs responded by calling in all the ASEAN ambassadors to inform them that the student demonstrations were spontaneous and not approved. Matters were further inflamed in January 2008 when China accused Vietnamese fishermen of attacking Chinese trawlers in the Gulf of Tonkin.

In an effort to manage growing friction, Vietnam and China moved quickly to contain the situation. A meeting of the China-Vietnam Steering Committee was convened in Beijing on 23 January. Co-chairs Chinese State Councilor Tang Jiaxuan and Vietnamese Deputy Prime Minister Pham Gia Khiem agreed to "properly handle the problems in bilateral relations" through "dialogue and consultation", and accelerate negotiations on the delineation of remaining areas of the Gulf of Tonkin and issues relating to the South China Sea.[35]

Tensions arising from incidents in the South China Sea were addressed at a summit meeting of party leaders in Beijing from 30 May to 2 June 2008. A joint statement issued after official talks between General Secretary Hu Jintao and Secretary General Nong Duc Manh declared that the two countries agreed to "uphold the use of peaceful negotiations to search for basic and long-term solutions acceptable to both sides, and at the same time to actively study and discuss the issue of joint development to find a suitable model and areas".[36] More notably, the two leaders agreed to raise the level of bilateral relations to a strategic partnership.

The issue of the South China Sea was barely mentioned in official Vietnamese media reporting of the summit; but what references did appear revealed deference towards China. Several news reports mentioned "problems left over from history" without further elaboration. A commentary in *Nhan Dan* on 30 May noted in passing that the "maintenance of stability in the East Sea" had been discussed. The Vietnamese press also reported that when Hu "suggested a proper solution to existing issues between the countries on the basis of friendly consultations and mutual benefit", Manh replied he shared Hu's views and that "the two countries should communicate promptly about their concerns". The two leaders agreed to "foster an effective cooperation mechanism between the foreign ministries and defence, public and security agencies". They also agreed that the joint Steering Committee was the most appropriate mechanism to manage bilateral relations.

Anti-Chinese nationalist sentiment was further aroused in Vietnam in August when a Chinese website posted an alleged "invasion plan" of Vietnam. Bloggers in both countries fired repeated salvos into cyberspace attacking each other.[37] Vietnam contacted the Chinese ambassador on at least two occasions to request that the invasion plan be removed from the website. In October, Prime Minister Dung held discussions in Beijing with his Chinese counterpart; they reaffirmed their commitment to "collaborate in maintaining peace and stability" in the South China Sea.[38]

Once again, Chinese words did not match Chinese deeds. In May 2009, China announced a unilateral three-month moratorium on fishing in the South China Sea (above the twelfth parallel) from 16 May to 1 August in order to preserve fish stocks, prevent illegal fishing, and protect Chinese fishermen. This was the height of the Vietnamese fishing season. Eight modern Chinese fishery administration vessels were dispatched to enforce the ban.[39] Vietnam lodged a diplomatic protest.

Also in May 2009, China tabled a protest with the United Nations Commission on the Limits of the Continental Shelf (UNCLCS) when submissions on extended continental shelves were presented jointly by Malaysia and Vietnam and by Vietnam in a separate submission.[40] Under the rules of the UNCLCS contested submissions were not eligible for evaluation. For the first time, China officially tabled a map containing nine unconnected lines to document its claims to virtually the entire South China Sea.[41]

In the midst of these developments, Vietnam temporarily suspended a website jointly maintained by their trade ministries when Chinese officials posted an article criticizing Vietnam's territorial claims in the South China Sea.[42] In August, Chinese authorities detained the crew of two Vietnamese fishing boats who sought sanctuary in the Paracels during a severe tropical storm.[43] Vietnam demanded the release of the fishermen and threatened to cancel a meeting scheduled to discuss maritime affairs. China released the fishermen[44] and the "border and territory" talks at deputy minister level were held in Hanoi as scheduled.

According to Vietnamese sources, China acted in a more aggressive manner than in the past. Chinese ships stopped, boarded, and seized the catches of fishing boats and chased other Vietnamese vessels out of the proscribed area. In one instance a Chinese fishery ship rammed and sank a Vietnamese boat.[45] On 16 June, China seized three Vietnamese boats and thirty-seven crew members in waters near the Paracel islands. After freeing two boats and their crews, China detained the third boat and its twelve crew members pending payment of a fine totaling US$31,700.[46] Chinese actions prompted outrage by local government officials in Quang Ngai province, the home of the detained fishermen, and yet another diplomatic protest by Vietnam's Foreign Ministry.[47] In December a Chinese naval patrol seized three more Vietnamese fishing boats near the Paracels.[48]

Conclusion

Vietnam's relations with China under conditions of mature asymmetry have proven remarkably robust over the last decade. Both sides have relied on past precedent to normalize their bilateral relations, first by relying on the restoration of party-to-party ties. Both sides have used regular high-level meetings by party leaders to set the direction and pace of the relationship. There is now a well-established network between their respective Central Committee departments and other party institutions. In recent years both parties have relied on inter-party seminars on ideology to underpin their relationship.

Vietnam and China have also developed a dense network of state-to-state relations based on the long-term cooperative framework agreement negotiated in 2000. Both sides regularly exchange high-level visits by State Presidents, Prime Minister/Premier, and ministerial level delegations. Since 2006, a joint steering committee at deputy prime minister level has coordinated all aspects of the relationship.

Defence relations between the Chinese PLA and the Vietnam People's Army have offered a further channel for the management of bilateral relations. Both armies were actively involved in demining the border so that commercial, trade, and other interaction could develop. The two militaries have sought common ground by exchanging experiences on various facets of army-building under state socialism. More significantly, both sides have conducted joint naval patrols in the Gulf of Tonkin and hosted port visits of each other's naval ships.

Finally, Vietnam has used membership in multilateral institutions such as ASEAN and the ASEAN Regional Forum to buffer its relations with China. As a member of ASEAN Vietnam has contributed to negotiating a range of key agreements to govern economic, political, security, and defence interaction. In 2010, as ASEAN chair, Vietnam will take responsibility for the ASEAN Defence Ministers Meeting Plus process of engaging ASEAN's dialogue partners, including China, in discussion on future defence and security cooperation.

In summary, Vietnam has employed this dense network of party, state, defence, and multilateral mechanisms to manage its relations with China under conditions of mature asymmetry. Vietnam continually reassures China that it is "ready, willing and able" to participate in cooperative endeavours in pursuit of common goals and interests.[49] For example, Lieutenant General Le Van Dung stated in an interview given in Hanoi after a visit to China in 2009 that "[t]hus, the situation will be stabilized gradually and we will keep strengthening our relations with China in order to fight the plots of the common enemy" (*Nhu vay thi tinh hinh se on dinh dan va chung ta van tang cuong quan he voi Trung Quoc de chong lai nhung am muu cua ke thu chung*).[50] Vietnam expects Chinese recognition of its autonomy in return for Vietnam's deference to China's power and role in the region.

Since 2007, the South China Sea has emerged as the single most important challenge to the robustness of mature asymmetry. As Alexander Vuving's chapter in this volume attests, anti-China nationalism has emerged in Vietnam as a particularly powerful force in domestic politics.[51] It has the potential to fuel "paranoia" among party and state leaders. In response to Chinese assertiveness, Vietnam's leaders have shored up Vietnam's capacity to defend its interests in the South China Sea by announcing plans to create an armed maritime militia, a new joint air-naval command, and a major arms procurement package that includes six conventional Kilo-class submarines, Sukhoi Su-30MK2 multi-role fighters and other defence equipment.[52]

Chinese assertiveness has also prompted Vietnam to raise its defence relations with the United States by conducting a political-military dialogue in October 2008. As a result of the visit of Vietnam's Defence Minister to Washington in late 2009, it appears likely that Vietnam and the United States will raise the scope of direct military-to-military contacts in 2010. But Vietnam's improved relations with the United States should not be seen as a sign that it is exercising the option of allying with another country to balance China. As early as June 1992, immediately after the normalization of relations with China, the third plenum of the VCP Central Committee concluded that political adversaries could both cooperate and struggle (*hop tac va dau tranh*) while maintaining relations of peaceful coexistence.[53] In July 2003, the VCP Central Committee's eighth plenum redefined its ideological approach to interstate relations with all countries by adopting the concepts *doi tac* (object of cooperation) and *doi tuong* (object of struggle), thus paving the way for ministerial-level defence contacts with the United States. In other words, Vietnam viewed its relations with both China and the United States as containing both cooperation and struggle (when either state adopted policies that affected Vietnam's national interests).

Vietnam and China will celebrate 2010 as the Year of Friendship to mark the sixtieth anniversary of diplomatic relations. Both have too much at stake to allow the present period of mature asymmetry to revert to hostile asymmetry. For Vietnam, the weaker party, the "tyranny of geography" dictates that it judiciously apply the levers of cooperation and struggle through various party, state, military, and multilateral structures in order to manage its relations with China under conditions of mature asymmetry.

Notes

[1]   Brantly Womack, *China and Vietnam: The Politics of Asymmetry* (New York: Cambridge University Press, 2006).
[2]   Ibid., p. 17.
[3]   Ibid., p. 20.
[4]   Ibid., p. 212.
[5]   Ibid., pp. 5 and 89–90.

[6]   Ibid., pp. 212–37.

[7]   Xinhua Domestic Service, 27 February 1999

[8]   Xinhua, 24 August 2006.

[9]   Vietnam News Agency (VNA), 25 December 2000.

[10] Between February 1999 and December 2000, the People's Republic of China negotiated long-term cooperative framework arrangements with all ten ASEAN members. See Carlyle A. Thayer, "China's 'New Security Concept' and Southeast Asia", in *Asia-Pacific Security: Policy Challenges*, edited by David W. Lovell (Singapore: Institute of Southeast Asian Studies and Canberra: Asia Pacific Press, 2003), pp. 92–95.

[11] "Vietnam, China Agree to Hotline: Ministry", Agence France Presse (AFP), 20 March 2009.

[12] Vietnam has established strategic partnerships with Russia, India and Japan and "strategic relations" with France.

[13] "China, Vietnam Premiers Promise Talks over Maritime Spats", Deutsche Presse-Agentur (DPA), 16 October 2009.

[14] "Chinese Diplomat Reaffirms Close Ties with Vietnam", Voice of Vietnam News, 7 January 2010.

[15] *Quoc Phong Vietnam* (Hanoi: Bo Quoc Phong, 2009), pp. 131–48.

[16] *Nhan Dan*, 8 April 2006. Cao was accompanied by Jia Qinglin, a member of the Politburo Standing Committee.

[17] *Xinhua*, 9 August 2006.

[18] "China-Vietnam Joint Communiqué", Beijing, 24 August 2006.

[19] "Tau chien Viet Nam tham Trung Quoc", BBC Vietnamese Service, 26 June 2009.

[20] Vietnam News Service, 25 October 2006.

[21] "Chinese Defence Minister Pledges to 'Deepen Ties' with Vietnam", *Xinhua*, 24 January 2008.

[22] Joint Press Release, "The First ASEAN-China Joint Cooperation Committee Meeting", Beijing, 26–28 February 1997.

[23] Plan of Action to Implement the Joint Declaration of ASEAN-China Strategic Partnership for Peace and Prosperity.

[24] VNA, 25 December 2000.

[25] VNA, Beijing, 21 January 2007 and *Quan Doi Nhan Dan*, 22 January 2007.

[26] Information provided to the author by a former high-ranking government official, Hanoi, December 2007.

[27] Dong Ha, "BP, PetroVietnam Rearrange Gas Pipeline Overhauls Plan", *Thanh Nien News*, 14 March 2007; Xinhua, *People's Daily Online*, 10 April 2007.

[28] Greg Torode, "Tussle for Oil in the South China Sea", *South China Morning Post*, 20 July 2008.

[29] "China Opposes Any Act Violating its Sovereignty", Xinhua News Agency, 27 July 2008.

30   "Vietnam Signals it Wants Exxonmobil Deal Despite China Warning", AFP, 24 July 2008.

31   Xinhua, *People's Daily Online*, 10 April 2007.

32   Xinhua, Beijing, 10 April 2007.

33   This section draws on Ian J. Storey and Carlyle A. Thayer, "The South China Sea Dispute: A Review of Developments and their Implications since the 2002 Declaration on the Conduct of Parties", in *South and Southeast Asia: Responding to Changing Geopolitical and Security Challenges*, edited by K.V. Kesavan and Daljit Singh (Singapore: Observer Research Foundation of India and the Institute of Southeast Asian Studies, 2010).

34   Press Trust of India, Beijing, 4 January 2007.

35   "China, Vietnam Agree to Properly Handle the South China Sea Dispute", Xinhua News Agency, 23 January 2008.

36   "China-Vietnam Joint Statement", Xinhua News Agency, 1 June 2008.

37   "Invade Vietnam: Plan A. One Battle to Set the Region in Order", Military Forum website; an English-language translation was provided to the author by Greg Torode.

38   "Vietnam, China Vow to Deepen Cooperation", VNA, 23 October 2008.

39   "Patrol Ships Trawl for Disorder in Beibu Gulf", *China Daily* (online), 28 May 2009; "One More Ship to Patrol South China Sea", *China Daily* (online), 15 May 2009; "Reinforced Patrol Sails from Hainan", *China Daily* (online), 19 May 2009.

40   Complete documentation may be found on the UNCLCS home page at: <http://www.un.org/Depts/los/clcs_new/clcs_home.htm>.

41   Unofficially, an earlier map had been in circulation based on a 1947 map drawn up by the Kuomintang government. The KMT map contained eleven dash lines; the PRC later deleted two dashes in the Gulf of Tonkin (Beibu Gulf).

42   "Vietnam Shuts Down Web Site in Dispute with China", Associated Press, 18 May 2009; DPA, "Vietnam-China Territory Dispute Moves to Cyberspace", 19 May 2009.

43   DPA, "China Detains Vietnamese Fishermen Fleeing Storms", 4 August 2009; DPA, "Vietnam Asks China to Release Fishermen", 5 August 2009; Beth Thomas, "China Releases Vietnamese Fishermen Seized Near Paracel Islands", Bloomberg, 12 August 2009.

44   "Chinese Nabbed Quang Ngai Fishermen Return Home", VNA, 15 August 2009.

45   "Controversial Chinese Ban Affects More Vietnamese Fishing Vessels", *Thanh Nien News*, 5 June 2009; "Fishermen Intimidated and Harassed by Chinese Patrol Boats", *Thanh Nien News*, 8 June 2009.

46   "MOFA Spokesman Answers Reporters' Question", *Nhan Dan Online*, 27 June 2009; "Calling for Signs of Goodwill from China", *Thanh Nien News*, 28 June 2009; "VN Official Asks for Chinese Counterparts' Help in Detained Fishermen Case", VietNamNet Bridge, 23 July 2009.

[47] "China Arrests Vietnamese Fishermen, Demands Astronomical Fines", Vietnam.net, 30 June 2009; "China Again Demands Money for Vietnamese Fishermen", Vietnam.net, 7 July 2009; "Fishermen team up for protection, Vietnam asks China to lift ban", *Thanh Nien News*, 8 June 2009.

[48] "China Seizes Vietnamese Fishing Boats", DPA, 14 December 2009. According to Vietnam's Maritime Police this was the fourth seizure of fishing craft from Quang Ngai this year by China.

[49] See the remarks by President Nguyen Minh Triet to Chinese State Councilor, Dai Bingguo, at the third session of the Joint Steering Committee; "Vietnam Wants to 'Address Discrepancies' in Ties with China: President", BBC Monitoring Asia Pacific, 20 March 2009.

[50] "Tim moi cach giai quyet van de bien Dong", *Tuoi Tre Online*, 24 December 2009. I am grateful to Alexander Vuving who supplied the reference and translation. According to Vuving, "My understanding is that Gen. Dung hopes that China and Vietnam will keep the security environment in the South China Sea stable so that the two communist countries can focus on combating their common enemy (the US, which is pursuing a peaceful evolution of China and Vietnam)", personal communication, 17 January 2010.

[51] In April 2009, Vietnam's Ministry of Information and Communication suspended *Du Lich* (Tourism) newspaper for three months for publishing a series of articles praising the patriotism of Vietnamese students who demonstrated against China in late 2007. Nga Pham, "Vietnam Paper Banned over China", BBC News, 15 April 2009.

[52] "Russia to Supply Vietnam with Six Diesel-Electric Submarines", Interfax-AVN Military News Agency website, 15 December 2009; "Vietnam Orders Russian Submarines, Fighter Jets", Associated Press, 16 December 2009.

[53] Hong Ha, "Tinh hinh the gioi va chinh sach doi ngoai cua Nuoc ta", *Tap Chi Cong San*, 1992, pp. 11–12. I am grateful to Nguyen Nam Duong for this point.